Blockchain Technology and Applications

Blockchain is an emerging platform for developing decentralized applications and data storage, over and beyond its role as a platform for cryptocurrencies. This reference text provides a comprehensive discussion on blockchain technology from research and application perspective.

- Discusses different approaches for building distributed applications (DAPPS).

- Provides detailed listing and discussion of blockchain technology applications in solving real-life problems.

- Covers proof of work (PoW) based blockchain consensus, and proof of stake (PoS) based blockchain consensus.

- Discusses blockchain algorithms including practical byzantine fault tolerance (PBFT) and simplified byzantine fault tolerance (SBFT).

It comprehensively covers important topics including blockchain consensus algorithms, Ethereum, Hyperledger, blockchain scalability, smart contracts with solidity, ERC20 standards, building DApp with Golang, building DApp using Hyperledger, building PoCs with Hyperledger fabric, blockchain as a server, blockchain security and privacy.

The text will serve as a useful text for senior undergraduate and graduate students in interdisciplinary areas including electronics and communications engineering, electrical engineering, computer science, and information technology.

Blockchain Technology and Applications

Edited by
Manoj Kumar M V
Annappa B
Likewin Thomas
Sourav Kanti Addya
Niranjanamurthy M

CRC Press
Taylor & Francis Group
Boca Raton London New York

CRC Press is an imprint of the
Taylor & Francis Group, an **informa** business

First edition published 2023
by CRC Press
6000 Broken Sound Parkway NW, Suite 300, Boca Raton, FL 33487-2742

and by CRC Press
4 Park Square, Milton Park, Abingdon, Oxon, OX14 4RN

CRC Press is an imprint of Taylor & Francis Group, LLC

ISBN: 978-1-032-05443-8 (hbk)
ISBN: 978-1-032-40864-4 (pbk)
ISBN: 978-1-003-35505-2 (ebk)

DOI: 10.1201/9781003355052

Typeset in Nimbus
by KnowledgeWorks Global Ltd.

Publisher's note: This book has been prepared from camera-ready copy provided by the authors.

Dedication

Dedicated to our beloved parents and teachers

Contents

Foreword

The Blockchain is initially developed as a way to support Bitcoin. Satoshi Nakamoto invented an unchangeable record of transactions that binds together data blocks using digital encryption to tackle the double-spending problem related to digital currency. While the concept works well for Bitcoin and other cryptocurrencies, blockchain technology has many additional uses. Blockchain greatly benefits money transfers, financial exchanges, lending, Insurance, Real estate, Secure personal information, Voting, Government benefits, securely share medical information, Artist royalties, non-fungible tokens, Logistics and supply chain tracking, Secure Internet of Things networks, Data storage, Gambling.

Different kinds of existing and potential activities in the blockchain revolution are segregated into three categories. Blockchain 1.0, 2.0, and 3.0. Blockchain 1.0 is money or cryptocurrencies in cash-related applications such as currency transfer, remittance, and digital payment systems. Contracts are the whole suite of economic, market, and financial applications that use the Blockchain beyond basic cash transactions: stocks, bonds, futures, loans, mortgages, titles, smart property, and smart contracts. Blockchain 3.0 refers to blockchain applications beyond currency, banking, and markets, focusing on governance, health, research, literacy, culture, and art.

Businesses are continually investigating new ways to use blockchain technology to assist their operations, despite having only been around for a dozen years. With the increasing usage of digital data in our lives, the data security, access, openness, and integrity that Blockchain can provide is becoming more critical.

The key challenges and the most difficult parts of using Blockchain Technology is a lack of knowledge and understanding of the Blockchain idea and how it works. The difficulties connected with legacy infrastructure in enterprises, as well as a lack of sufficient technical awareness, are essential roadblocks to Blockchain adoption in the mainstream. Adopting Blockchain also necessitates a culture shift away from old methods of doing things, as it decentralises the whole process. Compliance with existing rules and maintaining the needed data privacy and security for shared databases are essential hurdles to Blockchain adoption. Furthermore, with the continuous study and investigations in this domain, people will soon understand the immense potential of technology, resulting in a new wave of services and applications.

I heartily congratulate the Editors of the volume "Blockchain Technology and Its Potential Applications" for carefully scrutinising and presenting the chapters. The edited book illustrates various topics in Blockchain and its potential applications in diverse domains. This edited volume in book series: "Advances in Industry 4.0 and Machine Learning, to be published by CRC Press - Taylor & Francis Group, USA" has come excellent. This edited book will benefit the Academicians, Post-Graduate Students, Ph.D. Students, Researchers, Post-Doctoral Researchers, Innovators, Product Designers, Industry Practitioners are working in different sectors of Blockchain.

I want to convey my best wishes to all who are part of this book with the following saying by Vitalik Buterin, one of the co-founders of Ethereum.

"Whereas most technologies tend to automate workers on the periphery doing menial tasks, blockchains automate away the canter. Instead of putting the taxi driver out of a job, Blockchain puts Uber out of a job and lets the taxi drivers work with the customer directly."

Dr. H.C. Nagaraj
Former Dean, Visvesvaraya Technological University, Belagavi Member of Academic Senate, Visvesvaraya Technological University, Belagavi
Principal, Nitte Meenakshi Institute of Technology, P.B.No.6429, Yelahanka, Bangalore 560064.
principal@nmit.ac.in

Preface

Blockchain has been successfully implemented as a public record for transactions in digital money, such as bitcoin, as a potential mechanism for achieving decentralised agreement. Its safe architecture for enabling a distributed computing system with excellent fault tolerance has sparked widespread interest worldwide. Blockchain can lay new foundations for our socioeconomic systems by effectively creating trust between people and machines, lowering costs, and enhancing resource usage.

On the one hand, blockchain will play a critical role in securing decentralisation in developing industries such as the Internet of Things, Cyber-Physical Systems, edge computing, social networking, crowdsourcing, and next-generation wireless communications, among others. On the other hand, it should be developed further in scalability, security, privacy, efficiency, flexibility, availability, true decentralisation, and high reliability. The use of blockchain in day-to-day activities is a game-changer that adds trustworthiness. As a result, the goal of this edited book is to describe current blockchain breakthroughs and applications in real-world circumstances.

Decentralisation and trustworthiness are urgently needed, and blockchain technology provides both at a low or free cost. This book will serve as a forum for students, academics, researchers, and industry specialists to contribute their expertise and discoveries. The book's primary goal is to focus on two aspects: documenting the mechanics of how blockchain works and discussing real-life applications of blockchain through use cases. Anyone interested in learning about blockchain technology and its applications will find this book helpful.

The edited book describes the critical building elements of the blockchain ecosystem, such as various algorithms, methods, and services. The book is appropriate for undergraduate/postgraduate technical students, academicians, researchers, industry professionals, and anybody interested in technology.

We extend our heartfelt thanks to our reviewers, who have extended their support despite their busy schedules. A special thanks to all our authors for submitting the work. Our sincere thanks to Taylor and Francis - CRC Press publishers, for accepting our proposal for editing this book and supporting us extensively during the editing process. Our thanks to one and all who have directly or indirectly rendered the support for completing this edited book. We believe the efforts we rendered for editing the book are worthwhile only if this book is of any use for the ordinary end-users of our society. This satisfaction will fuel us to develop more edited books that will be useful for society at large.

Editors,

Dr. Manoj Kumar M V, Dr. Annappa, Dr. Likewin Thomas, Dr. Sourav Kanti Addya, Dr. Niranjanamurthy M

Editor Biographies

Dr. Manoj Kumar M V, is presently working as Associate Professor in Information Science and Engineering, Nitte Meenakshi Institute of Technology, Bengaluru. He has 10 years of academic experience which includes teaching and research. He has earned a Engineering and M.Tech. degree in Computer Science and Engineering from VTU Belgaum.

He earned his Ph.D. (with MHRD fellowship for 4.5 years) from the Department of Computer Science and Engineering, National Institute of Technology Karnataka (NITK), Surathkal. His research interests include: Process Mining, Data Mining, and some aspects of Machine learning. He has authored and published 35 papers in indexed International Conferences/Journals/Book Chapters. He has delivered 30+ research talks/workshops/FDPs at National and International levels on mobile application development and data science (Google certified mobile app developer).

He is a reviewer for reputed international journals in the field of Computer Science and Information Technology. He has received a gold medal award from the Federation of Karnataka Chambers of Commerce and Industry (FKCCI), for his notable findings in his Ph.D. thesis. He has successfully executed 03 consultancy projects worth ₹25 Lakhs, and one is under the development phase. He is currently executing the funded project worth ₹12 Lakh for TEQIP VTU.

A few of his research papers were honoured with the best paper award. My research includes solving the phenomenon of Concept drift (recurring, incremental and gradual) in the realm of Data Science.

He has visited 6 countries (Belgium, Hong Kong, Paris, Netherlands, Malaysia, and Sri Lanka) for research interaction, research lab visits, and paper presentations.

Annappa B is currently serving as a Professor at the Department of Computer Science and Engineering, National Institute of Technology Karnataka, Surathkal, Mangalore, India. He has more than 25 years of experience in teaching and research. He holds a Ph.D. and M.Tech. in Computer Science and Engineering from National Institute of Technology Karnataka, Surathkal and B.E. in Computer Science and Engineering from Govt. B.D.T. College of Engineering, Davangere affiliated Mysore University, Karnataka. He is a Fellow of

Institution of Engineers (India) and Senior member of IEEE and ACM. He is a Life member of Computer Society of India, Indian Society of Technical Education, Cloud

Computing Innovation Council of India and Advanced Computing and Communications Society. His research interests include Cloud computing, Big Data Analytics, Distributed Computing, Software Engineering and Process Mining. He has published more than 125 research papers in International conferences and Journals. He volunteered as the organizing chair of international conference ADCONS-2013 and DISCOVER-2020, general chair of DISCOVER-2019, TPC chair of DISCOVER'18, finance chair of DISCOVER'16, and he is in the Technical program committee of many International conferences and reviewer of Journals. He was the Chair of IEEE Computer Society Chapter India Council (2017–2018), and IEEE Mangalore subsection (2018). Six research scholars completed their Ph.D. under his supervision, and eight scholars are currently pursuing their research work in Computer Science and Engineering.

Dr. Likewin Thomas is currently working as Associate Professor in the Department of Computer Science & Engineering and Secretary of IEEE MSS. He is a Senior IEEE member along with lifetime ISTE member. He is also a program chair of IEEE DISCOVER conference 2020 and a member of National advisory committee of International Conference on "Contemporary Innovations in Engineering and Technology 2021".

He has completed his Ph.D. and masters from the field of Computer Science and Engineering at the National Institute of Technology Karnataka (NITK), Surathkal, Mangalore. He graduated from Visvesvaraya Technology University, Belgaum in the year 2004.

His research interest is in the field of machine learning and its application in the clinical area and process mining. He is interested in contributing his research excellence to the betterment and management of healthcare sectors. He has more than 30 papers published in international conferences like Springer, ACM, Elsevier, IEEE and Scopus. He has a couple of book chapters published and five international journals indexed by Scopus.

He holds more than 15 years of teaching and research experience including the industry. He has worked as a research scholar under the supervision of Dr. Annappa, Professor, NITK. He has been a resource person and a keynote speaker at many workshops and conferences. He, along with Dr. Annappa, has organized a workshop on machine learning and its application at an IEEE International conference, EmergiTech 2016, held at Mauritius.

Sourav Kanti Addya working as an Assistant professor in the Department of Computer Science & Engineering at the National Institute of Technology Karnataka, Surathkal, India. He received his Ph.D. in the Department of Computer Science & Engineering from the National Institute of Technology (NIT), Rourkela, India. He was a Post Doctoral fellow in the Department of Computer Science & Engineering, Indian Institute of Technology Kharagpur, India. He was a visiting scholar at San Diego State University, CA, USA. He obtained his M.Tech degree with a national level GATE scholarship, from NIT Rourkela, India and B.Tech from the West Bengal University of Technology. He

has several international collaborations and sound volunteer research experience as a reviewer of reputed international journals and TPC member of international conferences such as Mobile Networks and Applications, Springer, IEEE Systems Journal, IEEE Transactions on Sustainable Computing, IEEE Transactions on Dependable and Secure Computing, Computers & Electrical Engineering, Elsevier, COMSNETS 2020, IOTSm 2018, GLOBECOM 2015, etc. He has multidisciplinary research and technical interests include Cloud and distributed systems, Blockchain, Algorithm design, Computer networks, and Information security. Dr. Addya is a Senior Member of IEEE and a member of ACM. Further details about his works and publications can be obtained from https://souravkaddya.in/publication.html

Dr. Niranjanamurthy M, Assistant Professor, Department of AI and ML, BMSIT and M, Bangalore, Karnataka. He did his Ph.D. Computer Science (2016), MPhil-Computer Science (2009), Masters in Computer Applications at Visvesvaraiah Technological University, Belgaum, Karnataka (2007). BCA from Kuvempu University 2004 with University 5th Rank. He has 12* years of teaching experience and 2 years of industry experience as a Software Engineer. He published 15 books in top publishing houses like CRC Press USA, Wiley-SP USA, Springer and Scholars Press Germany. He is Series Editor in CRC Press, Wiley SP, and Nova Publishing House. He has published 80+ research articles in various National/International

Conferences and Reputed International Journals. Filed 25 Patents in that 5 were granted. Currently, he is guiding four Ph.D. research scholars in the area of Data Science, Edge Computing, ML, and Networking. He is a reviewer in 22 International Journals. Two times got the Best Research journal reviewer award. Got Young Researcher award - Computer Science Engineering, Received Patent Award from KSCST, India. Worked as National/International Ph.D. examiner. He conducted various National Level workshops and Delivered Lecture. Conducted National and

International Conferences. Member of Various Societies IAENG, INSC, IEEE, etc. Areas of interest are Data Science, ML, Augmented and Virtual Reality, Edge Computing, E-Commerce and M-Commerce related to Industry Internal tool enhancement, Software Testing, Software Engineering, Web Services, Web-Technologies, Cloud Computing, Big data analytics, and Networking.

Contributors

Annappa
NITK
Surathkal, India

Arun Kumar G Hiremath
BIET
Davanagere, India

Ajay Kumara M. A
Lenoir-Rhyne University
NC, USA

Anupam Pattanayak
IIIT Guwahati
Assam, India

Ahmet ÖZEN
Dokuz Eylul University
Buca-Izmir

Bangarugiri Sateesha
Bangarugiri Sateesha
India

Chandrasekhar Azad
NIT Jamshedpur
India

Divij Singh
University of Aizu
Japan

Digendra Rai
Sri Sathya Sai Institute of Higher
    Learning
India

Güzin ÖZDAĞOĞLU
Dokuz Eylul University
Buca-Izmir

Hardik Gohel
University of Houston, Victoria
TX, USA

Himanshu Upadhyay
International University,
Miami Florida, USA

T. Janani
NIT Tiruchirappalli
India

Kavitha H
SIT
Tumakuru, India

Likewin Thomas
PESIT-M
Shivamogga, India

Manoj Kumar M V
NMIT
Bengaluru, India

M. Brindha
NIT, Tiruchirappalli
India

Manoj Kumar M V
NMIT, Bangalore
India

Manoj Poudel
University of Aizu
Japan

Naveen Kumar K R
BIET
Davanagere, India

Nirmala C R
BIET
Davanagere, India

Niranjanamurthy M
MSRIT
Bangalore, India

Nukala Poorna Viswanadha Sravan
SSIHL
Anantapur, India

Jaydeep Howladerb
NIT Durgapur
India

Pallav Kumar Baruah
SSIHL
Anantapur, India

Prashanth B
SIT
Tumakuru, India

Prashanth B. S.
NMIT
Bengaluru, India

Prity Hansda
NIT Jamshedpur
India

Rashmi P. Sarode
University of Aizu
Japan

Sourav Kanti Addya
NITK
Surathkal, India

Sreenivasa B R
BIET
Davanagere, India

Sandesh R
New York University
New York, USA

Shiva Darshan S. L
NMIT
Bangalore, India

Santosh Joshi
Florida International University
Miami, Florida, USA

Shashank Shrestha
University of Aizu
Fukushima-Ken, Japan

Subhash Bhalla
University of Aizu
Fukushima-Ken, Japan

Sabri ERDEM
Dokuz Eylul University
Tinaztepe Campus, Buca-Izmir

Subhasish Dhal
IIIT Guwahati
Assam, India

Tamoghna Mandala
NIT Durgapur
India

Vinod Ramesh Falmari
NIT Tiruchirappalli
India

Yutaka Watanobe
University of Aizu
Fukushima-Ken, Japan

1 Blockchain Foundations and Methods

Blockchain technology is impacting practically every industry currently, and it's changing the way we do business. The Internet of Information was created by the first generation of the digital revolution. Using the second generation of blockchain technology, the Internet is a major platform that will revolutionise financial markets while also adding value to the existing order of human affairs. Blockchain is an open-source distributed ledger that operates on large devices and enables anyone to securely and anonymously move, store, and govern anything of value, such as currency, titles, actions, identities. Rather than relying on dominant intermediaries like banks and governments, reliability is generated via extensive engagement and sophisticated engineering. In 2008, Satoshi Nakamoto developed Blockchain Technology, which serves as the public ledger for the bitcoin cryptocurrency. The decentralised Bitcoin ledger, established by Satoshi Nakamoto, was meant to give consumers control over their money and prevent third parties, like the government, from accessing or monitoring it. Because of the blockchain's creation, Bitcoin became the first digital currency to address the issue of double-spending without relying on a trusted central authority or central server to do so. Several other programmes have modelled their designs after the bitcoin design [1].

1.0.1 TECHNOLOGIES BEHIND BLOCKCHAIN

The email was the first major application of internet technology (TCP/IP or HTTP) in the 1990s, while it was still in its infancy. New programmes, such as web browsers, appeared later. Bitcoin was the first big application to exploit blockchain technology when it was originally introduced, and then the trend was followed by other cryptocurrencies. Blockchain technology is currently being used for a variety of applications, including security and online voting. While computers can exchange data over the Internet, Blockchain enables them to store information securely. Essentially, the blockchain is a decentralised, immutable digital transaction database that can be used to record nearly any type of transaction that can be recorded in a digital format [1]. A block is a collection of records in the blockchain. A blockchain, then, is a continuously increasing list of linked and secured information known as blocks.

Individuals can be held to the highest level of responsibility imaginable thanks to the blockchain technology, which is being developed. When it comes to validating the legitimacy of transactions, blockchain can help by recording them in a central register and a distributed system of registers connected through a secure validation process. Each transaction on the blockchain is recorded and distributed decentrally. Each transaction is irreversible and double-verified by the majority of system

DOI: 10.1201/9781003355052-1

members before it is recorded on the public ledger. Due to the decentralised nature of the blockchain, every transaction can be independently verified.

Essentially, the blockchain is designed to produce a distributed consensus mechanism in the digital online world, and this is its fundamental hypothesis. It is possible for all parties involved to be confident that a digital event took place by producing an undeniable record in a public ledger. In contrast to a centralised digital economy, it creates conditions for establishing a democratic, open, and scalable digital economy. Even though this cutting-edge technology has immense potential, the revolution in this area has only recently begun to take hold. This white paper is a valuable resource to provide an overview of blockchain technology and several of its most appealing uses in the financial and non-financial sectors.

The chapter's main objective is to explore the foundations of the blockchain for framing dependable and stable decentralised solutions and the support of underlying principles. With a focus on the understanding of blocks, components of blockchain, the initial part of the chapter explores the role of the shared ledger and digital assets from the user's point of view. Further, a technical overview on the accomplishment of a decentralised data network (along with the methods of decentralisation), employment of cryptography and consensus mechanisms and the processes undertaken by the network miner nodes has been provided. The chapter extends to provide a brief inclusion of smart contracts that have risen to prominence as a result of Blockchain 2.0. Also, a discussion has been made on an Ethereum-like network that has grown in popularity due to the inclusion of smart contracts, which is a ground-breaking solution since the technology could be used to change any application where bringing in a third party would be both costly and unnecessary.

1.1 NEED FOR BLOCKCHAIN TECHNOLOGY

Businesses are the ones who benefit the most from blockchain technology in the vast majority of cases. Supervising a professional team is required; thus, it is best suited for businesses with the financial resources and drive to launch a blockchain initiative. The global blockchain sector is growing in tandem with the increase in the application of blockchain technology in business. Businesses benefit from eliminating intermediaries since it decreases expenses while also reducing the number of points of engagement, resulting in increased productivity [2]. In addition, the transaction pace has increased to previously unheard-of levels of rapidity. If businesses can keep their accuracy up, efficiency becomes a top goal for them. In addition, the business applications are exciting to investigate.

The use of blockchain technology to develop and operate a blockchain-based financial infrastructure is growing more popular among corporations and government organisations. While blockchain is fascinating and can change the way many businesses function, it is not the best option for every situation. But, if the business world intends to have secured digital actions and a transparent record of assets, especially between multiple partners [3]. Smart contracts, particularly, are ideal for making digital interactions and transactions more convenient. When the participants in a transaction agree that their criteria have been met, a smart contract can be used to unleash automated payments [4]. Moreover, blockchain is the better alternative when an intermediary service is too expensive in terms of time consumption with constantly changing data, and we want to record earlier acts. Anyone who benefits from a chronological trail of data and an instantly up-to-date record can't corrupt the data.

1.1.1 BLOCKCHAIN TECHNOLOGY AS AN INFRASTRUCTURE FOR THE MODERN BUSINESS

In considerations of transparency and accountability, it may be argued that the use of private blockchain as an open research foundation makes absolutely no relevance. An important principle of open science is that knowledge, the scientific method, and the results should be accessible to a broad audience, if not to everyone, regardless of criterion. A public blockchain is appropriate for this purpose, whereas a private blockchain would limit access [5].

A permissioned network's governance is not equitably distributed. In a permissionless network, everyone is equal, yet this opens the door to system abuse. Therefore, an appropriate consensus mechanism is necessary to make common judgments about the expansion of the underlying blockchain system and avoid network behaviour that is detrimental to the system's overall health [6]. The immutability of Blockchain Technology is a perfect property for preventing censorship of any type. The immutability of a blockchain is ensured via cryptographic hashing, a consensus process, and decentralisation. People involved in service could only add records to it, not change it.

1.1.2 BLOCKCHAIN AS A SERVICE

Even though blockchain is a game-changing technology, it is prohibitively expensive to set up and keep up to date. Organisations operating on a tight budget, on the other hand, can benefit from blockchain as a service to make the transition to the blockchain. Popular blockchain-as-a-service (BaaS) solutions are attempting to meet the demand. Businesses don't have to worry about infrastructure or upkeep because these are cloud-based solutions. To use it, customers simply have to pay for it the same way they would for any other service. However, the most well-known of them are Azure Blockchain Workbench and Amazon Managed Blockchain, Oracle Blockchain Applications Cloud, and SAP Blockchain (Cloud Platform Blockchain), which are currently available as blockchain-as-a-service providers [7].

1.2 BLOCKCHAIN LAYERED ARCHITECTURE

Figure 1.1 represents the layered architecture of the blockchain [26] and it consists of the following layers.

A. Hardware and Infrastructure Layer: The blockchain is stored on a server somewhere in the world, probably in a data centre. The client-server architecture will be used whenever clients browse the web or use apps because clients request

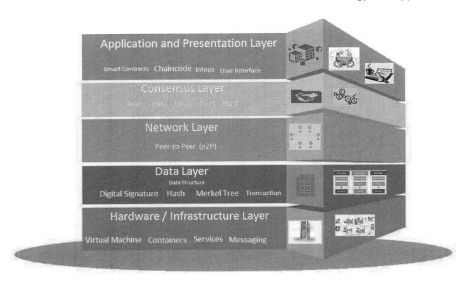

Figure 1.1   Layered architecture of blockchain

content or data from data centers [26, 27]. Users can now share data with one other. A P2P network is a group of nodes that share data. Blockchain is a decentralised, peer-to-peer computer network that records and manages transactions. Even better, this data is captured and stored in a distributed database. A P2P network node is a computer/node. Nodes verify transactions, store them in blocks, and broadcast them to the blockchain network. Nodes broadcast the block to the blockchain network and update their local copies of the ledger. Nodes. This layer has virtualisation components (creating virtual resources such as storage, network, servers, etc.). The nodes of this layer are vital. Any computer or other device connecting to the blockchain network is a "node". Decentralised blockchain nodes are scattered over a network.

B. Data Layer: Block chain data structures and physical storage are both kept at the data layer, where they should be stored. With the help of a list of linked blocks, known as Merkel trees, it is possible to construct a ledger that is subsequently encrypted using an asymmetric encryption algorithm. It is made up of the following components that make up the Data layer:

- Data Blocks
- Merkel trees
- Asymmetric Encryption
- BlockChain

i. Data Blocks: Blocks, which are data structures, are used by all nodes in the network to receive and process transaction requests. Miners are responsible for the construction of blocks. The metadata contained in a block header is used to determine whether or not a block is legitimate.

The following is a list of typical block metadata:

- version: Defines the block structure's current version
- previous block header hash (the reference this block's parent block)
- Merkle root hash cryptographic hash of all of the transactions included in this block
- time: the date and time at which this block was created
- nBits: the current difficulty with which this block was created.
- nonce ("number used once"): a random value that the originator of a block is free to manipulate in any way they see fit.

These six fields make up the block header. It is the miner who decides which transactions to keep in a block and which to discard. A blockchain's genesis block is the very first block. It is the ancestor of all other blocks in the blockchain, making it the universal parent. At least one block must be present in each blockchain.

ii & iii. Merkle Tree and Asymmetric Encryption: The Merkle tree is an essential part of blockchain [26]. Simplified, it's a statistical data structure that represents all transactions in a block and it is shown in Figure 1.2. It also allows for large-scale content vetting. It also helps verify data consistency and substance. Bitcoin and Ethereum both use Merkle Trees. This is a Merkle Tree. The Merkle Tree concept was patented in 1979 by Ralph Merkle. Each leaf node carries the cryptographic hash of a data block in this tree, while non-leaf nodes have the cryptographic hash of their child nodes' labels. The leaf node is the lowest node. A Merkle tree creates a digital fingerprint of all transactions in a block. It lets the user decide whether a transaction belongs in a block. Merkle trees are made by hashing nodes until only one remain. The Merkle Root or Root Hash. The Merkle Trees are built from scratch. The non-leaf node is a hash of its predecessor hashes. Having an odd number of leaf nodes is required for Merkle trees. A leaf node hash is replicated once for each transaction if the number of transactions is odd.

The blocks can be identified in two ways: the cryptographic hash and block height [27]. The Merkel Root is a block header that encapsulates all transaction data. Each block contains the root hash of the Merkel tree, which contains the actual transactions. Asymmetric encryption or public-private vital pairs protect the network transmission of blockchains. The Binary Merkle Tree is the most common and fundamental Merkle tree. A block's transactions are TX1, TX2, TX3, and TX4. As you can see, the Root Hash, or Merkle Root, is the hash of the entire tree. Their hashes are preserved in each leaf node, giving us Hash 0, 1, 2, and 3. Hashing Hash0 and Hash1 yields Hash01, and hashing Hash2, and Hash3 yields Hash23. The Root Hash is formed by hashing together Hash01 and Hash23. Merkle Root's data is in the header. As shown in Figure 1.3, the block header is the hashed component of a bitcoin block. This hash contains the Root Hash of all transactions in the current block as well as the previous block's hash, a Nonce. The block header includes the Merkle root, making the transaction secure. Due to the Root Hash containing all transaction hashes, this may result in disc space savings. The Merkle Tree protects the data. Changes in a transaction's details or order are recorded in its hash. This update would propagate up the Merkle Tree until it reached the Merkle Root, invalidating the block.

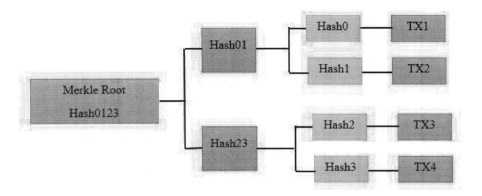

Figure 1.2   Merkle tree and asymmetric encryption

As shown, the Merkle tree allows for a quick and easy check to see if a transaction is in the collection.

iv. Blockchain: Each block contains the root hash of the Merkel tree, which includes the actual transactions. The root hash of the Merkel tree is contained in each block. Asymmetric encryption or public-private key pairs are used to protect the transmission of blockchains over networks like the internet.

C. Network Layer: The blockchain employs a distributed network, allowing anyone to download and interact with all of the information stored on the blockchain. The P2P network is used to propagate/broadcast transactions across nodes. Making the best use of the underlying network bandwidth is one of the most important considerations. Three types of networks are used by blockchain platforms. Centralised networks, Decentralised networks, Distributed networks.

Centralised Networks: They are not just geographically scattered, but also not colocated. This prevents centralization. The distributed network's basic idea is that everyone has equal access.

Decentralised Networks: A distributed network's nodes are not only geographically separated, but also not colocated. This entirely eliminates centralisation. The distributed network's basic tenet is that everyone has equal access.

Distributed Networks: The blockchain network consists of servers, edge nodes, and IoT nodes. These are usually linked as a P2P network, with identical permissions and participation.

D. Consensus Layer: Platforms based on blockchain technology necessitate the use of a consensus process. A consensus algorithm is used by each blockchain. The consensus layer may be the most important layer for any blockchain (Ethereum, Hyperledger, or any other). Consensus is in charge of validating, organising, and guaranteeing that consensus is achieved. The following are the most important aspects to keep in mind when it comes to the consensus layer:

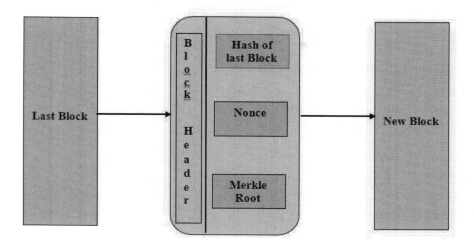

Figure 1.3 Block Header in Merkle Tree

- Unbreakable agreements between nodes in a distributed P2P network are provided via consensus techniques.
- Consensus keeps all nodes in sync. Nodes accept the truth through consensus.
- Consensus distributes and decentralises authority. Neither a single individual nor a group can control.
- Consensus ensures that only one chain is followed correctly.
- Consensus refers to the rules that nodes follow to validate transactions and blocks.
- Consensus occurs when all nodes in a network agree on something.
- Consensus also pays cryptocurrency to blockchain nodes for validating transactions and maintaining the network (for example, Ethereum).
- Consensus methods are not designed to be duplicated due to their high cost and time requirements.
- A consensus protocol ensures network reliability.

E. Application Layer: Smart contracts, chaincode, and decentralised apps (dApps) are all part of application layer. The application layer is divided into two sublayers: application and execution. Applications allow end users to interact with the blockchain network. There are scripts, APIs, UIs, and frameworks included. These apps communicate with the blockchain network via APIs and use it as a back-end technology. Smart contracts, underlying rules, and chaincode are all part of a sublayer. The actual code and regulations are contained in this layer. The semantic layer validates and executes transactions that have been propagated from the application layer (smart contracts and rules). The execution layer (chaincode in Hyperledger fabric) processes transactions and ensures the determinism of the blockchain (such as permissioned blockchain like hyperledger fabric).

1.3 BLOCKCHAIN PRINCIPLES

An adequate consensus mechanism is required to make common judgments about the extension of the underlying blockchain system and avoid network behaviour that is harmful to the system's general health [6].

1.3.1 IMMUTABILITY, TRANSPARENCY, AND DIGITAL FREEDOM

The immutability of blockchain excludes many alternatives for services that require immutability to operate in a competitive market, such as bitcoin exchanges. Immutability can be used by businesses to ensure that packages do not become damaged while in transit. Because blockchain is immutable, any alteration to the package information will result in an alarm [7]. Furthermore, because of the nature of public blockchain, it provides transparency. With blockchain, true digital independence is conceivable. Because there is no central authority, users are the sole owners and responsible persons for their possessions. It provides individuals with digital independence by depending heavily on blockchain technology as a foundation.

1.3.2 EXCELLENCE OF USE THROUGH TRULY DECENTRALISED SERVICES

The decentralised services that will form the backbone of future civilisation will be essential. There will always be decentralised services, no matter what type of business it is, asset management or energy management. Individuals will benefit from the strategy since it will provide them with easy access to currently inaccessible things. The availability of decentralised services is widespread across virtually every industry. A single example is not the only situation in which blockchain technology may be used successfully. As a result, distributed ledger (block chain) technology is a fantastic alternative for today's future. It is used in practically every industry, and the technologies used have a significant impact [8].

Blockchain adds an additional layer of protection to data kept on a network by encrypting the data as it is sent. Because of the decentralised structure of blockchain and the use of encryption, and processes (Figure 1.4) involved in validating every transaction, it offers a higher level of security than earlier systems in comparison. Data and services on the blockchain network are secured through cryptography, a mathematical procedure that is advanced in nature. Furthermore, each block on the network has its hash, ensuring that no data can be falsified or altered by hostile actors [9]. There is no longer any buffer required for effective network operation when no centralised authority is in place. Because there is no need to pay an intermediary, there are cost savings due to the lack of centralisation. The elimination of bureaucracy brought about by blockchain technology enhances the supply chain. In and of itself, documentation is expensive. Hiring staff to organise paperwork and

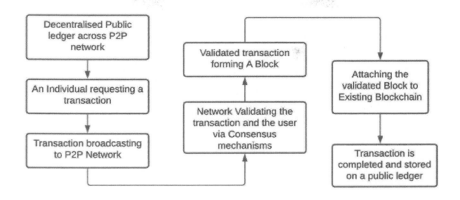

Figure 1.4 Overview of processes involved in blockchain technology

maintaining the middlemen's equipment are both additional costs. Another argument for the usefulness of blockchain is the increased efficiency it delivers. The reasons for this include increased security, the elimination of intermediaries, and the overall improvement of processes. Transactions, particularly international transactions, are completed in seconds rather than weeks, allowing for more efficient resources.

1.4 BLOCKCHAIN CORE COMPONENTS

Over time, blockchain technology has grown into three key versions: Blockchain 1.0, 2.0 and 3.0, all of which have opened up new methods to leverage the technology to create ever more complicated applications and initiatives. To put it another way, Ethereum is like an operating system in that it provides architecture. Without spending the time and money to set up a private blockchain, anyone can make apps. Using if-then clauses, Ethereum's smart contracts, which may be programmed in specialised languages like Java, GO, and Solidity, automatically enforce digital contracts. There are also plans to use SCs to create fully autonomous, decentralised organisations and automate governance and decision-making in these organisations using software [6].

1.4.1 DISTRIBUTED LEDGER TECHNOLOGY

Distributed ledgers are used in decentralised networks to maintain track of and share information about network transactions. A blockchain stores data in chronologically and cryptographically linked blocks, which distinguishes it from a database. The database may feature smart contracts and other consensus methods in addition to standard database capabilities.

In contrast to a traditional ledger, digital ledger technology (DLT) is a ledger for recording transactions based on an encrypted and shared library rather than on a single physical ledger. DLT is becoming increasingly popular due to its cutting-edge database solution and data architecture, which is gaining in popularity. Because every transaction upgrade is encrypted and verification is available throughout the particular Ethereum blockchain, each transaction update is encrypted and verified [10]. Application programming interfaces (APIs) must be built on the blockchain to connect off-chain (external) devices and applications to the blockchain network. It enables the transmission and exchange of data, as well as the sharing of information between systems. External web services can utilise the characteristics and capabilities of an existing blockchain for specific use cases in this manner [6].

1.4.2 SMART CONTRACTS

A smart contract can be used to record and execute contractual agreements using blockchain technology. It is regulated by the terms and conditions defined in the contract, and it is self-executing and self-enforcing. Before encoding the terms and conditions in the blockchain-stored smart contract code, the stakeholders must first negotiate and agree on the contract terms and conditions. Creating a blockchain-based smart contract is a time-consuming process that takes several steps. Smart contracts allow for the execution of secure transactions without the need for the intervention of a third party, as opposed to traditional contracts. It is a decentralised strategy that eliminates the need for middlemen to confirm trades on behalf of their clients. A smart contract automatically executes following the rules for which it was designed when certain specified terms and conditions are met [4].

Smart contracts require the presence of signatories, a subject, and certain terms. The signatories are the first to use the smart contract and digitally sign their agreement to the proposed terms. Second, the subject of the agreement is the smart contract ecosystem. The smart contract's terms are the final item to assess. They are mathematically expressed in a language compatible with the smart contract blockchain. This agreement will be followed.

1.4.2.1 Working of the Smart contracts

A smart contract is a computer application that encrypts application logic and executes it on a specialised virtual system embedded within a blockchain or other distributed ledger, much like a computer programme would. Initial and foremost, business teams must engage with developers to define the desired behaviour of a smart contract in response to specific events or circumstances. This is the first stage of the development process for a smart contract. Simple events include payment authorisation, delivery receipt, and metre reading thresholds for electric power, to name a few examples. The valuation of a derivative financial instrument and the completion of a derivative transaction, as well as the automatic release of insurance payment in the event of a person's death or natural disaster, may necessitate more extensive reasoning. The engineers then create the code, who test it on a platform for building smart contracts to confirm that it is functionally correct. After completing the program's development, it is sent on to another team for security testing.

It may be essential to hire a firm that specialises in screening smart contract security, or it may be necessary to hire an internal specialist. A contract is implemented on a blockchain or other distributed ledger infrastructure that already exists after approval [1]. As soon as the smart contract is implemented, it is set up to receive event updates from an "oracle," which is an effective streaming data source that is encrypted for security purposes. After receiving the requisite combination of events from one or more oracles, the smart contract will be triggered and will proceed to execution. Because of the immutability and security provided by the blockchain, it is a perfect platform for storing smart contracts and other data. Smart contracts hold encrypted data on a shared ledger, making it nearly impossible to destroy content.

A shared ledger encrypts smart contract data, making it extremely unlikely that the data contained within the blocks will be lost. Developers may use a blockchain to store nearly any type of data and choose from various transaction types. Blockchain smart contracts make financial transactions and other organisational procedures safer, more efficient, and cost-effective. The buyer receives a digital token when certain transactions occur, which they can use in conjunction with the traditional paper deed as proof of ownership. The use of blockchain-based smart contracts in supply chains can help a large number of organisations. Smart contracts can be used to automate healthcare payments, reducing overbilling and preventing fraud. A smart contract might be used in the music industry to ensure that payments are made when songs are utilised commercially and registered on the blockchain. The automobile sector might profit from smart contracts and blockchain by storing conveniently accessible information about vehicle maintenance, accidents, and ownership history [12].

1.4.2.2   Smart Contracts and Blockchain

The blockchain, a decentralised network, is at the heart of the transaction with these contracts. Smart contracts employ blockchain-based to evaluate, validate, collect, and impose requirements agreed upon by many people. Blockchain technology is used to check, validate, collect, and enforce conditions. Smart contracts allow anonymous individuals to perform blockchain transactions and agreements without requiring a central institution, external compliance, or a legal framework. Transactions that are transparent, irrevocable, and traceable Because of the immutability and security of any data saved on the blockchain, it is a perfect setting to develop smart contracts for use in cryptocurrency exchanges. The fact that smart contract data is encrypted and stored on a ledger ensures that it can't be lost, modified, or otherwise destroyed.

1.4.2.3   Smart Contract Platforms

There are a plethora of platforms for smart contracts that are presently available. In addition to the sort of technology, end-users (such as a bank) and geographic regions (such as the United States) are all classed in different ways (various countries of the world). To be sure, there are certain advantages to using smart contracts, such as increased bitcoin security, faster transaction speeds, and trustworthiness in the core network nodes. Still, some disadvantages must be considered. Decentralised applications were initially developed on the Ethereum blockchain platform, which was the first to feature code devoted to this purpose (dApps). Many competing systems have sprung up in reaction to Bitcoin's initial public offering, including Aeternity (formerly Cardano), Qtum (previously Stellar), Stellar Lumens (previously Stellar Waves), and Waves, among others.

When smart contracts were introduced to the cryptocurrency community as a whole, Ethereum, the well-known worldwide blockchain platform, was the first to do so. Ethereum is still the most sophisticated platform for building and executing smart contracts, according to the Ethereum Foundation. This open-source platform boasts one of the most active developer communities in the business, allowing it to adapt to a continuously changing environment without compromising its functionality or security. Aeternity facilitates the off-chain execution of Turing-complete smart contracts with a hybrid Proof-of-Work/Proof-of-Stake paradigm. Cardano is a cryptocurrency and distributed ledger technology effort. Cardano, like many other cryptocurrency initiatives, is an open-source project. Qtum, an open-source blockchain application platform, is distinguished by two critical characteristics: security and scalability. The Qtumteam has worked diligently to ensure smart contracts' appropriate execution, making the platform ideal for corporations and their corporate clients. Qtum is a Proof-of-Stake cryptocurrency with a decentralised governance protocol. In contrast to many other cryptocurrencies, Stellar was developed by developers for developers. As a result, it can deal with extremely complicated smart contracts. Stellar is a basic smart contract platform that enables developers to create more efficient smart contracts.

Waves is an open-source blockchain project that focuses on decentralised apps (dApps) and utilises Web 3.0 technology. Waves is a blockchain project that is open-source and free to use. Many online courses and other assistance are available to developers through Waves to make their cryptographic protocol project as straightforward as possible. Proof-of- Waves, among other smart contract applications, makes use of the stake concept.

1.4.3   BLOCKCHAIN CONSENSUS MECHANISMS

One of the strategies for obtaining consensus, trust, and security across a decentralised computer network is consensus. Consensus, like any distributed or multi-agent system, relies on a fault-tolerant method to achieve consensus across dispersed processes or multi-agents on a single value or region of operation. It is useful for a range of purposes, including inventory tracking [13]. The Proof-of-Work (PoW) consensus process is used to preserve the integrity of the Bitcoin blockchain, which demands computer power to solve a tough yet random issue to keep all nodes in the network honest.

1. **Proof-of-Work**
   The mining technology is called proof-of-work (POW) mining, and the miners are called nodes. Miners are tasked with difficult mathematical puzzles that

require a large amount of computer power to solve. Miners accomplish this by using various mining technologies, including CPU mining, GPU mining, Field-Programmable-Gate-Array (FPGA) mining, mining pools, and ASIC mining. After solving mathematical puzzles, a miner receives a block as a reward if they are the first ones to find the solution. Additionally, the puzzles can only be solved with trial and error. Hence, miners require an increasing amount of computational power for finding solutions quickly.

The difficulty level for the puzzles changes according to the speed at which the blocks are being mined. In case the blocks are created quickly, then the puzzles would get more difficult and vice versa. Therefore, new blocks have to be created within a particular time frame to adjust the difficulty level of puzzles carefully. Several popular cryptocurrencies like Bitcoin utilise the Proof of Work process. However, the Proof of Work consensus mechanism consumes resources at a staggering rate. According to sources, Bitcoin's current estimated annual power consumption is 51.13 TWh. Hence, this approach can be expensive.

2. **Proof-of-Stake**

Proof-of-Stake (POS) is a mechanism for picking the next block developer at random. Blockchain users may temporarily lock their tokens in order to qualify as validators. People who become validators can add blocks. Validators can also be determined depending on the blockchain's design. The user with the most stakes or coins for the longest amount of time is more likely to generate a new block.

Validators are typically paid for their efforts by receiving all or a portion of the transaction fees earned from transactions within their established block. Additionally, validators may be able to earn a specified quantity of coins as a result of inflation. The Proof of Stake approach employs this methodology to compensate validators for their efforts in sustaining the blockchain network. Compared to other blockchain consensus mechanisms such as Proof of Work, the proof of stake consensus process is more energy-efficient.

3. **Delegated Proof-of-Stake**

In the Delegated Proof-of-Stake (DPOS) mechanism, individuals can stake their currencies and vote for a certain number of delegates to represent them. User's/Customer's votes are given greater significance based on the amount of money they have put in the process. For instance, if a user "X" stakes 20 coins for a delegate and another user "Y" stakes 2, then X's vote will have more weight than Y's. The delegate that receives the highest number of votes gets a chance to produce new blocks. Delegates are compensated in the same way that other consensus processes on the blockchain, such as Proof-of-Stake, are compensated: with transaction fees or a fixed sum of cash. The DPOS consensus method is one of the most rapidly available blockchain consensus processes [14]. This mechanism can handle a higher number of transactions compared to the Proof of Work mechanism. Due to its stake-weighted voting system, DPOS is often considered a digital democracy.

4. **Proof-of-Capacity**

   In digital storage systems such as hard discs, the Proof-of-Capacity (PoC) approach is used to store solutions to complicated mathematical riddles that are difficult to solve. The term "plotting" refers to the entire process of creating a storyline. After a storage device has been filled with solutions to mathematical riddles, users can construct blocks of various shapes and sizes. Users that solve difficulties in the shortest amount of time are awarded the ability to create new blocks. As a result, people with the most available storage will be more likely to build a new block.

5. **Proof-of-Elapsed-Time**

   The Proof-of-Elapsed-Time (PoET) method picks the producer of a new block randomly and equitably based on the amount of time they have been waiting. Each user has a random wait time, and when that time expires, the first new block is generated by the user whose interval time has expired. This is accomplished by allocating a random wait time to each user. This consensus process is only effective if the system can verify that no user may simultaneously launch several nodes. As described above, the wait time is truly random [22].

6. **Proof-of-Identity**

   In Proof-of-Identity (PoI), a user's private key is compared to the private key of an authorised identity. Making the cryptographic claim that a user's private key has been cryptographically connected with a particular transaction is referred to as "cryptographically" proving a user's identity. A data block can be created by anyone who is recognised by the blockchain network, and this data block can be accessed by other members of the blockchain network. The integrity and veracity of information are ensured by using identity verification [15]. To provide an additional layer of protection, smart cities can leverage blockchain consensus techniques such as PoI to confirm their citizens' identities.

7. **Proof-of-Authority**

   When using this approach, network validators' identities are put at risk in exchange for a stake in the network, which is similar to the Proof of Stake procedure in its basic form. In this scenario, the identity is the correspondence between validators' personal identification and their official documentation to help verify their identity. These validators stake their reputation on the network. In Proof of Authority, the nodes that become validators are the only ones allowed to produce new blocks. Validators whose identity is at stake are incentivised to secure and preserve the blockchain network. Also, the number of validators is fairly small (i.e. 25 or less).

8. **Proof-of-Activity**

   Proof of Activity is a hybrid technique that combines PoW with PoS. It is used to verify that a person has done something. Proof of Activity is a game in which miners seek to solve a puzzle to get their reward. Alternatively, Proof of Activity blocks are templates, including the block's mining payout address and header data. Next, the header information is utilised to produce a random group of validators to sign a block using the information included in the header.

Validators with a higher stake have a greater chance of being chosen to sign a new block than those with a lower stake. A new block becomes a part of the network once it has been signed by the validators that have been specified. If certain validators determine that the block is unsigned, the block is discarded, and a fresh block is used in its place. The network fees collected during the process are divided between the successful miner and validators.

Despite having similar goals, various blockchain consensus mechanisms ensure consensus with varying approaches. A single reliable consensus mechanism does not exist yet, but the existing ones have evolved to meet the needs of blockchain technology. Additionally, predicting the type of blockchain consensus mechanism that will be popular and useful in the long run can be increasingly complex as the underlying technology is fairly new. Hence, business leaders who wish to introduce blockchain technology must be well informed about the various blockchain consensus mechanisms.

1.5   BUILDING A BLOCKCHAIN

At its most basic level, a blockchain is a tamper-resistant data structure that records the transfer of anything valuable or interesting from one owner to another securely and irreversibly. Digital assets such as cryptocoin, Word documents, and Microsoft Surface tablet serial numbers can all be considered "something" in this context. In actuality, blockchain technology may be used to track anything that has a unique digital fingerprint associated with it. By creating a protocol, enforcing transaction laws, and allowing nodes on a distributed network of computers to self-police the whole transaction process, blockchain technology differentiates itself from other kinds of computing. No central server or trust authority is required, and it works instantly and worldwide (that is, internationally). Some people are excited about this possibility because they believe it can cut or eliminate intermediaries and transaction costs, enhancing the efficiency of corporate-consumer interactions in the process [16].

It is possible for any node on the network, which is required to construct a blockchain, to read from and write to this public blockchain. An unremovable tamper-proof data storage should be used to store the binary hash chain data item that contains the transactions in the chain. The Merkle tree structure appears to be a promising candidate for usage as a blockchain because it can store transactions and is impenetrable by hackers. However, there are certain complications. Bill must have faith that the service or website will act as his agent and that the server will keep track of the hash structure of his digital investment. Because there is no central authority, any node can deal with Bill's pending transaction. A rogue dominating node may send incorrect or fraudulent transactions to honest nodes, which may alsobe relayed to other nodes. One possible approach would be for the network to assign Bill's transaction at random; however, this would once again centralise power and rely on the integrity of the random number generator. Blockchains use consensus mechanisms to tackle this challenge, which are discussed in greater detail below. Algorithms for Reaching Consensus Blockchain solutions avoid using a centralised data storage system and the problems associated with trust and authority. They accomplish this by following a protocol that oversees the addition and maintenance of blocks. They do it by enforcing a consensus algorithm, which leads to the construction of a blockchain. This section describes the PoW consensus algorithm's functioning and how it differs from other consensus methods. The PoW concept assumes that a node on the network must prove its worth by incurring a cost and devoting time to solve a computationally difficult problem. The network provides an incentive—often in the form of money—in the form of payments to node operators when they include a blockchain block to encourage them to join the system and follow its rules. Once transactions have been verified as complying with the blockchain's rules, nodes can earn money by solving a cryptographic challenge.

Previously, it was mentioned that a central authority might randomly select a node to handle a new batch of transactions. This strategy would necessitate the use of a central random-number-generator, which might be enraged or deactivated. In contrast, providing nodes with a challenging problem to answer accomplishes the desired result: the node that solves the riddle first cannot be predicted in advance, resulting in a node lottery that spreads throughout the entire network. One of the fundamental breakthroughs of blockchain technologies is that no central authority is required. It is also said that blockchains are decentralised, which means they are resistant to collusion. Unprocessed transactions from the channel are gathered by a node, which then constructs a Merkle tree, from which the Merkle root hash is computed to generate a block of transactions. To gain an advantage over other peers, a single node or group of nodes cannot join the network due to the time and processing resources required for PoW. PoW consensus removes the risk of a "51% assault", where a group of nodes gains 51% of the overall processing power. By the time the PoW puzzle is solved, the 256-bit block hash value will have been twice hashed, concatenated with a 32-bit integer known as the nonce, and checked to ensure that its hash yields a result with a specific number of leading zeroes. It is common to use the 32-bit nonce (0), generate the SHA-256 hash and check if it encompasses the desired number of prominent zeroes (i.e. the resulting value is less than an intended value). If it doesn't, the node increases the nonce value and tries again. Until the necessary number of leading zeroes is reached, continue step 2. Iterating through all nonce values fails, therefore the block hash value is recalculated and the procedure restarted. This assures a unique block hash value since the block header contains a timestamp used in the block hash computation. When a node checks a new block, it can include a different set of pending transactions (or add new pending transactions that have appeared since the previous check), which modifies the Merkle root hash-value, which modifies the freshly computed block hash value, and the timestamp, which is then updated on the blockchain. When computing the block hash, the node uses all 4 billion nonces in its memory.

Some network nodes eventually solve the cryptographic riddle by adding the new block to its duplicate of the blockchain (each node keeps a replica) and then broadcasting it to all other nodes on the network, allowing them to update their own blockchain copies in the process. Nodes that get a new blocly trust that it is legitimate and validate the block to confirm its authenticity to themselves. Validation is done by computing the SHA-256 hash of the block and concatenating it with a nonce value.

The answer is checked to see if it has the number of leading zeros defined by the PoW difficulty for that block.

The protocol updates the PoW difficulty values in some blockchains regularly, resulting in the generation of new blocks regularly, depending on how frequently it runs. A frequent adjustment must be made to the average processing power of the nodes because new and old nodes enter and leave the network regularly. Keep in mind that there is an incentive to contribute blocks to the blockchain in PoW, which is why node operators routinely update their hardware to compete for a prize. To ensure that blocks are added at a rate of 10 minutes per block, the difficulty number on the Bitcoin network is adjusted every 2016 block.

In the course of the game, branches can appear at any time. This is a concern due to the length of time required for new-block propagation on a large network. Nodes may solve their PoW puzzles during propagation, add new blocks to their local copies of the blockchain, and then broadcast those local copies to the network as a whole, all at once. If two distinct nodes at each end of a blockchain chain publish two new blocks, the result will be a branch that is linked to the same block. Yes, absolutely. According to the protocol, nodes will gradually add new blocks to the end of the "longest chain," until that chain has grown to infinity length. The chain with the most recent block timestamp may be the longest one given a branch. Abandoned branches will have their transactions returned to the unprocessed transaction pool once they have been deleted [12, 13, 17].

1.6   RECORD-KEEPING WITH BLOCKCHAIN

Due to the size of data, it is blockchain-dependent whether customers can store entire files on-chain or rely on off-chain storage such as a cloud or an Interplanetary-File-System (IPFS). IPFS is a P2P (Peer-to-Peer) distributed file system that enables the storage and sharing of data between users. It connects computing devices to a common data network, with each device storing and disseminating a small amount of the overall data. In the case of a blockchain, the chain simply stores the IPFS file's associated hash. Additional issues are raised and are an interesting research topic in and of themselves by off-chain (also known as "second-layer") blockchain solutions, but this is not the study's objective [18].

A blockchain is a type of database that only permits data reading and adding. The environment is a peer-to-peer network, meaning users (peers) communicate directly without trusted intermediaries or authorities. Numerous authors have referred to this as "trustless trust." A trade agreement's members agree to exchange physical or digital assets, such as currency, for one another. To verify that the transaction is complete and accurate, nodes from other network users apply the system's particular rules to analyse it. The requirement for verification comes from the immutability (tamper-proof) nature of all data and transactions on a blockchain. The network's consensus process is in charge of establishing how user verifications are conducted. As an illustration, we will look at the Proof-of-Work (PoW) consensus method. This technique is the most well-known and is used in the Bitcoin network, among other blockchains; nonetheless, it has been criticised for requiring excessive energy, which we will use to demonstrate our argument. The alternative is Proof-of-Stake (PoS), an energy-efficient and performant mechanism for verifying transactions and establishing consensus on them [6].

1.7   TYPES OF BLOCKCHAIN

Data privacy has become increasingly crucial in the digital era, as individuals and businesses conduct a range of transactions online, including purchasing goods and services, paying bills, and authenticating information. Due to the Strong Hash Key encryption, sending and receiving data over the internet without disclosing your genuine identity is incredibly safe. When a business is conducted over the blockchain's peer-to-peer network, the owner's identity is never revealed. By participating in the blockchain ecosystem, you will better understand and enforce your legal rights and liberties. As an excellent way to carry out an agreement between two parties, the Smart Contract on the blockchain is an excellent way to do so since it enables transactions to occur only once certain predefined benchmarks have been met and agreed upon by both sides [19].

1.7.1   PUBLIC BLOCKCHAIN

On a public blockchain, which is completely decentralised, everyone can read and send transactions, whereas, on a private blockchain, anyone can read transactions. The ledger maintains a record of all transactions. Cryptoeconomics, a combination of economic incentives and cryptographic verification, is used to safeguard public blockchains [7]. The quantity of economic resources added into the system determines how they influence the consensus process.

- Developers may use Ethereum to build distributed applications and perform smart contracts because it is a decentralised platform and programming language [20, 23].
- Blockstream is a blockchain technology company that places a strong emphasis on enhancing the capabilities of cryptography and distributed networks. Their goal is to establish an ecosystem that will address fraud, forgery, accountability, and transparency in financial systems by collaborating with other organisations.
- Factom—Developed the foundational blockchain data infrastructure for Factom technology, an open-source platform for distributed ledger technology.

1.7.2   PRIVATE BLOCKCHAIN

In a private blockchain, write permissions are centralised in the hands of a single organisation. The central authority has complete control over access and permissions in this system, and the capacity to modify them is restricted to that authority. This might be a concept that gets great interest from financial institutions and huge enterprises alike. The use of a private blockchain-based proprietary system will reduce transaction costs while increasing the efficiency of validation.

- Eris Industries is a blockchain client provider for multiple networks. It is a proof-of-stake blockchain with a programmable, smart contract-enabled architecture.
- Blockstack—Using blockstack.js APIs, developers may authenticate users, access data, and store it.
- MultiChain—Provides an open-source distributed database for financial transactions.
- Chain Incorporated—It's a blockchain architecture for enterprises, similar to Multichain, that enables firms to build improved financial services from the ground up [21].

1.8   LIMITATIONS OF BLOCKCHAIN TECHNOLOGY

Blockchain technology offers enormous promise for creating decentralised, trustless applications. It is, however, not without problems. Several impediments make blockchain technology unsuitable for general usage. The image below demonstrates the limitations of blockchain technology. Despite the enormous interest in blockchain technology these days, few people grasp its true utility or how to apply it in various settings. Today, numerous developers are available that can perform a wide range of activities in a wide range of industries. However, there aren't nearly as many developers with specialised knowledge when it comes to blockchain technology. As a result, a dearth of developers makes it difficult to produce anything on the blockchain. Every node in a distributed ledger, such as bitcoin that takes part in the transaction, must validate it. It restricts the number of transactions that a blockchain network can process at any given time. According to the protocol, the protocol allows for the creation of a new block to the blockchain every ten minutes. This is because each transaction must ensure that the blockchain network's blocks reach a shared consensus. The back-and-forth conversations required to reach a consensus on a blockchain can take a long time to complete, depending on the size of the network and the number of blocks or nodes in a blockchain. This can take a significant amount of time and resources. Finally, the immutability of blockchain technology and its core management characteristics may make certain transactions more difficult to complete.

1.9   FUTURE DIRECTIONS

The future of blockchain technology will either go in one of two directions or both directions. Those applications that demand decentralised, highly secure networks will fall into the first of these two categories. When used in blockchain technology, breakthroughs in artificial intelligence can significantly increase its value. Such advancements include the potential to decentralise ownership of big data, which is now owned entirely by enterprises, and the ability to democratise ownership and sharing by creating a marketplace for such data. Individuals will have control over their data and will be able to decide when and how their information is shared with third parties under this arrangement . Additionally, smaller artificial intelligence (AI) companies will use this data to improve AI, undermining the major corporations' data monopoly. Blockchain and artificial intelligence have the potential to be utilised in cybersecurity. Training machine learning algorithms to automate real-time threat detection and learn about attacker behaviour can provide a double layer of defence against cyberattacks, and decentralised blockchains can help alleviate the inherent vulnerability of centralised databases [24, 25].

The potential of blockchain technology to maintain anonymity and immutability can also be used to securely and immutably store highly sensitive, personal data essential for recognising patterns in delicate circumstances, such as those involving the healthcare industry. Blockchain can also assist in dissecting the AI black box by tracing how algorithms work and how their input influences machine learning output. At the same time, AI can significantly boost the efficiency of blockchain, considerably more so than humans or traditional computing. In addition, because Bitcoin has been widely regarded as blockchain's first revolutionary success, it can aid in the expansion of the technology's uses, increasing the attractiveness of both Bitcoin and artificial intelligence and its plethora of potential applications. Blockchain and artificial intelligence are still in their infancy, and much will be dependent on technology developments that are yet to be discovered in the future to be successful. However, the value and utility of their individual and combined utility have the potential to reach new heights in terms of value and usefulness. This was true with the Internet and all other new technologies, the utility of which was massively overstated at the time of their commercial launch.

1.10 CONCLUSION

The difficulty of encouraging secure commerce and other interactions among strangers has faced governments throughout history as civilisation has evolved beyond tribes and small groups of people to include people from all over the world. The purpose of providing a safe transaction means has not changed, even though the technologies used have gotten more diverse in recent years. The Internet of Things (IoT) and big data are transforming the world into an increasingly complex one. Blockchain will play a critical role in our digital world's financial and technological future, and it is already making headlines. Through the elimination of corporate intermediaries from global commerce, the bitcoin "blockchain" technology has the potential to trigger an innovation tsunami that will eliminate the middleman and make it possible to sell goods and services to anyone in the world without the need to go through a corporate middleman. A result of its decentralisation capability, it has the potential to completely decentralise civilisation by obviating the need for financial institutions, governments, corporations, and political leaders. Blockchain has already demonstrated its ability to disrupt current businesses due to its basic traits of decentralisation, durability (which can persist indefinitely), anonymity, and auditability, which are all characteristics of blockchain technology. The core concepts of blockchain technology were covered in detail in this section. A brief introduction to blockchain technology can make it easier to include crucial technological components, such as the critical attributes required for the development of blockchain-based apps, into a project's design. As a result, the discussion moved on to the various consensus procedures that are frequently employed in the context of blockchain technologies. In addition, the many types of blockchains (shown in the table 1.1), their limitations, and the roadblocks to further blockchain adoption are examined in greater depth in this chapter. In addition, the document contains some recommendations for possible future avenues to pursue. Applications that use blockchain technology are becoming increasingly popular, and we plan to undertake greater research into them in the future.

Table 1.1
Types of Blockchain

Public	Private	Consortium
It can be accessed by anyone	A single organisation can access	Multiple but few selected organisations can access
Participants can be permissionless & anonymous	Participants are permissioned with known identities	Participants are permissioned with known identities
Security via consensus mechanisms	Pre-approved participants with multi-party consensus	Pre-approved participants with multi-party consensus

Bibliography

1. Andrews George, A. (2021, APRIL 17). Blockchain Technology – Everything you need to know in layman's language. ClearIAS. https://www.clearias.com/blockchain-technology/

2. Marr, B. (2020). Why Use Blockchain Technology? Bernard Marr & Co. https://bernardmarr.com/why-use-blockchain-technology/

3. Simplilearn. (2021, September 29). What is Blockchain Technology and How Does It Work? Simplilearn. https://www.simplilearn.com/tutorials/blockchain-tutorial/blockchain-technology

4. IBM. (2021). What are smart contracts on blockchain? IBM. https://www.ibm.com/in-en/topics/smart-contracts

5. Weking, J., Mandalenakis, M., Hein, A., Hermes, S., Böhm, M., & Krcmar, H. (2019, December 23). The impact of blockchain technology on business

models – a taxonomy and archetypal patterns. Electronic Markets, 31(2), 285–305. https://doi.org/10.1007/s12525-019-00386-3

6. Leible, S., Schlager, S., Schubotz, M., & Gipp, B. (2019, November 19). A Review on Blockchain Technology and Blockchain Projects Fostering Open Science. Frontiers in Blockchain, 2, 1–28.

7. Iredale, G. (2021, February 9). Why Blockchain Is Important? 101 Blockchains. https://101blockchains.com/why-blockchain-is-important/

8. Ali, S., Wang, G., White, B., & Leslie Cottrell, R. (2020). A Blockchain-based Decentralised Data Storage and Access Framework for PingER. IEEE International Conference On Big Data Science And Engineering. https://www.osti.gov/pages/servlets/purl/1475405

9. LAKE, J. (2019, April 10). Understanding cryptography's role in blockchains. Comparitech. https://www.comparitech.com/crypto/cryptography-blockchain/

10. i-Scoop. (2021). Blockchain technology and distributed ledger technology (DLT) in business. i-Scoop. https://www.i-scoop.eu/blockchain-distributed-ledger-technology/

11. Lawton, G. (2021, June). Smart Contract. TechTarget. https://searchcompliance.techtarget.com/definition/smart-contract

12. Do, H. T., Truong, L. H., Nguyen, M. T., Chien, C.-F., & Tran, H. T. (2021, May 29). A Blockchain-Based Vehicle Condition Recording System for Second-Hand Vehicle Market. Wireless Communications and Mobile Computing, 2021, 10. https://doi.org/10.1155/2021/6623251

13. Frankenfield, J. (2021, August 4). Consensus Mechanism (Cryptocurrency). Investopedia. https://www.investopedia.com/terms/c/consensus-mechanism-cryptocurrency.asp

14. Sharma, N., Shamkuwar, M., Kumaresh, S., Singh, I., & Goje, A. (2021). Chapter 10 - Introduction to blockchain and distributed systems—fundamental theories and concepts. In Blockchain for Smart Cities (pp. 183-210). ScienceDirect. https://doi.org/10.1016/B978-0-12-824446-3.00002-8

15. Alsalamah, H. A., Alsuwailem, G., Bin Rajeh, F., Alharbi, S., AlQahtani, S., AlArifi, R., AlShargi, S., Alsalamah, S. A., & Alsalamah, S. (2021, June 30). eHomeCaregiving: A Diabetes Patient-Centered Blockchain Ecosystem for COVID-19 Caregiving. Frontiers in Blockchain. https://doi.org/10.3389/fbloc.2021.477012

16. Waldman, J. (2019, April 1). Blockchain Fundamentals. Microsoft Ignite. https://docs.microsoft.com/en-us/archive/msdn-magazine/2018/march/blockchain-blockchain-fundamentals

17. JOSHI, N. (2019, April 23). 8 blockchain consensus mechanisms you should know about. Allerin. `https://www.allerin.com/blog/8-blockchain-consensus-mechanisms-you-should-know-about`

18. Bhatt, S., Hotchandani, S., Gaur, K. R., & Sirsikar, S. (2020). Introduction to LifeBlocks: A Blockchain based Insurance Platform. ICETE, 77-81. `10.5220/0009854000770081`

19. Pramod. (2020, September 21). BlockChain Principle, Type & Application & Why You Should Care About It?, `https://medium.com/the-programmer/blockchain-principle-type-application-why-you-should-care-about-it-249417b516cc`

20. Joshua. (2021, September 21). INTRODUCTION TO SMART CONTRACTS. ethereum. `https://ethereum.org/en/developers/docs/smart-contracts/`

21. MaruthiT echlabs. (2020). Blockchain Technology and its Implications on the Financial Platform. MaruthiT echlabs. `https://marutitech.com/blockchain-technology-implications-financial-platform/`

22. Aggarwal, S., & Kumar, N. (2021). Chapter Eleven - Cryptographic consensus mechanisms. In Advances in Computers (Vol. 121, pp. 211-226). ScienceDirect. `https://doi.org/10.1016/bs.adcom.2020.08.011`.

23. De Meijer, C. R. W. (2020, September 30). Smart working with blockchain-based smart contracts. Finextra. `https://www.finextra.com/blogposting/19383/smart-working-with-blockchain-based-smart-contracts`.

24. Zibin Zheng, Shaoan Xie, Hongning Dai, Xiangping Chen, and Huaimin Wang. (2017). An Overview of Blockchain Technology: Architecture, Consensus, and Future Trends. 2017 IEEE 6th International Congress on Big Data.

25. Spyros Makridakis and Klitos Christodoulou. (2019) Blockchain: Current Challenges and Future Prospects/Applications, Future Internet 2019, 11, 258; `doi:10.3390/fi11120258`

26. H. -N. Dai, Z. Zheng and Y. Zhang, Blockchain for Internet of Things: A Survey, in IEEE Internet of Things Journal, vol. 6, no. 5, pp. 8076-8094, Oct. 2019, doi: `10.1109/JIOT.2019.2920987`.

27. W. Zhang, J. Yu, Q. He, N. Zhang and N. Guan, TICK: Tiny Client for Blockchains, in IEEE Internet of Things Journal, `doi:10.1109/JIOT.2020.3015476`.

2 Unraveling the Blockchain: A Study on Blockchain and Its Potential Applications

Blockchain is a decentralised, distributed, and public ledger shared among all the members of a distributed network. In Blockchain, data can be easily recorded and audited without being altered or manipulated. The information is stored in blocks, in chronological order, with the data being immutable and non-modifiable. Whenever a change is made, it is added as a new block, thereby keeping the previous information intact and easy to revert to [33]. Blockchain has all the potential to prove to be efficient in the current trustless environment. Given its decentralised nature and computational power, its use is growing every day.

Contrary to the centralised system such as modern financial institutions, Blockchain tends to use a decentralised network paradigm to regulate and protect the information nullifying the presence of centralised authority. The network comprises a set of authorised participants who hold the democratic power to condone or sanction any transaction over the blockchain network. As long as the participants have access to the Blockchain network, they have their copy of the ledger, which is immutable and shared across other users. A node or computer on one particular participant, if it corrupts the data, the other participants get an alert to review the change done and recover or sanction the difference if needed [49]. Therefore, the most common and typical blockchain network is a public blockchain. A wide range of information such as transaction receipts, billing information, signed digital documents, etc., can be accommodated on a blockchain. Still, the pivotal usage has been in the transaction ledgers. The data stored on Blockchain can be anything quantifiable: numbers, transactions, finances, etc. this easy storage and access to data, combined with its immutable, secure nature, makes Blockchain a preferred technology for all industries involved recording anything of value [13].

The technology has been introduced by Satoshi Nakamoto as a part of the bitcoin publication in the year 2008. Ever since its advent, continuous efforts were made by researchers, experts, and volunteers to inculcate the idea of virtual currency into the real world. The impact of blockchain technology has been walloping, but its practical implementation aspects still need further exploration. The systematic overview of evolution in blockchain technology is shown in Figure 2.1.

Blockchain quells the need of third-party companies, parties, or vendors and brings transparency between both parties of the transaction. The domain of banking, finance, and healthcare yields more from blockchain technology since these areas involve maintaining a large number of billings, transactions, and exchanges of money, etc. Even now, new Blockchain-based cryptocurrencies are being introduced

DOI: 10.1201/9781003355052-2

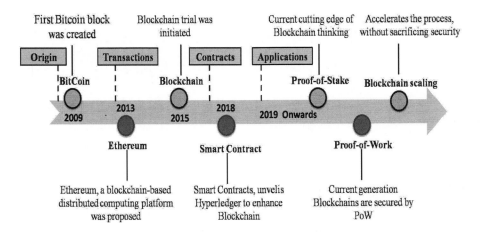

Figure 2.1   Evolution of blockchain technology

and had been sustaining in the market, and people are embracing the idea of virtual currency over the private networks willfully. Blockchain technology is not limited to just cryptocurrency, but it has its widespread applications in various domains. Today, Blockchain's widespread usage ranges from cryptocurrency transactions to recording assets to finance, and potentially anything of value, and has revolutionised the way information is used and exchanged [2].

The information inside the chain is usually encrypted using cryptographic techniques, which is of utmost importance in preserving the end-users' privacy and ensuring data integrity. The notable difference between the Blockchain and the typical RDBMS is in the way the information is stored. The difference is in the following terms,

- The data gets organised into a set of blocks, which are chained together
- A new block gets created for new incoming data
- Each new block is then tagged to the previous block and then chained together in the chronological order of their addition to the existing chain

Every innovation aims to solve a problem, and Blockchain is no exception. The benefits of employing blockchain technology in most emerging applications have brought up its usage to the maximum capacity, and giant firms such as Amazon, Google, and Facebook, have emerged to exploit the blockchain advancements efficiently. Moreover, Blockchain is believed to provide more security and immutability for storing individual's confidential information.

Blockchain technology is adopted in many domains and showcased to play a critical part in 5G and beyond networks. By empowering dynamic programing and confided transactions, smart contracts enable infrastructures among virtual network operators, infrastructure providers, and service providers. Blockchain devises to create a new business model for ephemeral networks for better inclusion and service. Further, the "Blockchain-as-a-service" ecosystem offers mobile operators and content providers to utilise the Blockchain infrastructure for access control and monetisation. Blockchain facilitates protection and security, identity management, and monetisation of the service for IoT networks. However, the Blockchain framework help to build up that evidence base, aggregate data from disparate sources, and be known to maintain integrity.

Blockchain's strength lies in its immutable nature, ensuring transparency of transactions while simultaneously privatising user details. This paper presents a systematic approach to exploring every possible way of using this valuable technology. This paper discusses the various technological facets of Blockchain, real-time applications, and future research directions. On a high level, the reader will be able to get the following knowledge upon reading this paper.

- Systematic inspection blockchain technology and it's working.
- Applications of Blockchain in various domains.
- Future possible research directions to explore.
- Systematic comparison of various alternatives for a task in blockchain technology.

Upcoming sections of this paper are as follows; Section 2.1 provides insights into the concept of decentralisation and its usage in the Blockchain. Section 2.2 discussed the consensus algorithms where the concept of proof of stake and proof of work is explored. Section 2.3 describes the Distributed ledger, the structure of the ledger, and its usage. Section 2.4 and 2.5 give the recent developments and platforms that incorporate blockchain technology. Section 2.7 and 2.6 cover the applications, challenges, and future research prospects in blockchain technology.

2.1 BACKGROUND

Bitcoin (digital currency) was the first significant innovation based on blockchain technology. The second significant innovation was to extend the underlying technology used in Bitcoin (i.e., blockchain) for all kinds of other inter-organisational transaction related operations [30]. The third innovation related to blockchain technology is Smart Contract, which was used in Ethereum (second-generation blockchain system) [39]. Ethereum is open-source blockchain and decentralised smart contract technology. Ethereum allows recording transactions related to financial instruments, loans, or bonds instead of only the cash-similar tokens of bitcoin. The fourth major advancement in the blockchain is Proof of Stake (PoS) and Proof of Work (PoW) consensus algorithms. Contemporary blockchains are protected by Proof-of-Work (PoW), wherein the individual (or group) who holds the highest total computational capacity plays a vital role and influences the outcome/decisions. The individuals/group who control the computational power are called miners, who own data centers and deliver safe cryptocurrency payments. Blockchain scaling is regarded as the fifth major innovation [46]. In the typical functioning of blockchain, it is necessary to access every transaction to be accessed by every computer, which causes error and delay in network. As opposed to this, the idea of scaled blockchain is to process the blockchain transaction without compromising security. Scaled blockchain estimates the number of computers (or amount of computational power) required to validate every transaction. Further, it divides up the work efficiently among miners.

This innovation landscape represents a mere ten years of work by an elite group of computer scientists, cryptographers, and mathematicians. From enterprises to MNCs to even countries, everyone is looking forward to building a better future with the help of Blockchain, a vital component of the fourth revolution that the world is currently witnessing. The fourth Industrial revolution magnanimously changed the world's perception of the business, with technological advancement contributing for the most. The innovations in connectivity and end-devices available at affordable prices pushed the business leaders to reassess their business strategy [15]. Table 2.1 summarizes the roles and responsibilities of various endusers/entities involved during a Blockchain transactions.

2.1.1   STRUCTURE OF BLOCKCHAIN

The Blockchain data structure utilises hashing algorithm to determine each block's unique indices; all the transactions get chained as a Linked list that we can access bi-directionally. Individual blocks can be stored on flat files or in the traditional databases. The hash computed uniquely for each block is stored in the block header and is used to identify each block uniquely. A block data structure is a form of a container that wraps all the information related to transactions. A set of blocks together forms the public ledger. The basic structure of the block comprises of header and a long list of transactions. The block header comprises metadata which provides information about the transactions and the block itself. Metadata information in the header consists of the following fields,

- *Index* – indicates the position of the block inside the block chain. Indexing starts with 0, 1, and so on.
- *Hash* – hash generated by hash function uniquely identifies the data present in each block
- *Previous Hash* – each block is linked to its predecessor. The chaining promotes immutability, as a slight change in the block data, causes an immense difference in the whole computation in the rest of the chain.
- *numTx* – stores the number of transactions added to the block.
- *Nonce* – stores the integer used for the mining process
- *Transaction* – An array inside the block's body that holds the summary of all transactions that occured on it to date.

The Blockchain is composed of blocks chained together to constitute the public distributed ledger. Each block has a unique hash which is the digital signature of itself. The transactions occurring on the Blockchain gets verified by consensus algorithm such as Proof-of-Work (PoW), Proof-of-Stake (PoS). To validate the transactions, miners over the blockchain network solve the cryptographic puzzle for rewards.

Table 2.1

Roles and Responsibilities of Entities in Blockchain

Role	Explanation	Example
Customer	A customer is someone who sends and accepts requests in the Blockchain network. They create or run their node in the Ethereum network. In a token-based platform, the user is considered to be a participant, who is rewarded based on an auction mechanism. If the customer invests in the Blockchain network, he can also be considered an investor. He carries out transactions using cryptocurrencies	Any individul or organisation who wish to store information using Blockchain
Infrastructure Provider	The provider of the infrastructure provides users with a platform to carry out their activities and transactions. The provider also sets the rules and conditions based on which the users must act upon.	Hyperledger, Bitcoin, Ethereum
Application Provider	These providers offer applications that are linked to online services and offline services. A large part of application providers revolves around wallets. These wallets, designed to store cryptocurrencies, come with their features and security. One of the main functions of application providers is to ensure the smooth operation of their services to the end-users. The providers must be aware of the system at all times.	Databroker, Power Ledger, Binded
Miners	The miners are responsible for keeping track of all the transactions taking place on the network. As a reward for their work, the miners are given cryptocurrencies in payment. Whether or not miners are involved in the network depends on the type of Blockchain platform used.	Bitfury, Antpool
Mining Solution Provider	These providers give the hardware and software required for the process of mining. This includes repair and maintenance. Besides proving complex hardware for computing, mining providers also provide cloud-mining solutions for those unable to handle hardware mechanism.	MinesGate, Canaan, Genesis Mining
Blockchain Community	The Blockchain community is vital in running the Blockchain network. Consisting of individuals deeply invested in Blockchain, this community discusses the prospects of a new currency, applications, etc. this community is vital in break-throughs and innovations in the Blockchain sphere.	Reddit, Blockchain Community
Blockchain Consulting Services	When an organisation wishes to inculcate or leverage Blockchain technology, they often consult experts in the Blockchain domain. These services explain the requirements, cost, maintenance, etc., to the organisation. Generally, mining service providers seek the expertise of consulting services in cases of technical glitches.	Accenture, Consensys, Cisco, IBM, etc.

Though the data storage is similar to traditional databases, the key difference is how the data is structured. A set of transactions are cumulated together and get stored under a block. Each of the blocks has varying capacities when filled are chained together to form the Blockchain, which is immutable over time. Any new information added gets compiled to create a new block and then gets added to the chain upon validation from consensus algorithms [14].

Another critical difference between databases and blockchain is that databases store the data into tables, whereas the latter gets stored as a set of blocks. This organisation also creates an irreversible timeline of data over decentralised networks. Since the timestamp is another entity that gets tagged along with data, the transactions are inherently foolproof. When the block gets filled, it undergoes validation and becomes part of the blockchain, and none can deny its existence over time once it gets added to the chain [28].

2.1.2 BLOCKCHAIN TYPES

There are primarily three types of Blockchain – Public, Private, and Hybrid Blockchains.

Public Blockchain – Transactions taking place here is completely transparent. All the users have the facility to examine the details of the transaction. Public Blockchains are designed to be completely decentralised, meaning no single individual has complete control over the Blockchain functionality. However, given its open nature and transparency, users, irrespective of their location, nationality, etc., can join this network, making it extremely difficult for authorities to trace and shut them down. This system is based on tokens. Meaning, the system rewards its users for using and participating in the network.

Private Blockchain – This is also known as Permissioned Blockchain. These have several notable differences compared to public Blockchains. Primarily, to join this network, users must need consent from the authority handling it. The transactions carried out here are completely private and are visible only to users within the network. Unlike public Blockchain, they are centralised, meaning an authority supervises the operations. Private Blockchains are very valuable to businesses who prefer to hide details of their transactions from the public. These Blockchains may or may not have a token-based system.

Hybrid Blockchain – This Blockchain is a combination of both Public and Private Blockchains. The advantage of the transparency of public Blockchain and permissioned status of private Blockchain is that it allows businesses with great flexibility to share data either in public or keep it private. Another advantage is the ability to form InterChains, meaning this Blockchain allows easy connectivity to other Blockchain protocol. The ability to carry out multiple public Blockchains at once increases the transaction's security as well, as the combined hash power is high.

2.1.3 RELATED WORKS

Many existing works of literature outline the methodology that employs Blockchain technology, their evaluations, and comparisons [13]. However, representing the systematic mapping process of Blockchain technology into the various domains is required to highlight its functionality. Figure 2.2 illustrates the mapping of Blockchain Technology applications' taxonomy in various domains.

2.1.3.1 Current Research on Blockchain Technology

The authors [45] focused extensively on currency transactions using cryptocurrencies. According to their research, Blockchain is best suited for banking transactions,

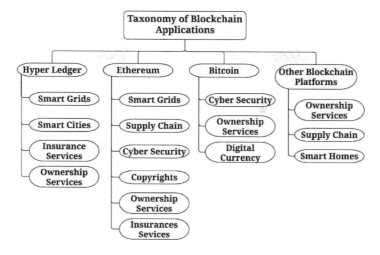

Figure 2.2 Platform based taxonomy of blockchain applications

given its security features and scalability. However, it poses its set limitations. High integrity and security, combined with the privacy of nodes, are needed to prevent on-line attacks, and attempts to imbalance transactions in Blockchain [36] [48]. Besides, these transactions require considerable computational power and capacity.

2.1.3.2   Technology in Healthcare

Authors et al. [26] have shifted their focus from viewing Blockchain just as a financial related technology to its diverse use in the healthcare domain. With instances of public healthcare management to user-oriented medical research, the use of this disruptive technology is vast [25]. While Blockchain has its influence on various domains, one of them aims at societal development.

2.1.3.3   Securing Smart Cities Using Blockchain Technology

Authors et al. [12] proposed using the Internet of Things (IoT) with Blockchain. They intend to completely automate an entire city using Blockchain and provide the platform to secure users' devices from tampering and ensure secure communication. This, however, remains a proposal with varied problems of its own.

2.1.3.4   Blockchain Technology in the Chemical Industry

Authors et al. [37] explored the use of Blockchain in the trading of electricity between two electricity-producing machines and one electricity-consuming machine in the context of the chemical industry. The paper contributes a proof of implementation and discusses the use of Blockchain in revolutionising industries further [17].

2.1.3.5   Blockchain Technology in the Insurance

Earlier to the evolution of Blockchain technology, digital currency or e-currency was considered to record the transactions by ensuring no redundancy in the process, utilising digital signatures [43]. However, over the years the issue related to anonymity, compatibility, and centralisation persisted which showcased to introduce bitcoin. The pioneer of bitcoin ensured to overcome these issues by employing the concept of consensus mechanism exhibiting PoW and ledger information among the distributed machines. Further, perceived the technique behind the bitcoin, there exists a Blockchain technology that has ledgers sharing information, employing cryptographic proof of transactions and consensus recording of transactions, shared across the connected machines [31].

The application of cryptography in bitcoin insists on less intervention of the third party to record transactions since the same process could be done through the system permitting to substantiate through a consensus algorithm [27]. The cryptographic signature is essential in the Blockchain to record the transactions of any ledger [20]. The Blockchain technology has made an impact on the insurance application, and many applications have proposed using this technology at different sectors, including: the Government employs this technology to empower an autonomous governance system to bring transparency in recording the citizen's votes or any political programs [3][42]; Intellectual property to validate the authorship of a document with evidence [5]; Internet to diminish censorship, by utilising the immutability of information put away in the Blockchain [32][7]; Finance for the money transaction between two parties without having dependent on banks [47]; Commerce to reduce the market of counterfeit by recording the luxury good's characteristics and ownership [24]; Internet of Things (IoT) employs Blockchain technology to dynamically process the information that is originated from sensors by exploiting smart contracts, to let intelligent machines communicate with one another and autonomously take actions when explicit circumstances happen [40]; In education to accumulate the information on qualifications obtained by learners, to diminish the job application frauds, universities and training institutions could write qualification information accomplished by a person on the Blockchain; human staff can get to know the competency about the information from where and when that were obtained.

2.2   CONSENSUS ALGORITHM

While dealing with cryptocurrencies, it is always important to keep track of the balance of users. This is done with the help of Blockchain, where a copy of the database is distributed to the user. Public-key cryptocurrency ensures that users do not spend each other's currencies. In order to main maintain coordination and transparency, the method of PoW was introduced. As an alternative, where specialised workspaces and complicated hardware were not required, PoS was introduced, requiring a normal and regular PC for users to use. Each of these are discussed as follows:

Proof-of-Work (PoW) – In this method, the users, referred to as miners, hash the data until the desired output has been obtained. A hash is a random string of letters and numbers that are run through a hash function. By running the same data over and again, the output does not change. Through hash, a slight change can produce a completely different output. In PoW, the protocol defines conditions to make a block valid. For example, a hash beginning with 02 is considered valid. The only way to ensure a hash is created with the same combination is by using brute-force inputs and guessing until the hash is correct. This way of finding the right hash takes high computational power, electricity, and time. If right, the reward is worthwhile, else large amounts of electricity and time are wasted in vain.

Proof-of-Stake (PoS) – Unlike PoW, which involves complex mechanisms, PoS focuses more on storing the funds in a wallet. Here, the user takes his chance/bets on the block selected, and the protocol decides which one to choose. If selected, a portion of the transaction fee is given to the user who bets correctly (depending on the stake). If a user cheats by proposing invalid transactions, a portion of the stake is withdrawn. PoS is, therefore, deployed in minor currencies where the stakes are not high.

2.3   DISTRIBUTED LEDGER

A shared and synchronised database across different platforms and multiple users accessing from diverse geographical locations is called a Distributed Ledger. The transactions carried out here have witnesses. Users at the end of each node can access the recordings of transactions shared across the network. They are also permitted to own a copy of the same. Any changes induced in the ledger are reflected across all the copies in a matter of seconds. A Distributed Ledger, unlike its counterpart, a Centralised Ledger, is highly immune to cyber-attacks and fraud. Besides, it evades the single-point failure persistent in Centralised Ledgers. This system allows the elimination of a central authority in maintaining security. All the information is stored securely using cryptography methods and can only be accessed through keys and cryptographic signatures.

2.3.1   ETHEREUM

Ethereum is a decentralised open-source platform based on Blockchain, used mainly for its currency transaction (Ether). It promises high computation, eliminates fraud and interference from the third party [50]. Their currency, Ether, is comparable to a vehicle-like token that moves around the entire platform and is coveted by application developers working on Ethereum [23]. The main function and purpose of Ether are classified as follows – a digital currency and to run applications inside Ethereum. The complete structure is very identical to that of Bitcoin. Meaning, a copy of the transaction history is shared among users accessing their respective nodes [41] [16]. Also, every time a user wishes to perform some action, all the other nodes must acknowledge this action.

2.3.2   HYPERLEDGER

The Hyperledger project, whose subsidiaries include various other projects, was mainly developed to build open-source Blockchain and other related applications whose usage is deemed to span a wide range of industries. It also aims at facilitating businesses to run their operations effectively and smoothly. Hyperledger is essentially a cryptocurrency network. However, it does not support cryptocurrencies like Bitcoin, rather provides resources and a platform to develop infrastructure for Blockchain-based systems designed for industrial use. Some of the various projects being developed under this are as follows – Hyperledger Fabric [8], Hyperledger Composer [44], Hyperledger Cello [9], Hyperledger Explorer [22], Hyperledger Burrow [35], Hyperledger Sawtooth [6], and Hyperledger Caliper [21]. All of these projects follow a methodology that allows security, expandable, and concise approach. The main components in the architecture of Hyperledger include:

- Consensus Layer – meant for authenticating correctness and agreements.
- Smart Contact layer – responsible for authorising only valid transactions.
- Communication Layer – user-to-user message transfer.
- Identity Management Service – maintaining and validating identities to ensure trust.
- API – enables external clients and applications to interfere with Blockchain.

2.4   RECENT DEVELOPMENTS IN BLOCKCHAIN TECHNOLOGY

Blockchain has taken the FinTech sphere by storm. Its embedment in finance industries, its rising popularity among cryptocurrencies, and its potential to create applications have seen Blockchain's use grow exponentially. Commercially carried out transactions using Blockchain technology share specific vital characteristics, such as – Real-time records, immutable records, anonymity, cybersecurity risk, and tax implications [4]. Blockchain's flexible nature has been utilised to fulfill demands and developments in various other domains too.

2.4.1   COMPANIES ACTIVELY INVOLVED IN BLOCKCHAIN RESEARCH

With the world moving towards Blockchain technology, the demand for customised and advanced applications is constantly rising globally. With many companies wanting to capitalise on this, the journey has never been easy. The development of Blockchain applications is not an easy walk for many of them. However, a few prominent companies around the globe have traversed great lengths to achieve this feat. Some of them are discussed below:

IBM – One of the most prominent players in the technology sphere, IBM has embraced the use of Blockchain extensively. With over $200 million invested in the research and development of Blockchain, IBM is leading the way for companies to inculcate Hyperledger and IBM cloud into their systems [1]. IBM continues to help small businesses to build Blockchain tools and applications.

Circle – This FinTech company was build to provide a platform for online money transfer and cryptocurrency investment. The application allows users to transfer currencies online without charging a transaction fee[1]. With the company has introduced its own set of 7 different cryptocurrencies, its exponential rise in the market is primarily attributed to rapid developments in the Blockchain domain.

Gemini – The NewYork based company allows its users to purchase, sell, and trade cryptocurrencies. This company extensively relies on Blockchain to ensure transaction and security. Individuals and organisations are welcome to trade currencies ranging from Bitcoins to Ether to Litecoin[2]. Its partnership with Samsung Blockchain to power Samsung Blockchain Wallet allows users to access crypto at their fingertips through a smartphone alone.

Celsius Network – This company works to provide loans by leveraging users' cryptocurrencies. The company uses a different approach than the conventional way of determining loan amounts based on credit scores. It uses the Loan-to-Value ratio. Meaning, it evaluates how much collateral the user can offer before determining the loan interest[3]. The company is powered entirely by Blockchain technology.

TraDove – The California-based company social network like platform connects the buyers to their sellers. The Blockchain platform also manages the supply chain acts as a medium for communication between buyers and sellers. Commercial giants like Amazon, John Deere, IKEA, etc., use this platform to identify the right customers[4].

Doc.AI – This company amalgamates Blockchain with machine learning for predicting the health conditions of an individual. The platform works by combining all possible medical records under an umbrella application. The app also allows patients to input their data and produces a predictive analysis of the same[5]. The data stored is further used for medical research, with the permission of the user.

2.5 BLOCKCHAIN PLATFORMS

2.5.1 COMMON BLOCKCHAIN TOOLS

The rise of Bitcoin brought Blockchain technology to the forefront by utilising its decentralised payment system. Ever since Blockchain has continued to widen its horizon. To understand the usage and functioning of Blockchain technology, let us understand the tools used for these purposes:

1. *Geth*: This program acts as a node to the Ethereum Blockchain. With Geth's help, one can mine ether tokens, transact tokens, create smart contracts, and explore the entire block history.
2. *Remix*: A compiler by design, it is used for compiling relatively small contracts. Written in JavaScript, Remix allows users to function both online and

---

[1] https://www.circle.com/en/

[2] https://www.gemini.com/fees/marketplace/section-gemini-block-trading

[3] https://celsius.network/about/

[4] https://www.tradove.com/login

[5] https://doc.ai/

offline. It mainly supports debugging, testing, and deploying of smart contracts. Its code analyser ensures that programmers write their best code.

3. *GanacheCLI*: Considered as one of the fastest Blockchain emulators, GanacheCLI simulates the Ethereum network on a single computer and allows the user to engage to the Blockchain without causing any hassle to the Ethereum Node.

4. *EtherScripter*: A software designed for upcoming developers, EtherScripter provides an easy interface for programmers to create smart contracts. All one needs to do is simply drag and drop to create a contract.

5. *Ethers.js*: This library was designed for ethers.io. Its main functionality was to make coding JavaScript on the client-side much easier. The implementation of Ethers.js eliminates the need to use contract addresses. Instead, it proposes the use of an Ethereum Name Service (ENS) name. It handles key management and Ethereum Blockchain interactions in a way convenient to the users.

6. *Truffle*: A deployment environment provides an excellent framework for Ethereum development. It also consists of a support library that connects sophisticated Ethereum apps and allows smart contracts to be made in a simple way. It also features an automated contract testing, configurable build pipeline, scriptable deployment, and instant rebuilding of assets during development.

7. *MyEtherWallet*: Wallets are by far the most common modes of storing currencies. There are, however, two types of storage – hot and cold. Meaning, in hot storage, cryptocurrencies are linked to the internet. Whereas in cold storage, the currencies are stored in offline mode. MyEtherWallet is a type of cold storage. The keys are in the form of barcodes. The positive of this wallet is that all the transactions carried out by the user is are under complete control of the user only.

2.5.2   LAYERS OF BLOCKCHAIN TECHNOLOGY

Like the Internet, Blockchain too has a few layers, each with its function, as shown in Figure 2.3. Each of these is discussed below:

1. *Data Layer*: This layer assists in providing valuable methods for manipulating data collected from various sources. All this data is stored in nodes in a Blockchain network as completely encrypted blocks. A typical block consists of two parts – a head and a body, as illustrated in Figure 2.4. The blocks are arranged in chronological order. Time-stamp is considered to be an important component of the Blockchain network. It helps in tracing and positioning Blockchain data. It also helps in identifying recurring data.

2. *Network Layer*: This layer describes the different communication models required for data forwarding, verification, and distributing the network. All participating nodes in the network have equal opportunities and privileges without any central authority governing everyone. Data gets broadcasted continuously by ever active nodes based on standard checklist [29]. During the situation of

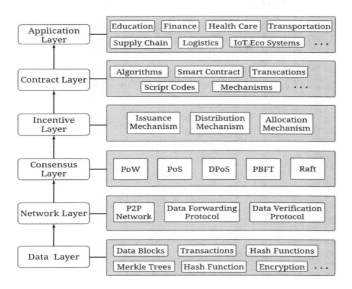

Figure 2.3 Layers in blockchain

worst-case scenario, data stored on each node can be restored and synchronised to other nodes with at most efficiency. This plays a vital role during the situation of interaction and communication with decentralised entitie [10].

3. ***Consensus Layer***: Blockchain utilises a variety of consensus theorems to ensure data is consistent and fault-tolerant. It is generally used in a completely closed ecosystem where the entities trust each other, where primitive algorithms are sufficient to reach consensus efficiently. However, a large number of Blockchain models concentrate on environments that contain a large number of trustless entities that can cause errors or faults. This is done to employ more complex algorithms that look to eliminate faults. For instance, PoW is a frequently used algorithm that asks nodes to perform complex mathematical operations to ensure data validity and authenticity [1].

4. ***Incentive Layer***: This layer is meant for rewarding the users in the Blockchain network. The entire network is designed so that trust is ensured between all the nodes, and these nodes are rewarded for maintaining this trust. The incentive layer is the driving force for Blockchain, especially those based on public Blockchain. This layer, however, is optional in a private Blockchain environment where users communicate with each other without any financial benefits whatsoever.

5. ***Contract Layer***: This layer contains various smart-contracts. Smart-contracts also self-verify, execute and enforce rules that are contained and secured by a Blockchain, as depicted in Figure 2.4. A contract can be codified only if

a group of parties agrees upon a set of rules. Once agreed, the contract is contained in a block on the ledger. The necessary actions associated with the conditions get activated with predefined conditions, and self-executing occurs without any human intervention. This method increases autonomy and programmability.

6. *Application Layer*: All use cases of Blockchain and application scenarios are carried out in this layer. Although Blockchain is in its progressive stage, many companies have come forward by developing centralised and decentralised applications, with security being their top priority.

2.6 CHALLENGES

Despite being revolutionary in its development, Blockchain has its own set of drawbacks. The main ones being – Scalability, Privacy Leakage, and Selfish Mining. Each of these is discussed below.

2.6.1 SCALABILITY

As a large number of transactions take place every day, the storage space is massive. Also, each transaction details have to be stored for validation and verification. Since a block's capacity is limited, the smaller transactions may be ignored indefinitely as bigger transactions with higher fees are given prime importance. Consequently, larger blocks take up more space and lead to delays and more computation power consumption. The problem of scalability is prominent [1]. There are, however, ways proposed to tackle this and can be categorised into two types – Storage Optimisation Blockchain: According to this method, all the nodes in the system do not need to store information about the transaction for validation. Instead, a lightweight client can be used to help fix this problem. Here, large computations are outsourced. This way, the results can be compared with multiple servers.

2.6.2 REDESIGNING BLOCKCHAIN

This method's main idea is to bifurcate the block into two parts – key block for elections and micro block for storing transactions. Miners compete with each other to become a leader. The leader would be responsible for the micro block until another leader is selected. In this way, the Blockchain is redesigned, and the tradeoff between block size and network security can be taken care of [11].

2.6.3 PRIVACY LEAKAGE

Blockchain is considered very safe for transactions as the user's identity is concealed and only transaction addresses are used. However, during an information leak, a user may generate multiple addresses. This does not guarantee transaction privacy since all values of the transaction are made visible. Many methods have been proposed to maintain the anonymity of the user.

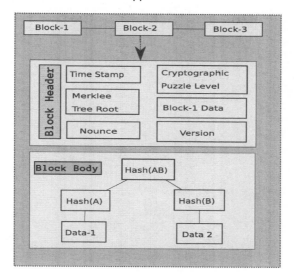

Figure 2.4   Enabling smart-contracts

2.6.3.1   Mixing

– While making a transaction, users generally prefer to use the same address frequently. Mixing service allows transferring from multiple input addresses to multiple output addresses. An intermediary is used that encrypts users' requirements, including transfer amount and date of the transaction with a private key. If the intermediary does not transfer the money, it is clear that the intermediary cheated and can be verified by anyone. To prevent this, output addresses are mixed.

2.6.3.2   Anonymous

– In this method, miners need not validate a transaction using digital signatures instead of using coins against a list of valid coins. Earlier payment sources were hidden to prevent transaction graph analysis. The amount and destination were visible. In the new method, the amount and destination are hidden completely.

2.6.4   SELFISH MINING

There are a lot of selfish miners wanting to exploit. It has been shown that with even a small hash power in hand, the miners can use it to cheat [11]. Selfish miners usually don't broadcast the mined blocks, and they keep it for themselves. The public display of the private branch happens only when there are specific conditions/requirements are met. The majority of miners generally admit that the private branches span in more length than public branches. Honest miners would be draining their time and resources on branches with little to no value, while selfish miners mine on private chains without any competition, generating more significant revenue. With selfish

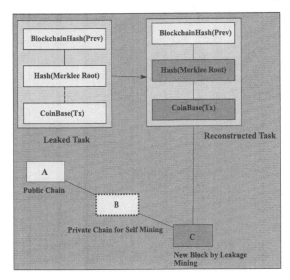

Figure 2.5 Selfish mining process

mining, many other attacks have been put forward, indicating Blockchain is not safe. Small miners use selfish mining strategies to derive profits compared to simple and plain selfish mining. Even with the computational power of >25%, a selfish miner could still stand a chance to gain something. To solve this problem, an approach was proposed where honest miners could choose the branch of their choice [34]. Another method suggests that each block must be generated and accepted by the network within a maximum interval [14]. Figure 2.5 can be explained as an example.

2.7 APPLICATIONS OF BLOCKCHAIN TECHNOLOGY AND FUTURE DIRECTIONS

Blockchain technology has diversified its functionalities in many domains including, asset protection, standardisation, smart contracts, and big data. It has shown its immense potential and leads to explore its venture furthermore in the future.

Investors get lured by Blockchain technology due to huge profits in its various application areas. Firstly, it is necessary to evaluate this technology's suitability and capability for a given real-life application. Such evaluation further demands the standard testing framework for technologies based on Blockchain. It is essential to evaluate the trade-offs between various parameters if Blockchain applies to the solution. The future of Blockchain holds many answers for innovation. Some of it discussed below in Table 2.2.

Various industries maintain humongous amounts of data about their clients, transactions, purchases, orders, audits, inventory, etc. They maintain this confidential information in their private databases either on the physical server or on the

Table 2.2
Major Application Domains of Blockchain Technology

Domain	Application	Utilising Companies
Finance	Blockchain is considered to increase financial efficiency by eliminating or reducing manipulation. It also incorporates transparency, a trait valuable and welcomed by many. A single database in design, it hold all the transaction details, and is also immutable in nature. With the use of smart-contracts, compliance with customers and government will also increase.	Australia Stock Exchange, Webank, JP Morgan
Healthcare	Blockchain technology has revolutionised the healthcare industry too. This has helped patients keep complete control of their medical records, allowing doctors to access only those files that are granted access to. Also, patients can connect to their hospitals and obtain their medical data hassle-free.	MedicalChain, Patientory
Transportation	Blockchain provides a way to authenticate and track vehicles easily. This could be done using a digital ledger. It could also be used in logistics to maintain track of assets and supply chain. It is also an immediate solution for tracking orders, and in case of cancellation, an efficient means of refund mechanism.	Koopman, UPS
Supply Chain Management	Blockchain affects everything from warehouse storage to delivery to payment while maintaining complete transparency. Blockchain provides consensus. There is no discrepancy in the chain, as all transactions are maintained by the same version of the ledger.	Walmart, British Airways
IoT	Tracking of million devices can be done with the help of Blockchain. It also enables easier tracking, coordination, and authentication. Data is secure and is maintained in a single database server.	Helium, Filament
Public and Social Services	Blockchain provides a system for records to be shared by members of the network and eliminates the need for a different ledger. It is immutable and tamper-proof. No one can delete the records, not even the administrator. Blockchain does not entertain malpractices; hence, only users with privileges are allowed access.	IBM, Stanley Morgan
Reputation System	A decentralised reputation system allows identification of users to eliminate bots or duplicates. It also facilitates a mechanism to allow up-voting and down-voting for users' feedback. Aggregates the reputation of different users across the platform in the network.	Block Armour, Hacken
Security and Privacy	Blockchain employs asymmetric cryptography to ensure the trust between the users for transactions. Since hackers can't predict the private key from the user's public key, it is inherently secure.	Sentinel Protocols, Gladius
Privacy	A Blockchain is a public, distributed shared database that keeps track of all transactions in an immutable ledger. Blockchain technology secures, and authenticates transactions and data through cryptocurrency.	Megahoot, OpenAVN

private cloud such as AWS Eucalyptus, Azure, etc. The idea of maintaining the data on a centralised physical server or the 3rd party cloud servers does not provide transparency. It is susceptible to attacks for data theft over the internet. Another area that demands alternative implementation with Blockchain is in the supply chain management, which requires stringent monitoring and access control continuously in a timely manner [18]. The above issues can be addressed with Blockchain implementation and with the help of cryptocurrency. [19] propose an approach for introducing a Blockchain technology for the global supply chain that involves many companies to deliver products to the customers on a need basis. The approach uses Blockchain to maintain the logistics among the various vendors who pitch in during the procurement of items, packaging, and delivering the product. A similar implementation can be found in [38] which introduces an agri-food supply chain traceability system using Blockchain. Industries like IBM, Consensys provide real-time end-to-end Blockchain solutions addressing the various needs of industry 4.0 and being active in the domain of supply chain management in particular.

The financial sector domain that works based on Blockchain technology is still in infancy, although it had got a broad research area. To date, the prime emphasis was on the functionalities of Blockchain prototypes for proof of concepts. However, to implement and adopt the Blockchain in the financial sector, the main factor is to adopt interoperability that requires to be defined. Henceforth, the researchers have to focus on the interoperability issue and the process of standardisation. Blockchain-based financial applications are characterised by interoperability, data privacy, speed, scalability, and data security. Adopting them is challenging and open research gaps that require further investigation to bring confidence among stakeholders to adopt Blockchain technology for the financial sector.

Future research on the adoption of Blockchain technology in healthcare mainly concerns employing smart contracts. Adopting this to the healthcare domain could enhance customer service by performing efficient information exchange between stakeholders. Information security and privacy play an essential role in healthcare to secure users' privacy and the information stored in Blockchain-based systems where researchers need to look at service development-oriented research. In concern to this future research focus mainly on the designing protocols to ensure authenticated use of private keys and avoid data breaches due to mismanagement of keys. Blockchain has proven to be an effective choice for the implementation of maintaining one database for all the patient-related data (EHR) and storing it in a distributed manner. One such successful implementation is in called EHRchain[6]. The EHRchain provides full control to the patient about his/her medical records, which can be sharable to the doctors or institution on a need basis or with permission. The work proposed in called ACTION-EHR[7] presents a hybrid data storage approach for storing the EHR data upon encryption and using permission-based data access between the Patient and Medical facility. The ready-to-deploy Blockchain implementation called Medicalchain for EHR data management is presented that stores the data in the distributed environment upon encryption[8]. Blockchain technology has shown promising implementation for storing, processing, and accessing the electronic health record (EHR) data efficiently and securely.

The significant design of IoT ecosystems includes smart contracts with edge computing in the future. However, to sort out the smart contract system's computational overheads, the Blockchain generation needs to handle on the edge

---

[6]https://ehrchain.world/
[7]https://www.jmir.org/2020/8/e13598/
[8]https://medicalchain.com/en/whitepaper/

computing infrastructure. These issues are open challenges that need to be addressed by designing edge computing interfaces with compatible protocols since IoT will ease adaptable components in future smart cities.

The subscribers to telecommunication in the recent era are growing exponentially, and to manage them, Blockchain-based smart contracts are the best solutions in the future. Moreover, managing such an enormous number of subscribers comprising industrial sensors demands expanding communication infrastructure. In real-time, the access control to the user data must be ensured, and to do so, the Blockchain-based smart contracts are seen to be the best emerging where more research is required to be carried out.

Blockchain-based smart contracts are extensively used for data provenance in the supply chain industry and logistics. The application of smart contracts for autonomous functioning requires improved optimisation for optimal operation. The block synchronisation is a prerequisite functionality to identify whenever the smart contract nodes require to operate with an unstable network where the nodes are located in the sea. In such a scenario, error handling procedures are necessary to handle the inconsistent blocks that occur because of unstable network connections that require further enhancements. The emerging smart contract platforms can divaricate a novel approach for logistics-related services in future use.

It has been predicted that many industries will adapt to Blockchain oriented smart contracts in the coming days. There are several dimensions of research and opportunities to explore with respect to smart contracts and their applications. The characteristics of smart contracts (such as scalability, minimum latency, improved throughput) will benefit many industries. The domains such as military and space research can yield more from Blockchain oriented smart contracts.

2.8 CONCLUSION

Blockchain has taken the world of technology by storm, it has revolutionised the way information is used, stored, and exchanged. Today, Blockchain's widespread usage range from cryptocurrency transactions, recording assets, to finances, and potentially anything of value.

Blockchain's role in rapidly transforming and commoditising how society agrees, trusts and transacts is significant. Through this paper an attempt has been made to demonstrate the working, recent developments, challenges, and applications of Blockchain technology.

Bibliography

1. Tareq Ahram, Arman Sargolzaei, Saman Sargolzaei, Jeff Daniels, and Ben Amaba. Blockchain technology innovations. In *2017 IEEE technology & engineering management conference (TEMSCON)*, pages 137–141. IEEE, 2017.

2. Shaik V Akram, Praveen K Malik, Rajesh Singh, Gehlot Anita, and Sudeep Tanwar. Adoption of blockchain technology in various realms: Opportunities and challenges. *Security and Privacy*, 3(5):e109, 2020.

3. Walid Al-Saqaf and Nicolas Seidler. Blockchain technology for social impact: opportunities and challenges ahead. *Journal of Cyber Policy*, 2(3):338–354, 2017.

4. Omar Ali, Ashraf Jaradat, Atik Kulakli, and Ahmed Abuhalimeh. A comparative study: Blockchain technology utilization benefits, challenges and functionalities. *IEEE Access*, 9:12730–12749, 2021.

5. Ibrahim Alnafrah, Elena Bogdanova, and Tatyana Maximova. Text mining as a facilitating tool for deploying blockchain technology in the intellectual property rights system. *International Journal of Intellectual Property Management*, 9(2):120–135, 2019.

6. Benjamin Ampel, Mark Patton, and Hsinchun Chen. Performance modeling of hyperledger sawtooth blockchain. In *2019 IEEE International Conference on Intelligence and Security Informatics (ISI)*, pages 59–61. IEEE, 2019.

7. Merlinda Andoni, Valentin Robu, David Flynn, Simone Abram, Dale Geach, David Jenkins, Peter McCallum, and Andrew Peacock. Blockchain technology in the energy sector: A systematic review of challenges and opportunities. *Renewable and Sustainable Energy Reviews*, 100:143–174, 2019.

8. Elli Androulaki, Artem Barger, Vita Bortnikov, Christian Cachin, Konstantinos Christidis, Angelo De Caro, David Enyeart, Christopher Ferris, Gennady Laventman, Yacov Manevich, et al. Hyperledger fabric: a distributed operating system for permissioned blockchains. In *Proceedings of the thirteenth EuroSys conference*, pages 1–15, 2018.

9. A Averin and O Averina. Review of blockchain frameworks and platforms. In *2020 International Multi-Conference on Industrial Engineering and Modern Technologies (FarEastCon)*, pages 1–6. IEEE, 2020.

10. Seyed Mojtaba Hosseini Bamakan, Amirhossein Motavali, and Alireza Babaei Bondarti. A survey of blockchain consensus algorithms performance evaluation criteria. *Expert Systems with Applications*, page 113385, 2020.

11. MR Biktimirov, AV Domashev, PA Cherkashin, and A Yu Shcherbakov. Blockchain technology: Universal structure and requirements. *Automatic Documentation and Mathematical Linguistics*, 51(6):235–238, 2017.

12. Kamanashis Biswas and Vallipuram Muthukkumarasamy. Securing smart cities using blockchain technology. In *2016 IEEE 18th international conference on high performance computing and communications; IEEE 14th international conference on smart city; IEEE 2nd international conference on data science and systems (HPCC/SmartCity/DSS)*, pages 1392–1393. IEEE, 2016.

13. Fran Casino, Thomas K Dasaklis, and Constantinos Patsakis. A systematic literature review of blockchain-based applications: current status, classification and open issues. *Telematics and informatics*, 36:55–81, 2019.

14. Sara Cohen, Adam Rosenthal, and Aviv Zohar. Reasoning about the future in blockchain databases. In *2020 IEEE 36th International Conference on Data Engineering (ICDE)*, pages 1930–1933. IEEE, 2020.

15. Jeff Daniels, Saman Sargolzaei, Arman Sargolzaei, Tareq Ahram, Phillip A Laplante, and Ben Amaba. The internet of things, artificial intelligence, blockchain, and professionalism. *IT Professional*, 20(6):15–19, 2018.

16. Gabriel Estevam, Lucas M Palma, Luan R Silva, Jean E Martina, and Martín Vigil. Accurate and decentralized timestamping using smart contracts on the ethereum blockchain. *Information Processing & Management*, 58(3):102471, 2021.

17. Ge He, Yagu Dang, Li Zhou, Yiyang Dai, Yi Que, and Xu Ji. Architecture model proposal of innovative intelligent manufacturing in the chemical industry based on multi-scale integration and key technologies. *Computers & Chemical Engineering*, 141:106967, 2020.

18. Petri Helo and Yuqiuge Hao. Blockchains in operations and supply chains: A model and reference implementation. *Computers & Industrial Engineering*, 136:242–251, 2019.

19. Petri Helo and AHM. Shamsuzzoha. Real-time supply chain—A blockchain architecture for project deliveries. *Robotics and Computer-Integrated Manufacturing*, 63:101909, jun 2020.

20. Akanksha Kaushik, Archana Choudhary, Chinmay Ektare, Deepti Thomas, and Syed Akram. Blockchain—literature survey. In *2017 2nd IEEE International Conference on Recent Trends in Electronics, Information & Communication Technology (RTEICT)*, pages 2145–2148. IEEE, 2017.

21. Murat Kuzlu, Manisa Pipattanasomporn, Levent Gurses, and Saifur Rahman. Performance analysis of a hyperledger fabric blockchain framework: throughput, latency and scalability. In *2019 IEEE international conference on blockchain (Blockchain)*, pages 536–540. IEEE, 2019.

22. Dongcheng Li, W Eric Wong, and Jincui Guo. A survey on blockchain for enterprise using hyperledger fabric and composer. In *2019 6th International Conference on Dependable Systems and Their Applications (DSA)*, pages 71–80. IEEE, 2020.

23. Andrea Lisi, Andrea De Salve, Paolo Mori, Laura Ricci, and Samuel Fabrizi. Rewarding reviews with tokens: An ethereum-based approach. *Future Generation Computer Systems*, 120:36–54, 2021.

24. Zhiyong Liu and Zipei Li. A blockchain-based framework of cross-border e-commerce supply chain. *International Journal of Information Management*, 52:102059, 2020.

25. Thomas McGhin, Kim-Kwang Raymond Choo, Charles Zhechao Liu, and Debiao He. Blockchain in healthcare applications: Research challenges and opportunities. *Journal of Network and Computer Applications*, 135:62–75, 2019.

26. Matthias Mettler. Blockchain technology in healthcare: The revolution starts here. In *2016 IEEE 18th international conference on e-health networking, applications and services (Healthcom)*, pages 1–3. IEEE, 2016.

27. Du Mingxiao, Ma Xiaofeng, Zhang Zhe, Wang Xiangwei, and Chen Qijun. A review on consensus algorithm of blockchain. In *2017 IEEE international conference on systems, man, and cybernetics (SMC)*, pages 2567–2572. IEEE, 2017.

28. Muhammad Muzammal, Qiang Qu, and Bulat Nasrulin. Renovating blockchain with distributed databases: An open source system. *Future generation computer systems*, 90:105–117, 2019.

29. Suyel Namasudra, Ganesh Chandra Deka, Prashant Johri, Mohammad Hosseinpour, and Amir H Gandomi. The revolution of blockchain: State-of-the-art and research challenges. *Archives of Computational Methods in Engineering*, pages 1–19, 2020.

30. Nawari O Nawari and Shriraam Ravindran. Blockchain and the built environment: Potentials and limitations. *Journal of Building Engineering*, 25:100832, 2019.

31. M Niranjanamurthy, BN Nithya, and S Jagannatha. Analysis of blockchain technology: pros, cons and swot. *Cluster Computing*, 22(6):14743–14757, 2019.

32. Daniel E O'Leary. Configuring blockchain architectures for transaction information in blockchain consortiums: The case of accounting and supply chain systems. *Intelligent Systems in Accounting, Finance and Management*, 24(4):138–147, 2017.

33. Deepak Puthal, Nisha Malik, Saraju P Mohanty, Elias Kougianos, and Chi Yang. The blockchain as a decentralized security framework [future directions]. *IEEE Consumer Electronics Magazine*, 7(2):18–21, 2018.

34. Bina Ramamurthy. *Blockchain in Action*. Manning Publications, 2020.

35. Mohammadreza Rasolroveicy and Marios Fokaefs. Performance evaluation of distributed ledger technologies for iot data registry: A comparative study. In *2020 Fourth World Conference on Smart Trends in Systems, Security and Sustainability (WorldS4)*, pages 137–144. IEEE, 2020.

36. Ashish Rajendra Sai, Jim Buckley, Brian Fitzgerald, and Andrew Le Gear. Taxonomy of centralization in public blockchain systems: A systematic literature review. *Information Processing & Management*, 58(4):102584, 2021.

37. Janusz J Sikorski, Joy Haughton, and Markus Kraft. Blockchain technology in the chemical industry: Machine-to-machine electricity market. *Applied energy*, 195:234–246, 2017.

38. Feng Tian. An agri-food supply chain traceability system for china based on rfid & blockchain technology. In *2016 13th international conference on service systems and service management (ICSSSM)*, pages 1–6. IEEE, 2016.

39. Anna Vacca, Andrea Di Sorbo, Corrado A Visaggio, and Gerardo Canfora. A systematic literature review of blockchain and smart contract development: Techniques, tools, and open challenges. *Journal of Systems and Software*, page 110891, 2020.

40. Wattana Viriyasitavat, Tharwon Anuphaptrirong, and Danupol Hoonsopon. When blockchain meets internet of things: Characteristics, challenges, and business opportunities. *Journal of industrial information integration*, 15:21–28, 2019.

41. Ziyu Wang, Jianwei Liu, Qianhong Wu, Yanting Zhang, Hui Yu, and Ziyu Zhou. An analytic evaluation for the impact of uncle blocks by selfish and stubborn mining in an imperfect ethereum network. *Computers & Security*, 87:101581, 2019.

42. Merrill Warkentin and Craig Orgeron. Using the security triad to assess blockchain technology in public sector applications. *International Journal of Information Management*, 52:102090, 2020.

43. Marcia Narine Weldon and Rachel Epstein. Beyond bitcoin: leveraging blockchain to benefit business and society. *Transactions: Tenn. J. Bus. L.*, 20:837, 2018.

44. Ruksudaporn Wutthikarn and Yan Guang Hui. Prototype of blockchain in dental care service application based on hyperledger composer in hyperledger fabric framework. In *2018 22nd International Computer Science and Engineering Conference (ICSEC)*, pages 1–4. IEEE, 2018.

45. Jesse Yli-Huumo, Deokyoon Ko, Sujin Choi, Sooyong Park, and Kari Smolander. Where is current research on blockchain technology?—a systematic review. *PloS one*, 11(10):e0163477, 2016.

46. Haifeng Yu, Ivica Nikolić, Ruomu Hou, and Prateek Saxena. Ohie: Blockchain scaling made simple. In *2020 IEEE Symposium on Security and Privacy (SP)*, pages 90–105. IEEE, 2020.

47. Li Zhang, Yongping Xie, Yang Zheng, Wei Xue, Xianrong Zheng, and Xiaobo Xu. The challenges and countermeasures of blockchain in finance and economics. *Systems Research and Behavioral Science*, 37(4):691–698, 2020.

48. Rui Zhang, Rui Xue, and Ling Liu. Security and privacy on blockchain. *ACM Computing Surveys (CSUR)*, 52(3):1–34, 2019.

49. Qiheng Zhou, Huawei Huang, Zibin Zheng, and Jing Bian. Solutions to scalability of blockchain: A survey. *IEEE Access*, 8:16440–16455, 2020.

50. Maryam Zulfiqar, Filza Tariq, Muhammad Umar Janjua, Adnan Noor Mian, Adnan Qayyum, Junaid Qadir, Falak Sher, and Muhammad Hassan. Ethreview: An ethereum-based product review system for mitigating rating frauds. *Computers & Security*, 100:102094, 2021.

3 Interoperability Across Blockchains

In modern days data is an invaluable resource, which guides business decisions. There is a scope of data tampering which leads to serious problems in decision taking in any industry. This is true in centralised databases. Especially in Financial Industry the data should be secured and tamper-proof. Blockchain promises the data integrity and control of data to its owner.

The interoperability of blockchain alludes to the exchanging of information across blockchains. It is mainly persuaded by two prerequisites common in distributed frameworks: data accessing and getting to functionality that is accessible in other frameworks. The first requirement is accessing information in other frameworks, which has been already achieved by utilising of dispersed inquiry dialects, SPARQL Federated Inquiry 1.1 [24], and the Asset Portrayal System 1.1 [25]. The second requirement is getting to functionality in other frameworks, which has been accomplished by Common Object Request Broker Design (CORBA) [27], and Representational State Exchange (REST) [28], Remote Procedure Calls (RPC) [26].

Blockchain framework works mostly in environments of untrusted/trusted. Previous frameworks have worked with implicit trust. Implicit trust is believed in the results of query languages of distributed systems that hit queries to single servers. Essentially, substances It is assumed that calls getting executed in remote procedure calls often will be of less or zero authentication. Considering all these aspects, Byzantine Fault Tolerant (BFT) is embedded into Blockchain systems by handling node failure, bad actors, failure of a network. Blockchain works on consensus [32] mechanism across nodes for the validity of transactions, rather than a single source.

Interoperability technique helps nodes on destination blockchain that nodes at source blockchain have agreed on some fact, their by trusting each other. Interoperability on the blockchain requires both a technological and a business justification to exist. Blockchain technology must be distinguished from the business applications of blockchain and the business model of blockchain-based solutions. Multiple blockchain implementations, some businesses can exist and drive value even if they are not connected to the same blockchain for example Blockchain Technology in Health Insurance – Integration of 8 Stake Holders who are operating in different blockchain frameworks.

Bitcoin emerged as the discovery of Satoshi Nakamoto [1], thus making Bitcoin the first crypto-currency that drove the strength of Blockchain Technology. This technology offers a novel way of building distributed systems that are tamper-proof and transparent.

Blockchain is a distributed ledger that has all transactions that have not yet been executed in the system. Blockchain is widely applicable to many industrial areas

DOI: 10.1201/9781003355052-3

where there is a need for transparency and trust among distributed different parties in the network. This technology introduces a new kind of governance with more decentralised and peer2peer decision-making. It is a Peer2Peer network where every full node stores a copy of the Blockchain ledger. There is no central authority that manages the Blockchain database. The Consistency of the ledger is achieved by using various consistency protocols involving all parties in the network. The selection of consensus protocol depends on the trust model and the business environment. Each blockchain has its own ideal, purpose, culture, and different advantages and disadvantages. In the network when the consensus is reached each node updates the ledger's copy locally. There are many blockchains that are existing and many of them exist independent of each other and can't interact with each other to share information.

The Internet has revolutionised the entire mankind, and it became possible that anyone can easily exchange information and deliver a message to others across the globe. The enormous amount of transactions that are happening at each and every second on the Internet has created a huge amount of Big Data which revolutionised many industries. Many networking concepts have been used for the huge success of the Internet. Encryption techniques, different consensus algorithms, and mining techniques in the blockchain replaced the old-fashioned centralised systems. This technology has replaced the middleman's trust by using the private key concepts and network of nodes that validate the set of transactions defined in their smart contracts. Rules defined in the smart contract ensure whether the transaction is valid or not accordingly transactions are written to the blockchain.

3.0.1   ADVANTAGES AND DISADVANTAGES OF USING BLOCKCHAIN

Blockchain has its ways of advantages like Traceability, Integrity, faster processing and some of them are as follows.

1. Transparency: The data in the blockchain is visible to all the participants allowing transparency in all dealings.
2. Availability: The presence of multiple nodes in a blockchain network ensures that the failure of one node does not bring down the entire system leading to almost zero downtime with the ledger data being available to all participants at all times.
3. Reliability: Any asset of value including money, titles, deeds, music, art, etc. can be securely stored and transferred using blockchains.
4. Trusted: Blockchains are risk-free by design and can safeguard against tampering, fraud, or cybercrimes. Trust in blockchains is not maintained by centralised bodies but by technology that cannot cheat.
5. Secure: Blockchains can be made provably secure using strong cryptography and a network that is collaborating to maintain the security of the system through complex algorithms. Bitcoin itself is the best example of this. In more than eight years of operation, the only thefts of Bitcoins have been owing to weaknesses in the wallets while the core protocol itself has remained secure.

6. Cost Effective [21]: Blockchains enable the movement and storage of value in a simpler, fast and cheaper way. They can be used to automate trusted processes and allow proprietary solutions tailored to the need of the organisation rather than generalised solutions by trusted third-parties.
7. Efficiency: By exposing all relevant data to the concerned parties, blockchains can increase the efficiency of transactions. Supply chains, for example, can now be monitored more efficiently since all the institutions involved manufacturers, shippers, banks, governments, etc. can see the necessary data immediately.

There are many hurdles to blockchain adoption, despite the above advantages. These concerns that need to be addressed for widespread blockchain deployment are as follows:

- Speed/Scalability: One of the biggest problems currently preventing the adoption of blockchain systems is their inherent inability to handle large volumes of transactions and system activity. Blockchain implementations are currently in very primitive forms that cannot scale to the requirements of today's applications. Though many blockchain applications are being developed scalability is the biggest limitation, factors that affect scalability are chain size, digital signature [22], transaction per second, block size. Solution for this scalability can be based on on-chain, off-chain, interchain.
- Privacy: While it is important to expose relevant data to authorised bodies, there is also a need for increasing transaction privacy to enable the routing of even confidential transactions through blockchains.
- Implementation: Recent years have seen the proliferation of a number of blockchain implementations each with its own set of protocols and transaction formats. There is a need to establish standard tools and administration interfaces to enable easy adoption of blockchains in businesses.

We did a study on different blockchain applications like Bitcoin [1], Ethereum, R3 Corda [10], etc., and found that countless decentralised applications are built on Ethereum using smart contracts [31] which run on the Ethereum Virtual Machines. However, all these blockchains have its own limitations and there is no communication across these chains.

An Ideal solution to this problem is allowing multiple blockchains to communicate with each other, without compromising on their security aspects through Interoperability. Many layers [159] of Interoperability exists [159]: Legal, Semantic, Organizational, Technical, Governanace of Interoperability. Our work in this paper is focused on technical interoperability. We have implemented a network architecture to address this issue. Other Interoperability layers are left for future work.

Our focus in this paper is developing a protocol technique, that helps nodes on destination blockchain and nodes at source blockchain have agreed on some fact, their by trusting each other, their by sharing information across blockchains. We created a platform/protocol that enables diverse blockchains to communicate with each other, without depending on an external intermediary.

Paper is organised as follows Introduction, Diversified Implementation of Blockchains and Literature Review, System Architecture, Detailed Design of the Router for communication across Blockchains, Prototype and experiments, Conclusion.

3.1   DIVERSIFIED IMPLEMENTATION OF BLOCKCHAINS

A lot of research work has been on to develop a variety of blockchains. Currently, there is an abundance of blockchain implementations with each having its own set of properties. These implementations include public/ private /consortium blockchains. Popular public blockchains include Bitcoin, a decentralised currency system. and Ethereum, a decentralised platform for applications with smart contracts. Other implementations like Multichain [23] and the Hyperledger Fabric are suitable for enterprise needs with permissioned access and a lot of flexibility in deployment. Some of the implementations are aligned to a specific use-case like Ripple that seeks to provide efficient international payments while BigchainDB aims to be a scalable, blockchain implementation suitable for Big Data requirements. Corda is an open-source consortium blockchain that enables contract management between mutually trusting organisations. This platform has a high edge in the Financial Industry. Each of the above blockchain implementations has its consensus mechanism like the PoW (proof-of-work) in Bitcoin, PoS (proof-of-stake) in Ethereum and Multichain, voting in Ripple and BigchainDB, PBFT in Hyperledger Fabric, Notary in Corda. A lot of energy consumption by PoW has led to the development of PoS based consensus in decentralised cryptocurrencies, a notable example being Peercoin. Based on the various strategy of consensus mechanism blockchain interoperability mechainsm has become challenging as their is no standard protocol for bridging gap among them. In this chapter, we explore these blockchain implementations highlighting the important protocol decisions, properties and, the utility of each.

BITCOIN

Bitcoin is a peer-to-peer currency system that operates without the need for a central regulator for currency issue or trade. It was introduced in 2008 by an individual or group with the pseudonym Satoshi Nakamoto. The state of the system is recorded through transactions in a proof-of-work blockchain. It is a decentralised system where any node can join/leave the network. Curve25519 public-private key pair is used for signing transactions by every user in the Bitcoin network. Users in the Bitcoin network are identified with their public keys. Bitcoins are owned by these public keys and only users with the corresponding private key can spend the acquired coins.

New Bitcoin transactions are gathered together in a block. The blocks are chained by adding a cryptographic hash of the previous block in the current block. The hash used is SHA-256. This provides a mechanism for tamper proof since a change in the previous block will change the hash of the block that is stored in the current block. Thus, such a change can be detected and this holds all the way back to the genesis block. This chaining of blocks is where the name "blockchain" is derived from. Thus, the Bitcoin blockchain is a record of all the Bitcoin transactions ever made. The current blockchain data can be downloaded by any node to recreate the whole history and establish the current ownership of Bitcoins. Bitcoins are mined as mining rewards and the total number of Bitcoins that will ever be mined is capped at roughly 21 millions.

MINING

Bitcoin employs the proof-of-work mining where users are expected to solve a mining puzzle for mining blocks. The mining puzzle involves finding a nonce such that the hash of the block header is less than an agreed upon mining difficulty target. Checking a solution for the mining problem is very easy and involves the calculation of just one hash. Finding the solution can be made arbitrarily difficult by adjusting the difficulty target accordingly. The difficulty target is adjusted every 2016 blocks that amounts to roughly 14 days. The adjustment is made in order to maintain the average time between blocks at 10 minutes. The block time of 10 minutes is chosen to ensure that mined blocks have sufficient time to be propagated across the network to reduce the number of forks in the blockchain. The Bitcoin mining process is computationally very expensive and consumes a lot of resources including electricity since it requires the checking of quintillions (1018) of hashes. It is against these mining costs that Bitcoin nodes are incentivised through the mining reward.

It could happen that two different blocks are mined over the same block leading to forks in the chain. To maintain a single chain, Bitcoin uses the longest chain as the main chain. The idea is that the longest chain is the one on which most work has been done, and is thereby most secure.

CONFIRMATIONS

Lets say a transaction t has been mined in a new block B0 mined over block B. B' is then broadcast to the Bitcoin network. Depending on the network latencies some nodes may not hear about B' and it could happen that another block B" is mined over B simultaneously. If it happens that most nodes hear about B" before B', then the main chain will record the block B" and not B'. Hence while the transaction t had been mined in a block, we cannot be certain if that block, and thereby t, would be a part of the main chain. Hence it is suggested that to confirm a transaction, users ought to wait for blocks to be mined over the block in which the transaction was recorded. The transaction is said to receive one confirmation if one block is mined over the transaction's block and soon. It is currently agreed that if a transaction receives six confirmations then it can be considered to have been permanently recorded.

ETHEREUM

Ethereum [51] utilises the blockchain technology to enable the development of decentralised applications. Such decentralised applications, also called smart contracts, are executed on every node in the Ethereum network without any possibility of down-time, censorship or third-party interference. A consensus is reached among the nodes using a proof-of-work algorithm to update the global state based upon the execution of the contracts. The embedding of legally binding contract logic in smart contracts ensures its correct execution thereby precluding any possibility of fraud. Smart contracts can significantly reduce enforcement and helps in the smooth running of businesses. Using Ethereum, users can create numerous decentralised applications which could even include crypto-currencies. Applications that can benefit from Ethereum include those that automate interactions between various parties or those that can facilitate coordinated group action across a network. Ethereum has the power to support a Web 3.0 which is decentralised and secure.

ETHEREUM VIRTUAL MACHINE

Code of smart contracts will be executed on Ethereum Virtual Machine. Ethereum has currency called ether (ETH) which will paid as fee for computations done by EVM.

3.1.1 TRANSACTIONS

Every transaction has recipient address and signature which recognises sender, amount of ether, data field, gas price and start gas values. Start gas defines the threshold for code execution by EVM and gasprice is ether which will be paid for a unit of gas utilised.

3.1.2 ETHER AND GAS

Ethereums network currency is Ether (ETH). The sender will be paid for each transaction he executes, including the volume of storage and computation are done in the smart contract. This cost is represented in gas. Gas and Ether are different from each other value of ether keeps changing based on the market, a gas value is constant. Each computation is associated with gas price. The decision of gas-price is done by miners. Miners are the one who validates whether a transaction is valid or not using the Proof-Of-Work consensus mechanism.

3.1.3 ETHEREUM ACCOUNTS

Ethereum supports two types of accounts: Externally Owned Account (EOA) and Contract Account. EOA is accessed using the private key, can transfer ethers to other members of the Ethereum network. Transactions done by EOA will be written to the blockchain. A Particular function in the smart contract is triggered by receiving a transaction from the EOAs. The behaviour of the contract is dependent on the business logic embedded into the code.

The state of the Ethereum blockchain involves the state of every account in the network. Ethereum with the ability to build decentralised applications [13,14]. All transactions in Ethereum are essentially state transitions involving the transfer of value/asset through ethers, or the transfer of information between the accounts. The EOAs are user-controlled and can use transactions to either transfer value to another EOA or to execute code stored in contract accounts. Contract codes cannot be executed natively without activation by EOAs to ensure strict determinism in the execution. An EOA must pay for the computation and memory storage that they use by activating a contract. This is paid in the form of transaction fees collected by the miners in ether.

3.1.4 SMART CONTRACTS

Smart contract is just a logic which include both a code and data. This logic or code can be used to transfer money, asset or anything that can be represented by a value. The execution of this smart contract on the blockchain lead to a correct deterministic execution with zero down time, no fraud or no third party interference. Smart contract enables credible transactions which is irreversible and easily verifiable by the network. Smart contract code can be used for a validation rule, transferring asset only when certain conditions are met etc. This smart contract is deployed on the Blockchain as bytecode. This bytecode contract is replicated by all ethereum nodes and whenever this contract logic is activated, this bytecode is run and all the ethereum node executes this logic and performs the necessary actions for state updation. There are many high level languages for writing this smart contract. This contract are compiled into the EVM bytecode and stored in a Ethereum Blockchain.

The language for writing this contract includes:

- Solidity: JavaScript-like language
- Serpent: Python-like language
- LLL: Lisp-like language
- Mutan : C-like language Apart from these work towards Java and Python is on the process

Ethereum uses "Greedy Heaviest Observed Subtree (GHOST)" [19] protocol, which is an innovation first introduced by Yonatan Sompolinsky and Aviv Zohar. Unlike a bitcoin network where a valid blockchain is considered the longest blockchain formed so far, in Ethereum the valid blockchain is considered the heaviest blockchain. For calculating the heaviest blockchain it includes the stale/uncle blocks into consideration. This inclusion of uncle block for calculating the heaviest blockchain also helps to combat centralisation issue. The block includes the uncle block gets an Ether reward of 1/16 and the uncle block gets a reward of 15/16. So, this reward for uncle inclusion for valid blockchain calculation is what incentives the miners and abates centralisation issue. The Ethereum version of Ghost only goes down seven levels or back seven levels in the height of the blockchain.

3.1.5 FEES AND CONTRACT EXECUTION

Executing code or transferring a transaction in Ethereum results in the updation of the Ethereum state. This computation requires usage of resources and Ethereum has defined a fees structure which is paid in a value called Ether. Each operations in Ethereum is assigned a gas which specifies the minimum amount of computation which this operation requires for successful execution. For example; ADD uses 3 gas, MUL requires 5 gas, basic transaction transfer cost 21000 gas and contract transaction takes 21000 gas plus extra gas for further complex operation execution. The gas [15] per operation is fixed but the price to be paid per gas, called gasPrice is dynamic and depends on market value. gasPrice represent the value which the user will be willing to pay for execution the required operations. The users specifies the gas price in Gwei. The total fees that a user pays for an operation execution is measured as: totalfees = gasPrice × gasUsed. The gas used is dependent on the operation execution and the gas used by EVM. The total gas for a transaction execution is specified by the user at the start of the transaction execution as gasLimit. If the user specifies less amount of gas to execute an operation, then the EVM will result in an error and all the gas consumed during the execution will be lost, else the remaining gas is returned to the user of the transaction.

3.2   BIGCHAIN DB

BigchainDB [18] was started by Trent McConaghy. BigchainDB provides an abstraction of blockchain which is built on a distributed database. It is meant to fill the gap in a decentralised ecosystem. This strategy gives a transaction throughput of million transactions per second, storing tera to peta bytes of data and sub-second latency. BigchainDBs permissioning capability ranges from a permissioned and a private blockchain network to an open public blockchain database. It is complementary to decentralised blockchain processing platform like Ethereum, Bitcoin and a decentralised file system like the InterPlanetary File System (IPFS).

The underlying design of BigchainDB is a Distributed Database, MongoDB. The characteristics of a Blockchain is added to this database using concepts like "Blockchain Pipelining." This features give BigchainDB the unique characteristics of a decentralised control, immutability and creation and movement of digital assets. Unlike Bitcoin where the performance is restricted with 8000 to 10000 nodes, BigchainDB scales linearly in throughput with the increase in the number of nodes. BigchainDB relies on the underlying consensus algorithm of the distributed database, viz., Paxos, etc. for the correct ordering of the transactions and the correct copy of all the transactions in all the nodes. It inherently uses the features of a distributed database like sharding for improving performance throughput and conserving storage. BigchainDB's aim is to allow the underlying distributed database to improve performance and capacity while providing the Blockchain characteristics. BigchainDB operates or provides this Blockchain features by building a consortium of nodes called the federation of nodes. This federation of nodes is a peer-to-peer node where their main objective is to vote for a transaction. For a transaction to pass through, it must have a certain quorum of votes

This federated nodes can vary from five to six hundred nodes. All the transactions that comes to the federation nodes are bundled into blocks and are written to the underlying database. The database then use it's consensus algorithm for ordering and storing the blocks of transactions. The work of the federation nodes is to vote for the validity of every new transactions that are submitted to them.

The main building block of BigchainDB is the concept of "Blockchain Pipelining." In Blockchain pipelining all the transactions are laid into a row and put in the database. The validation of the transactions by voting happens later. This separation of storing the transactions block into the database where as many as transactions gets stored and then validating as two separate layer is what provides a performance in transactions throughput. The transactions block that gets a majority of a valid votes is considered valid, else it is marked invalid. In order to keep the main chain of blocks unaffected both the valid and invalid blocks are maintained in the chain. If the transactions is considered invalid it can be taken out of a block put in a queue and then re-validated later by putting in the next coming block. This enables the invalid transactions to get a fair chance of getting validated and form a part of the main blocks in the blockchain. Insights into "chainfication at voting time" refers to the chaining of blocks taking place during voting time and not during the writing of blocks to the database. The blocks which gets voted by a federation of nodes over time are required to have an id of the previous block. The votes have the chain information rather than the blocks. BigchainDB is meant to scale wherein the scaling capability allows the legally binding contract and certificates can get stored directly on the distributed database. It can be used side-by-side with decentralised storage IPFS, processing; Ethereum and high level computation and communication systems. The security of the Blockchain rests in the honesty and trust built in the federation of nodes. The PoW protocol rests its security on the hardness 2.5 Blockchain Implementations 31 of solving the cryptographic puzzle by the miner nodes which also decides the security of the network. Here, the network security is completely on the federated nodes. If a majority of nodes decides to act against the network or all the nodes has a weak security than the security of the network gets breached. However, if a small fraction of nodes has a strong security than the whole network is secure.

3.2.1   R3 CORDA

Corda is open source consortium blockchain which enables the contract management between mutually trusting organisations. This platform has a high edge in the Financial Industry. Expressing the financial contracts are the most popular research areas. Peyton-jones,Seward,Eber had done seminal work "Composing Contracts" PJSE2000 [12] in this, financial contracts are done with library of Haskell combinators, these models which will be used for valuation of deals. In Blockchain System the contract acts different than PJSE but the underlying concepts are adapted to corda as well.Contracts in Corda can be upgraded with the co-ordination of convincing large participants to update the contract.Corda does execution of JVM byte code. A better example for this is Whiley language by Dr. David Pearce [11] which checks the integrity of program proof's at compile time.

3.2.1.1 Architecture

This architecture has 2 components:

- Accessing the records depends on the type of actors.
- Computer code describes the agreements behaviour of the system, which enables legitimacy.

3.2.1.2 Key Features

- In this platform sharing of information is done without centralised controller.
- This platform involves supervisory observer and regulatory nodes.
- This platform supports plugable consensus mechanism.
- There is no native currency concept in this framework.
- Sharing of information is done, depending on the roles defined in the network.

3.2.1.3 PBFT Consensus

Parties involved in the transaction process must reach to the agreement whether a transaction is valid or not depending on the rules defined in the smart contract with all the required signatures. Parties should reach to a certainty that the output states are created by the input states consumed by that transactions. Every state has an associated notary. Table 3.1 describes different aspects of Ethereum and R3 Corda.

The PBFT mechanism fundamentally centers around providing a Byzantine state machine replication that endures Byzantine faults through a supposition that there are independent node failures and manipulated messages propagated by particular, independent nodes. PBFT is designed for working in asynchronous systems.

Assumption in PBFT is number of malicious nodes cannot simultaneously equal or exceed 1/3 of the overall nodes in the network at a given time. If there is increase in the nodes of the network, at that point the more mathematically improbable it is for a number moving towards 1/3 of the overall nodes to be malignant. PBFT effectively provides both liveness and safety as long as at most (n-1/3), where n is total nodes. In addition,the PBFT consensus algorithm, the common nodes only synchronise the new block information from leader's nodes without taking part in the consensus.

3.2.2 LITERATURE REVIEW

We categorise Blockchain Interoperability Frameworks into Public Connectors, Chain of Blockchains.

3.2.2.1 Public Connectors

2015 could be a starter for starting the public connectors such as atomic swaps [33,34,35], atomic swap concept has been used in the router that is implemented

Table 3.1
Ethereum vs Corda

	Ethereum	R3 Corda
Smart Contracts	Solidity Programming	Kotlin Programming
Consensus	Proof of Work	Preferred mostly PBFT
Currency	Ether	No Native Currency
Mode of Operation	Public Blockchain	Consortium Blockchain
Use Case	Popular with generalised applications and largely used for P2P operations.	This runs on the specialised distributed ledger platform for the financial industry.

and discussed in this paper. Huge transactions are being batched before submitting to the main blockchain [36,37,38] through Sidechains. Sidechains work in both environments of public and permissioned blockchains [39]. Some side chains have a sidechain consensus algorithm and use Ethereum for bidirectional transfers [42]. BTC Relay has a consensus of sidechain and relay scheme identifies transactions on other chains, as a flow of information is unidirectional [43]. Simple relay schemes, which verify transactions on other chains, such as BTC Relay, have a simple sidechain consensus, as the information flow is unidirectional [43]. Block headers transmission is done using aggregation chains [45] or using users. POA [44], Liquid [41] works on the consortium of validators by running on hardware for smart contract execution and validation. Wanchain [40] works on consortium but not on hardware.

Limitations on Sidechains: Sidechains always assume that the mainchain network cant be attacked successfully, if compromise happens on the mainchain then the whole concept of sidechains will fail. More centralisation is observed in sidechains than mainchains based on the trade-off of decentralisation performance. Based on this observation, having reasonable validators of a quorum to sign each transaction. HTLC's are the first category in a trustless way for the exchange of assets. Cryptocurrency trades are performed using public connectors by moving non-fungible and fungible assets to public blockchains.

3.2.3   CHAIN OF BLOCKCHAINS

Cosmos [46] and Polkadot [47,48] are most prominent in this area. These frameworks provide reusable data, consensus, the network for customised blockchain creation their by interoperating each other.

Building a network of Blockchain networks [48] was Wood's proposal for Polkadot. Polkadot gave the foundation for parachains. Parachains are parallelised chains that involve in the Polkdadot network. Independent chains are linked using bridges (specialised parachains [48]). It is a framework for creating decentralised sytems and other cryptocurrencies. Polkadot provides integration with other technologies, interoperability is enabled on validation of transition state which is done through chain-relay validators. Cross-chain message-passing protocol, is used for Parachains communications. The scalability of Polkadot is up to 100 parachains by connecting directly to the relay chain.

Parallel blockchains (zones [48]), that are independent and all connected in a decentralised way through Cosmos. Zones are Tendermint Blockchains [49]. Transferring of data between zone can happen directly or through hubs. Double spending is avoided and minimises connections between zones are done by Hubs.

Use case, zone Test1 connects to zone Test2 using Hub C and receives tokens from zone Tests. Test1 zone trusts the token of Hub c and Zone Test2. This helps the zone to maintain fewer connections. Inter blockchain communication protocol (IBC) [50]. IBC (inter blockchain communication) is similar to the network layer for routing packets across blockchains. Ex: Blockchain A knows that certain packets are received from another blockchain. IBC has many steps for doing transactions across zones. Tracking of headers of each blockchain will be done and then transfer initiation. Asset locking will happen in the origin chain when the transfer is initiated. After this proof will be sent to the target blockchain,It therefore, reflects the assets that have been locked. This allows for Interoperability across blockchains.

A protocol known as the Application Blockchain Interface connects the application layer to the Tendemint BFT engine. WASM8 is the language in which smart contracts are compiled which is provided by cosmos SDK at the application layer.

During our research, we encountered that there are different frameworks that are available for Interoperability across different environments of blockchains, in our work we looked into Corda and Ethereum frameworks of Interoperability.

3.3   HIGH LEVEL DESIGN OF ROUTER

We made a study on cross chain communications [2,12] as discussed in literature review. We had come up with our own router to connect different blockchains. Routing architecture of the Internet [6] is the basis for designing a router for cross blockchain communication. Recent studies [2,12] on blockchains communication,we made a study on cross chain communications. We had come up with our router concept. Different networks are connected together using the router. They also connect different nodes in that network to the Internet. This architecture ensures the same underlying philosophy of Internet architecture.

3.3.1   BASIC GOALS

Designing ARPANET and Internet favoured many values like survivability, high performance, flexibility over commercial goals [5] which in turn affected how the Internet has evolved and used.DARPA [3] view at the time of the 1960s and 1970s there were set of goals among which three are most basic. Internet fundamental goals are [3,4]:

- Ability to support different types of communications.
- Internet must accommodate different kinds of networks.

- Loss of networks or gateways should not interrupt Internet communications, which is the basic goal of the Internet.

When there is a failure in one of the network there should be another network which offers the same services that are offered by the network that is down. It should dynamically reconfigure its status of routing information to handle the communication failures. All this should happen without a lot of latency and the security should not be compromised. Decentralisation, distribution of resources, etc. are the other goals of the internet.

Distribution of routing information can be divided into intra-domain routing and inter-domain routing. IP packet routing within a network is called intra-domain and routing across networks is called inter-domain routing. All the routers in an autonomous system are unique which is the precondition for routing. Devices visibility in a domain is limited to that domain. The router acts as dispatcher and analyses the data being sent across the network. Each device is identified by unique IP address. The router maintains a routing table that reflects the address that it can jump to, and different routers are connected together using the network topology. Routers can also share the information across.

We will be using these fundamental goals of the Internet for achieving the cross chain communications.Architecture of the interoperability across blockchain systems should allow all the entities to be uniquely authenticated,identifiable and also the transactions should be uniquely referenced across domains irrespective of permission:

Gateway does the boundary for permissioned blockchain's for identifier resolution. On referencing transaction-identifier externally and resolved to ledger in the permissioned blockchain,gateway objects that transaction request as external requests. All Gateways could do the implementation of a transaction-identifier resolution service, like Domain Domain Name Service (DNS and DNS-SEC) [16, 17].

Each blockchain (Ethereum, Corda, Bitcoin, HyperLedger Fabric) is considered a unique network, once the transaction is commited and approved by the peers in its respective chain's, that approved transaction will be sent to the router with all the necessary headers inorder to differentiate the request packet from each blockchain. Router identifies each packet and its origin and sends to other blockchain their by transmitting the information. Communication across blockchains can happen only via the router. The router routes the requests that are coming from different chains.

Router maintains the information of all the chains periodically. In order to communicate with other chains, each chain has to be registered with the router. Exchange of information is done between the router and other chains Figure 3.1. From Figure 3.1 BC is the Blockchain, BC1 could be Ethereum, BC2 could be Hyperledger Fabric, BC3 could be R3 Corda, etc. Router ensures the smoothness of communication in the connected block-chains. There is a possibility of packets getting corrupted in the process of sending and receiving requests in a router, in order to overcome this issue different encryption and decryption algorithms like RSA and DSA are used and the usage of this algorithms is decided dynamically by the router.

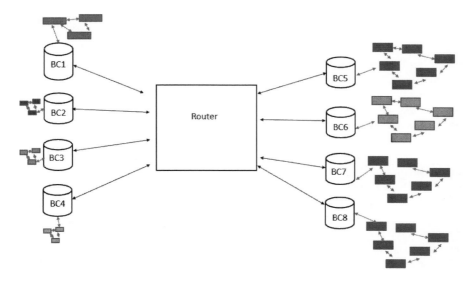

Figure 3.1 Router connected with different blockchain's

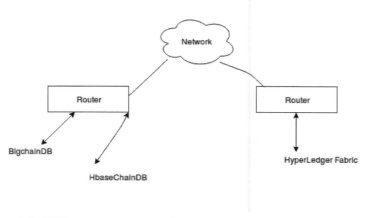

Figure 3.2 Different routers connected via network

Cross chain communication is the major requirement to become the core components of future Industries. Each blockchain handles its own user requirements and business logic. Our router helps to share the information across these different chains by breaking the communication barrier. This protocol design serves a more robust ecosystem of business. Each router can handle a set of chains which will be called a cluster and each of the routers are connected via network Figure 3.2. Router can grow linearly with the increase of connections blockchains.

3.4 DETAILED DESIGN OF THE ROUTER

3.4.1 VARIOUS COMPONENTS

3.4.1.1 Adapter

Adapter links the router and different chains and this connection are done using the sockets and the role of the adapter is to establish the connection between different chains, handles sending and receiving requests from different chains. Each chain has its own consensus mechanism. Once a particular request is commited in the chain and it has been approved in its quorum or consensus algorithm such commited request will be sent to Adapter. Thread will be running in each blockchain apart from its normal functionality their by intimating the Adapter about the current state of the blockchain and how many commits or size of the chain. Adapter collects all the information of each chain. Any transactions that happen in each sub-chain will be recorded in the router, thereby maintaining the up-to-date information and each transaction is signed with the corresponding signature.

3.4.2 ATOMIC SWAPS

Atomic Swap [7] technique has been integrated with the designed router for handling the double spending. Double spending is a big problem in digital currency like bitcoin, ether, ripple, etc. because this currency will be digital, so reproducing this digital currency is easier. In bitcoin, this problem is handled by committing every transaction to the public blockchain. This ensures the valid owner of the bitcoin. In order to understand the need of atomic swaps, we must realise the exchange of assets or currencies or goods needs trust for certain level mainly when these kind of transactions are not involved with humans. Example- There is no assurance that individual x will send cash subsequent to getting merchandise from other individual y and the other way around, these are the transactions that are happening in the same blockchain. The answer to this problem is to identify a confided escrow or party to intercede transaction. Doing this will add generous extra expense to the transaction and does not ensure escrow as a confided source.

To have a decentralised, trust-less system we need to use atomic swaps. The main motive for this atomic swap is rather than two transfers occurring, i.e. the trading of merchandise pursued by the trading of cash, a solitary, subordinate exchange swaps the two values without a moment's delay. This is finished by making the two sides of the exchange subject to one another their by implying that trade of cash is subject to the trading of products. A programming logic is made to safeguard that it is incomprehensible for just a single side of the exchange to happen: either the two sides of the exchange are finished or not one or the other. Atomic swap is modelled as directed graph D, whose vertices are parties and whose arcs are proposed asset transfers and hashed time lock contracts are been used for timely delivery.

The point to note here is in-case if the requester chain fails to deploy the contract while the requestee blockchain follows through, requestee's blockchain contract will be self-destructed and funds will be remitted back to the respective accounts.

In order to make sure the payments are done in timely manner,each chain pings respective contracts,invoking a Hash-time-lock method. If the contract is too many blocks behind the agreed upon time-lock, the contract is destroyed due to non-compliance.

3.4.3   SOCKETS

A network socket is a point of communication flow between different nodes running in the network. Sockets which were created are utilised with function calls. Each of the blockchains that are connected to the router will be communicated through sockets. There are diverse socket families, in order to make sure that there will not be any kind of failure in communication, a router is designed in such a way to accept connection from different blockchains. Socket family that is chosen for this purpose is UDP, on choosing TCP/IP if their the router is down then entire communication will be interrupted and this will be like server-centric to overcome this issue we used (MulticastSocket) family of UDP socket, as we had tested in local-lan their is no packet dropping or sequencing issue, as UDP dont guarntee sequencing. We used master and slave concept, on receiving request packet to Adapter component, Adapter component will post the request packet to multicast group. Their will be a master component which will observe the heartbeat of each system, incase of any failure in system, master will pickup one of the system/process to act as a router incase of current router down, this mechansim is done using MulticastSocket.

3.4.4   COMMUNICATION MECHANISM

Each blockchain has its own limitations, advantages, and disadvantages. Packet always carries the current updated information of its chain along with hash value of validators, committed transactions in the chain etc., all the packets will be encrypted with the public key of router Figure 3.3, and router decrypts the key using its private key and vice-versa, this helps to overcome the problem of manipulating the content of packet, etc.

3.4.5   COMMUNICATION PROTOCOL

Each chain is registered initially with a router, the router maintains all chain's information similar to routing table. The size of the routing table increases linearly if there is an increase in the number of chains in the network. When transaction is commited in a chain, thread that is running in the chain will send request to router, that request will be sent to the router which internally writes to its own blockchain. The job of a router is divided into two parts one for management of sending and receiving of requests and other is to record all these requests into BigchianDB[8], and the reason for choosing BigchainDB is, it handles both the distributed database world with blockchain characteristics. Requests that are triggering from different chains can be written to any other databases like Mysql or MongoDB, etc. but these do not guarantee the tamper-proof, transaction irreversibility and the transparency etc.,

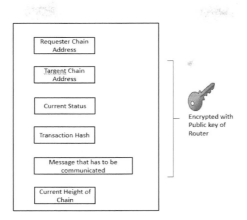

Figure 3.3   Structure of packet

these databases are centralised whereas BigchainDB overcomes all these problems. In a centralised database if the server is down we can't record all the transactions that are happening. In BigchainDB several nodes will be participated, in case any one node is down another node will accomplish the task, because each and every node maintains the complete details of all the transactions that had occurred.

Writing a transaction to BigchainDB is based on the Federation of voting nodes. Once a cross chain communication request is triggered by a specific chain, the adapters send the request to the router, router checks the validity of the request by verifying the transactionId in its routing table. Once the verification is done in routing table, router routes that packet to the requestee chain for the required information. If the requested information is not present router sends a message saying that requested information is not available else it sends the necessary package details accordingly.

The router should be always synced with the latest information of its chains, each blockchain also should maintain the information of router like router's ID, latest block that is committed in the routers. Time to live can be set for each of the requests that are coming to the router. The router maintains the communication status of each request Figure 3.4, and same is shown in the table 3.2.

Table 3.2
Router's Communication Status

Sender/Receiver	Router's Communication Status
Sender sends packet	Pending
Receiver receives packet	Transmitted
Sender received packet as "Transmitted"	Received

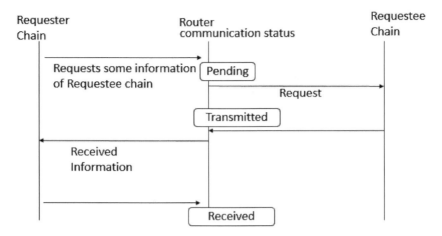

Figure 3.4   Communication status maintained by router

3.4.6   TACTICS FOR AVAILABILITY

To check the availability of the services that are provided by the system is consistently monitored using HeartBeat tactic. In our case router should be ensured that all the chains are alive and in order to service the requests that are coming from different chains and also to keep up to date information of each of its sub-chain and vice-versa. In our case, different Blockchains emits a periodic heartbeat message to router and router listens. If there is a failure of receiving HeartBeat messages from registered chains within a particular time period, the router assumes that particular chain is down. Along with heartbeat message it also carries the current status of the chain, Figure 3.5. This refers to the degree to which a product or system can maintain operational services. This tactic helps to identify which chain is down at a time.

3.5   PROTOTYPE AND EXPERIMENTS

In our set up we have tested with 2 frameworks Ethereum, R3 Corda for the proposed Cross Chain Communication for business use case of Health Insurance [20]. These 2 frameworks are able to share the data across each other using the router and the same has been tested with use case of Health Insurance where some entites of Health Insurance are implemented in Ethereum and some are in Corda, when there is need to share information between these entites in this business domain that sharing of information across these blockchains are done via router. The experiments were carried out on a system with a quad core intel i5 processor and 15.6 GB RAM, Ubuntu 16.04(64 bit), LAN speed 15 Mbps.

Figure 3.8, explains about serving the request that is being received by each blockchain. Figure 3.9, explains about how the messages are serviced by router

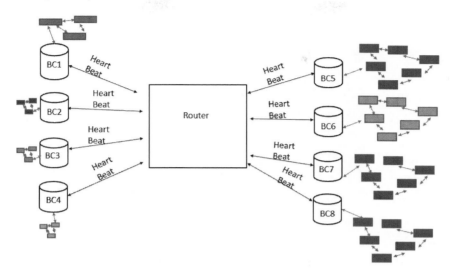

Figure 3.5   Communication status maintained by router

between chains by preserving Blockchain Characteristics. Each time request triggered by the blockchains to router it checks in routing table whether it is valid chain or not, accordingly it passes information by recording all the valid (send/receive) requests in BigchainDB.

In order to transfer the information from a blockchain to the router we use buffer and router does its own operations such as encryption, decryption and storing the information in blockchain. As the number of transactions per second increases their by sending lot of bytes to the router, because of the set of operations involved at router we observed some of the transaction are dropped as shown below. The same is shown in the Figure 3.6.

We had observed as we change the buffer size() and keeping some latency at the router we had seen their is no dropping of information at router side as seen in Figure 3.7. From figure 3.7 we can see 2 transactions are getting dropped at router when buffer size is 65535, when buffer size is 65000 their is drop of 1 transaction, when it is 64450 their is no drop, similarly for other transactions.After tweaking the buffer size with various sizes, we found having buffer size with 64450 their is no drop of transactions at router. Decrease in the buffer size much more will create lot of latency at router, so we observer keeping buffer size to 64450 is giving optimal latency at router.

Figure 3.9, gives detailed picture of different chains having different consensus models, connecting to router through the sockets for passing information. Router handles every request that is coming from different chains and each request is considered as a transaction,router passes that message to BigchainDB consensus algorithm which uses Federation of nodes for validation of the transactions. BigchainDB

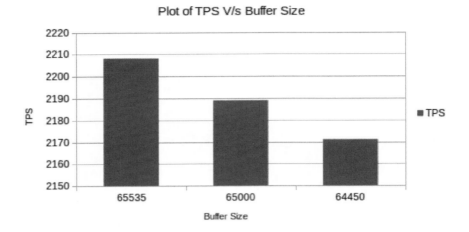

Figure 3.6 Number of TPS at router with different buffer sizes

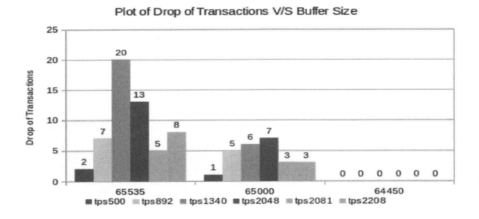

Figure 3.7 Plot of drop transactions vs. buffer size

consensus algorithm adds the transaction to chain only when it gets majority of votes,if there is 50 percentage of votes for committing and 50 percentage for not committing, such transactions will be put in uncle block for a certain period,once the time limit exceeds that transaction will be aborted and dropped from the chain. With this design, router is following each and every property of blockchain there by not violating any characteristic's of blockchain.

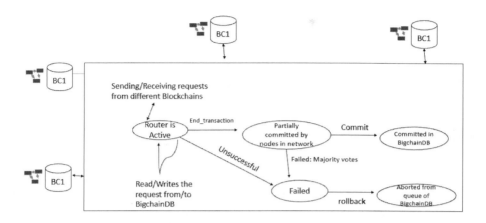

Figure 3.8 Servicing the requests of chains by router

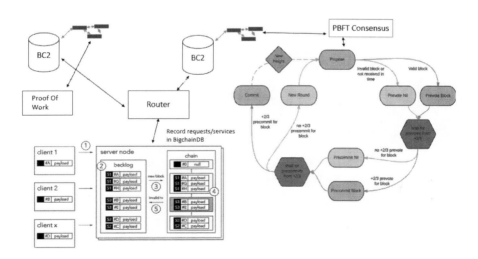

Figure 3.9 Detailed view of router with blockchain Characterstics

3.6 CONCLUSION

We proposed a working model of router to provide, totally decentralised environment to handle communication across different chains with transparency and data integrity.

In Future, we will be developing a mechanism to handle the large data that generally shoots up when communication happens across the chains with large number of nodes in the network via router and storage becomes bottleneck for handling huge data. A study will be made for understanding the scalability issue and the same will be implemented in the router for efficient storage and cost effective.

ACKNOWLEDGMENT

Our work is dedicated to Bhagawan Sri Sathya Sai Baba, Founder Chancellor of Sri Sathya Sai Institute of Higher Learning.

Bibliography

1. Satoshi Nakamoto, *Bitcoin: A Peer-to-Peer Electronic Cash System*, 2008.

2. Ethan Buchman and Jae Kwon, *Cosmos: A Network of Distributed Ledgers*, `https://github.com/cosmos/cosmos/blob/master/WHITEPAPER.md`, 2016

3. D. Clark, *The Design Philosopy of the DARPA Internet Prtocols*,ACM Computer Communication Review - Proc SIGCOMM 88, vol. 18, no. 4, pp. 106-114 ,August 1988

4. V.G. Cerf and R.E. Khan, *Protocol for Packet Network Intercommunication*,IEEE Transactions on Communications, vol.22, pp. 637-648, 1974

5. J. Abbate, *Inventing the Internet*, MIT Press, 1999

6. T. Hardjono,A. Lipton and A. Pentland, *Towards a design philosopy for interoperable blockchain systems*,arxiv [online] Available: `https://arxiv.org/abs/1805.05934`, 2019

7. Maurice Herlihy *Atomic Cross-Chain Swaps*, arxiv 2018 [Online]. Available: `https://arxiv.org/pdf/1801.09515.pdf` ,

8. Trent McConaghy *White Paper on BigchainDB 2.0 The Blockchain Database*, 2018 May

9. Juan Benet *IPFS- Content Addressed,Versioned, P2P FileSystem*,`https://arxiv.org/abs/1407.3561`, 2018

10. Mike Hearn *Corda: A distributed ledger*, [Online] Available: `https://www.corda.net/content/corda-technical-whitepaper.pdf`

11. David J. Pearce and Lindsay Groves, Designing a verifying compiler:Lessons learned from developing whiley, Science of Computer Programming , 113, Part 2:191 – 220, 2015

12. Simon Peyton Jones, Jean-Marc Eber, and Julian Seward Composing contracts: An adventure in financial engineering (functional pearl), SIGPLAN-Not., 35(9):280–292, September 2000

13. Ethereum Blockchain App Platform, [Online] Available: `https://ethereum.org/`

14. Etherscan, Ethereum Charts and Statistics, [Online] Available: `https://etherscan.io/charts`

15. Ethereum Homestead Documentation,Available: `https://ethereum-homestead.readthedocs.io/en/latest/index.html`

16. P. Mockapetris, *Domain names:Concepts and facilities*,RFC 882,Internet Engineering Task Force, Nov.1983, obsoleted by RFCs 1034, 1035, updated by RFC 973. [Online] Available: http://www.ietf.org/rfc/rfc882.txt

17. D.E. 3rd, Domain Name System Security Extensions,RFC 2535(Proposed Standard),Internet Engineering Task Force, Mar. 1999, obsoleted by RFCs 4033, 4034,4035,updated by RFCs 2931, 3007, 3008, 3090, 3226, 3445, 3597, 3655, 3658, 3755, 3757, 3845. [Online]. Available: `http://www.ietf.org/rfc/rfc2535.txt`

18. Trent McConaghy, Rodolphe Marques, Andreas Muller, Dimitri De Jonghe, Troy McConaghy, Greg McMullen, Ryan Henderson, Sylvain Bellemare, and Alberto Granzotto. Bigchaindb: a scalable blockchain database. white paper, BigChainDB, 2016.

19. `https://eprint.iacr.org/2013/881.pdf`

20. Nukala Poorna Viswanadha Sravan, Pallav Kumar Baruah, Sathya Sai Mudigonda, and Phani Krihsna K, Blockchain Technology in Health Inusrance-Integration of 8 Stake Holders.

21. Abdullah Ahmad Zarir, Gustavo Ansaldi Oliva, Zhen Ming (Jack) Jiang, Developing Cost-Effective Blockchain-Powered Applications: A Case Study of the Gas Usage of Smart Contract Transactions in the Ethereum Blockchain Platform.

22. Junfeng Xie, F. Richard Yu, Tao Huang, Renchao Xie, Jiang Liu, and Yunjie Liu , A Survey on the Scalability of Blockchain Systems, 0890-8044/19 2019 IEEE

23. Dr Gideon Greenspan, MultiChain Private Blockchain — White Paper.

24. E. Prud'hommeaux and C. Buil-Aranda, "Federated Query, W3C Recommendation," 2013. [Online]. Available: `https://www.w3.org/TR/sparql 11-federated-query/`

25. R. Cyganiak, D. Wood, and M. Lanthaler, "RDF 1.1 Concepts and Abstract Syntax, W3C Recommendation," 2014. [Online]. Available: `http://www. w3.org/TR/rdf11-concepts/`

26. B. J. Nelson, "Remote procedure call," Ph.D. dissertation, Carnegie Mellon University, 1981. [Online]. Available: `https://dl.acm.org/citation. cfm?id=910306`

27. Object Management Group, "Common Object Request Broker Architecture Specification Version 3.4," 2021. [Online]. Available: `https://www.omg. org/spec/CORBA/`

28. R. T. Fielding, Architectural Styles and the Design of Networkbased Software Architectures, Ph.D. dissertation, UNIVERSITY OF CALIFORNIA, IRVINE, 2000. [Online]. Available: `https://www.ics.uci.edu/fieldi ng/pubs/dissertation/restarchstyle.htm`

29. Fakhar Ul Hassan, Anwaar Ali, Siddique Latif, Junaid Qadir, Salil Kanhere, Jatinder Singh, and Jon Crowcroft. 2019. Blockchain And The Future of the Internet: A Comprehensive Review. arXiv e-prints (2019). `https://arxi v.org/abs/1904.00733`

30. Aviv Zohar. 2015. Bitcoin: Under the Hood. Commun. ACM 58, 9 (8 2015), 104–113.

31. Nick Szabo. 1997. Formalizing and securing relationships on public networks. First Monday 2, 9 (1997). Manuscript submitted to ACM

32. Zibin Zheng, Shaoan Xie, Hongning Dai, Xiangping Chen, and Huaimin Wang. 2017. An Overview of Blockchain Technology: Architecture, Consensus, and Future Trends. In Proceedings - 2017 IEEE 6th International Congress on Big Data, BigData Congress 2017. Institute of Electrical and Electronics Engineers Inc., 557–564

33. Matthew Black, Tingwei Liu, and Tony Cai. 2019. Atomic Loans: Cryptocurrency Debt Instruments. `http://arxiv.org/abs/1901.05117`

34. Christian Decker and Roger Wattenhofer. 2015. A fast and scalable payment network with bitcoin duplex micropayment channels. In Lecture Notes in Computer Science, Vol. 9212. Springer Verlag, 3–18

35. Maurice Herlihy. 2018. Atomic cross-chain swaps. In Proceedings of the Annual ACM Symposium on Principles of Distributed Computing. Association for Computing Machinery, New York, New York, USA, 245–254.

36. Sergio Lerner. 2015. RSK Whitepaper. Technical Report. RSK.

37. Joseph Poon and Vitalik Buterin. 2017. Plasma: Scalable Autonomous Smart Contracts. Technical Report. Plasma. `https://plasma.io/`

38. Amritraj Singh, Kelly Click, Reza M. Parizi, Qi Zhang, Ali Dehghantanha, and Kim Kwang Raymond Choo. 2020. Sidechain technologies in blockchain networks: An examination and state-of-the-art review. Journal of Network and Computer Applications 149 (2020).

39. Wenting Li, Alessandro Sforzin, Sergey Fedorov, and Ghassan O. Karame. 2017. Towards scalable and private industrial blockchains. In ACM Workshop on Blockchain, Cryptocurrencies and Contracts. Association for Computing Machinery, Inc, 9–14

40. Wanchain Foundation. 2019. Wanchain Roadmap. `https://www.wanchain.org/learn/`

41. Johnny Dilley, Andrew Poelstra, Jonathan Wilkins, Marta Piekarska, Ben Gorlick, and Mark Friedenbach. 2016. Strong Federations: An Interoperable Blockchain Solution to centralised Third-Party Risks. Technical Report. BlockStream. `http://arxiv.org/abs/1612.05491`

42. Alberto Garoffolo, Dmytro Kaidalov, and Roman Oliynykov. 2020. Zendoo: a zk-SNARK Verifiable Cross-Chain Transfer Protocol Enabling Decoupled and Decentralised Sidechains. Technical Report. V.N.Karazin Kharkiv National University

43. Ethereum Foundation and Consensys. 2015. BTC-relay: Ethereum contract for Bitcoin SPV. `https://github.com/ethereum/btcrelay`

44. V Arasev. 2017. POA Network Whitepaper. Technical Report. POA Network. `https://www.poa.network/for-users/whitepaper`

45. Peter Robinson and Raghavendra Ramesh. 2020. General Purpose Atomic Crosschain Transactions. arXiv (11 2020). `http://arxiv.org/abs/2011.12783`

46. Jae Kwon and Ethan Buchman. 2016. Cosmos Whitepaper. Technical Report. Cosmos Foundation

47. Jeff Burdges, Alfonso Cevallos, Peter Czaban, Rob Habermeier, Syed Hosseini, Fabio Lama, Handan Kilinc Alper, Ximin Luo, Fatemeh Shirazi, Alistair Stewart, and Gavin Wood. 2020. Overview of polkadot and its design considerations. arXiv 2005.13456 (2020), 1–40.

48. Gavin Wood. 2016. Polkadot: Vision for a Heterogeneous Multi-Chain Framework. Technical Report. 1–21 pages. `https://github.com/w3f/polkadotwhite-paper/raw/master/PolkaDotPaper.pdf`

49. Tendermint. 2016. Tendermint BFT. `https://github.com/tendermint/tendermint`

50. IBC Ecosystem Working Group. 2020. Inter-blockchain Communication Protocol (IBC). `https://github.com/cosmos/ics/tree/master/ibc`

51. Vitalik Buterin. 2014. Ethereum: A next-generation smart contract and decentralised application platform. `https://github.com/ethereum/wiki/wiki/White-Paper`

4 HBasechainDB 3.0 Scalable Implementation of Blockchain on HBase with Capability for Smart Contract

Blockchain [13] is a distributed ledger of transactions shared among the network of peers. It is a growing list of records/transactions that has been executed by all the parties in the network. The transactions can only be appended, this is achieved by hash chaining. The difficulty in inverting the chained hashes imparts the immutability to the list. Each transaction is to be verified by the majority of the network peers. Participation of the peers in the validating process happens through different consensus mechanisms.

Blockchain is the main technology for digital cryptocurrency Bitcoin. Satoshi Nakamoto, a person or group of individual, had published a white paper named Bitcoin [6]: A peer to peer electronic cash system in 2008 through which the blockchain technology has gained its popularity. The transaction records can not be manipulated since they are distributed over the network. Transactions can be anything of value like Cars, Buildings, etc. Blockchain contains data in the form of blocks and each block has a header and set of transactions. A block contains hash of the transactions to produce a fixed-length hash output that is applied to the block header. Each subsequent valid block must contain the previous block header's hash output once the first block is created. The hash of the previous block header contained in each block serves as the chain connecting each valid block to the previous block. Thus a chain of blocks (blockchain) is established by linking each block to the preceding blocks.

Blockchain has many applications in various fields like Finance, Insurance, Supply Chain and Banking, etc. Blockchain increases the transparency of transactions as each peer has the copy of ledger which makes the ledger tamper-proof.

It has a trust less, decentralised, immutable consensus network. The feature of security makes blockchain a prime technology. It uses public key cryptography for encrypting the data on the blockchain. It is highly disruptive innovation and potential game-changer in the digital world. Proof-of-Work is one of the consensus mechanisms used in the blockchain. It is the most important concept in Nakamoto's white paper [6] as it provides trust less and distributed consensus. PoW (a original consensus algorithm in a blockchain network) makes expensive calculations which is considered as mining. Mining is used for validating the transactions and the miners

DOI: 10.1201/9781003355052-4

should solve a mathematical puzzle to validate the transaction after which miner gets the reward of tokens.

The main objective of the proposed model is to have a blockchain framework with higher throughput and smart contract ability. Existing HBasechainDB1.0 and HBasechainDB2.0 frameworks have higher throughput but has no smart contract ability. So, we have designed this system to have both abilities.

The scope of this model is Hyperledger fabric kind of smart contract ability and HBasechainDB(1.0 & 2.0) kind of throughput. We have added smart contract ability to HBasechainDB2.0 then the throughput is compromised to some extend. There is scope to increase throughput further but it may effect smart contract ability.

4.1 BACKGROUND AND RELATED WORK

The idea of smart contract was introduced even before the blockchain came into existence. It was proposed by Nick Szabo in 1994. Szabo is a scholar, computer scientist, and cryptographer.

Nick Szabo [11] describes a smart contract as a set of promises, specified in digital form, including protocols on which the parties perform according to these promises. Smart contracts [11] are defined as self-executing contracts with the terms of agreement between buyer and seller being embedded in the code. It is used to verify, facilitate and enforce the performance of a contract. The code and agreements exist across the blockchain network. Smart contracts allow trustworthy transactions and agreements to take place between independent, anonymous parties without the need for a framework for central authority, legal system or external compliance. It makes transactions irreversible, traceable and transparent.

Smart contract working can be understood easily through examples. Lets assume an item has to be delivered to Bob by Alice. Bob agrees to pay for the item upon delivery. Alice would also like to be assured that she will receive payment from Bob once the item is delivered. This makes the need for a third party to ensure the conditions agreed in advance are met. This is where smart contracts are used. Rather than send the payment to Alice before he receives the delivery or Alice faces the possibility that Bob will not pay, the terms of exchange can be defined in the smart contract by both parties. On the day Alice sends the item to him, Bob would then transfer the money for the item to a smart contract. When Bob confirms the delivery of the item as stated in the contract, the smart contract will retain the sum and serve as an escrow. The sum payable by Bob will then be released to Alice after delivery and confirmation.

The conditions, that are placed inside a contract, can be self-verified by the smart contract by interpreting the data. The following steps describe the smart contract usage:

- At first, the smart contract has to be written into the blockchain as code.
- The contract and transaction information is recorded but the parties involved may remain anonymous on public ledgers.

- The contracts are easily interpreted and executed based on the terms written in the code by setting the triggering events like due date, expiration date, strike price or other conditions.

Continuous recording of data in real time and immediate feedback is possible with these self-verifying contracts. Smaller processes that are associated with the legally binding contracts can be automated by smart contracts. Finally, it provides speed and ease of use, cost-savings, immutability, a level of autonomy, security, trust, reliability, and accuracy.

Smart contracts are more flexible as they not only set the conditions but also executes the terms of agreements in the contracts. The potential use cases of smart contracts are Mortgages and Land Title Recording, Supply chain, IoT, Auto insurance, Financial Data Recording, Digital Identity, Trade, Finance, Derivatives and Securities.

4.1.1   ETHEREUM

Ethereum [4] is used for building decentralised applications by utilising blockchain technology. These decentralised applications are also called smart contracts that are executed on all nodes in Ethereum network. Contract logic is embedded in smart contract which ensures the correct execution and avoid any possibility of fraud. Smart contract has lines of code representing the legal contract which is executed by all network participants using a type of operating system called Ethereum virtual machine (EVM) [4]. This works without any intermediary and downtime of the network. Ether is a cryptocurrency for Ethereum platform. It is used for virtually any kind of transaction lower than the cost of traditional payment systems. Proof of Work consensus algorithm is used for checking the consistency on all the nodes after the execution of smart contract. Every node comes to an agreement on the global state using Proof-of-Work algorithm.

Services like naming and identity services can benefit from Ethereum as these services can be decentralised over Ethereum platform. It has power to support Web 3.0 that is highly secure and decentralised. Secure economic interactions can be made using this platform without any intermediary.

In Ethereum, the smart contract is a piece of code which can be deployed and executed to perform business processes. This code is stored as byte codes on the blockchain and it is immutable once created. On each node the complied code is run using Ethereum EVM (ethereum virtual machine). Each contract has its own address and the Ether must be paid by the caller to deploy and execute the smart contract. A token or currency is also considered as a smart contract. Solidity language is used to write the smart contracts in Ethereum. User can define their own currency as a smart contract. The contracts address is similar to the public address of private key based accounts. The only difference it has no associated private key. Execution of smart contracts byte code is triggered when the transaction is sent to the contract's address. The contract's code can do similar tasks by calling the address of the code on the contracts, sending funds to other address. The contract cannot initialise the transaction but normal address can. Private key base addresses initiates the transactions on the Ethereum.

Smart contracts are considered as an agreement or contract (It contains instructions like *"if A is found then B will happen"*) which works on the Ethereum network. The commands or instructions which are in the form of code are distributed throughout the Ethereum network. On ETH blockchain, the distributed code is executed. User must pay the fee called gas to the nodes in the network for executing these smart contracts. The smart contract is executed on Ethereum Virtual Machine (EVM) after distributing the code to all the nodes.

Today, Ethereum processes about 500,000 transactions a day, and can process about *13 transactions a second* at full capacity. The main reason behind Ethereum's bottleneck for scalability is that *every node in the network has to process every transaction*.

4.1.2   WORLD OF BIGDATA

This section discusses various factors of big data.

4.1.2.1   Apache HBase

[9] A scalable, distributed Big Data store and it is built on the Hadoop ecosystem. It supports real-time, random read/write access to Big Data. This data store is designed to be distributed, open-source, versioned, non-relational database designed from the inspiration of Googles Bigtable. HBase makes maximum use of fault tolerance feature of HDFS, which makes it an important component in the Hadoop ecosystem. It has low-latency arbitrary writes and reads over HDFS. Regions are the basic element of distribution and availability for tables. They comprise of a Store per Column Family. HBase Regions are continuous, sorted set of rows which are stored together. A region contains all rows in the table between the regions start key and end key. They form a subset of table data. HBase is a master slave design which has a single master hub i.e. HMaster and a few slaves known as region-servers. Every region-server has group of regions, and a region can be served just by a solitary region server. The client requests are directed to the corresponding region-server by the HMaster. HMaster, Region-server and ZooKeeper are the three important components of HBase architecture. HMaster is a procedure which is said to be lightweight that allocates regions to region-servers of the Hadoop group for balancing the load. Region Servers are the worker nodes which are responsible for handling write, read, delete, and update requests from clients. Region Servers keeps running on each hub of the hadoop network.

ZooKeeper can be used as coordination service in distributed environment, by HBase, for region assignments and recovering any region server crashes by loading them into other region servers which are working. It is a centralised monitoring server that provides distributed synchronisation and maintains configuration information. Zookeeper is the gateway for communication with Region Servers. HMaster and region servers should get registered with ZooKeeper service, client needs to access ZooKeeper quorum to access HMaster and region servers. In the case of node failure within an HBase cluster, ZKquoram will trigger error messages and start repairing failed nodes.

4.1.2.2   BigchainDB

[12] A decentralised database, at scale. It focuses for higher throughput and low latency. The BigchainDB configuration begins with a distributed database (DB), and through an arrangement of advancements includes blockchain qualities: decentralised control, immutability, and creation and development of digital resources.

BigchainDB acquires qualities of current distributed databases: linear scaling in throughput and limit with the quantity of hubs, a full highlighted NoSQL query language, productive querying, and permissioning. Being based on a current conveyed DB, it additionally acquires venture solidified code for the greater part of its codebase. Scalable capacity means that legally binding contracts and certificates may be stored directly on the blockchain database. The permissioning framework empowers setups running from private venture blockchain databases to open blockchain databases.

Consensus on the validity of BigchainDB transactions is achieved through voting by the federation nodes. The federation itself can have a high barrier of entry based on trust and reputation thereby preventing Sybil attacks and the resulting swamping of votes on transactions. The transactions submitted to the BigchainDB federation nodes are bundled into blocks and these blocks are then written to the underlying database. BigchainDB allows the underlying database consensus mechanism decide the block ordering. Once the blocks have been written to the underlying database, all the federation nodes are informed about the new block who then proceed to vote upon the validity of the block. The key contribution of BigchainDB that enables the performance benefits is its method of blockchain pipelining. In this method, blocks are written to the underlying database with no waiting for a vote upon its validity. Voting happens as a separate layer over the databases consensus. If a block acquires a majority of valid votes then it is considered valid, else it is marked invalid. To keep the chain unmodified, both valid and invalid blocks are retained in the chain.

Another idea unique to BigchainDB is that the chaining of the blocks does not happen during the block writing but at the voting time. The ordering of the blocks is unknown during the writing of the blocks and blocks are not required to store the id of the previous block. Instead votes appended to the block over time by the federation nodes are required to have a previous block id. This is what is meant by chainification at voting time - the votes have the chain information rather than the blocks themselves.

4.1.2.3   HBasechainDB

[3] [10] A peer-to-peer network handled by using a federation of nodes. Federation nodes share same privileges which makes it a decentralised system. This network takes the inspiration from Internet Domain Name System. Transactions or blocks can be submitted or retrieved by network parties but blockchain can only be modified by

the federation nodes. The federation is not fixed but it can increase or decrease during the execution of operations of HBasechainDB. It seems like a centralised system but by choosing federation nodes appropriately makes the system more decentralised. It provides a tamper-proof data store even if federation nodes don't trust each other. The system can be compromised if there exists a majority of malicious nodes.

Whenever any transaction is submitted by any client, it is randomly assigned to one of the federation nodes. Let there be k federation node N1, N2, N3,..., Nk. If a transaction is assigned to a federation node say Nk,then this node is responsible for checking its validity. Validation of a transaction can be done by verifying the contents of transaction hash if it is tampered, signature of the participating entities, inputs to transactions if it is spent already. After validating a set of transaction by the node Nk, it combines them together to form a block and this block will be added to the blockchain.

The block contains specified maximum number of transactions. When a block is appended to the blockchain its validity is not finalised. Blocks contains a voters list based on the existing federation as this federation nodes increase or decrease during the course of execution of operation of HBasechainDB. All nodes in the list of voters (nodes) participate to validate the block. A block is validated by validating each transaction in the block.

A block is considered to be valid if all its transactions are valid, otherwise it is invalid. The block status can be changed from undecided to invalid or valid based on the majority of invalid or valid votes respectively. Transactions of a valid block is stored in the blockchain whereas the invalid blocks are not considered but both valid and invalid blocks are retained. For answering any query for transactions, only the valid transactions are considered. Invalid blocks may not contain all invalid transactions so the transactions of this kind are reassigned to federation node randomly.

This helps when a rogue node tries to put an invalid transaction to the blockchain, but it is reassigned to another honest node the second time, it is dropped by this honest node. The blocks are recorded in HBase in the lexicographical order of their ids when the blocks are entered into HBasechain table. After the voting, blocks are chained. Block creation and validation happens independently which removes unnecessary delay. It may appear that each federation node has different view of the blockchain depending upon the order in which they see the incoming blocks. But in practice in HBasechainDB, the blocks which have to be voted upon are sequenced based on their timestamp because of strong consistency nature of HBase. So all the nodes see the blocks in the same order.

If any adversary has to change any block in the blockchain, he/she will have to change the block, resulting to a change in its hash. The vote information for the block in the votes table and the hash will not match. So adversary has to change the vote information all the way upto the current block. During vote time, the nodes must append their signature to the vote.

Adversary cannot modify the nodes votes unless he/she forges the signature which is not possible due to the encryption used. He/She has to forge many signature to make any modification in the blockchain which is computationally hard. Such design makes HBasechainDB a tamper-proof, scalable blockchain system over HBase. High performance Computing and Data (HPCD) Group, Department of Mathematics and Computer Science (DMACS), Sri Sathya Sai Institute of Higher Learning has proposed HBasechainDB [10]. There exist two versions of HBasechainDB i.e. HBasechainDB1.0 [3] and HBasechainDB2.0 [10]. These two follow the same validation procedure as discussed above. HBasechainDB1.0 modifies the architecture of BigchainDB [12] and builds a query mapper which converts MongoDB queries to HBase queries and vice-versa. It is implemented in python. It provides better performance in terms of transaction throughput. HBasechainDB2.0 builds a new scalable blockchain framework and it doesn't have any query mapper. It is implemented in java. It provides higher performance than BigchainDB and HBasechainDB1.0. Figure 4.9 shows the performance of BigchainDB, HBasechainDB1.0 and HBasechainDB2.0.

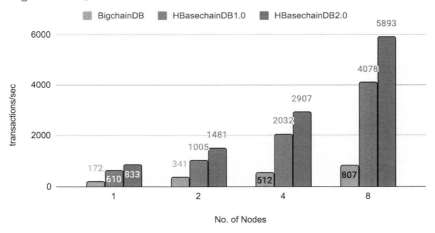

Figure 4.1   Performance of BigchainDB, HBasechainDB1.0, and HBasechainDB2.0

HBasechainDB 3.0: The subject of this paper is a modified design of HBasechainDB which not only performs better than the previous versions but also facilitates Smart contract. We discuss some of the features in the next sections.

4.2   PERFORMANCE OF HBASECHAINDB THROUGH FORKING

Forking is one of the critical issue that hinders good performance of a Blockchain. Any of the Blockchain network following PoW or BFT type of consensus mechanism falls into this trap of Forking. In the next section we describe this with respect the Hyperledger fabric. Also discuss as to how to get better of the same. We demonstrate the avoiding forking will lead to an overhead on performance. This discussion is important in the context because we claim that HBasechainDB does not fall into get trapped into the Forking problem. We also discuss the comparative performance of HBasechainDB against Hyperledger Fabric, with and without Forking.

4.2.1   FORKING PROBLEM IN HYPERLEDGER FABRIC

The Hyperledger Fabric architecture makes users to choose an orderer service which implements a consensus algorithm that better fits their application. One desirable property is Byzantine fault tolerance (BFT) [7], that says the orderer can do its job even in the presence of rogue actors.

It applies to the transaction ordering in Hyperledger Fabric [2] only. Its job is to ensure that each peer has the same list of transactions in their ledger.

In Fabric, the Ordering Service is the sub-system that is tasked with putting together a block of transactions. Then the ordering service transmits the block to all nodes. The ordering service in Hyperledger Fabric is a pluggable module, meaning one can choose to use any existing consensus protocol. The ones currently being used (Solo, Kafka (CFT) and PBFT) [2] achieve consensus deterministically. In Hyperledger Fabric, the Kafka ordering service consists of a cluster of Ordering Service Nodes (OSNs) used for transaction ordering deterministically. Transactions are received by any of the OSN nodes which will be posted to a Kafka [5] partition. The transactions are consumed by all OSNs including the one which posted it into the Kafka cluster. Each OSN consumes all transactions from the Kafka partition and stored into their local ledgers. A block is cut when one of three conditions is satisfied: (1) the block contains the specified maximum number of transactions; (2) the block has reached a maximum size (in bytes); or (3) an amount of time has taken since the first transaction of a new block was got. So every OSN creates the block from the transactions stored in the OSNs local logs. The above mentioned process is currently happening in the Kafka ordering service. We know that Kafka orderer is not Byzantine Fault Tolerant (BFT) so byzantine attacks can occur. Consider a scenario where transaction stream sent to the OSN was tampered by a byzantine attacker on Kafka. One more scenario where block signature stream sent to OSN was tampered by a byzantine attacker on Kafka. This kind of scenarios will be addressed and safety guarantees will be assured by our model. Finally, this model makes the Kafka ordering fork resilient. Forking means blocks mismatch at Ordering service nodes. Figure 4.4 shows the forking problem in Hyperledger fabric, where the OSN0 and OSN1 have two different blocks C and C'(C != C'). Suppose block C contains two transactions, and block C' contains those same two, but in opposite order and account A has a balance of & $10.

In transaction1, it says "transfer &$10 from A to B"

In transaction2, it says "transfer &$10 from A to C"

If in block C, the order is transaction1, transaction2, and in block C' the order is transaction2, transaction1, then in block C, account B ends up with the money and account C gets nothing, while in block C', account C gets the money and account B gets nothing. This is commonly known as a "Double Spend [1]," where transaction1 spends the money, transaction2 spends it again. Only one can be valid, and it will be the first one which is processed.

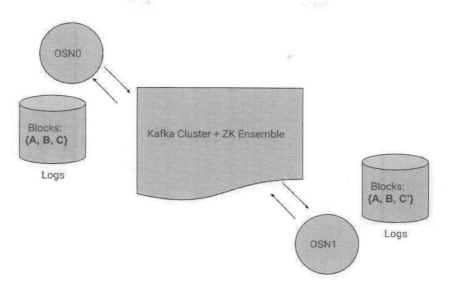

Figure 4.2   Forking in hyperledger fabric

So, if the blockchain is forked, it's possible to convince two parties that they have each been paid & $10, when there is only & $10 initially in the account.

4.2.2   PROPOSED MODEL

Our proposed model is shown in Figure 4.3, to avoid forking situation in the Kafka orderer, we perform the following steps:

- Create a second partition in the Kafka topic for each channel apart from the first partition from where the OSNs consume the transactions.
- Have each OSN produce its signature over the block header, but before committing it, produce the signature and block header into the second partition.
- Have each OSN wait on this other partition for a "sufficient" number of matching signatures.
- Each OSN commit their block into their local logs after getting a sufficient number of matching signatures from the second partition and all these signatures must be added into block metadata.

The above proposed algorithm (Algorithm 1) is used for finding forked blocks in Kafka orderer of Hyperledger Fabric. Today, orderers/OSNs do not share blocks with each other, they assume that the blocks are the same because they were generated deterministicall (all OSNs take the transactions from the same partition). The modification we propose, is to have a second round through Kafka where they share

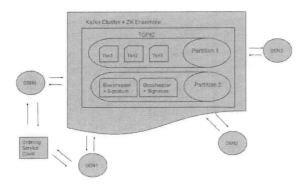

Figure 4.3   Modified Kafka orderer with the second partition in a Kafka topic

---

Algorithm 1 Finding block forks in Kafka Orderer of Hyperledger Fabric

---

Majority ← Count of majority of the Kafka ordering nodes
OSN ← 2D array of ordering nodes with final signature(Blockheader signed with Signature)
Counter ← 1
repeat
    if OSN[0][OSNSignature] ≠ OSN[Counter][OSNSignature] **then**
        return *Fork Occurred*
    end if
    Counter ← Counter + 1
until the Counter reaches the count of Majority

---

block header hashes and signatures, and require a certain number of them before committing. Block contents are shown in the **Figure 4.4**.

'DataHash' is a hash over the transactions in the Data section of the current block and 'PrevHash' is the hash of the previous block header.

The overall process of the proposed model as follows:

- Each Orderer/OSN generate a block and its header by invoking "Create-Block" function and sign it.
- It then pushes the blockheader and signature to the second partition as shown in Fig 4.4.
- Because every orderer does this, eventually, the orderer will consume enough block headers and signatures, and may combine those signatures before invoking "WriteBlock" function.
- Each OSN would check for matching signatures and if majority matches then it will commit the block.

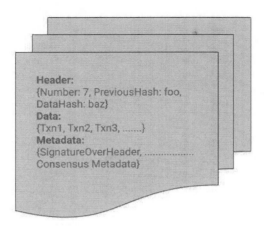

Figure 4.4   Block contents in Hyperledger Fabric

With today's Kafka Fabric Ordering Service [2], each block only has one signature. But, the field in the block metadata for signatures is arbitrary in length. This was always part of the design to support BFT protocols in the future. So, instead of only having one signature, the OSN would collect a majority of signatures, before committing the block. Because an orderer only ever signs once, it's impossible to get two sets of majority signatures for two different blocks. Hence, the fork cannot occur. So, the stated goal of preventing a fork is achieved and the method also provides the safety guarantees.

4.2.3   FORKING PROBLEM IN HBASECHAINDB 3.0

In HBasechainDB 3.0, the *forking problem can't happen as there exists no ordering service* in it. Each federation node handles different blocks so one block can't be handled by more than one federation node. So forking situation can't arise in the any versions of HBasechainDB.

4.3   HBASECHAINDB 3.0

4.3.1   DESIGN FEATURES

HBasechainDB 3.0 is a scalable blockchain framework which provides efficient and flexible development domain. It supports smart contract facility. The interface shown in **Figure 4.5** must be implemented by the user to write smart contract in HBasechainDB 3.0. Transactions can be created by using one of the methods in ScUtil interface. User can define the operations to be performed on the transaction using

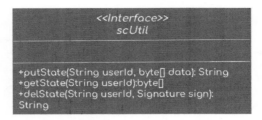

Figure 4.5   ScUtil interface

the methods of ScUtil interface. A smartcontract can be created by implementing ScUtil interface. Participating parties must agree upon the created smartcontract.

HBasechainDB 3.0 has been designed to operate with a federation of nodes and every node has equal privileges in the federation. The federation is formed from the participating nodes in the blockchain network. This setup makes it a decentralised network. The smart contract has business logic which has to be deployed as blockchain transaction. Clients can submit smart contracts to blockchain network and transactions will be generated from those smart contracts. Each of the transactions generated is allocated at random to one of the nodes in the federation.

4.3.2   STRUCTURAL DESIGN

HBasechainDB 3.0 follows the same process as HBasechainDB follows from the transaction validation to finality. The blockchain can only be modified by the federation nodes. Assume that there exists n federation N1, N2, ..., Nc in the network and when a transaction is submitted by the clients it is tagged to one of the federation nodes, say Nc, randomly. Then the node Nc is accountable for checking validity of this transaction and entering the same into the blockchain. A transaction is valid if it has correct transaction hash and correct client signature. Besides all these validations, the transaction is checked against double spending condition. All the valid set of transactions have to be bundled into a block which will then be added to the blockchain. A specified maximum number of transactions can be allowed inside a block. A block validity is not decided when it is added to the blockchain. Blocks has a voters list based on the current federation as this federation nodes increase or decrease during the course of execution. This list of voters (nodes) in the block indicates that all these nodes has been validated the block. Validating the block involves validating all the transactions of the block. A block is considered as a valid if all its transactions found to be valid, otherwise it is invalid. The block status can be changed from undecided to valid or invalid based on the majority of valid or invalid votes respectively. Transactions of a valid block is recorded in the blockchain whereas the invalid blocks are ignored but both valid and invalid blocks are retained. For answering any query for transactions, only the valid transactions are considered. Invalid blocks may not contain all invalid transactions so the transactions of this kind are reassigned to federation node randomly. This helps when a rogue node tries to add

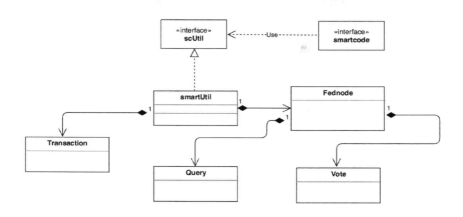

Figure 4.6   Class diagram of HBasechainDB 3.0

an invalid transaction to the blockchain, but it is reassigned to another honest node the second time, it is dropped by this honest node. When the blocks are loaded into the hbasechain table, the blocks are placed in HBase [9] in the lexicographic order of their ids. The time when voting happens then this the time when the blocks are actually chained. Block creation and validation happens independently which removes unnecessary waiting. It may look for a different view of the chain for each federation node depending on the order in which the incoming blocks are viewed. But in practice in HBasechainDB 3.0, the blocks to be voted upon are ordered based on their timestamp as HBase has the strong consistency. So All the nodes see the blocks in the same order. If any opponent has to tamper with any block in the blockchain, he/she will have to modify the block, which leads to a hash change. That hash would not match the voting information in the voting table for the block. So adversary has to change the vote information all the way upto present. During vote time, the nodes must append their signature to the vote. Adversary cannot modify the nodes votes unless he/she forges the signature which is cryptographically not possible. He/she has to forge multiple signatures to make any changes to the computationally difficult blockchain. In this way HBasechainDB 3.0 is blockchain over HBase that is tamper proof. The class diagram and the transaction flow of HBasechainDB is shown in Figures 4.6, 4.7, and 4.8.

4.3.3   STRUCTURAL DESIGN

4.3.3.1   Block Creation Algorithm

- Pick the transactions allocated to that node from the smartLog table.
- All the transactions are checked for validity. All the valid transactions are kept in valid list and invalid ones are in the invalid list.

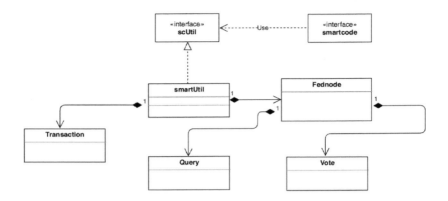

Figure 4.7 Class diagram of HBasechainDB 3.0

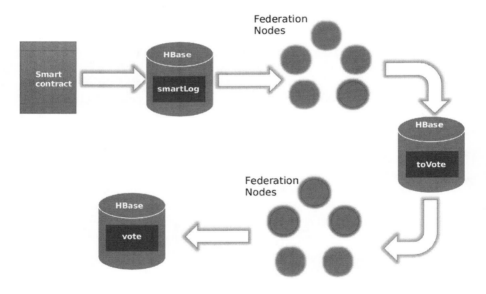

Figure 4.8 Transaction flow in HBasechainDB 3.0

- A HBasechainDB block is created with all the valid transactions.
- The newly created block is signed.
- The block being created is inserted into 'Block' table.
- All the transaction details of transactions which are there in newly created block have to be inserted into smartBase table.
- Update the toVote table after which all the federation nodes get updated

about the newly created block.
- Federation nodes cast the vote on the newly created block.
- All the transactions, which are retrieved in step 1, are deleted from the 'smartLog' table.

4.3.3.2 Transaction Validation Algorithm

- Check the signature of the client who submitted the smart contract.
- If the signature is valid return transaction is valid else return transaction is invalid.
- Check the transaction detail hash for the integrity and if it is not tampered return it is valid else return invalid.
- Check if the value is being double spent. If it is found to be spending twice return invalid, else return valid.

4.3.3.3 Block Validation Algorithm

- Check if all the transactions in the block are valid or not.
- If all transactions are valid then return block is valid else return invalid.

4.3.3.4 Voting Algorithm

- A newly created block information is taken from the toVote table.
- Validity of the block is checked.
- After the validation check, the vote is signed by the voter.
- The vote is inserted into vote table.
- The notification from toVote table is deleted

4.3.3.5 HBasechainDB 3.0 Life Cycle

- Smart contracts [11] submitted by the clients are submitted to the backend of the HBasechainDB 3.0. Then the transactions are generated from the smart contract and inserted into smartLog HBase table. These transactions are assigned to one of the federation nodes randomly.
- The federation node takes all the assigned transaction and performs validation checks. Checks involve content integrity, client's signature verification, double-spending, matching transaction Id with transaction hash. After the validation, each federation nodes create a block from these valid transactions. Next it performs the following steps:
    - Block-chaining. The block created for incorporation into the chain is first added to the smartBase table. This is in line with the blockchain pipe lining concept where blocks are applied to the chain without waiting for the blocks to be checked.
    - Putting transaction details into smartBase table. After block formation all the transaction details found in that block are moved to the table smartBase.

- Block Voting Indication. All the federation nodes get notified about the voting of the new block. This can be carried by putting the block details in toVote table.

- Block voting. The federation nodes obtain the list of blocks on which to vote table. All the federation nodes check the validity of all the blocks. Then the valid blocks are indicated in the vote table.

4.4 PERFORMANCE ANALYSIS

We have tested HBasechainDB 3.0 for scalability over homogeneous HBase cluster with two parameter such as Transaction latency and Transaction throughput.

Throughput: It indicates the number of transactions that are processed and recorded in the blockchain per second.Transactions that are generated from the smart contracts are stored in the smartLog table beforehand to find the peak throughput. The peak throughput is the result observed then.

Latency: It indicates the time taken from the submission of the transaction to HBasechainDB 3.0 until its get validated.

4.4.1 EXPERIMENTATION ON HOMOGENEOUS HBASE CLUSTER

4.4.1.1 Experimental Setup - I

Initially, We have tested HBasechainDB 3.0 after *disabling smart contract feature and making transaction as object format* using 8 nodes with the following configurations:

- Each node is configured with a quad core Intel i5 processor with capacity of 16 GB RAM and 1TB disk storage running Ubuntu 16.04 (64 bit) OS with LAN speed of 15 Mbps.
- We have installed Apache Hadoop (version 2.9.2) cluster using these nodes after which HBase (version 1.4.10) cluster is installed on it.
- HBase region-servers are running on 8 nodes and a HBase master is running on one of these nodes.
- HDFS has replication factor of 3 and HBase has 3 quorum zookeeper.

We have tested HBasechainDB 3.0 over 8 nodes for scalability on transaction data size ranging to few MBs. We have also tested BigchainDB on the same data (of same size) by setting up BigchainDB in the same hardware. The throughput of HBasechainDB 3.0 and BigchainDB is shown in **Figure 4.9**, and **Figure 4.10** shows the latency of BigchainDB and HBasechainDB 3.0. The throughput of HBasechainDB 3.0 has linear scalability as we add the nodes. It is much higher in HBasechainDB 3.0 compared to BigchainDB.

In HBasechainDB 3.0, we have used an approach similar to BigchainDB's approach. Despite using MongoDB as the underlying database, we have used the Hadoop database, Apache HBase. It is a distributed, scalable Big Data store. It supports random, real-time read/write access to Big Data. It is an open-source, distributed, versioned, non-relational, column-family oriented database modelled after

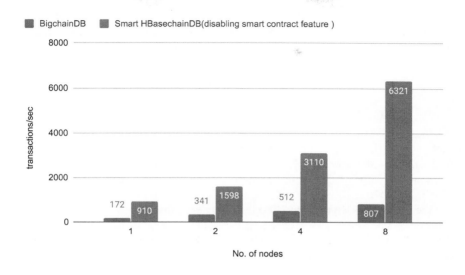

Figure 4.9   Performance of HBasechainDB 3.0 and BigchainDB

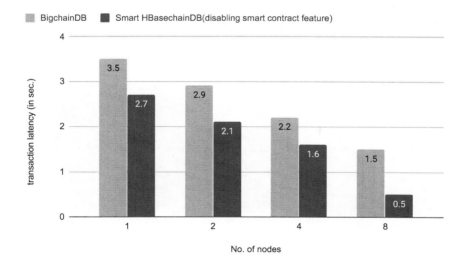

Figure 4.10   Latency of BigchainDB and HBasechainDB 3.0

Googles Bigtable. HBase features both linear and modular scaling, in addition to strongly consistent reads or writes. HBase tables are distributed on the cluster via regions. It supports automatic sharding by splitting and re-distributing regions automatically as data increases. HBasechainDB 3.0 is a decentralised, scalable, data store similar to BigchainDB.

4.4.1.2 Experimentation Setup - II

In HBasechainDB [10], transactions are first converted from object format to JSON format and then stored in HBase. While retrieving a transaction it has to be converted back object format from JSON format. This serialisation and deserialisation takes a huge amount of time. This can be improved by storing the data directly in object format in HBase.

We have tested HBasechainDB 3.0 by *disabling smart contract feature and with transaction in a object format* over 8 HBase nodes with the workload of 10000 transactions. Each node is configured with a quad core Intel i5 processor with capacity of 16 GB RAM and 1TB disk storage running Ubuntu 16.04 (64 bit) OS with LAN speed of 15 Mbps. We have installed Apache Hadoop (version 2.9.2) cluster using these nodes after which HBase cluster is installed on it. After making changes to HBasechainDB 3.0, We have also compared performance of HBasechainDB 3.0 with HBasechainDB [10]. **Figure 4.11** shows the performance of HBasechainDB and HBasechainDB 3.0 (after disabling smart contract feature).

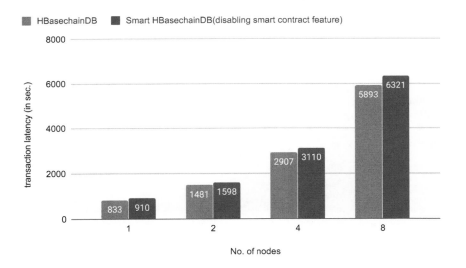

Figure 4.11 Performace of HBasechainDB and HBasechainDB 3.0 *(after disabling smart contract and with transaction in object format)*

4.4.1.3   Experimentation Setup - III

We have tested HBasechainDB 3.0 over 7 nodes for scalability with workload of 10000 transactions. The configuration of 7 nodes as follows:

- Each node is configured with a quad core Intel i5 processor with capacity of 16 GB RAM and 1TB disk storage running Ubuntu 16.04 (64 bit) OS with LAN speed of 15 Mbps.
- We have installed Apache Hadoop (version 2.9.2) cluster using these nodes after which HBase cluster is installed on it.
- HBase region-servers are running on 6 nodes and a HBase master is running on one of these nodes.
- HDFS has replication factor of 3 and HBase has 3 quorum zookeeper.

The throughput of HBasechainDB 3.0 on varying number of nodes is shown in **Figure 4.12**. HBasechainDB 3.0 scales as the computation of double spending and transaction's validity is handled at server side. So if we increase HBase nodes, the system scales but not linearly (keeping the federation nodes constant) In Hyperledger

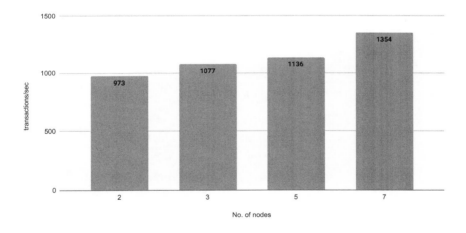

Figure 4.12   Scalabilty of HBasechainDB 3.0 upto 7 nodes

Fabric, the scalability means changes happen in throughput and latency as network size grows. We have also tested Ethereum and Hyperledger Fabric for scalability. The experiment is conducted with the workload of 10000 transactions over 7 nodes with a quad core Intel i5 processor with capacity of 16 GB RAM and 1TB disk storage running Ubuntu 16.04 (64 bit) OS with LAN speed of 15 Mbps. This setup is done by taking the help from the authors of research article "Performance Analysis of Hyperledger Fabric Platforms [8]." From the **Figure 4.13** it is evident that HBasechainDB 3.0 has better throughput than Ethereum and Hyperledger Fabric but it is not scaling linearly.

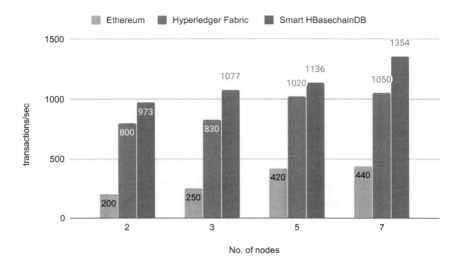

Figure 4.13 Performance of ethereum, Hyperledger Fabric *with forking problem* and HBasechainDB 3.0

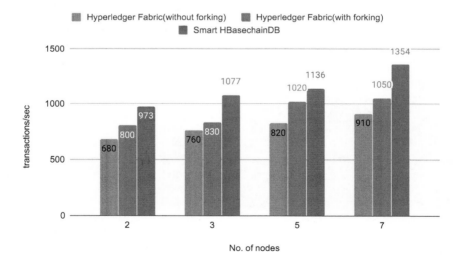

Figure 4.14 Performance of Hyperledger Fabric *without forking problem*, *with forking problem* and HBasechainDB 3.0

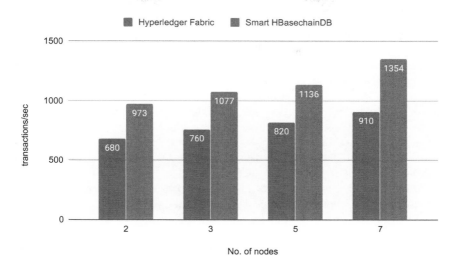

Figure 4.15 Performance of Hyperledger Fabric *without forking problem* and HBasechainDB 3.0

This throughput difference comes from many reasons include peer communication overhead, consensus overhead, mining issues, etc. No communication overhead in HBasechainDB 3.0 but it exists in Hyperledger Fabric. HBasechainDB 3.0 doesn't use any consensus model for transaction ordering as HBase takes care this issue but Hyperledger Fabric need consensus model for transaction ordering such as Kafka, Raft, etc. HBasechainDB 3.0 doesn't perform any mining process as it exists in Ethereum.

Under the same setup the Hyperledger Fabric, after incorporating fork resilience module, is tested for scalability. The performance of Hyperledger Fabric is compared with HBasechainDB 3.0. The *forking problem in Hyperledger Fabric is addressed by us*. So no forking problems crop up in Kafka ordering service. In HBasechainDB 3.0, the forking problem can't arise so the transaction throughput remains intact. After addressing forking issue in Fabric, we have compared its performance with HBasechainDB 3.0. From **Figure 4.15** it shows that HBasechainDB 3.0 has better throughput than Hyperledger Fabric.

By making Kafka orderer a fork resilient, the performance of Hyperledger Fabric get reduced as we are making extra checks. We can control Byzantine faults partially by the proposed model at the cost of performance. So HBasechainDB 3.0 performs better than Hyperledger Fabric in this scenario. Standard Hyperledger Fabric has forking problem which we are referring here as *Hyperledger Fabric with forking problem*. The **Figure 4.14** shows the performance of *Hyperledger Fabric (after addressing forking problem by us), Standard Hyperledger Fabric (with forking problem), and HBasechainDB 3.0.*

4.5   CONCLUSION

Our investigation has driven us to the conclusion that there is an expanding acknowledgement of private endeavour blockchains moving far from the first simply decentralised model. Further, alternative consensus protocols like proof-of-stake, PBFT and voting are by and large progressively used to get rid of the expenses of mining in the proof-of-work consensus utilised as a part of the Bitcoin blockchain. The presence of a native asset like Bitcoins or ether in Ethereum acts as barrier to entry and newer implementations like the Hyperledger Fabric or Multichain allow specification of a native asset by choice.

We have investigated different use cases for blockchain technologies and it is apparent that there is a requirement for blockchain-based Big Data solution. A key worry that emerges when investigating such Big Data solution is whether the blockchain frameworks today can deal with the volumes of information that are created. The Bitcoin blockchain fails miserably in such matters. The pinnacle throughput that the Bitcoin blockchain can bolster is only 7 transactions for each second with transactions latencies of around 10 minutes. Likewise, capacity of the whole blockchain on every one of the node puts overwhelming capacity prerequisites on the nodes and with increment in the quantity of members and a relating increment in the volume of transactions, nodes may soon come up short on space for putting away the blockchain.

BigchainDB endeavours to address the worries of blockchain versatility by confining the decentralisation to a federation of nodes.While numerous endeavours have been made to address these implementation worries over blockchains, BigchainDB has bulit a blockchain on scalable distributed database store. Besides decentralisation and unchangeability (got from blockchain), this gets the feature of underlying database's scalability. BigchainDB uses RethinkDB and MongoDB databases whereas we have built using HBase.

Smart contract is a facility which allows the blockchain application de- veloper to define his own transaction validation protocol. This brings a great flexibility to the blockchain users. We have re-architectured HBasechainDB [4] to support smart contract which has got a whole lot of flexibility to the users. This re architecture system is HBasechainDB 3.0. HBasechainDB 3.0 has been built by integrating blockchain with Hadoop ecosysem which has high throughput. It is used for analysing data present on blockchain. The throughput and scalability of HBasechainDB is superior to BigchainDB.

4.6   ACKNOWLEDGEMENTS

Our work is dedicated to Bhagawan Sri Sathya Sai Baba, Founder Chancellor of Sri Sathya Sai Institute of Higher Learning. We acknowledge Adarsh Saraf from Google, Bengaluru, India and Manuj Subhankar Sahoo from HCL technologies, Bengaluru who have contributed to the work on HBaschainDB while at SSSIHL. .We acknowledge Jason Yellick from IBM Research, North Carolina, USA, for his help and support.

Bibliography

1. Bill barhydt, 2018 the double-spend (what bitcoin's white paper solved forever). available at: https://www.coindesk.com/the-double-spend-what-bitcoins-white-paper-solved-forever (accessed: 23 august 2021).

2. Hyperledger documentation, available at: https://hyperledger-fabric.readthedocs.io/en/release-2.2/ (accessed: 2 september 2021).

3. Naveen H. Adarsh Saraf, Sanju Singh and Pallav Kumar Baruah. Hbasechaindb – blockchain infrastructure for the hadoop ecosystem over hbase.

4. Vitalik Buterin. A next generation smart contract & decentralized application platform. 2015.

5. Rishika Shree; Tanupriya Choudhury; Subhash Chand Gupta; Praveen Kumar. Kafka: The modern platform for data management and analysis in big data domain. 2017.

6. Satoshi Nakamoto. Bitcoin: A peer-to-peer electronic cash system. 2008.

7. Haiyong Wang College of Computer, Nanjing University of Posts Science, and China ; Kaixuan Guo Telecommunications, Nanjing. Byzantine fault tolerant algorithm based on vote. 2019.

8. Manar Abu Talib Qassim Nasir, Ilham Qasse and Ali Bou Nassif. Performance analysis of hyperledger fabric platforms.

9. Vijayalakshmi Bhupathiraju; Ravi Prasad Ravuri. The dawn of big data - hbase. 2014.

10. Manuj Subhankar Sahoo and Pallav Kumar Baruah. Hbasechaindb – a scalable blockchain framework on hadoop ecosystem. 2018.

11. Nick Szabo. The idea of smart contract. 1997.

12. Andreas Muller Dimitri De Jonghe Troy McConaghy Greg McMullen Ryan Henderson Sylvain Bellemare Trent McConaghy, Rodolphe Marques and Alberto Granzotto. Bigchaindb: A scalable blockchain database. 2016.

13. Zibin Zheng; Shaoan Xie; Hongning Dai; Xiangping Chen; Huaimin Wang. An overview of blockchain technology: Architecture, consensus, and future trends. 2017.

5 An Analysis of Blockchain Technology: A Security and Privacy Perspective

A distributed ledger technology that took over the world in recent days is Blockchain technology. It is simply a list that grows continuously holding the records of the transactions and data records securely in the form of blocks. It is also referred to as technology similar to linked lists where blocks are interlinked to each other [20]. A header block and the body block are the two main components of each block in the blockchain [41]. Usually, the header block holds the information about the management information of the block and the chain. The nodes of the blockchain communicate directly with each other through a peer-to-peer network. Every node consists of its digital signature [30] to validate the transactions.

Blockchain technology brings the features like transparency, decentralisation, anonymity, and audibility. These features have gained the interest of both researchers and industries. Nowadays blockchains are extensively used in the fields of finance, medicine, agriculture, transportation, and Internet of Things [25] [38]. But we need to consider the security and privacy-related challenges in order to effectively use this new technology.

Today most of the researches are going on the security and the privacy issues of the blockchain. The researches mainly focus on two concepts, analyzing the attacks which have been suffered by the blockchain recently and proposing some of the countermeasures against the type of attack. However, there are very little researches that provide an in-depth analysis of these issues

The focus of this chapter is on examining current trends in blockchain security and privacy problems. The chapter is laid out in a fairly orderly fashion. The first portion of the chapter covers the fundamentals of blockchain technology, including the various types of blockchains, blockchain architecture, and consensus methods. The most recent and likely cyberattacks and issues on blockchains are described in the next section. The solutions section lists some of the legitimate current countermeasures to the attacks presented. Finally, the article highlights the unresolved concerns that will need to be handled effectively in the future.

5.1 OVERVIEW OF BLOCKCHAIN TECHNOLOGY

Bitcoin was the first blockchain, introduced in 2008 by Satoshi Nakamoto, an unknown individual or group of persons. [29]. The blockchain used a number of cryptographic techniques, including the use of cryptography for encryption, digital

DOI: 10.1201/9781003355052-5

signatures, and a consensus algorithm that validates the network's integrity and security. [30].

The blockchain's structure may be thought of as a connected list of blocks. The hash pointer connects each block to the one before it. The pointer's hash value aids in the chain's integrity throughout the network.

5.1.1 ARCHITECTURE OF BLOCKCHAIN TECHNOLOGY

There can be several layers in the blockchain architecture, and the number of layers is not set. The number of layers is determined by the application for which the blockchain is employed, and it varies from one user to the other user depending on the application [14]. A basic blockchain contains the following six layers. Figure 5.1 [33] shows the architecture of basic blockchain.

5.1.1.1 Data Layer

This is the foundation layer of the blockchain's architecture. This layer serves as the blockchain's and physical storage's data structure. The data layer is made up of chunks. [38]. Miners generate blocks, and each block includes metadata that aids in the verification of its authenticity. Version, preceding block header hash, Merkle root hash, time, nBits, and nounce are among the block's metadata.

5.1.1.2 Network Layer

Blockchain extensively works on the principle of distributed network technology. Every participating node is required to download and interact with the blockchain's information. The network layer's goal is to determine whether or not the transactions created are legitimate. Data propagation, data verification, data authentication, data forwarding, and distributed networking are all part of this layer. [39].

5.1.1.3 Consensus Layer

In the blockchain, consensus strategies are employed to decide on the network. Blockchain cannot maintain uniformity among the network's participating nodes without a consensus protocol. Consensus is a method in which all of the network's nodes agree on a modification and maintain the ledger synced at all times. Some of the most frequently used consensus protocols are Proof of Work (PoW), Proof of Stake (PoS), practical Byzantine fault tolerance (PBFT), and delegated proof of stake (DPOS) [39].

5.1.1.4 Incentive Layer

The inclusion of this layer is solely dependent on the blockchain's established consensus processes. The layer is concerned with distributing the incentives received by the network's nodes for their efforts in reaching a consensus. This layer handles economic aspects including economic incentive issuance, allocation methods, and distribution mechanisms [39, 38].

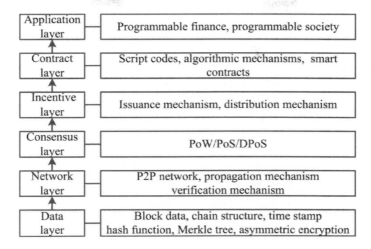

Figure 5.1 Layers of blockchain

5.1.1.5   Contract Layer

The contract layer enables the blockchain to be integrated with other technologies. It is made up of optional components and services that make integration possible. The smart contracts, algorithms, and other scripts are all included under this layer [39, 38].

5.1.1.6   Application Layer

The application layer is the top layer of the blockchain architecture. It contains the blockchain's concept and concepts. Scripts, APIs, user interfaces, and frameworks may be included to assist the end-user in interacting with the blockchain [39, 38].

5.1.2   TYPES OF BLOCKCHAIN

Blockchains are majorly divided into three types, which are public blockchain, consortium blockchain, private blockchain [20]. Figure 5.2 shows different types of blockchain.

5.1.2.1   Public Blockchain

The main aim of the public blockchain was to remove the middle man in any asset exchange scenario. Figure 5.3 shows the architecture of public blockchain. Most of the public blockchains employ Proof of Work (PoW) as the consensus mechanism and usually open source. Anyone may download the code and start running as a public node on this blockchain. The public node can validate the transactions, Hence it takes part in the consensus process. Anyone may view the data on the blockchain

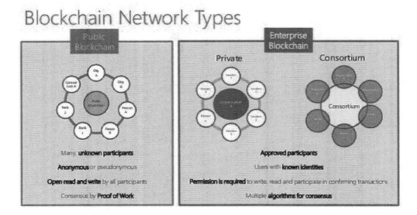

Figure 5.2 Types of blockchain [28]

in a public blockchain. i.e transactions will be transparent at the same time it will be anonymous [20, 30].

5.1.2.2 Private Blockchain

The private blockchain again brings the middle man inside the network. Figure 5.4 shows the architecture of private blockchain. The centralised entity will have the writing capability to the blockchain. Reading capability may be or may not be restricted to the users, it depends on the application it is used for. The private blockchains again put the risk of the data breach as considered in the centralised system. The private blockchains have their use cases where privacy rules and regulatory issues are considered. They have their security advantages as compared to the public blockchains. In this system, the transaction costs are reduced and legacy systems are replaced. This simplifies the data handling gets rid of semi-manual compliance mechanisms [20, 30].

5.1.2.3 Consortium Blockchain

In Consortium or Federated blockchain, unlike the private blockchain, the writing permission is given to the group of trusted entities. Figure 5.5 shows the architecture of federated blockchain. Federated blockchains are faster compared to public blockchains and provide privacy. These blockchains are majorly used in financial institutions. The consensus protocols in these blockchains are controlled by a set of pre-defined nodes. The permission to read the transactions can either be public or can be restricted to the participants [20, 30].

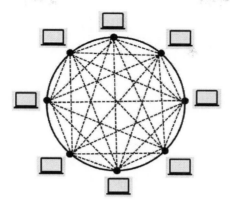

Figure 5.3 Architecture of public blockchain

5.2 CHARACTERISTICS OF THE BLOCKCHAIN

Blockchain technology has a number of distinguishing properties that set it apart from previous technologies. The following are some of the most important characteristics of blockchains.

5.2.1 MULTIPLE WRITERS

On the blockchain, all nodes in the network operate as contributors. Multiple parties can write to the blockchain at the same time using blockchain technology. The data will be kept on the blockchain and all transactions will be based on a consensus method. This guarantees a simple data backup whenever a database replica is required.

5.2.2 SHARED DATABASES

Multiple sources can contribute to a single blockchain, making it the universal record of transactions. Blockchain serves as a shared ledger that records all transactions and makes them available to all parties. Despite the fact that the data are shared among users, the blockchain's features prevent them from being tampered with or updated.

5.2.3 DISTRIBUTED TRUST

The blockchain serves as a centralised record of all transactions, and it serves as the source of truth for all transactions. In a centralised database, it may be impossible to track down the person who began the transaction, but with blockchain, each and

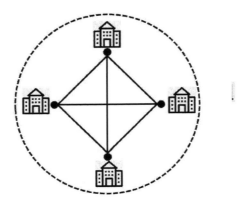

Figure 5.4   Architecture of private blockchain

every transaction is recorded and visible to all the participating nodes, hence making it accountable.

5.2.4   NO INTERMEDIARIES

The major issue in any trustless system is the usage of intermediates for data storage and update during transactions. In the case of blockchain, the goal is to eliminate intermediaries and allow each member to interact directly inside the network. As a result, blockchain attempts to eliminate intermediaries in the network.

5.2.5   TRANSACTION DEPENDENCY

A set of stated dependencies must be satisfied for a transaction to be executed in the blockchain. It is accomplished by the use of a mutually agreed-upon method known as the consensus protocol, which must be followed in order for the network transaction to be completed properly.

5.2.6   TIME STAMPING

Blockchain heavily relies on time-stamping to record the creation or alteration of every minor elements in the blockchain. Using the timestamping approach, this assures immutability in the database so that even the highest authorised persons in the network can also be held accountable.

5.2.7   TRANSACTION RULES

The transaction rules assure the transactions and roles of the network's members. The network's transaction rules must be properly followed. It grants privileges to higher

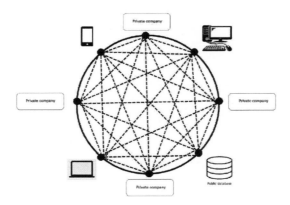

Figure 5.5 Architecture of hybrid blockchain

authority entities and curtails privileges as the hierarchy descends. It is critical to keep the network's role-based functions operational. Usually these rules are defined in the private or consortium blockchains.

5.3 CONSENSUS ALGORITHMS

Consensus is a protocol where each node mutually agrees on an agreement dynamically in a group-based protocol [9]. The main function of the consensus is to ensure the validity and authenticity of a blockchain transaction. Consensus can be defined as the acceptable resolution even if it not the favour of each individual in the network. Without the consensus protocol, the blockchain can fail wholly.

5.3.1 PROOF OF WORK (POW)

The Proof of Work (PoW) protocol was designed for the Bitcoin blockchain by Satoshi Nakamoto [29]. It overcomes the Byzantine Generals problem where a malicious entity in the network could secretly create a conflicting message between the users. The PoW has two properties: it is extremely difficult and time-consuming for the prover to generate the proof, yet it is extremely simple and quick to check the evidence for accuracy. The PoW consensus is an extension of the Hashcash [3] system with some modifications. Roughly to append a new block using the PoW consensus it takes around 10 minutes to mine a block.

5.3.2 PROOF OF STAKE (POS)

The Proof of Stake (PoS) was introduced in the Ethereum blockchain as an alternative type of distributed consensus [30, 41]. It introduced the penalty-based approach over bitcoin's incentive-based approach. Unlike the PoW where any participant on the network can involve in the mining process, Here participants are considered for mining only if they had locked up their deposit (Stake). The miners place bets on a specific block, if the block gets appended all the miners will be rewarded proportionally. There is no block creation prize in PoS, but the transaction cost is split among eligible validators.

5.3.3 PROOF OF AUTHORITY (POA)

The Proof of Authority (PoA) is a consensus algorithm that focuses on the fast transactions of blocks [22]. PoA employs the right to approve the transaction and new blocks only with the validators. In the network each node has to earn a reputation, When the reputation crosses the specified limit the node can become a validator. The validator is unable to approve the two successive blocks in this consensus, preventing centralised trust.

5.3.4 BYZANTINE FAULT TOLERANCE CONSENSUS ALGORITHM (BFT)

The failure tolerance capabilities of a system against the Byzantine Generals' Problem is characterised as Byzantine fault tolerance. When Byzantine failures occur, most traditional distributed computing systems feature central authority that coordinate and determine what to do next.

When it comes to blockchains, they're kept as a global ledger with replicates at each node, which makes it difficult to recover from byzantine failure. Miguel Castro and Barbara Liskov suggested Practical BFT (PBFT) [10] for high-performance Byzantine state machine replication. The AlgoRAND algorithm is capable of handling Byzantine fault tolerance. It is more efficient compared to its previous versions, and it's the first to have a new feature called player replaceability, which offers greater security in a distributed setting. [19]

5.3.5 PROOF OF ELAPSED TIME (POET)

Intel invented the Proof of Elapsed Time (PoET), [12] which achieves fairness among the nodes and consumes less computational power by leveraging Software Guard Extensions (SGX), an Intel trusted computing platform. Here each node has to wait for a certain random period after which the node will be granted to generate the new block.

5.3.6 COMPARISION OF CONSENSUS ALGORITHMS

We may separate consensus algorithms into two categories when using them in practice: strong consistency algorithms and eventual consistency algorithms.

Table 5.1

Types of Attacks on Blockchains

Attack	Cause
51% Attack	Consensus mechanism
Private key security attack	Encryption scheme in network
Double spending	Delayed Transaction verification
Transaction privacy leakage	Transaction design flaws
Selfish mining	Dishonest nodes
DAO attack	Program design flaw

Strong consistency algorithms are generally employed in private or hybrid blockchains when there is a potential of centralised authority or trustworthy users, and they primarily concern Byzantine flaws. Consistency algorithms like PoW and PoS are widely utilised in public blockchains, where there is no central authority and the number of nodes is typically high and difficult to ensure integrity and accuracy. As blockchain is still evolving the consensus algorithms are also developing eventually according to the applications.

5.4   TYPES OF ATTACKS ON BLOCKCHAINS

This section discusses the many sorts of cyberattacks that a blockchain can face, as well as potential attack vectors. This section focuses on the real-world assaults that occur often in blockchain networks. Table 5.1 provides the attack and respective underlying cause for particular attack.

5.4.1   LIVENESS ATTACK

Liveness attack tries to delay the acknowledgment transactions of the target. The three stages in liveness attack are preparation, transaction denial, blockchain delay [24]. The main aim of the attack is to delay the transaction confirmation time. The attacker tries to gain an advantage over the honest nodes in the initial stage. Attacker tries to postpone the legitimate block transaction in the latter phase. If this is unsuccessful, the attacker advances to the blockchain render phase, where they attempt to reduce the chain transaction rate.

5.4.2   DOUBLE SPENDING ATTACK

When a successful transaction is replicated using the same amount that has previously been spent, it is known as double spending. [23]. The attack occurs due to the potential flaw that the same token can be spent more than once to perform the transaction. The attacker makes the digital copy of the cryptocurrency or digital asset and tries to make a transaction while keeping the original with himself. Even if the blockchain consensus process confirms all transactions, it is impossible to avoid double-spending.

Double spending attacks include Race attack, where a merchant accepts the payment before the block confirmation, Finney attack, similar to race attack, 51% attack, Where attacker tries to control more than half of networks hash rate.

5.4.3　51% ATTACK

Blockchain is a distributed peer-to-peer network that relies on the consensus mechanism for maintaining mutual trust. The 51 percent attack is a flaw in the consensus system in which an attacker tries to take control of more than half of the nodes in order to compromise the whole network. By performing the 51% attack the attacker tries to manipulate and change the blockchain data. 51% attack can reverse the transaction which makes a window for double-spending, exclude or remove some of the transactions, disrupt the mining operation among the miners [40].

An attacker may simply reverse the transaction and begin a double-spending assault, exclude and specify transaction orders, hinder other miners' general mining activities, and impede the verification of regular transactions by executing the 51% attack.

5.4.4　PRIVATE KEY SECURITY ATTACK

The private key of a user is created once and can not be recovered if it is lost. This key allows the users in accessing their funds and verifying the transactions. The private key of a user is an attractive target for an attacker. Malicious entities perform different types of actions to steal the key from custodial service. Once a private key is stolen it is very difficult to recover the blockchain information and track any related criminal activity [8].

5.4.5　PRIVACY LEAKAGE

Transaction privacy in the blockchain protects the user from the traceability of their behaviour in the network. However still, confidential pieces of information like cryptographic keys and other sensitive information tends to leak which might encourage the attacker to commit real-world crimes [4]. There is a chance for wallet privacy leakage, where the crypto wallet operations leak some confidential information. There are several real-world cases where these leakages have been exploited.

5.4.6　SELFISH MINING ATTACK

In selfish mining a malicious miner node even if has found the new block, doesn't broadcast the block instead keeps it private and mines further blocks. whenever the private branch of this node is at least two blocks bigger than the public blockchain then this node will broadcast its private chain. The length of the broadcasted chain will be two blocks larger, hence it will become the new longest valid chain. This attack tries to waste the computational power of the honest miners [37].

5.4.7   ECLIPSE ATTACK

In the eclipse attack, the attacker's main intention is to isolate and attack a specific target, rather than the complete network. This attack is possible in the decentralised network because a node connects to a selected group of other nodes, which are again connected to several other nodes forming a distributed network. A malicious user tries to hijack the neighbor nodes on which the target node is dependent. Once successful the attacker can perform attacks like double spending, selfish mining, etc [21].

5.4.8   DAO ATTACK

The Decentralised Anonymous Organizations (DAO) is a code where a set of smart contracts are connected together and perform governance operation. The DAO framework was developed by slock.it and deployed on Ethereum in 2016. It was assaulted and the perpetrator took about US$60 million after being deployed for 20 days and raising around US$120 million. It was the most serious assault against the Ethereum consensus model to date. The attacker created a smart contract with a malicious callback function that allowed him to steal all of DAO's ethers. [15].

5.5   SECURITY ISSUES IN BLOCKCHAIN

This section describes the many sorts of blockchain issues that might be exploited by malicious users. This section brifely explains basic issues connected to blockchains that, if not addressed effectively, might develop into potential risks.

5.5.1   NETWORK SECURITY

A network attack is a situation where an attacker tries to control the pieces of network communication. The attacker tries to logically divide the network so that the delay can be increased. A simple example is an eclipse attack, where the attacker hides the information from the targeted nodes. Which may potentially delay the delivery of the block and can result in selfish mining and double-spending attacks [17].

5.5.2   MALLEABILITY

In the event of contractual transactions, the agreement will not cover all of the hashes transaction's components at the same time. As a result, the node has a window in which to modify its network transaction. Some of the researchers have defined malleability as when a transaction is intercepted, modified, and re-broadcasted, making the legal node believe that the original transaction is still not confirmed [16].

5.5.3 PRIVACY

Privacy is the biggest concern in blockchain technology because each node can access data from another node on the network and can view all the transactions. The issues in privacy raise due to the property of transparency in the blockchain. The data transmission in the network will be huge and these issues can be exploited by Man in the Middle attack (MitM) and Denial of Service attacks. The studies have found some solutions to overcome these issues, But they cannot be applied to all applications [2].

5.5.4 REDUNDANCY

The redundancy in the centralised system can be achieved parallelly, but in the case of blockchain, it has to traverse and process each node. The redundancy of the blockchain affects the performance severely. In the case of financial institutions, it is illogical to have redundant brokering. Banks will not perform transactions with every bank, So such duplications will only increase the costs with no added benefits [26].

5.5.5 VULNERABILITIES IN SMART CONTRACT

A smart contract is not an invulnerable piece of code, when the program gets executed in the blockchain smart contract can pose vulnerability due to flaws in its code. Studies have found that smart contracts can be vulnerable to bugs like timestamp dependence, mishandled exceptions, transaction ordering dependence, etc. The vulnerabilities in the smart contracts may lead to a breach in security, privacy, and a complete takeover of the system [13].

5.6 EXISTING SOLUTIONS TO SECURITY ATTACKS

This section goes through some of the strategies that may be used to defend against the security attacks described above. These approaches can aid in the effective management of network security concerns. Table 5.2 shows some of the available defending solutions for the attacks on blockchain.

5.6.1 LIVENESS ATTACK

Conflux's consensus protocol encapsulates Li et al's distinct block generating techniques [25]. The active liveness assault is combated by Conflux's consensus. The best plan aims for rapid confirmation, whereas the conservative method ensures consensus advancement. This protocol aids in high throughput and quick confirmation of network blockages. To achieve an integrated consensus, the protocol employs an adaptive weight mechanism to merge the two techniques.

Table 5.2
Blockchain Attacks and Solutions

Attack	Defending Solution
51% Attack	Merged mining, Chainlocks, Two-phase PoW
Private key security attack	Public key Infrastructure, Group key management
Double spending	Multi-stage secure pool, Distributed timestamping
Transaction privacy leakage	Ring signatutres, Homomorphic cryptosystem
Selfish Mining	Honest Mining, Self confirmation height

5.6.2   51% ATTACK

Sayeed and Macro-Gisbert's [36] research focused on combating the 51% attack. To study the 51% attack, they concentrated on low hashing power and attempted to expose a flaw in the consensus protocols. The authors provided the five security mechanisms against the 51% attack which are, A penalty system for delayed submission, delayed Proof of Work, Pirlgaurd, ChainLocks, and Merged Mining. The latest works against the 51% attack include defensive mining, where a permapoint system is used to control the chain re-organisation.

5.6.3   DOUBLE SPENDING ATTACKS

Nicholas and wang [31] proposed the Multi-stage secure pool (MSP) to overcome the double-spending attacks. The framework is divided into four stages: detection, confirmation, forwarding, and broadcasting. Begum et al. [5] provided a set of solutions to counter the limitations of the above framework.

5.6.4   PRIVATE KEY SECURITY ATTACK

The public key infrastructure [32] can be used in the blockchain technology to authenticate the entities, Which helps in countering a key security attack. The technique can be used to maintain integrity in the network. A group key management system is also presented, which allows a group of users to communicate in a secure manner while maintaining secrecy.

5.6.5   TRANSACTION PRIVACY LEAKAGE

The security loopholes while carrying out transactions were presented in the works of Bushan and Sharma [6]. They have suggested a more secure transaction scheme in their works. The proposed system includes the ring signature, homomorphic cryptosystem, and other security mechanisms to decrease the threats in the network and to increase the reliability of the transaction.

5.6.6 SELFISH MINING ATTACK

Some of the researchers have proposed solutions to the selfish mining attacks [34]. The proposed approaches include relying on honest mining, which can calculate the truth state for all blocks and assign a self-confirmation height to each transaction.

5.7 EXISTING TECHNIQUES TO SECURITY ISSUES

This section goes through some of the strategies that may be used to combat the security problems described above. These approaches can be used to improve the blockchain's security and privacy concerns.

5.7.1 MIXING

The blockchain will not guarantee the anonymity of the user, the pseudonymous addresses used in the network can be verified publicly. This makes anyone identify the address of the user with a simple analysis. When the address is leaked the real-world, identity and all transaction details can get breached. The mixing services prevent the user's addresses from being leaked. Mixcoin [7] provides the anonymous transactions in the blockchains, it allows the set of users to mix coins simultaneously. The accountability mechanism is used in the technique to identify the stealing of cryptocurrencies. It ensures that all users mix coins rationally without stealing any cryptocurrencies. Coinjoin [27] also uses the mixing protocol, where a user finds the other user who wants to make payment and they make the joint payment together. Hence in Coinjoin, it is difficult to find the exact direction of the money movement.

5.7.2 ATTRIBUTE BASED ENCYPTION

Attribute-based encryption (ABE) is a cryptographic method, in which attributes are the defining and regulating factors for the ciphertext encrypted using the secret key of a user. If the user's characteristics match those in the ciphertext, the encrypted data may be decrypted using the user's secret key.

Initially, the idea of attribute-based encryption was presented with a single authority [35]. Later, it was expanded to allow several authorities to create users' private keys at the same time [11]. Permissions on a blockchain might be represented by ownership of access tokens. All nodes in the network that have received a certain token will be provided access to the token's particular rights and privileges. The token allows the authoritative body that distributes the token to track who possesses certain attributes, and this tracking should be done in an algorithmic and consistent manner. Tokens should be utilised similar to badges that reflect attributes.

5.7.3 ANONYMOUS SIGNATURES

A digital signature that aims at providing anonymity to the user can be called an anonymous signature. Group signature and Ring signature are the two important signatures used for maintaining anonymity.

In group key signature [18], The member of the group can sign for the entire group without revealing its identity, on the other end anyone can verify the validity by verifying using its public key. The group key signature mechanism verifies the membership of the user to a particular group and not the true identity of the user. There will be a group manager who manages the members of the group. In ring-key signature there will be no group manager and the identity of the user will not be revealed even in the time of dispute between the group. Ring-signature can be effective in public blockchains.

5.7.4   NON-INTERACTIVE ZERO KNOWLEDGE PROOFS

Non-Interactive Zero-Knowledge Proofs (NIZK) [1] are powerful cryptography techniques that preserve privacy. A certifier can show to the verifier that the claim is true using zero-knowledge proof without disclosing any sensitive information to the verifier. The NIZK is a non-interactive technique in which the verifier and certifier never communicate. A common string will be shared by both the certifier and the verifier. The zk-SNARK (zero-knowledge Succinct Non-interactive ARgument) is another version that was introduced and utilised in the Zcash protocol.

5.8   OPEN ISSUES

As seen in the above sections the research in the field of security and privacy is moving at a faster pace and many solutions are being proposed. Considering the present developments some open research challenges arise in the infrastructure, zero-day attacks, key exchange mechanisms, combined attacks, resource utilisation, and performance trade-offs, etc these challenges must be addressed efficiently to resolve the issues related to security and privacy. Despite offering a robust decentralised network, blockchains are still vulnerable which put forth a big challenge for the researchers.

Although blockchain technologies may be utilised with high confidence, security safeguards must be established at every point in the network. To make the information more secure, the blockchain user's private key address must be carefully coded. Before implementing a blockchain network, network designers must be aware of potential network threats. The system must have attack detection software.

5.8.1   PROPER FRAMEWORK AGAINST THE COMBINED ATTACKS

Many security solutions and application for blockchain have been studied and suggested, each of which is meant to address specific security concerns and threats. The major question entails creating a framework that can withstand many combined attacks while also taking into account the implementation practicality of the suggested solutions.

5.8.2 ZERO-DAY ATTACK POLICIES

A zero-day attack is a software module method that happens when there are no countermeasures in place to prevent a vulnerability from being exploited. It's difficult to see the danger of such assaults, because they can compromise any device.Software must be constantly tested for vulnerabilities, and security updates must be issued as quickly as feasible by software distributors.

5.8.3 EXCHANGE OF SECURITY KEYS

It plays a vital role in securing end-to-end communications in a cryptographic system. It is a network pillar for attack prevention. It should be ensured that a key is safely shared throughout the network.

5.8.4 INFRASTRUCTURE

Storing data on the blockchain database entails storing non-deletable information on the network's nodes. This means that maintaining these nodes in a decentralised network will be extremely expensive.

As the blockchain increases in size, it becomes more expensive to maintain. In addition, the blockchain infrastructure includes address management and fundamental communication protocols. The blockchain infrastructure must, in particular, guarantee the dependability of devices with substantial computational capacity.

5.8.5 UTILISATION OF AVAILABLE RESOURCES

The use of memory and power can conserve the operation for a longer period of time. In a blockchain transaction system, the unique network design may effectively use resources for each purpose. Other technologies, such as fog computing, edge computing and other distributed approaches, can help with resource utilisation and security.

5.8.6 TRADE-OFF'S IN PERFORMANCE

The performance of the system, as well as how well it performs jobs, is critical. In addition to security, the system's calculation speed must be maintained. During parallel operation, one should not ignore the system's performance. There must be proportional trade-off between all the operations.

5.8.7 INSIDER THREAT MANAGEMENT

It protects employees by preventing threats, countering them, identifying and monitoring them. To identify and prevent false alarms in components of the blockchain system, non-compromised models are necessary.

5.9 CONCLUSION

Blockchain has created a revolution in the field of Information technology. It aims to bring the governments and companies together. It gathered an enormous interest of researchers and industrialists due to its nature of decentralised characteristics. The chapter started with the basic architecture of the blockchain and broadly categorised the different sorts of attacks on the blockchains concerning recent trends. The chapter also focused on the recent advancements in countering the issues of the blockchain concerning security and privacy. With blockchain as the trending concept today we can expect more innovative solutions as the research in this field is continually evolving day by day. Still, there are a lot of open research questions which need to be addressed for the efficient and secure implementation of blockchain technology.

Bibliography

1. Shahla Atapoor. On privacy preserving blockchains and zk-snarks. 2020.

2. Adam Back, Matt Corallo, Luke Dashjr, Mark Friedenbach, Gregory Maxwell, Andrew Miller, Andrew Poelstra, Jorge Timón, and Pieter Wuille. Enabling blockchain innovations with pegged sidechains. *URL: http://www. opensciencereview. com/papers/123/enablingblockchain-innovations-with-pegged-sidechains*, 72, 2014.

3. Adam Back et al. Hashcash-a denial of service counter-measure. 2002.

4. Jaume Barcelo. User privacy in the public bitcoin blockchain. *URL: http://www. dtic. upf. edu/jbarcelo/papers/20140704 User Privacy in the Public Bitcoin Blockc hain/paper. pdf (Accessed 09/05/2016)*, 2014.

5. A Begum, AH Tareq, M Sultana, MK Sohel, T Rahman, and AH Sarwar. Blockchain attacks, analysis and a model to solve double spending attack. *International Journal of Machine Learning and Computing*, 10(2):352–357, 2020.

6. Bharat Bhushan and Nikhil Sharma. Transaction privacy preservations for blockchain technology. In *International Conference on Innovative Computing and Communications*, pages 377–393. Springer, 2021.

7. Joseph Bonneau, Arvind Narayanan, Andrew Miller, Jeremy Clark, Joshua A Kroll, and Edward W Felten. Mixcoin: Anonymity for bitcoin with accountable mixes. In *International Conference on Financial Cryptography and Data Security*, pages 486–504. Springer, 2014.

8. A Bryk. Blockchain attack vectors: vulnerabilities of the most secure technology. *Accessed: Sep*, 14:2019, 2018.

9. Christian Cachin et al. Architecture of the hyperledger blockchain fabric. In *Workshop on distributed cryptocurrencies and consensus ledgers*, volume 310. Chicago, IL, 2016.

10. Miguel Castro, Barbara Liskov, et al. Practical byzantine fault tolerance. In *OSDI*, volume 99, pages 173–186, 1999.

11. Melissa Chase. Multi-authority attribute based encryption. In *Theory of cryptography conference*, pages 515–534. Springer, 2007.

12. Lin Chen, Lei Xu, Nolan Shah, Zhimin Gao, Yang Lu, and Weidong Shi. On security analysis of proof-of-elapsed-time (poet). In *International Symposium on Stabilization, Safety, and Security of Distributed Systems*, pages 282–297. Springer, 2017.

13. Nicolas Christin. Traveling the silk road: A measurement analysis of a large anonymous online marketplace. In *Proceedings of the 22nd international conference on World Wide Web*, pages 213–224, 2013.

14. Gaoying Cui, Kun Shi, Yuchen Qin, Lin Liu, Bing Qi, and Bin Li. Application of block chain in multi-level demand response reliable mechanism. In *2017 3rd International Conference on Information Management (ICIM)*, pages 337–341. IEEE, 2017.

15. Phil Daian. Analysis of the dao exploit. *Hacking, Distributed*, 6, 2016.

16. Christian Decker and Roger Wattenhofer. Bitcoin transaction malleability and mtgox. In *European Symposium on Research in Computer Security*, pages 313–326. Springer, 2014.

17. Casimer DeCusatis, Marcus Zimmermann, and Anthony Sager. Identity-based network security for commercial blockchain services. In *2018 IEEE 8th Annual Computing and Communication Workshop and Conference (CCWC)*, pages 474–477. IEEE, 2018.

18. Rafaël Del Pino, Vadim Lyubashevsky, and Gregor Seiler. Lattice-based group signatures and zero-knowledge proofs of automorphism stability. In *Proceedings of the 2018 ACM SIGSAC Conference on Computer and Communications Security*, pages 574–591, 2018.

19. Yossi Gilad, Rotem Hemo, Silvio Micali, Georgios Vlachos, and Nickolai Zeldovich. Algorand: Scaling byzantine agreements for cryptocurrencies. In *Proceedings of the 26th symposium on operating systems principles*, pages 51–68, 2017.

20. Manav Gupta. Blockchain for dummies. 3rd ibm limited edition, 2020.

21. Ethan Heilman, Alison Kendler, Aviv Zohar, and Sharon Goldberg. Eclipse attacks on bitcoin's peer-to-peer network. In *24th {USENIX} Security Symposium ({USENIX} Security 15)*, pages 129–144, 2015.

22. Leila Ismail and Huned Materwala. A review of blockchain architecture and consensus protocols: Use cases, challenges, and solutions. *Symmetry*, 11(10):1198, 2019.

23. Ghassan Karame, Elli Androulaki, and Srdjan Capkun. Two bitcoins at the price of one? double-spending attacks on fast payments in bitcoin. *IACR Cryptol. ePrint Arch.*, 2012(248), 2012.

24. Aggelos Kiayias and Giorgos Panagiotakos. On trees, chains and fast transactions in the blockchain. In *International Conference on Cryptology and Information Security in Latin America*, pages 327–351. Springer, 2017.

25. Xiaoqi Li, Peng Jiang, Ting Chen, Xiapu Luo, and Qiaoyan Wen. A survey on the security of blockchain systems. *Future Generation Computer Systems*, 107:841–853, 2020.

26. Christopher Mann and Daniel Loebenberger. Two-factor authentication for the bitcoin protocol. *International Journal of Information Security*, 16(2):213–226, 2017.

27. Felix Konstantin Maurer, Till Neudecker, and Martin Florian. Anonymous coinjoin transactions with arbitrary values. In *2017 IEEE Trustcom/BigDataSE/ICESS*, pages 522–529. IEEE, 2017.

28. medium.com. types of blockchain, 2018. [Online; accessed October 22, 2021].

29. Satoshi Nakamoto and A Bitcoin. A peer-to-peer electronic cash system. *Bitcoin.–URL: https://bitcoin. org/bitcoin. pdf*, 4, 2008.

30. Arvind Narayanan, Joseph Bonneau, Edward Felten, Andrew Miller, and Steven Goldfeder. *Bitcoin and cryptocurrency technologies: a comprehensive introduction*. Princeton University Press, 2016.

31. Kervins Nicolas and Yi Wang. A novel double spending attack countermeasure in blockchain. In *2019 IEEE 10th Annual Ubiquitous Computing, Electronics & Mobile Communication Conference (UEMCON)*, pages 0383–0388. IEEE, 2019.

32. Om Pal, Bashir Alam, Vinay Thakur, and Surendra Singh. Key management for blockchain technology. *ICT Express*, 2019.

33. researchgate. Architecture of blockchain, 2018hain. [Online; accessed October 22, 2021].

34. Muhammad Saad, Laurent Njilla, Charles Kamhoua, and Aziz Mohaisen. Countering selfish mining in blockchains. In *2019 International Conference on Computing, Networking and Communications (ICNC)*, pages 360–364. IEEE, 2019.

35. Amit Sahai and Brent Waters. Fuzzy identity-based encryption. In *Annual international conference on the theory and applications of cryptographic techniques*, pages 457–473. Springer, 2005.

36. Sarwar Sayeed and Hector Marco-Gisbert. Assessing blockchain consensus and security mechanisms against the 51% attack. *Applied Sciences*, 9(9):1788, 2019.

37. Yuzhe Tang, Qiwu Zou, Ju Chen, Kai Li, Charles A Kamhoua, Kevin Kwiat, and Laurent Njilla. Chainfs: Blockchain-secured cloud storage. In *2018 IEEE 11th international conference on cloud computing (CLOUD)*, pages 987–990. IEEE, 2018.

38. Junfeng Xie, Helen Tang, Tao Huang, F Richard Yu, Renchao Xie, Jiang Liu, and Yunjie Liu. A survey of blockchain technology applied to smart cities: Research issues and challenges. *IEEE Communications Surveys & Tutorials*, 21(3):2794–2830, 2019.

39. Yong Yuan and Fei-Yue Wang. Blockchain and cryptocurrencies: Model, techniques, and applications. *IEEE Transactions on Systems, Man, and Cybernetics: Systems*, 48(9):1421–1428, 2018.

40. J Leon Zhao, Shaokun Fan, and Jiaqi Yan. Overview of business innovations and research opportunities in blockchain and introduction to the special issue, 2016.

41. Zibin Zheng, Shaoan Xie, Hong-Ning Dai, Xiangping Chen, and Huaimin Wang. Blockchain challenges and opportunities: A survey. *International Journal of Web and Grid Services*, 14(4):352–375, 2018.

6 Blockchain Technology and Its Potential Applications

Blockchain, concept and its technique, has recently received widespread attention. Blockchain serves as a decentralised, immutable ledger for all transactions [73]. It acts as an enabling technology to form a peer-to-peer (P2P) network-based system. Blockchain technology may be seen as an alternate logging system for recording state changes, similar to a database log. Blockchain technology forms the basis of a decentralised peer-to-peer mechanism to handle database transactions in a distributed system of participants [57].

6.0.1 BLOCKCHAIN'S CORE CHARACTERISTICS

In brief, blockchain technology possesses the following key characteristics:

i. **Decentralisation:** Traditional centralised transaction systems need each transaction to be validated by a trusted third party (such as the central bank), which results in high transaction costs as well as performance bottlenecks at the central servers. While the centralised paradigm necessitates the use of a third party, blockchain does not. Data consistency across distributed networks is ensured by consensus techniques employed in blockchain [73].

ii. **Persistency:** Honest miners will not submit faulty transactions because they can be validated quickly. It's nearly hard to erase or turn back a transaction after it's been added to the blockchain. There is a quick way to find blocks that include invalid transactions [73].

iii. **Anonymity:** Users can communicate with the blockchain anonymously by utilising a randomly generated address. Due to blockchain's inherent constraints, it cannot ensure absolute privacy protection [73].

iv. **Auditability:** Users' balances are stored in the blockchain's Unspent Transaction Output model (UTXO): A reference to previously unspent funds is a requirement for any transaction to take place. The state of the referred unspent transactions switches to spent once the current transaction is uploaded to the blockchain. As a result, it's simple to verify and track transactions [73].

6.0.2 ARCHITECTURE OF BLOCKCHAIN

Unlike a public ledger, a blockchain is a peer-to-peer network that stores a complete record of transactions. Figure 6.1 presents an illustration of the blockchain. If the hash of a previous block appears in the block header, then the block has only one parent block. Significantly, the hashes of uncle blocks (the children of the parent block) will be preserved on the blockchain. The first and only block that does not have a parent is called genesis block. [73].

 i. Rules for validating blocks are specified by the block version argument.
 ii. Merkle tree root hash: the hash value of all transactions in the block.
 iii. Timestamp: current time as seconds in the universal time since January 1, 1970.
 iv. nBits: the maximum length of a valid block hash.
 v. Nonce: a 4-byte field that typically begins with 0 and increases with each hash calculation
 vi. A 256-bit hash value that points to the previous block is referred to as the parent block hash [73].

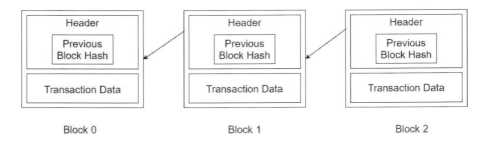

Figure 6.1   Blockchain example: sequence of Blocks

An example of a block's structure can be seen in Figure 6.2. Specifically, the block header provides the following information:

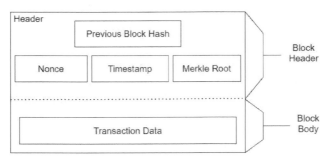

Figure 6.2   Block structure

The block contains transactions and a transaction counter. Only a finite number of transactions may be stored in a block that is large enough. Asymmetric cryptography is used by Blockchain to verify transaction authentication. Asymmetric cryptography-based digital signatures are employed in untrustworthy environments [73].

6.1   GLOBALISATION AS A TREND AND CHALLENGE TO ADOPT THE TREND

In the last few decades, digitalization has made it easier for countries to communicate with each other and share information. Products, services, capital, people, data and ideas are all moving across borders in a global economy. There has been an increase in global innovation due to the global spread of information and technology, which has resulted in countries creating more favourable investment conditions [48].

Globalisation is viewed in perspectives such as political, economic and cultural. The World Trade organisation (WTO) aims to negotiate between countries. Similarly, World Bank and International Monetary Fund (IMF) make efforts to end poverty and share prosperity. These banks provide support to developing nations in eradicating poverty [42].

In the following lines, the drawbacks of globalisation are mentioned. globalisation expands markets and increases profits with wider access to resources, it creates competition at the same time and decreases demand for local products [42]. However, globalisation also poses its own drawbacks like unequal economic growth, fall of local businesses, possibilities of increase in global recession, cheaper labour markets or human resources being exploited and job displacements. Besides these globalisation also possibly develops terrorism, currency fluctuation and price instability [21]. People are hesitant to accept globalisation because it has the ability to curb free movements across borders, control over extraction of natural resources and restrain the use of human resources [69].

Also, globalisation poses risks such as global excess liquidity, growth of debt, increase in geopolitical conflicts and surge in social instabilities. Such risks make aspirants apprehensive in adopting globalisation [56].

Thus, globalisation and integration of business and economic activity promotes inter-organisation activities and higher levels of monetary and information exchanges. This is in contrast to the previous ways of individual organisation managed activities.

6.1.1   THE GROWING PROMINENCE OF DECENTRALISED LEDGER

In the past few decades, data has replaced oil as the most valuable resource. With the advent of technology in the form of smart phones and the internet, almost everyone with digital access could predict trends in many avenues including purchases and health to name a few. The need to decentralize knowledge and the prospects of blockchain to provide the same, is widely recognised across the globe [56].

Blockchain has shattered obstacles to transfer money and minimised dependence on financial institutions for this purpose. Advent of bitcoin, blockchains and irreversible records of transactions are widely appreciated by aspirants in numerous fields. New digital platforms and services have enabled distribution of transaction and ledger systems as a result of which blockchain developers and applications are moving towards advanced methods of interacting with the internet [56]. Touted as a significant innovation, decentralised ledgers have made transaction immutable, consistent and effectual linear storage of events, thus giving rise to transactions based on smart contracts. The abolishment of middleman and manipulation is the notable highlight here [56].

6.1.2   DECENTRALISED LEDGERS AND BLOCKCHAIN ARE NOT THE SAME

Though blockchain and decentralised ledger look similar, they are not the same. Unlike blockchain, the decentralised ledger does not require data structure in blocks. The information is just spread across sites and individuals. Though all blockchains are decentralised ledgers, it is not vice versa. The transparency of decentralised ledgers, mitigation of time to complete transactions, control over operational inefficiencies, security and tamper proof logs are a few of the attributes that hail the technology [66].

Blockchain is based on distributed ledger technology, in which every node has a copy of every transaction. decentralised ledger lacks a sequence, whereas blockchain does. While blockchain employs Proof-of-Work mechanism to access control, decentralised ledger does not require such consensus and is more scalable than the former. While blockchain technology is already adopted by governments and institutions, decentralised ledgers are still in developing stages. While blockchain has cryptocurrencies and other tokens, decentralised ledger do not require such elements. Clear knowledge about the distinction between the two enables better revolutions in this concern [4].

6.2   BLOCKCHAIN CONSENSUS ALGORITHM

Consensus is a fault-tolerant process used in blockchains to bring distributed nodes together to agree on a single network state. These mechanisms ensure that all nodes are in sync with one another and agree on genuine transactions that are added to the blockchain. They are responsible for ensuring the transactions' validity and authenticity. They keep the network in sync and agree on which transactions are genuine and should be added to the blockchain. These methods are utilised by the blockchain network. With each new person that joins the blockchain and uploads data, all nodes in the network verify and confirm transactions using the consensus method continuously. If there is no agreement, anyone can launch a DoS attack, a distributed denial-of-service attack, or even a sybil attack [1].

The most prevalent consensus techniques include Proof-of-Work (PoW), Proof-of-Stake (PoS), Delegated Proof-of-Stake (DPoS), Practical Byzantine Fault Tolerance (PBFT), Proof-of Capacity (PoC), Proof-of-Activity (PoA), Proof-of-Publication (PoP), Proof-of-Retrievability (PoR), Proof-of-Importance (PoI), Proof-of-Burn (PoB), Proof-of-Elapsed time (PoET) and Proof-of-Ownership (PoO). All of these mechanisms will be explained in depth as follows:

Proof-of-Work (PoW) Bitcoin and Litecoin are two of the most popular cryptocurrencies that use PoW as its consensus mechanism. Miners are the nodes that engage in the PoW process, which is called mining. Mathematical problems that take a long time to solve require powerful computers and processing capacity. The first miner who successfully completes the challenge and builds a block receives a bitcoin reward [1]. Proof-of-work consensus is intended for public blockchains with a constantly fluctuating number of participating nodes. On the plus side, an adversary would have to spend a lot of money to get enough processing power to dominate mining on a large network. On the other hand, the amount of energy used in mining is enormous [61].

Proof-of-Stake (PoS) When it comes to adding blocks in PoS, nodes having a large stake in the blockchain's currency are prioritised. This rule cannot be followed in its entirety since it would provide control of the chain to a single most excellent stakeholder. As a result, the probability of a node's mining success increases in proportion to its stake. Blocks can be mined at a different rate by changing the stake requirements and difficulty of mining. There are a plethora of proof-of-stake protocols to choose from. It's possible that they may list both the total stake and the length of time the stake was held. This stake or a portion of it may be requested to be kept dormant for an extended period in the future. A proof-of-stake mechanism is difficult to fine-tune. If an adversary is able to add blocks to forks other than the longest one at a cost that is too minimal, one should be on the alert [61].

Delegated Proof-of-Stake (DPoS) Consensus can be reached quickly using DPoS, a consensus technique included in the EOS (blockchain-based platform). First, we define the term "delegate." Those who can generate network blocks are referred to as a node person or a group. It receives rewards when it builds a block with the most votes from all network nodes. During inflation, either transaction fees or the creation of a specific quantity of coins compensates delegates. The DPoS consensus mechanism is the second step in the process. Nodes on the network can vote for delegates by putting their coins on the stake. The stakes determine the significance of a vote [1].

Practical Byzantine fault tolerance Byzantine fault tolerance (BFT) refers to the ability of a distributed computer system to accept component failures. The NEO platform employs this kind of consensus. BFT can be used to demonstrate the difficulties faced by distributed computing systems. PBFT was created as a solution to the problems associated with administering a distributed computing system in BFT. In this consensus method, the blocks are picked by an election mechanism after a validation process based on the BFT principle for verifying [1].

Proof-of-Capacity (PoC) Plotting consensus is the goal of the PoC procedure. Unlike PoW, where miners utilise computational power to select a solution, PoC uses memory-hard drives to store solutions. The miners use their workstations to create a map of the stored data and it is known as Plotting. When the storage data is plotted and miners participate in it, block production begins. Mining capacity is enhanced by the number of solutions a miner can store. A new block will be constructed if miners have a large enough storage capacity, thus making this procedure more efficient [1].

Proof-of-Elapsed Time (PoET) Miners are chosen at random and equitably via PoET's consensus method. It also chooses a miner to be the one to start a new block. To use this consensus method, the miners must have waited for a block to be created for a certain period of time before proceeding. Each network node is given a random and equal wait time as a result of the operation. The right to produce a new block is awarded to the node in the network with the shortest wait time. This strategy works well for verification when there are no multiple nodes in the system and the wait time is assigned at random [1].

Proof-of-Activity (PoA) In comparison to PoW, the PoA consensus technique requires a lot more work, but it's simpler to use. It also takes longer to find a solution because the time it takes can vary greatly. It's a method that incorporates both PoW and PoS elements. Before the conversion to PoS, miners were able to solve cryptographic challenges in the same manner as they had before the switch. Blocks rather than transactions hold template information like headers and the address of the reward for mining.It's important to limit the time it takes to manufacture each block to a minimum so that the chain can continue to grow. To counteract network flooding, spam transactions aren't permitted [1].

Proof-of-Publication (PoP) In order to identify whether or not a specific piece of information was published in Bitcoin at a specific time and date, the PoP is used. As part of the Bitcoin consensus process, a secure hash of some plain text is encoded in the blockchain [1].

Proof-of-Retrievability (PoR) A server confirms that a client has downloaded and received a target file from the server using the PoR consensus mechanism. Efficiency is the key advantage of PoR over other consensus methods. In contexts where files are replicated across numerous systems, it is most commonly employed [1].

Proof-of-Importance (PoI) During the New Economy Movement (NEM), the PoI consensus approach was developed to authenticate blockchain transactions by checking the entity responsible [1][].

Proof-of-Ownership (PoO) PoO is used to find out who owns a specific piece of data at a given point in time. Corporate organisations, for example, might use this consensus approach to certify the integrity, publication date, and ownership of their inventions or contracts.. CodeChain has incorporated it [1].

Proof-of-Burn (PoB) A PoS and PoW alternative consensus protocol. PoB miners must show that they have created a new cryptocurrency by burning an existing one, or they will be sent to an address where they can't be used. The unrecoverable burning of tokens is critical to PoB's usefulness. It's easy to prove but difficult to undo in comparison to PoW and PoS [1].

6.3 TYPES OF BLOCKCHAIN

Blockchains which controls participants' transactions and maintains their identity are known as permissioned blockchains and accommodates only known nodes. A blockchain operated by a bank is a good example for permissioned blockchain. Permissioned blockchains in industries and businesses may be role limited. For instance, a manufacturer takes care of supply chain management which involves logistics partners, banks and vendors in its fold, who in turn have role limited implementations [26].

Permissioned blockchains are dictated by the owner of the network who decides on membership eligibility. They do not have consensus based protocols and are predefined in their decisions. The permissioned blockchains are partially decen-tralised or completely centralised and are rarely transparent [23].

Bitcoins on the other hand allow anyone to participate as a miner. Anyone can take read only roles or make changes by adding new blocks and this is done on Blockchains known as **Permissionless or Public blockchains**. Permissionless blockchains are equipped with elements including anonymity, transparency, decentralization and tokens [26]. Permissionless blockchains have been used to implement global peer-to-peer cryptocurrency networks [57]

While anyone can add nodes in Permissionless blockchains, such permission is restricted to pre-authorised members in permissioned blockchains. Though Permissionless blockchains are more secure, they are also slower and allow a limited number of transactions in a given time. Permissioned blockchains are more efficient. Permissioned blockchains are not as secure as permissionless ones and are prone to manipulation [26].

6.4 BLOCKCHAIN TRANSACTIONAL FLOW

The very first block in a blockchain is known as the genesis block, and it serves as the foundation for all subsequent blocks and it's a standard part of every blockchain implementation. A series of events links every new block to the one before it. Expanding a blockchain occurs when new blocks are added to an existing chain [32].

A blockchain transaction is the same as any other distributed or OLTP data transaction (TPP Council 2010). Traditionally, blockchain applications (such as Bitcoin) represent monetary transactions between two parties (or users). In order to maximize efficiency, each valid transaction is recorded in a block. Strong cryptographic characteristics like hashing provide immutability [32].

Figure 6.3 depicts the three primary processes that each blockchain application must go through in order to create a new block. The client sends a transactional request to one of the participants. The client request is broadcast to all other nodes by this participating node. To put it another way, we call this process "Transaction Dissemination." Nodes begin a consensus mechanism once they have received a copy of all client requests. When it comes to time complexity and resource usage, the underlying consensus method counts. As soon as an agreement is reached on the next block, it is sent to all nodes. Transmitting in this manner is equivalent to creating an additional record (block) in the global distributed ledger [32].

6.5 BLOCKCHAIN SCALABILITY

The ability of the blockchain to accommodate more transactions and more nodes, also known as scalability is inevitable for a successful run of blockchains. The consensus, network latency, node infrastructure, smart contracts, transaction payload size, transaction pooling or queuing are a few of the entities that decide the blockchain's scalability. Scalability however remains an unsolved problem and is a hindrance for not only blockchain adoption but also for applications [71].

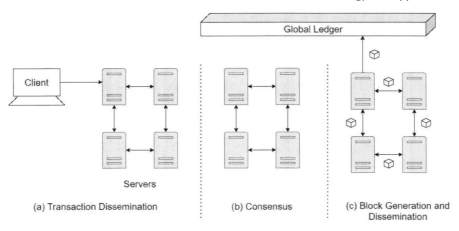

Figure 6.3   Blockchain transactional flow

Quoting Deloitte Insights, "Blockchain based systems are comparatively slow. Blockchain's sluggish transaction speed is a major concern for enterprises that depend on high-performance legacy transaction processing systems [41]."

Customers using Bitcoin and Ethereum were subjected to long wait times and exorbitant fees in 2017 and 2018. While dealing with scalability, an increase in block size and mitigating hash complexity does not suffice. Reportedly, while Visa makes 1,736 transactions per second, bitcoin takes 4.6 transactions per second [41].

Transactions on e-commerce platforms that leverage Blockchain technology must deal with a high volume of transactions. These systems must be scalable. When it comes to finding a solution to this issue, the Bitcoin's Lightning Network may be the best option. These are a set of rules established on top of the Bitcoin blockchain for micropayments. In other words, the Bitcoin Lightning Network is a layer two solution to the problem of Bitcoin. In 2015, Thaddeus Dryja and Joseph Poon introduced the idea. These two young developers greatly improved Satoshi's original plan by proposing a decentralised network of lightning fast transactions [33].

Through a series of routed transactions, Bitcoin Lightning Network can connect many users. It eliminates the majority of Bitcoin's drawbacks while retaining the currency's primary feature, decentralization. As is the case with Bitcoin, the Bitcoin Lightning Network is a permissionless network in which any node can join or leave at any time. Additionally, nodes can establish payment channels with one another and terminate them at any time. Figure 6.4 depicts the Bitcoin Lightning Network [33].

Payment channels are the fundamental concept underlying Bitcoin Lightning Network. When two users want to transact on the Blockchain, they create a "off-chain" payment channel. From that point forward, the payment channel is open for business, and any number of transactions can occur directly between them — without ever touching the main blockchain. As a result, funds can be transferred at the speed

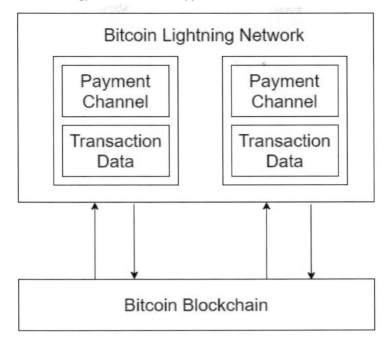

Figure 6.4 Bitcoin lightning network

at which users' wallets can communicate over the internet. A "closing transaction" blockchain is initiated when they're ready to close their business, thereby settling all of our prior transactions [33].

Users can "jump" between connected payment channels on the Bitcoin Lightning Network, which solves this problem. Using network channels, payment channels can converse with one another without directly exchanging data. A user who has a payment channel with a buddy who also has a payment channel with his brother will be able to use both channels. An open payment channel allows the user to ask a friend to make a payment on his brother's behalf. Once the user provides evidence of payment, he or she can quickly refund their friend [33].

It's called network channels, and it makes the Bitcoin Lightning Network much stronger in Bitcoin. In order to conduct business with somebody, you must first find a way to contact them through another network user. Irrespective of how many intermediaries are involved, the Bitcoin Lightning Network is globally scalable because of the routed channels [33].

6.6 SECURITY AND PRIVACY IN BLOCKCHAIN

Though blockchain is observed as secure and unalterable, it is susceptible to hacking when one or more miners gain control over half of the mining process. When miners

create a second version or forks, transactions are not reflected and different transactions are designated as the true version of blockchain. Hackers thus double spend
cryptocurrency [22].

Hackers exploit security glitches and steal money because the fraudulent activity
is not detected. The money could be retrieved only when a fork is recognised by all
participants. Most hacking occurs at exchanges where cryptocurrency is used and
when security is weak and hackers have access to data [22].

However, asymmetric cryptography can secure transactions. Since calculating a
private key from another public key is deemed impossible, the technique enhances
security from hackers. When encryption of data is a solution to secure globally published data, losing the key to decrypt the same, the data may be lost for good. When
a key is stolen and published, the entire data faces havoc [22].

Blockchain aims to improve security, especially for identity and access [47].

In Man in the Middle (MITM) attacks, Certificate Authority may be led to provide the user with forged keys, later leading to decryption of sensitive information.
Projects like "okTurtles" are working to solve this issue [47]. Attacks like those of
"Mirai botnet" are impossible when blockchains are based on DNA technology. Data
thus distributed are transparent and secure and cannot be easily tampered with [47].
The most promising research on blockchain privacy is "zkSNARKs" which are implemented by zCash and Ethereum to execute anonymous payments, blind auctions
and voting systems [47].

To address the traceability concerns, Hyperledger is developing a method for establishing the precise date and location of a medicine's production using blockchain
technology and time stamps. While blockchain is best recognised as the technology
that powers Bitcoin, it can also be used to track the movement of items through the
supply chain, with each transaction validated by the blockchain network. The provenance of the product and its components, as well as any transfer of ownership, are all
recorded in the distributed ledger and are verifiable by anyone with access, making
it simple to monitor and identify counterfeit, diverted, or stolen items. According
to Mbanefo, the technique can assist combat both falsified/fraudulent medicines and
inferior drugs by making it evident where a product was created [63].

6.7   BLOCKCHAIN AS A SERVICE (BAAS)

BaaS (Blockchain as a Service) is a solution for people who don't want to invest in
the technology directly. In this approach, the user is able to utilise the applications
most economically. According to reports, BaaS will generate USD 24.94 billion in
revenue by 2027 [5].

organisations interested in adopting blockchain are constrained by technical issues and operational costs related to development, configuration, operation and maintenance of the infrastructure. BaaS accommodates such requirements without much
hassles. The users could focus more on the benefits without worrying about the constraints [5].

BaaS is like a web hosting provider. Either the user can host websites on their
own server, administer tasks and hire resources for this purpose or host their site at

elsewhere hosting provider and give them the authority to administer the site. BaaS provides the latter services. It relieves users from the woes of carrying out blockchain activities [5].

Amazon Managed Blockchain is a fully managed solution that enables users to easily join public networks or build and administer scalable private networks based on the famous open-source frameworks Hyperledger Fabric and Ethereum. Amazon Managed Blockchain is a fully managed solution that enables you to quickly and easily join public networks or create and maintain scalable private networks. Amazon Managed Blockchain removes the costs associated with establishing a network or joining an existing public network, and automatically grows to meet the needs of thousands of apps processing millions of transactions. Once your network is operational, Managed Blockchain makes managing and maintaining your blockchain network simple. It keeps track of your credentials and makes it simple to welcome new users to the network [2].

6.8   HYPERLEDGER FABRIC

Open source Hyperledger Fabric is the modular blockchain framework and the de facto standard for enterprise blockchain applications. Enterprise-grade applications and industrial solutions are designed to be built on top of the open, modular framework. For a wide range of applications, it uses plug-and-play components. Because of its unique consensus technique, Hyperledger Fabric is able to grow performance while still ensuring the data privacy organisations require, thanks to the combined efforts of more than 120,000 participating companies and over 15,000 contributing engineers [35].

A distributed ledger platform that is open, tested, and reliable is Hyperledger Fabric. Only data shared with the network's "permitted" (known) participants is subject to these privacy measures. Using self-executing terms written in lines of code between the parties, smart contracts document commercial operations that are designed to be automated. The blockchain network's code and agreements are spread out and decentralised. Because transactions can be tracked and are irreversible, they promote confidence within the organisation. As a result, businesses can make better-informed decisions more quickly, saving both time and money while also reducing the risk [35].

IBM advises companies against developing a blockchain production solution purely using open source code. Commercial distributions receive tools and support from IBM (as well as other suppliers). There is a retail distribution of Hyperledger Fabric, the open-source technology, called the IBM Blockchain Platform, which provides full $24 \times 7 \times 365$ support and service level agreements (SLAs). The most complete set of productivity tools for building, administering, and running blockchain systems is included. The Hyperledger Fabric blockchain platform and code base are being used by innovators from a variety of industries — including finance, banking and healthcare — as well as the Internet of Things (IoT), supply chain, manufacturing and technology [35].

Instead of creating a single standard, it encourages blockchain technology development guided by the community. So open development and gradual implementation of important standards are encouraged. Developed by Hyperledger, the Hyperledger Fabric project is a blockchain project. It makes use of a ledger, smart contracts, and a platform for users to manage their transactions, just as other blockchain technologies. Hyperledger Fabric is a private and permissioned blockchain system that sets itself apart from the competition. The Hyperledger Fabric network enrolls users via a trusted Membership Service Provider (MSP) rather than an open permissionless system that permits participation by unknown identities (to confirm transactions and secure the system, it needs methods like proof of work) [34].

6.8.1 SHARED LEDGER

This ledger subsystem uses the world state and transaction log from the Hyperledger Fabric distributed ledger. Each Hyperledger Fabric network participant has a copy of the ledger available to them. It's the ledger's database, hence the world state component contains the ledger's current status. The transaction log component acts as a history of updates to the world state, recording all transactions that have led to the present value. As a result, the ledger is built from a combination of the world state database and a chronological history of transactions. Data on the present state of the planet is stored in the ledger's replaceable data storage. This database's key-value store type is set to LevelDB by default. It's not necessary to have a pluggable transaction log. It only keeps track of the ledger database's previous and subsequent values [34].

6.8.2 SMART CONTRACTS

Non-blockchain applications can communicate with the ledger using Hyperledger Fabric smart contracts written in chaincode. Rather of interacting with the transaction log, chaincode frequently queries the world state, the ledger's database component. It is possible to implement chaincode in a wide range of programming languages. Currently, chaincodes written in Go, Node.js, and Java are supported [34].

6.8.3 PRIVACY

Depending on the network's demands and requirements, business-to-business (B2B) network participants may be exceedingly cautious when it comes to the amount of information they transmit. The privacy of users on other networks will be less important. To enable a wide range of network architectures, Hyperledger Fabric offers support for both private and public networks (through channels) [34].

6.8.4 CONSENSUS

Even if various groups of network participants are involved, transactions must be recorded in the ledger in the sequence in which they occur. As a result, the transaction order must be determined and a system for rejecting erroneous transactions accidentally (or deliberately) entered into the ledger must be implemented. Even in the face of corruption, PBFT (Practical Byzantine Fault Tolerance) can sustain communication between file replicas. Alternately, in Bitcoin, orders are placed through a process known as "mining." Competing computers compete to solve a cryptographic issue that specifies the order in which all future processes are built on [34].

Using Hyperledger Fabric, network initiators can choose the consensus technique that best portrays the relationships between network participants' members. From highly organized networks to more decentralised networks, there is a wide range of privacy requirements [34].

6.8.5 BENEFITS OF HYPERLEDGER FABRIC

- **Permissioned network**: Rather than an open network of anonymous users, establish decentralised confidence in a network of known members.
- **Confidential transactions**: Exhibit only the data which has to be shared with the parties.
- **Pluggable**: utilise a pluggable design to tailor the blockchain to industry demands rather than a one-size-fits-all approach.
- **Easy to get started**: Instead of learning new languages and architectures, program smart contracts in the languages already being used [35].

6.9 ETHEREUM

Ethereum is a decentralised public blockchain network focused on the execution of decentralised application programming code. Simply said, it is a global platform for the dissemination of unalterable knowledge [67]. Ethereum is a decentralised blockchain platform that features its own cryptocurrency, Ether (ETH) or Ethereum, and its own programming language, Solidity [24]. Besides being a tradable coin, ether fuels the Ethereum network by covering transaction costs and providing computing functions. Ether lays the groundwork for the development of a more sophisticated financial platform [67].

Ethereum is a decentralised public ledger that uses blockchain technology to verify and record transactions. Users of the network can create, publish, monetise, and use applications on the platform, and pay with the network's Ether money. Insiders refer to the network's decentralised applications as "dApps" [24]. Ethereum is a decentralised blockchain platform that enables the creation of a peer-to-peer network capable of securely executing and verifying application code known as smart contracts. Smart contracts enable participants to conduct business without relying on a trusted central authority. Transaction records are immutable, verifiable, and securely disseminated throughout the network, ensuring that participants retain complete ownership and visibility over transaction data. User-created Ethereum accounts are used to send and receive transactions. Senders must sign transactions and pay Ether, Ethereum's native coin, as a cost of processing transactions on the network [3].

The Ethereum creators were among the first to investigate the potential of blockchain technology for applications other than a secure virtual currency exchange. Its ETH token was first designed as a means of payment for applications established on its network. Its invulnerability to hackers and other snoopers has enabled the storage of sensitive data ranging from healthcare records to voting systems. The network's dependency on bitcoin allows programmers to construct and promote games and business apps [24].

An characteristic of the blockchain over traditional databases is that data is organized in a "chain" rather than a "block" hierarchy. Each transaction involving an Ether token, for example, needs to be verified and put to the coin's unique blockchain. A blockchain is commonly compared to a ledger because of the sequential documentation of each transaction. More than just Ether money transaction records can be stored on the Ethereum blockchain. Games and commercial programs known as dApps can be created and distributed using this platform. These users are looking to take advantage of the low risk of storing private information on the Internet [24].

6.9.1 IS ETHEREUM BETTER THAN BITCOIN?

Unlike the Bitcoin blockchain, which was built to support a cryptocurrency, the Ethereum blockchain was not created to support a cryptocurrency. The Ether coin was intended to serve as an internal currency for Ethereum-based applications. In other words, Ethereum aspires to greater heights. It aspires to be a platform for all types of applications capable of securely storing data. Regardless of their disagreements, the two are the developers of virtual currencies that have developed into investment rivals. They are virtual currencies that do not exist physically but are represented by a string of codes that may be exchanged at a price agreed upon by a buyer and seller [24].

6.9.2 HOW LONG DOES IT TAKE TO MINE ONE ETHEREUM?

The time required to mine Ethereum and earn Ether mining rewards varies according to hash rate, power consumption, electricity cost, and any fees paid to a mining pool and hosting service associated with the mining operation. These factors also directly affect profitability, increases in mining difficulty targets, and the crypto market's overall price performance. Mining one ETH is expected to take 51.8 days using the default calculations of a popular Ethereum mining calculator [24].

6.9.3 BENEFITS OF BUILDING ON ETHEREUM

As a platform for building decentralised apps, Ethereum is exceptionally easy to use owing to the Ethereum Virtual Machine and the native Solidity scripting language. decentralised apps built on Ethereum benefit from the wide range of developer tools available, as well as the protocol's growth. There are wallets like Metamask and Argent that make it easy for users to interact with the Ethereum network and its smart contracts. Additionally, the Ethereum application user experience has improved. Decentralizing applications like DeFi and NFTs, which have a large Ethereum user base, makes it easier for developers to deploy their services on the network. A more scalable network for building decentralised apps with higher transaction throughput requirements will be possible in the future with Ethereum 2.0's backward-compatible protocol, which is currently being developed [3].

6.10   THE COMPETITION THAT BLOCKCHAIN FACES

Blockchain has a plethora of competitors and still counting. After blockchain (2011) evolved, Coinbase (2012), Hedera Hashgraph (2017), Cosmos Network (2017), Polkadot Network (2017) and Circle (2013) followed suit [15].

Ethereum is contended by QTUM, which has the best of bitcoin and ethereum. Tangle is more scalable and swift than blockchain and is free of cost. Tangle does not charge to verify transactions. In blockchain, however there are either few miners or expensive fees [55].

We will discuss the competitors in detail in the following sections.

6.10.1   HEDERA HASHGRAPH

Hedera Hashgraph is a cryptocurrency network that aims to serve as a platform for anybody to transact and build applications under the supervision of a group of businesses. Hedera Hashgraph's most significant distinguishing feature is its hashgraph-based data structure for grouping transactions, which the company says processes more transactions more efficiently than existing blockchains. The Hashgraph is a patented technique in which all nodes constantly communicate with one another. It was created for private usage. The Hedera Hashgraph is the algorithm's first iteration in a public network [40].

6.10.1.1   Hashgraph Consensus Service

Hedera Hashgraph uses the Hashgraph consensus method, powered by two types of nodes, to ensure that all computers in its distributed network agree on its transaction history. Consensus nodes determine the order and history of transactions, whereas mirror nodes communicate this information to other network stakeholders. By relying on a small number of nodes to reconstruct its history, the Hedera model ensures that transactions cannot be undone later. This contrasts with most traditional blockchains, which obtain consensus through users proposing blocks to be added to the chain in open market competition. As a result, Hedera Hashgraph asserts that it combines the benefits of public and private blockchain networks [40].

6.10.1.2   Hedera Governance

Hedera Hashgraph is governed by the Hedera Governing Council, responsible for administering the consensus nodes that determine transaction ordering. By 2020, the council will have 39 members, including Google, IBM, and Boeing. The council's role is to govern the software, vote on improvements, allocate funding properly, and ensure the network's legal status in various jurisdictions. The council has a limited number of seats. Each member may serve a maximum of two consecutive three-year terms. Members have an equal vote during this period on network and platform decisions. While members of the Governing Council currently run mainnet nodes, the Hedera team aims to open it up in the future to anybody interested in operating nodes [40].

6.10.2 COSMOS

Cosmos is a thriving decentralised network of autonomous, interconnected blockchains that manages over $ 140 billion in digital assets and is powered by the Cosmos Hub. They place a premium on interoperability, scalability, and usability. That is why they are developing a new sustainable internet—the Internet of Blockchains—that disrupts old monopolies, promotes new business models, and empowers everyone to participate in its ownership. They gain the ability to transfer value peer-to-peer through blockchains, enabling users to form decentralised communities in which products and services can be exchanged outside the constraints of today's financial system. Before Cosmos, blockchains were isolated, incompatible with one another, and impossible to develop. They had a low transaction throughput, which made them vulnerable to network congestion and hefty transaction costs [14].

6.10.3 POLKADOT NETWORK

All kinds of data, not simply tokens, can be exchanged over Polkadot networks. Since Polkadot supports cross-chain registrations and computations, it is a genuine multi-chain application environment. It is possible to transmit data across public and private blockchains using Polkadot. Applications that can access private blockchain data and use it on a public blockchain can now be developed and tested. For example, a private, permissioned academic records chain at a university may communicate proof to a public chain's degree-verification smart contract [50].

Polkadot permits for the construction of an open, decentralised web where users retain ownership. To integrate private and consortium chains, public and permissionless networks, oracles, and new technologies, Polkadot is being developed. The Polkadot relay chain facilitates the creation of a trustless internet by allowing different blockchains to share data and transactions. decentralised applications, services, and institutions have never been easier to create and connect with Polkadot. By empowering entrepreneurs to construct better alternatives, they are attempting to free society from its reliance on a faulty network in which its massive institutions cannot betray our trust [49].

6.10.4 CIRCLE

Financial technology startup Circle aims to empower businesses of all sizes to use digital currencies and public blockchains to facilitate payments, commerce, and financial transactions around the world. USD Coin (USDC) is Circle's principal currency, and it has become the fastest-growing digital currency in the world. A year ago, USDC transactions totaled about $ 700 billion, making it the world's second-largest digital currency. Now Circle is providing the infrastructure for the next generation of banking and commerce applications that can help the world's economy grow through frictionless monetary value exchange. [11].

6.10.5   COINBASE

Coinbase is a safe and secure online platform for purchasing, selling, transferring, and storing digital money. Their objective is to build a global open financial system and to be the premier global brand for converting digital currency to and from local currencies. They simplify the process of purchasing and selling digital currency. It's completely free to send and receive digital money between Coinbase wallets, friends, and merchants. They take care of security and backups and are a "one-stop-shop" - they combine a wallet, an exchange, and merchant tools into a single, straightforward interface. Coinbase is a platform that enables the development of several applications through the use of their API [12].

Coinbase and other cryptocurrency exchanges are distinct from conventional US exchanges. They frequently function as a custodian of crypto assets in addition to exchange—a position they have taken on to circumvent the technological restrictions of the majority of current blockchain networks. Accounts on a blockchain network are referred to as "wallets," and moving cryptocurrency between wallets might take minutes or even hours if the network is busy [25].

As a result, Coinbase's technology verifies that users have transferred their cryptocurrency to the exchange before trading. Due to the fact that both parties to the deal are on Coinbase's platform, the coins never leave Coinbase's wallet. Coinbase records the trade internally and keeps it off the blockchain until one of the traders requests a withdrawal from the exchange. When crypto assets are added or removed from the platform is a transaction recorded on a blockchain network, enabling free cryptocurrency trading without the delays or expenses associated with blockchain networks. While functioning as an asset custodian addresses the transaction speed issue, it also makes the exchanges a perfect target for theft. Users entrust billions of dollars in assets to startups with a limited operating history and cyber security knowledge [25].

Part B: Applications

6.11   APPLICATIONS WITH ILLUSTRATIONS

In this section, we discuss various applications of Blockchain with illustrations.

6.11.1   E-COMMERCE

Blockchain technology and distributed ledgers are employed in e-commerce to develop decentralised online buying and selling platform which ensures security and speed in the transactions. Ethereum and bitcoin technologies are used in e-commerce where the former serves as a platform and the latter is a mode of payment. The well defended blockchain technology reduces expenses of inventory management and enhances payment processing effectually. These elements of business along with product descriptions and images and other business activities mitigate maintenance. Besides, cryptocurrencies also slash the banking charges for completing transactions [59] [19].

Blockchain technology, through distributed ledgers, offers security against cyber attacks which threat to steal consumer data and cash. Such security helps retailers to effortlessly face competition and gain consumer confidence. Blockchain technologies such as Waves, enable speedy payments unlike previous conditions where users need to wait for hours to complete payment transactions. Speedy payments enable transactions to move to the shipping process easily [59].

Smart contracts not only realise the transactions but also minimise staff hiring for the process and thus slash labour costs, besides controlling inventory management effectually. Receipts and product warrants are stored easily. Content creators are notable elements of blockchain technology. Content creators are rewarded with cryptocurrencies by retailers through digital wallets for the appealing posts that they create. Content creators can convert the cryptocurrency bestowed on them to their chosen currency. In addition to these loyalty programs and supply chain monitoring are carried out smoothly by executing blockchain technology [59].

Examples of blockchain e-commerce include Gemini, Circle, Coinbase, Chronicled, IBM besides popularly known Ali Baba and Amazon. Amazon uses Ethereum blockchain framework for its transactions, while Ali Baba uses Tmall e-commerce platform.

On a concluding note, Blockchain influences e-commerce with aspects like revamped payment methods, enhanced supply chain, transparency, security and genuine reviews and offers [51].

6.11.2 GOVERNMENT

From a political perspective or with a view of governing any country, blockchain is indisputably an answer to curb corruption. Though blockchain cannot single handedly prevent crime, it can definitely curb or control the same. Tamper-free and permanent databases can tackle corruption and effectually handle proceedings with the aid of smart contracts. Sweden, Estonia and Georgia are few examples where these countries employ blockchain technology for land registry whereby many parties hold copies of the registry to resolve property disputes and mitigate distrust. Many countries such as Honduras and India are probing possibilities of enhancing transparency and establishing property rights to check corruption in land acquisition. Distributed ledgers enable land owners to establish their rights [53].

However, countries which do not previously recorded land registers or those which possess improper information, would have to tediously format information before executing blockchain based registry. Government contract or public procurement is globally vulnerable for official corruption where vendor selection is complex and lacks transparency. Such corruption is in almost same magnitude all over the world irrespective of whether the country has low income or high income.

Blockchain, with its transparency and automated smart contracts can definitely answer this issue. However, this concept still has shortcomings such as spamming and draining attacks [53] [37].

Blockchain can possibly play a powerful role in establishing the election of a country's government. India, for instance, is reportedly probing the idea of shifting from EVMs (Electronic Voting Machines) to blockchain based e-voting, which is likely by 2024 general elections. Election Commission of India is working with IIT-Madras, in this regard. Still, this system is vulnerable to vote manipulation, paper trial erasure and is susceptible to electoral chaos. Government disbursements to support education, humanitarian aid and social assistance to mention a few, can be made transparent through blockchains and avert middlemen, so that financial diversions are curbed [53] [54].

6.11.3   HEALTHCARE

Blockchain plays a prominent role in digitalising healthcare with benefits such as supply chain transparency, electronic health records, insurance based smart contracts, authenticating medical staff and IoT security for remote monitoring, to name a few. Purchase of medical goods gain visibility and while counterfeit prescription medicines and the deaths that they might cause, are curbed. MediLedger, is one of the blockchain protocols that tracks prescription drug supply and verifies the credibility of the medicines, such as expiry date to name one [45].

Medicalchain in collaboration with healthcare providers executes blockchain enabled EMR (electronic medical record) which acts as a comprehensive single source of patient's medical records. Patients can with researchers for a given period of time. Medical insurance is processed swiftly with such blockchain facilities. Medicalchain also develops a platform for virtual consultations and enables medical data exchange where patients can sell anonymised medical information to support digital health application development called Medtokens, to acquire population level analytics solutions [45].

Chronicled, Curisium are few blockchain based systems who authenticate players in health sector and enable digitalization and automated contracts. These distributed ledgers mitigate disputes over payment claims. The chargeback claims which follow change in pricing structures are disputed widely and such disputes are solved or averted through blockchain infrastructures. Hiring process for healthcare organisations are streamlined with blockchain based applications. US based ProCredEx is one such instance which has designed a medical credential verification system. IoT security for remote monitoring is enhanced with blockchains and DDoS and man in the middle attacks are reduced [45].

MedRec enables health practitioners to gain remarks for previous care provider, without which patient's medical history is invisible and crippling present consultations and prescriptions. SimplyVital Health blockchain technology determines the gross cost of patient's care which comprises multiple organisations. phrOS enables transparency between medical institutions by compiling patient's medical information in blockchain and securing it through decentralised ledger technology.

FarmaTrust tracks medicine when it is altered and throws light on the lifecycle of the medication [68].

Estonia's healthcare system has been transformed by the introduction of innovative e-solutions. Patients and physicians, as well as hospitals and the government, gain from the convenience and cost savings provided by e-services. Each person in Estonia who has visited a doctor has a trackable online e-Health record. With the electronic ID-card as a means of identification, the health information is maintained entirely secure while remaining accessible to authorised individuals. KSI system makes use of blockchain technology to assure data integrity and to reduce internal risks to the data [20].

NITI Aayog and Oracle signed a Statement of Intent (SoI) to pilot a real-world pharma supply chain leveraging blockchain distributed ledger technology and Internet of Things (IoT) software to fight India's escalating counterfeit drug problem. This project will be a collaboration between Apollo Hospitals and Strides Pharmaceutical Sciences. NITI Aayog CEO Amitabh Kant stated that the counterfeit drug problem is substantial, costing the Indian pharmaceutical industry billions. As a result, the patient is at greater danger as well. This agreement with Oracle and collaboration with Apollo Hospitals and Strides Pharma have enabled Indian pharmaceutical businesses to gain access to cutting-edge, standards-based technology – blockchain and Internet of Things – that will aid in the eradication of counterfeit medication distribution [10]."

Blockchain technology will be especially beneficial for securely transmitting information across the supply chain, as each exchange of information in the supply chain is recorded, making it impossible to tamper with or delete any trace of drug transportation. To prevent manipulation, the manufacturer's medical supply chain utilises blockchain technology to permanently preserve a drug's data (including serial number, labeling and scanning). In real time, this system keeps tabs on every point of hand-change, from the manufacturer to logistics to distribution to hospitals and pharmacies to customers. A discrepancy will be detected if the medication is a fake. It is also possible to track important information such as chemical composition or temperature control for life-saving medications or vaccines [10].

6.11.4   ENTERTAINMENT

Entertainment is one of the spectrum of industries, which finds possibilities of accommodating blockchain technology. By executing decentralization, writers and musicians could deliver their works to patrons, thus saving the revenue that is dispatched to traditional distribution channels. Blockchain ensures security of intellectual property besides ensuring transparency in payments, funding and contract enforcement, to name a few. Users could choose to access a part of the content and pay a smaller fee [36].

Collection and distribution of royalty payments is accentuated when blockchain technology is implemented in entertainment streaming. Disputes over accuracy and compensation rates are minimised or averted. However, blockchain in entertainment industry is still in the evolving stage and adopters in this early stage are wary about the possible challenges and costs. The location where the intellectual property would be stored is yet to be decided. Arriving at a common ground where all entities agree, is yet to be worked upon [36].

Enterprise Ethereum enables artists to digitise their creations and time-stamp their IP rights and store them in an immutable ledger [13]. Blockchain plays a vital role in streamlining royalties. Mediachain, Rebel AI, Fluz Fluz, Steemit, Civil, Dot Blockchain Media and Binded are a few of the blockchain players in the entertainment sector [17].

6.11.5 REAL ESTATE

Blockchain technology in real estate effactually controls buyers and sellers and cuts revenue shelled out to intermediaries. ATLANT, a blockchain based platform, tokenizes assets and conducts online transactions as stocks would be done in an exchange. The tokens are exchanged for fiat currency and buyers have percentage stake on properties [44].

Liquidity status of real estate receives a new perspective and is no more an illiquid asset waiting for a buyer. They are readily exchanged for fiat currencies and partial value of the property is still obtained. Fractional ownership allows investors to pool their money to secure bigger ticket properties and avoid managing woes such as maintenance and leasing. Blockchain also enables access to global asset distribution as well as secondary market opportunities. The concept thus enables investment decisions and portfolio management [44]. Propy, Harbor, ShelterZoom and Ubitquity are few of the blockchain organisations based in the United States and are working on the real estate sector [64].

6.11.6 CORPORATE MANAGEMENT

Blockchain when integrated in corporate administration removes administrative burden and minimises risks of frauds, if any. It is interesting to note that blockchain is fast moving towards the mainstream of any corporate. Blockchains enable to maintain accurate records of stock ownership. Statutory filings from corporate to registrars and exchange of information are also facilitated. They enable effactual trading and protect piracy of intellectual property. Blockchain plays a prominent role in real time accounting, smart contracts execution, corporate voting [16].

Blockchain helps brands to track supply chain and manage them, so that illegal and unethical practices are averted. Corporate such as Walmart, Nestle and Tyson are reportedly employing blockchain to solve such issues. Quoting Chainyard, a blockchain consulting company, "creating new supplier categories and finding qualified vendors within each category is an onerous process." He further adds, "With blockchain, however, you can easily access supplier records, information from government agencies and insurers, and prior verifications completed by trusted parties, all in one place." Blockchain enables tracking, agreements and secure payments besides eliminating supply chain disputes. Besides mitigating click fraud, blockchain enables advertising managers to track investments and streamline accounting practices [29].

6.11.7   CROSS-BORDER PAYMENTS

The World Bank estimates 6.51% as transaction fees for cross border remittances in Q4 of 2020 which is 11% for transactions initiated through banks. An average international payment takes 2 to 3 days to get processed which is an issue for migrant workers who send money to their homes. G20 governments had resolved to mitigate this to 5% and are working over it in the past decade [31].

Ripple vouches to empower cross border payments and currency exchange and invites banks and money transfer institutions to join its distributive ledgers and hold funds in XRP tokens. Ripple's CTO, David Schwartz, claims to complete cross border transaction in 5 to 7 seconds. Blockchain enables cross border payment between innumerable banks without the need for an intermediary to carry out the process. The transaction is also secure, speedy and cheap [31].

Unlike SWIFT, the global payment innovation which was susceptible to fraud in Punjab National Bank case, reportedly no such issue crops up in Ripple, which notifies transactions to concerned banks before transferring funds. If the funds are not transferred the banks involved are informed [31].

IBM has also joined the cross border payments ledger, which is known as IBM World Wire where exchange currencies are Stellar cryptocurrency. Difficulty to purchase cryptocurrencies and hesitance to adopt are two obstacles keeping blockchain cross border payments in developing stage. Various regulatory ambiguities are one of the prominent obstacles for blockchain. Taavet Hinrikus, CEO of TransferWise expressed skepticism to join Ripple, until other banks agreed to do so. Western Union, which expressed the same, later in 2019 signed contract with Coins.ph, a Philippines based blockchain startup [38].

SatoshiPay's blockchain-based instant payments technology enables business-to-business cross-border money transfers and frictionless micropayment processing. Satoshipay eliminates the need for ads and paywalls by enabling customers to micropay for online content. SatoshiPay enables publishers to integrate a Stellar wallet widget into their websites, allowing users to pay for online content in small quantities. There are no login requirements, no waiting periods, and (virtually) no charges. On their website, publishers include a Satoshipay widget with a built-in Stellar wallet. The wallet can be topped up with XLM, USD, or any other Stellar-network cryptocurrency. They can click on pay-per-view content while browsing any site that includes the Satoshipay widget and immediately access it without requiring a login. It's a completely private, smooth, and ad-free experience [58].

6.11.8   ASSETS MANAGEMENT

Blockchain enables open collaboration and creates transparency when applied in assets management besides assuring consistent records. It also improves aspects such as data security. Blockchain improves operational efficiency, where nodes need not send information to one another. When one node is updated, the others relevant to this node are updated accordingly. Blockchain technology is also applied in client onboarding and management, portfolio management, speeding clearance processes, supporting regulatory compliance and sales automation through smart contracts. Though blockchain supports the three pillars of financial market namely transparency, speed and security, it could not gain pace in assets management owing to slow adoption and developing regulatory framework [46].

Two types of Crypto Hedge funds exist where one is exclusively portfolio of cryptocurrencies while the other manages a mix of cryptocurrency and other assets. The fund enables investors to comprehend the market movements of established coins such as Ethereum, Ripple and Dash. Increasing numbers of people are willing to invest in the rather volatile market [43].

6.11.9 SHARE MARKETS

Stocks are tokenised in blockchain technology and are easily transferred. Blockchain technology mitigates the otherwise cumbersome process and lengthy time that security traders, representatives and brokers experience to complete exchanges. Not only fund raising and asset management, blockchain technology is also beneficial in margin financing, post-trade settlement, tracking securities lending and monitoring systematic risk [6]. Leading stock exchanges like NASDAQ and ASX have recognised and adopted blockchain. LSE or London Stock Exchange is probing the possibilities from a critical perspective. Reportedly a projected tokenised asset of 24 trillion dollars are predicted in 2027, which includes tangible assets like listed and unlisted equities and intangible assets such as patents, copyrights and trademarks [6].

In 2017, cryptocurrency trading become an interesting area for both experienced and inexperienced investors. Crypto trading entails speculating on the market's future price changes. Crypto trading, in its simplest form, is the act of purchasing and selling cryptocurrencies in a manner that results in profit. To reach this goal, they must have a clear grasp on how to execute it, the various types of cryptocurrencies, and the factors that affect their market movements. Cryptocurrencies, as decentralised digital assets, rely on a computer network to verify the network's overall state and legitimacy. It is not comparable to fiat currencies such as the dollar, as these coins are not backed by a central authority or government. Unlike them, cryptocurrencies are based on mathematical principles that minimise human participation, allowing the world to finally have a truly unique financial asset [7].

It is critical to remember that cryptocurrencies exist solely as a decentralised ledger of digital ownership. As a result, no one may handle or touch cryptocurrencies, as these assets exist solely in the digital environment. No cryptocurrency transaction is complete unless it is verified and added to the blockchain by miners or network nodes. Nowadays, individuals can trade a variety of different types of blockchain assets. Each investment carries with it trading and regulatory responsibilities. These must be followed. Security tokens, cryptocurrencies, and utility are the three primary types of blockchain assets available on the market today [7].

Binance, a cryptocurrency trading platform was able to enter the market in 2017. Its objective is to simplify the trading process for casual visitors. Chang-peng Zhao, the firm's founder, is well-known in the FinTech field as a developer of high-frequency trading software. Due to his technological expertise, he established a unique user experience for Binance, which solidified the company's position as the market leader. Due to the exchange's simplicity, it was able to grow considerably. Binance overtook Coinbase as the world's largest cryptocurrency exchange in terms of trading volume in 2018. It has maintained a hegemonic position in this area to the present day. Since then, Binance has been able to launch a number of platforms, including Binance Australia, Binance KR, Binance DEX, and Binance US [7].

6.11.10   BANKING

Blockchain is not a competitor to banks, but is just a technology that anyone can use and integrate to their products. Since the inception of cryptocurrency, debate exists over blockchain versus traditional banking. While they cannot replace one another, it is gradually evolving merger. Anyone who vouches about blockchain killing banks, are not enlightened about both the concepts [65].

Blockchain is a solution to issues such as scalability, throughput, security and speed that banks encounter. Banks are compelled to accommodate cryptocurrency, which is here to stay. The process may take a decade or more, but banks are pushed to adopt blockchain. Few banks have begun to develop their own cryptocurrency, but would take time to be recognised. While few banks are coming together to create a cryptocurrency, others are adopting existing ones offered by Ripple, for instance [65].

Consider the following activities of several prominent Indian banks in Blockchain Technology [60]:

   i. Reserve Bank of India (RBI)—Blockchain has piqued the interest of India's banking regulator, the RBI. Research is being conducted by the IIDRBT, India's Institute for Development and Research in Financial Technology, a division of the RBI.

   ii. YES Bank—It has also been preparing to deploy blockchain technology. Bajaj Electrical and 32 additional vendors will be included to the bank's invoice finance blockchain. Currently, the invoicing process takes four days to complete due to the verification, presentation, recording, and reconciliation of bills prior to disbursing working capital loans. The bank will save time and money by implementing this technology.

   iii. Axis Bank—Axis Bank has developed a blockchain-based inward remittance system. It will serve retail consumers in the Middle East through RAKBank, and corporate trade remittance through Standard Chartered Bank (Singapore). Ripple's cross-border transaction network powers Axis Bank's blockchain-based remittance services, which are powered by the bank.

   iv. ICICI Bank—ICICI Bank is building a closed-loop wallet for intra-campus transactions to help with blockchain adoption. The bank also works with Emirated NBD on two blockchain-based remittance and trade finance solutions.

v. SBI or State Bank of India—It also has plans to use blockchain technology for smart contracts and Know Your Customer information (KYC).

The crux of the issue is that India's banking sector is utilising blockchain technology to assist clients and also to develop a network that is significantly more safe and secure than the current methods used by banks and other NBFCs (Non-Banking Financial Companies).

6.11.11   IDENTITY MANAGEMENT

Besides adding value to the business sector in parameters such as transparency and security, blockchain is attempting to transform the identity management and make it more effectual. While the existing system lacks security and requires multiple authorised cards such as Voter ID, Passport and Pan Card, blockchain attempts to decentralize. Though government institutions, banks and credit agencies are vulnerable to threat, citizens could still manage identity through distributed ledgers. The current identity management faces issues such as identity theft, user words and passwords combination, KYC onboarding and lack of control [62].

Reportedly, 56 records are stolen each second. While each platform asks for user name and password, users struggle to remember them all. KYC (Know Your Customer) companies are bound to answer multiple entities like banks, immigration officials to name a few. KYC requires more resources to process verifications and this makes the task more expensive. Personally Identifiable Information (PII), struggles for security for which blockchain would be a suitable solution. By using blockchain, the information would be safe from theft, individuals can create their own digital identities and need for multiple user names and passwords are averted [62].

Five technical components such as native android/iOS app for individuals, native android/iOS app for third party company verification, interplanetary file system to store user's PII, Microservices programmed using Node.JS and permissioned block chain component are required for blockchain based Identity management process. Four steps including installation of app, uploading documents, smart contract trust score generation, and third party company's access request, complete the process [62].

6.11.12   TRANSPORTATION

Blockchain makes order tracking and authentication easier. For instance, smart contracts facilitate customs clearance and enables logistics ecosystem, which dwells in data validation. Even if a shipment requires acknowledgement of more than 30 organisations in more than 200 communications, they are done impeccably and swiftly with blockchain technology. Few examples of blockchain technology in transportation include BiTA (The Blockchain in Trucking Alliance), Chronicled, ShipChain, Modum, 300cubits, SkyCell, Sweetbridge and Provenance [70] [18].

All the above Applications are summarised in the Table 6.1

Table 6.1
Industries in Blockchain and Work Done So Far

Industries in Blockchain	Work Done So Far
E-commerce	Inventory Management and Payment, security against cyber attacks
Government	Land Registry, E-voting
Healthcare	Electronic Health Records, Counterfeit Drug Prevention, supply chain transparency, authenticating medical staff, IoT security for remote monitoring
Entertainment	Royalty payments, uploading of art works
Real Estate	Online transactions, tokenization of assets, liquidity status of real estate
Corporate Management	Real time accounting, corporate voting, track supply chains, securing payments
Cross-border payments	Instant payments, wallet-based payments
Assets Management	Onboarding and Management, Portfolio Management, speeding clearance processes, supporting regulatory compliance and sales automation
Share Markets	Margin financing, post-trade settlement, tracking securities lending, monitoring systematic risk
Banking	Remittance, trade finance, secure payments
Identity Management	Creation of digital identities, KYC more secure
Transportation	Order tracking, authentication

6.12 BENEFITS OF BLOCKCHAIN, CURRENT SITUATION AND WHAT CAN BE ANTICIPATED

Blockchain offers multiple benefits from a plethora of perspectives and throws light on tomorrow's world. It is a technology that must undoubtedly be embraced. Adoption, the only issue that the technology faces, can be mitigated through proper explanation which answers every skeptic issue. Blockchain in future, will revolutionise commerce, given that more people accept it [30].

The following are some of the many benefits of Blockchain technology in numerous fields:

- **Instant Settlements:** Transactions can be completed in a matter of minutes or seconds, whereas settlements now take up to a week. With Blockchain, settlements become more user-friendly, which saves both parties substantial time and money. Due to the instantaneous settlement of transactions, blockchain eliminates the need for a large number of middle office and back office workers at banks. As such, banks have a strong incentive to investigate Blockchain for the purpose of enhancing settlements, and some banks begin with internal possibilities, while others begin with interbank options [9]. The current breakthroughs in blockchain technology enable the creation of a network that goes beyond merely a messaging service similar to SWIFT to one that optimises transactions via the use of smart contracts to complete the settlement lifecycle. Participants in such a network can transact and have the transaction transparent and settled between parties in minutes, if not seconds, rather than days, resulting in considerable advances in transparency and efficiency along with cost savings [72].

- **Greater Transparency:** The most distinguishing feature of blockchain is that its transaction record for public addresses is publicly accessible. This provides an unparalleled layer of accountability to financial systems and organisations, requiring each sector to operate with integrity towards the company's growth, its community, and customers [39]. Today's supply networks incorporate blindspots, which blockchain's inherent properties address. For instance, the distributed nature of blockchain reduces the lag between an event occurring in the supply chain and the system updating the status. Inventory and financial data are updated in real time, and anyone with the appropriate permissions can see exactly where things are at any given time. For the first time, comprehensive transparency into transactions between retailers, suppliers, and banks is possible [27].

  This facilitates cooperation and streamlines communications between participants, while the immutability of the blockchain increases trust. For example, suppliers can monitor when a merchant takes out a loan to refill a product. This enables them to begin preparing a shipment immediately upon receipt of the client's order, minimising delays and even assisting in the avoidance of shortages through priority product placement [27].

  Without a doubt, blockchain technology possesses a slew of unique qualities that make it an ideal fit for supply chain management. It enables you to accurately record every transaction and provides real-time tracking for every item in your whole supply inventory. Most importantly, it establishes a degree of trust and openness in supply chain management that was previously impossible [27].

- **Reduced costs:** Additionally, the decentralised nature of blockchain technology enables enterprises to save money. It improves transaction processing efficiency. Additionally, it automates manual duties such as data aggregation and amendment, as well as reporting and auditing processes. Experts emphasised the cost reductions that financial institutions realise when they implement blockchain, adding that the capacity of blockchain to expedite clearing and settlement directly translates into process cost savings. More broadly, blockchain enables organisations to save money by eliminating the middlemen – vendors and third-party providers – who have historically provided the processing capabilities of blockchain [52].

- **Improved security and privacy:** Another significant advantage of blockchain-enabled technologies is their security. The greater security provided by blockchain is a result of the way the technology works: With end-to-end encryption, blockchain generates an unalterable record of transactions, preventing fraud and unauthorised conduct. Additionally, blockchain data is distributed across a network of computers, making tampering extremely impossible (unlike conventional computer systems that store data together in servers). Additionally, blockchain technology can handle privacy problems more effectively than traditional computer systems do by anonymising data and requiring permissions to restrict access [52].

- **True Traceability:** Businesses may concentrate their efforts on developing a supply chain that works with both vendors and suppliers when they use blockchain. It is difficult to trace products in a typical supply chain, which can result in a variety of issues, including theft, counterfeiting, and loss of commodities. The supply chain becomes more visible than ever before using blockchain. It enables all parties to track and guarantee that commodities are not replaced or abused along the supply chain process. Additionally, organisations can leverage blockchain traceability by deploying it in-house [28].

Blockchain technology is expected to speed digital supply chain integration and will undoubtedly revolutionise supply chain management, as well as the transportation and logistics industries. Due to the effectiveness of blockchain technology in advancing peer-to-peer transactions in privacy without the intervention of a third-party, a blockchain-based solution can mitigate risks associated with data manipulation, compromised privacy, and compliance with government rules and regulations, all while lowering auditing costs. Numerous experts have identified supply chain management as a sector that might benefit from blockchain deployment by gaining radical transparency and so transforming supply chain traceability. As a result, blockchains have been increasingly implemented in industries that require increased traceability, such as food, fashion, and logistics [8].

Bibliography

1. Shubhani Aggarwal and Neeraj Kumar. Cryptographic consensus mechanisms. In *Advances in Computers*, volume 121, pages 211–226. Elsevier, 2021.

2. Amazon. *Amazon Managed Blockchain*, 2021.

3. AWS Amazon. *What Is Ethereum?*, 2021.

4. Hasib Anwar. *Blockchain Vs Distributed Ledger Technology*, 2019.

5. Varun Bhagat. *What is Blockchain-as-a-Service & its Business Benefits?*, 2020.

6. Vinith V Bhandarkar, Akshay A Bhandarkar, and Aditya Shiva. Digital stocks using blockchain technology the possible future of stocks? *International Journal of Management (IJM)*, 10(3), 2019.

7. Binance. *What is Crypto Trading*, 2021.

8. Oliver Bischoff and Stefan Seuring. Opportunities and limitations of public blockchain-based supply chain traceability. *Modern Supply Chain Research and Applications*, 2021.

9. London Speaker Bureau. *Blockchain – 7 Benefits for the Financial Services Industry*, 2020.

10. Press Information Bureau. *NITI Aayog and Oracle sign a Statement of Intent to pilot drug supply-chain using blockchain*, 2021.

11. Circle. *About Circle*, 2021.

12. Coinbase. *What is Coinbase?*, 2021.

13. CONSENSYS. *Blockchain in Media and Entertainment*, 2021.

14. Cosmos. *Building the Internet of Blockchains*, 2021.

15. Craft. *Blockchain Competitors*, 2021.

16. Cygnetise. *Blockchain as a Tool for Corporate Governance*, 2018.

17. Sam Daley. *From Stopping Fake News to Producing Movies, Blockchain in the Media Industry is Creating Bold Possibilities*, 2019.

18. Sam Daley. *Making Moves: 21 Companies using Blockchain's Logistics Capabilities to Excel*, 2019.

19. Sam Daley. *Retail Revolution: 8 Blockchain Companies Giving Buyers and Sellers an Edge*, 2021.

20. e estonia. *healthcare*, 2020.

21. Edusson. *Positive and Negative Effects of Globalization*, 2021.

22. Epiq. *Yes, Blockchain Can Be Hacked: 3 Ways It Can Be Done*, 2021.

23. Jake Frankenfield. *Permissioned Blockchains*, 2020.

24. Jake Frankenfield. *What Is Ethereum?*, 2021.

25. Emelia Fredlick. *Coinbase: Everything You Need to Know*, 2021.

26. Freemanlaw. *Permissioned and Permissionless Blockchains*, 2021.

27. Robert Galarza. *How Blockchain Technology Can Create More Transparent and Traceable Food Supply Chains*, 2021.

28. Diego Geroni. *Top 5 Benefits Of Blockchain Technology*, 2021.

29. Serenity Gibbons. *3 Practical Ways To Use Blockchain In Your Business In 2020*, 2019.

30. Marcell Gogan. *Blockchain Technology in the Future: 7 Predictions for 2020*, 2020.

31. Navin Gupta. *Impact on Real-Time Cross-Border Payments*, 2018.

32. Suyash Gupta and Mohammad Sadoghi. Blockchain transaction processing. *arXiv preprint arXiv:2107.11592*, 2021.

33. Steven Hay. *Bitcoin's Lightning Network Explained Simply*, 2020 (accessed April 4, 2020).

34. Hyperledger. *Hyperledger Fabric Introduction*, 2020.

35. IBM. *What is Hyperledger Fabric?*, 2021.

36. JPMorgan. *The Future of Blockchain in Media and Entertainment*, 2018.

37. Richard McConkie Kate Boeding. *3 Potential Benefits of Blockchain for Government*, 2021.

38. Sam Klebanov. *A Look at Blockchain in Cross-Border Payments*, 2021.

39. Ilker Koksal. *The Benefits of Applying Blockchain Technology In Any Industry*, 2019.

40. Kraken. *What is Hedera Hashgraph? (HBAR)*, 2021.

41. Kenny L. *The Blockchain Scalability Problem & the Race for Visa-Like Transaction Speed*, 2019.

42. Lumen Learning. *Current Trends in Global Business*, 2021.

43. Joe Liebkind. *The Rise of the Crypto Hedge Fund*, 2019.

44. Joe Liebkind. *How Blockchain Technology is Changing Real Estate*, 2020.

45. STL Advisory Limited. *5 Blockchain Healthcare Use Cases in Digital Health*, 2017.

46. Gilad David Maayan. *How is Blockchain Changing the Face of Asset Management?*, 2019.

47. Chris Wojzechowski Matteo Cagnazzo. *Security and Privacy in Blockchain Environments*, 2017.

48. Library of Congress. *Globalization: A Resource Guide*, 2010.

49. Polkadot. *About Polkadot*, 2021.

50. Polkadot. *Polkadot Technology*, 2021.

51. Mayank Pratap. *5 Ways Blockchain is Transforming eCommerce*, 2019.

52. Mary K. Pratt. *Top 10 Benefits of Blockchain Technology for Business*, 2021.

53. Ashley Lannquist Rachel Davidson Raycraft. *Blockchain Alone Can't Prevent Crime, But These 5 Use Cases Can Help Tackle Government Corruption*, 2020.

54. Harshit Rakheja. *India Explores Blockchain-Based E-Voting By 2024 General Elections*, 2021.

55. John Ryan. *Blockchain Vs Tangle: Which Is Better?*, 2019.

56. Burcu Sakiz and Aysen Hic Gencer. Blockchain technology and its impact on the global economy. In *International Conference on Eurasian Economies*, volume 10, page c11, 2019.

57. Rashmi P Sarode, Manoj Poudel, Shashank Shrestha, and Subhash Bhalla. Blockchain for committing peer-to-peer transactions using distributed ledger technologies. *International Journal of Computational Science and Engineering*, 24(3):215–227, 2021.

58. SatoshiPay. *SatoshiPay*, 2014.

59. Sergii Shanin. *How Blockchain Technology is Going to Revolutionize Ecommerce*, 2021.

60. Toshendra Kumar Sharma. *Which Indian Bank Uses Blockchain Technology?*, 2020.

61. Abraham Silberschatz, Henry F Korth, Shashank Sudarshan, et al. *Database System Concepts*, volume 4. McGraw-Hill New York, 2020.

62. Akash Takyar. *Blockchain Identity Management: Enabling Control over Identity*, 2021.

63. Phil Taylor. *Applying Blockchain Technology to Medicine Traceability*, 2016.

64. YouTeam Editorial Team. *14 Blockchain Startups in Real Estate to Watch*, 2018.

65. Waves Tech. *Does Blockchain Pose a Threat to Banks?*, 2018.

66. TRADEIX. *The Difference Between Blockchain and Distributed Ledger Technology*, 2018.

67. Blockchain Wallet. *Ethereum For Beginners*, 2021.

68. Bryan Weinberg. *14 Major Real Use Cases of Blockchain in Healthcare*, 2019.

69. Wikipedia. *Anti-globalization movement*, 2021.

70. WINNESOTA. *How Blockchain is Revolutionizing the World of Transportation and Logistics*, 2018.

71. Wipro. *Improving Performance & Scalability of Blockchain Networks*, 2019.

72. Haohan Xu. *Blockchain Technology Will Remove Barriers to Instant International Settlement*, 2020.

73. Zibin Zheng, Shaoan Xie, Hongning Dai, Xiangping Chen, and Huaimin Wang. An overview of blockchain technology: Architecture, consensus, and future trends. In *2017 IEEE international congress on big data (BigData congress)*, pages 557–564. IEEE, 2017.

7 Cryptoassets Inheritance: Needs, Challenges, and Solutions

An asset is something that contains an economic value and/or future benefit. An asset may be tangible, intangible, or virtual. Tangible assets are the physical quantities that carry some value. Examples of tangible assets are fiat currency, gold, real estate, etc. Intangible assets do not exist physically. Examples of intangible assets are work experience, patents, private keys, software keys, etc. Nowadays, an asset can be virtual too. Virtual assets are the digital representations of values that can be digitally traded or transferred and used for payment and investment. Examples of virtual assets are Bitcoin, cryptikitties, ERC20 tokens[1], etc. Virtual assets, whose ecosystem is based on cryptographic primitives, are called cryptoasset. The concept of cryptoasset emerged from Bitcoin technology, the primitive form of cryptocurrency. The underline structure of Bitcoin is Blockchain technology. Blockchain has the unique feature of the decentralised public ledger and immutable record keeping. The sanity of the records is governed by a consensus mechanism, known as *proof of work* and the majority's approval. It may be noted that the existence of Blockchain is not completely virtual because every user has a copy of the last updated Blockchain. However, the records on the Blockchain refer to completely virtual cryptocurrencies.

So far, we have seen that Blockchain is used for the accounting of virtual assets. In addition to that, Blockchain can also embed some logic programming, called a *smart contract*. The transaction is not simply deterministic even that transfer some amount from one account to another, rather depends on some condition checks and cryptographic primitives. In Bitcoin, conditions are imposed by the sender (who wants to pay) as a challenge string, and the receiver (who is supposed to accept the payment) presents a valid response to the challenge. A `scripting` language is used to represent this challenge-response mechanism in Bitcoin. The challenge string is called `ScriptPubkey`, and the response string is called `ScriptSig` [2]. `ScriptPubkey` contains the address or *ScriptHash* of the receiver. Bitcoin address is a unique identifier of a virtual location where the cryptocurrency can be sent and stored. The address is derived from the public key of an asymmetric key pair. Generally, Elliptic Curve Cryptography (ECC) [21] is used for Bitcoin and other related Blockchain applications. An address is the cryptographic hash (`SHA256` followed by `RIPEMD-160`) of the ECC public key. Therefore, every address is pertaining to some

---

[1]Cryptokitty is an online video game. Every cryptokitty is a non-fungible token. Every cryptokitty has a unique identity and owner. Cryptokitty cannot be replicated, transferred without the user's permission. Owner can interact, can buy or sell or breed the cryptokitties. It is worth noting that cryptokitty artwork is not the party of Blockchain, instead created and released by AxiomZen.

see `https://ethereum.org/en/developers/docs/standards/tokens/erc-20/`

DOI: 10.1201/9781003355052-7

ECC key pair. A software application, called a wallet, maintains all the addresses the entity possesses and provides related interfaces to transact over the Blockchain. On the other hand, `ScriptSig` contains the proof that the receiver knows the preimage of the address, i.e., the corresponding public key of the address and a valid signature for authentication. The proof of knowledge is not sufficient to ensure the integrity of the transaction. It only guarantees that the transaction transfers the amount to the legitimate receiver. To include the transaction on the Blockchain, a mining operation is required. There are miners who form blocks, solve the *Proof-of-Work* (PoW) and post the block on the Blockchain. Dishonest miner miners (or any adversary) may tamper with the transaction before it is included in a block. Therefore, a digital signature is purposefully done to ensure the integrity and authenticity of the transaction.

Bitcoin `Scripting` has a little scope of programming. The advent of Etheream changes Blockchain technology a lot. Ethereum is an opensource Blockchain platform with smart contract functionality. The original Blockchain, namely Bitcoin, tracks the state of Bitcoins and their ownership. The Blockchain may be viewed as a distributed state machine, where a transaction is a global *state transition* and causes the *state change* of two *addresses*. The consensus mechanism of the Blockchain constrains the state transition. Ethereum can also be modelled as a distributed state machine. Ethereum is not limited to the state of ownership, but every state reflects general-purpose data storage and execution. The Ethereum address can store any data expression and logic program that operates on the data. The transaction encapsulates the alteration of stored data and the transfer of values from one address to other. In some way, this serves the same purpose as infinite linear memory (tape memory) and the general purpose stored-and-compute model of Universal Turing Machine (UTM).

The ability to store and program data on the Blockchain unfolds a new arena, called decentralised applications (DApps). DApps are a growing movement of application developments that use Ethereum and disrupt the existing business models or invent new ones. The philosophy behind DApps is a smart network that enables security, peer-to-peer communication, and computationally validated transfer of assets. The asset may be either virtual-money or tangible-intangible items or contractual arrangements. The network is inherently intelligent to identify, validate, confirm and route the asset from one address to other. The intelligence to the network is imparted by software programs, i.e. smart contracts. Thus an "Algorithmic Trust" model emerges. The model disrupts traditional human-centric institutions, like banks, notaries, custodians, etc., that usually validate the transaction and enforce obsolesce.

The earliest form of DApps was the cryptocurrency, e.g. Bitcoin. Ethereum ERC20 token [3] changes the spectrum. Though Bitcoin is a form of token, but only contains the monitory value. However, the Ethereum ERC20 token can store any fungible items, e.g., keys, voting rights, hall tickets, etc. Furthermore, a non-fungible token, Ethereum ERC721 [3], has enriched the tokenisation process by including the non-exchangeable physical assets, like real estate, ownership, precious metal, etc. ERC721 simulates the signed legal documentation regarding the ownership of property or right for public reference. We sometimes refer ERC721 token as a *deed*.

There are salient differences between token and cryptocurrency. Unlike *Ether*[2], the Ethereum protocol does not implicitly operate on the token. Transaction of *Ether* is an intrinsic action. Whereas owning or transferring a token is a function call. *Ether* can only persists on an address. Token can be stored and maintained by a contract. In brief, token is a part of data that has a specific structure and can be programmed. Present days, almost every DApps on Ethereum implements some sort of token. It is obvious to ask - Is tokenisation a Pied Piper? Do all DApps need tokens? The answer may be affirmative. In practice, token becomes the ultimate management or organisational tool. Developers are using tokens in one of the two ways: *utility* tokens or *equity* tokens. The use of *utility* token is to gain access to a specific storage on the Blockchain. For example, I have access to some cryptographic keys stored on the Blockchain. Like I possess a movie ticked. The ticket is a virtual entity stored on a Blockchain. On the other hand, *equity* is used to represent the possession of some shared values control or own an item, either physical or virtual. For example, I have the key of a cryptokitty.

7.0.1 REPRESENTING CRYPTOASSET - IS IT A FANTASY?

In practice, who do we possess an asset? Say, I have a car. I do not manufacture the car. Factory manufactures and dispatched to the outlet. Every car comes with a pair of unique identification: Engine Number and Chassis Number. These numbers are the primary identity of the car. As I procure the car, I register my ownership to the registration authority, generally under the Department of Motor Vehicle. The registration authority issues another unique identification number, called Vehicle Number. The Vehicle Number, primarily, reflects a particular geographical location where the car has been registered. At the backend, Vehicle Number links the car with the owner, along with all the relevant testimonies. For example, one can verify the up-to-date taxes on this car or the accident records of the car.

We have seen that two sets of identification numbers are applied to the car. The first one, Engine Number and Chassis Number is intrinsic and assigned with the release of the vehicle from the factory. This identity only describes the vehicle, not its ownership or other legal attestations. The second one, Vehicle Number, is the second identity of the vehicle issued by the registration authority. This is analogous to naming the vehicle with a unique number. Registration authority maintains all records related to the vehicle throughout its life span.

So, the ownership of the car is a registration under the competent authority. There is valid documentation (either in digital or paper form). A vehicle is only owned if the registration is completed. The ownership can also be transferred when the vehicle is re-registered to another owner. However, the Vehicle Number remains unchanged. This is because Vehicle Number previous the previous records of the Vehicle.

Can the possession of the car be a cryptoasser? Before answering this let discuss some inherent properties of cryptoasset.

---

[2]*Ether* is the unit of cryptocurrency on Ethereum Blockchain.

7.0.1.1 Cryptoassets are Inherently Secure

The notion of security may be of different dimensions.

- Firstly, cryptoassets are unforgeable. Blockchain basically maintains the record of ownership of asset. Though the records are publicly accessible, they are immutable. Moreover, the transfer of cryptoasset requires the involvement of a private key, which is only under the owner's possession. Therefore, an adversary cannot execute the transfer unless the privacy is compromised.
- Secondly, cryptoasset provides the privacy of information. A software, called smart contract backs up every DApps. The responses of the DApps are predetermined and governed by the use cases. Unlike the human-centric system which may deviate, DApps do not. In practice, the smart contract defines a set of functionalities by which the outer world retrieves information about the cryptoasset. To prevent unauthorised leakage of information, developers have to design the prototype of those functionalities very carefully.
- Finally, cryptoasset confirms the authenticity of the transfer. This is obvious for any Blockchain application. In a Bitcoin application, receiver has to satisfy the challenge of the sender. We sometime call the Bitcoin as Unspent Transaction Output (UTXO) which has been referred to some address, the *addressee* has to produce the proof (i.e. valid `ScriptSig`) to redeem the coin. Similarly, Ethereum Blockchain also provides condition checking to impose certain constrain on the transaction. Ethereum smart contract may call the functionalities of other smart contracts. This opens up the vulnerability of "Code Reentrancy." Developer has to follow certain secure coding practices to avoid such vulnerability.

7.0.1.2 Cryptoassets are Certifiable

We have seen that ownership is a process of registration. There must be some regulatory institution under which the registration is performed. In the case of cryptoasset, the underline structure is Blockchain technology. Blockchain provides the framework of decentralise ledger. The ledger is immutable and distributed in nature. This solves the purpose of registration for cryptoasset. However, Blockchain is self-severing in nature

Ethereum Blockchain is an opensource movement, and philosophically does not involve a central controlling authority. At the same time, Ethereum does not restrict the developers to design DApps with specific controls. The only hurdle is that Governments do not frame proper regulation for DApps.

Ethereum tokens, like ERC20, ERC721, provide a set of standard interfaces for managing fungible and non-fungible items. The standards include

- totalSupply this is a data variable. Returns the total units of this token.
- balanceOf this is a data variable. The data structure is a mapping from address to uint. Returns the balance units of token of a given address.

- transfer this is a function. Given an address and amount, the function transfers the amount of tokens to that address from the balance of the invoking address.
- transferFrom this is a function. Given a sender address, receiver address and amount, the function transfers token from sender's account to receiver. This is always used in combination with approve.
- approve this is a function. The function authorises another address to execute several transfers up to the remaining balance from the caller's account.
- allowance this is a function. Given owner's address and spender's address the function returns the remaining balance that the spender has approved to withdraw from the owner's account.
- Transfer this is an event. The function triggers the event upon successful transfer. The event logs the _from address, _to address and _value.
- Approve this is an event. The function triggers the event upon successful call to approve. The event logs the _owner address, _spender address and _value.

In addition to the above, ERC721 provides the following interfaces.

- balanceOf ERC721 defines this as a function. Given an address the function returns the remaining balance of token of that account.
- wonerOf this is a function. The function maps the deedID to an address. ERC721 defines an interface to set the identification number, called deedID, to the token. This function is a reverse mapping, i.e. deedID to address.
- setApprovalForAll this is a function. This function approves or removes an address as an operator for the caller address. If the address is approved, the address can execute transferFrom or safeTeansferFrom of any token owned by the caller.
- safeTransferFrom this is a function. The function is similar to transferFrom, but if the receiving address is a contract then the implementation of IERC721Receiver.onERC721Received is a must.
- ApprovalForAll this is an event. The function triggers the event when the owner enables or disables an approval or setApprovalForAll.

Token standards are the minimum specifications for a token implementation. The primary purpose of these standards is to encourage interoperability between contracts. The standards are descriptive rather than prescriptive. The implementation of the interfaces is left for the developers. It is also important to note that ERC20 and ERC721 tokens have some optional interfaces. We can name a token with the name function and symbolize a token using symbol function. For example, a token can be named Maruti Sedan and symbolized as BS6.

Tokenisation and Ownership: Ethereum tokens are suitable for representing the ownership of some item. The concept is to attach unique identification or deedID to the item and map the deedID to some address or vise-versa. One can inherent the token and implement any cryptoasset DApps. Figure 7.1 shows a snippet of contract Car that inherits the OpenZeppelin ERC721.

```
pragma solidity ^0.8.0;
import "@openzeppelin/contracts/token/ERC20/ERC20.sol";
contract Car is ERC20{
    .
    .
    .
}
```

Figure 7.1   Inheriting the `OpenZeppelin` ERC721 token

7.0.2   RISK IN CRYPTOASSET

Bitcoins and other Blockchain applications are essentially using cryptographic primitive to execute the transaction. The Blockchain ecosystem defines two types of entities: user and smart contract. Every entity's activity, irrespective of the user or smart contract, is uniquely identified by an address. A user may possess multiple addresses. This is analogous to the situation where the user has multiple bank accounts. Here address acts as a pseudonym of the user. Thus a user may have multiple pseudonyms to remain anonymous in the network. Transaction transfers assets from one address to another addresses. In fact, Blockchain only records the state changes of the *addresses*. A software, called wallet, seamlessly maintains the *addresses* of a user and the corresponding balances. It also provides the necessary interfaces to perform transaction on the Blockchain. Therefore, wallet contains the private keys of the user. Every user must have his own wallet. The challenging part of the wallet software is to storing and maintaining the private key. The wallet must be shielded with specific access control mechanisms, like biometric, passcode, airdrop, etc., to prevent private key leakage.

The most significant risk in any Blockchain application is the "lost of key". If you lost your private keys, your immediately lost the fund and control forever. This is because:

- Key and address are the complement to each other. If the key (private key) is lost, the address becomes inactive.
- DApps often require a digital signature to make a transaction successful. The signing process requires a private key. Therefore, loss of key results in the stop-making-transaction.

There is no easy method to recover the private key. Insights reported that - around 20% of the Bitcoin has not moved from its current state to another address in the last five years. This Bitcoins are considered as the lost coin. Ironically, the 50 BTC allocated to Satoshi Nakamoto at the inception of Bitcoin was lost forever.

Another significant risk of cryptoasset includes - people remain reluctant to plan for the heirs. This is because people often want to keep their digital content private even after death. Our *digitality* requires privacy and protection. When we are alive, we want to keep our Twitter, Facebook, Netflix accounts private. What to do with

Figure 7.2 "My cryptoasset estate plan" - a survey on Twitter

those digital rights after the death? We don't have a specific answer. The present scenario keeps those accounts inactive. On the other hand, certain digital rights must be passed on to others. For example, your bank account access right, cryptocurrency wallet key, etc. In some cases, transfer of rights is oblivious. For example, the CEO of the company has to transfer the rights as he retires or leaves the company. A well define inheritance mechanism should be incorporated for hassle free transfer of ownership. Following, we present two surveys and a case study.

Pamela Morgan, educator, and entrepreneur, surveyed on the topic "My cryptoasset estate plan (for who gets what when I die)"[3]. There were 5291 participants; among them, 55% of people said that they had not planned for the cryptocurrency to be passed on to their loved ones. Only 5% of people had prepared the cryptographic "will" or crypto trust to pass on this wealth to their heirs. In the line, only 25% of people had programmed (smart contract) their cryptoasset to be transferred to their heirs. Figure 7.2 shows the survey report in short.

In another online survey, conducted by Cremation Institute [10], among 1150 participants during October, 2019 to June, 2020. The objective was to collect the views of cryptoasset users regarding their heirs' plan. The survey was made among broad range of age groups, i.e. 19 to 73 years. The survey revealed that 89% of cryptoasset owners were worried about their assets "what would happen to their asset after the death." Yet, only 23% of them had documented the heirs' plan. Youngers were less interested to have the heirs' plan. Only 18% within the age group of 19-34 years had documented heirs.

According to the above surveys, knowing that untimely death may cause massive loss of cryptoasset, people are reluctant to plan their assets for their heirs. The death incident of Gerald William Cotten, founder-CEO of Quadriga Fintech Solutions, taught us the lesson to plan for our cryptoasset heirs [9]. Quadriga was the largest cryptocurrency exchange in Canada. The company was declared bankrupt with a huge amount as the CEO of the company, Cotten, died in December 2018

---

[3]The Twitter of @pamelawjd . Feb 11, 2018

at the age of 30 years. Approximately 190 million CDA in the form of Bitcoin and other cryptocurrency were locked forever and became inaccessible since Cotten was the only person who knew the private key. In another incident, James Howells, an IT worker, had mined 7,500 bitcoins and stored the cryptocurrenct in his hard drive. While cleaning his house in 2013, by mistake, he put the drive into a waste bin and lost the drive forever. Howells knew how the cryptocurrency was converted to waste but had no alternative. The present value of Howells Bitcoins are worth approximately 255 million USD [17]. Howells's incident points out that physically storing the keys is not enough; rather a software solution is more desirable.

We organise the chapter into seven sections. After the introduction, we focus on safeguarding the wallet. The second section describes the security issues of wallet and their remedies. Following, we briefly describe the regulation related to the cryptocurrency of different countries. The fourth section highlights some practical implementations of safeguarding the private keys, either online or offline. Those are the existing mechanisms of inheriting cryptoassets by the heirs. We introduce the concept of cryptographic "will" in the fifth section. Here, we are focusing on modelling the traditional "will" into a cryptographic "will". Those models are not decentralised. Our final contribution is in the sixth section, where smart contracts are deployed for inheriting the cryptoasset. We conclude our discussion in the seventh section.

7.1   WALLET SAFEGUARD MECHANISM

A wallet is a special device or program used to send and receive cryptocurrency. This is analogous to our money wallet. Instead of storing fiat currency, the wallet stores cryptographic functionalities which help us to access and transfer cryptocurrencies. To make a transaction, the owner has to produce the `ScriptSig`. The `ScriptSig` contains a digital signature. Private key is involved in every signature. In Bitcoin (or similar type of cryptoassets), private key is a 256-bit string, and a private data to the owner. Remembering the 256-bit string is impossible. Therefore, a wallet is proposed to hold the private keys and their corresponding UTXOs. A user may possess multiple private keys, so the wallet maintains the list of all private keys and their easy retrievals. Wallet acts as the first and foremost device to control cryptocurrencies.

The great concern of storing, trading, exchanging, and investing cryptocurrency is the security and privacy of the private keys. Wallet is one of the central menaces and risks to the cryptoassets. Wallet does not keep the cryptocurrencies, but it contains the private keys, the most sensitive information, that control the cryptocurrencies. Anyone who obtains access to your wallet, viz. private key, can execute fraudulent transactions or burglarize your cryptocurrencies.

From the functional point of view, wallet performs two things,

- Manages the private keys and provides interfaces to control the cryptoasset.
- Provides a hackle free recovery of private keys.

The primary consideration of wallet design is to tread off convenience and privacy. The most convenient wallet maintains only one private key, and uses that private key for every transaction. Unfortunately, such a wallet is catastrophic for privacy. It is easy to track all your transactions on the Blockchain. The best assurance of privacy is to use different private keys for every new transaction. Managing so many private keys would be a mess. This is analogous to remember and recall all individual's birthday of your class.

On the other side, wallet generates the keys on behalf of the users. Wallet is equipped with the functionalities to produce random keys. But, wallet is a device or software that may fail, damage, destroy, or be misplaced, or uninstalled. Once your wallet malfunctions, you basically lose your cryptocurrencies. Therefore, the generation of keys is not purely random. Wallet accepts multiple pass-phrases from the user, then applies at different layers of hashing to generate pseudo-randomness. This pseudo-randomness is used for the generation of keys. The pass-phrases are easy to remember for the users. Therefore, in case of wallet failure, user can deploy a new wallet and recover the lost keys from the pass-phrases. Following, we present different models of cryptocurrency wallets.

Desktop Wallet: The desktop wallet is installable software that works in unison with other utility software, like antivirus, Internet security, etc. The private key is reposed in a virtual layer on the local machine. `Bitcoin Core`, `Exodus`, and `Electrum` are just a few examples of desktop wallet. Generally, the wallet, does not require user's pass-phrase for key generation. The recovery of private key is not possible.

Web Wallet: The private key is placed on a web server maintained by trusted third party. The accesses to the private keys is through a web address or application. Cryptocurrency exchanges, like `Coinbase`, `Kraken`, `WazirX`, `Bittrex`, `CoinDCX`, etc., are using web wallet to maintain the private keys. Web wallet is often protected by passcode along with Two-Factor Authentication (2FA). The 2FA is advisable because it implements the authenticity of the owner. Web wallet are often called hot wallet.

Hardware Wallet: The private key is embedded on physical devices. A small display unit along with a USB connector forms a portable device for storing the private key. Hardware wallet is separated from the web and is often called cold wallet. Separation from the web reduces the risk of being hacked and lost of keys. Hardware wallets such as `Ledger` and `Trezor` are becoming popular among cryptoasset owners.

Mobile Wallet: Mobile wallets are similar to web wallets, except they are designed for use on a mobile or other smartphone. These wallets offer a simple graphical platform that enables operations simple. Mobile wallets are primarily smartphone programs that keep secret keys in the crypto world. A mobile wallet allows its owner to transfer and receive cryptocurrency and hold them. These apps are available on popular app stores such as the Google Play Store for Android and the Apple App Store for iOS. Some examples of mobile wallets are `Mycelium`, `Electrum`, `Exodus`, `Bitcoin Wallet`, `Binance Wallet (WazirX)`, and `Coinbase Wallet`.

Paper Wallet: A paper wallet is a printed paper containing keys, often in the form of QR codes. Paper wallets are generally safe options as they are not connected to the Internet. However, it is the owner's responsibility to keep the paper wallet private.

The security of wallets is determined by how the owner maintains them. The most severe threat to cryptocurrency safety is the loss of the secret key by an individual client. Online wallets (Hot Wallets) are the smoothest to install and use, but they seem most vulnerable to hacking. Using an offline wallet (Cold Wallets) rather than an online wallet is one approach to keeping your cryptocurrency safe.

Web wallets are often linked, making them vulnerable to malware and cyber-attacks. Mobile wallets are somewhat safer than web wallets. However, the secret key could be disclosed, and losing or breaking your phone could permanently lock you out of your mobile wallet. Dealing at home with a desktop wallet over a secure connection is safer. However, because it is still connected to the internet, the wallet's security is worrying. Although paper wallets are primarily safe from hackers and viruses, retrieving a key from a stolen or destroyed wallet is impossible. A hardware wallet's data is never linked to the internet, providing a very secure solution. The most severe worry with hardware wallets is being locked out and the chance of losing this costly hardware.

7.1.1 WALLET DESIGN AND RECOVERY OF PRIVATE KEY

Once a record is logged in Blockchain, it cannot alter. This is also applicable to the compromised key. Even the network realizes that transaction is fraudulent; there is no way to recover the cryptoasset. Therefore, wallet that contains private keys should be well protected. Generally, wallets are often protected by passcode and 2FA. Sometimes user forgets the passcode of the wallet. This is analogous to the scenario where we lost our physical wallet. Following, we present some safeguard mechanisms to recover the keys when our wallet becomes nonfunctional. The recovery mechanism depends on how the keys were generated earlier.

7.1.1.1 Non-deterministic and Randomised Wallet

In this case, the keys are generated independently from a uniform random distribution. All keys are independently, and there is no correlation among the keys. While non-deterministic mechanism seemed to be good from the security viewpoint, but there is a huge overhead to maintain the keys. Every key and the randomness that constructs the key must be put in safe custody. A non-deterministic wallet gradually increments the list of keys. Therefore, regular backup is essential for non-deterministic wallet. You may lose the access to your cryptoassets in case of key failure.

Some cryptocurrencies, such as Ethereum, employs a *Keystore* file. The *Keystore* file is a JavaScript Object Notation (JSON) encoded file. The file contains single randomly generated private key which is encrypted with a passphrase for additional security. The *Keystore* format is defended by the Key Derivation Function (KDF). This is often known as a password stretching technique. To put it another way, the passphrase does not encrypt the private key directly, instead expanded by multiple hashing.

7.1.1.2 Deterministic Seeded Wallet

A deterministic wallet generates keys from a single starting point, known as a seed. The seed is randomly generated from a uniform distribution and combined with other index numbers or chain-codes to form the private keys. The seed enables a user to backup and restores a wallet in case of an emergency. As the seed is enough to recover all of the keys, a single backup of the seed value is enough to restore the wallet with all lost keys. The seed can also be used for export or import a wallet, thereby making it simple to migrate keys across the cross platform.

7.1.1.3 Hierarchical Deterministic Wallets

Like a deterministic seeded wallet, a hierarchical deterministic wallet (HD) uses a seed to produce several keys generated and stored in hierarchical order. The advantage of using HD wallet over the deterministic wallet is - deterministic wallet topically produces a single "chain of keys". As a result, sharing the seed is either disclosing all the derived keys, otherwise reveals nothing. Whereas HD can share a substructure of the derived keys, keeping the other substructures private. HD builds a

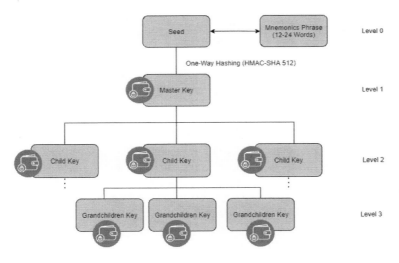

Hierarchical Deterministic (HD) Wallet Structure

Figure 7.3 Hierarchical deterministic wallets and the key structure

tree like structure. The seed is a random string of 256 bits that forms the master key. The master key derives a series of child keys, and child keys further derive another series of grandchild keys, and so on. At every level, a parent key can derive at most 2^{31} children. Every key in the hierarchy is indexed with a tuple of level and index. The 4th child of the master key is indexed as $m/0/3$ where 0 indicates level 1, and 3 indicates the 4th child. The index $m/0/0/3$ indicates the second level 4th derived key. The Bitcoin Improvement Proposal BIP32[4] describes the HD key generation mechanism. HD also provides an easy way to represent the seed. Instead of managing the random seed, encoding is used to convert the random string of 256 bits into a 12 to

---

[4]see https://github.com/bitcoin/bips/blob/master/bip-0032.mediawiki

24 words English word. Bitcoin Improvement Proposal BIP39 [5] defines the encoding process. The owner can remember the 12-24 words. BIP39 has described the 12-24 words as a *mnemonic phrase*. Figure 7.3 shows the HD and the key derivation.

7.1.1.4 Multi-Signature Wallet

Multi-signature states several keys rather than a single sign to validate a transaction. There are n private keys, and any m private keys are required to transfer the cryptocurrency. A multi-signature wallet defines a threshold structure for validating a transaction. A multi-signature wallet is shared among two or more users called co-payers. Depending on the signing application, two or more co-payers participate in the transaction process.

Do the wallet safeguard mechanism help cryptoasset inheritance? The answer is affirmative. The deterministic and hierarchical deterministic wallets provide a key recovery technique based on seed value. This seed value is often mnemonics of 12 words written or stored on a paper or devices. The owner of cryptoasset prepares a "will" mentioning the cryptoasset and the paper and/or device where the seed value is maintained. The paper and/or device must be kept in safe custody, e.g. bank locker, attorney, or trusted friend. In case of the owner's demise, the heirs can assess the cryptoasset after legally occupying the paper and/or device.

7.2   CRYPTOCURRENCIES JURISDICTIONS AND REGULATIONS

Cryptocurrencies, cryptoassets, decentralised finance industries, and non-fungible tokens are all part of the new rise of information transactions for investments, exchanges, and market tradings, and each has its own set of advantages, disadvantages, and complications. Countries from all over the world have attempted to accept cryptocurrency under a particular format or another. Similarly, several governments have started developing cryptocurrency legislation to oversee cryptocurrency interactions. The regulatory structure surrounding digital assets is still immature, and constructing one is often challenging and imprecise. Absolute limits are uncommon and tricky to execute, but Government bodies and Regulators are trying to ascertain guidelines to make sure of crypto's increasing boom. Different countries have their very own judicial systems for governing cryptocurrencies. Several countries have implemented legislation to either restrict or encourage the use of cryptocurrencies. In contrast, others are hesitant or evolving, and only a few governments have permitted cryptocurrency usage. Following we list of nations and their cryptocurrency and cryptoassets in terms of jurisdictions and regulations:

North America - Canada: Canada hosts several cryptocurrency businesses and start-ups, and it sees cryptocurrency as a viable payment option in the long term. In Canada, cryptocurrency is categorized as consumable, which indicates that all cryptocurrency operations are legally recognised. When it comes to cryptocurrencies, the Canadian government wants to ensure that rigorous anti-money trafficking rules are in place. The FINTRAC (Financial Transactions and Reports Analysis Centre of

---

[5]see https://github.com/bitcoin/bips/blob/master/bip-0039.mediawiki

Canada) [15] is the regulatory body in Canada. Paper currency and coins produced by the Bank of Canada and the Royal Canadian Mint Act are the only legal money in Canada. The Canadian Securities Administrators (CSA) and the Investment Industry Regulatory Organization of Canada (IIROC) have released recommendations requiring cryptocurrency exchange services and traders to connect with concerned authorities in Canada. Companies that deal in cryptos must register with Canada's Financial Transactions and Reports Analysis Centre (FINTRAC). For the Income Tax Act, the Canada Revenue Agency (CRA) treats cryptocurrencies as a commodity.

North America - United States: Cryptocurrencies are not governed by any comprehensive regulations in the United States of America. The Financial Crimes Enforcement Network (FinCEN) [14] considers cryptocurrencies to be money exchangers. The Internal Revenue Service (IRS), on the other hand, views cryptocurrencies as a form of digital property. Digital currencies, on the other hand, are subject to the Bank Secrecy Act (BSA) [6]. Furthermore, the Securities and Exchange Commission (SEC) of the United States considers cryptocurrencies securities for which financial security laws apply. Now, the Treasury Department and other authorities are focusing intensively on a fast-growing commodity known as Stablecoin as a priority for more robust regulation. Stablecoins will act as a link between crypto space and the regular system.

Central America - Brazil: In Brazil, cryptocurrencies are mainly uncontrolled. Some cryptocurrencies have been certified by the Brazilian Securities and Exchange Commission [6], or CVM (Comisso de Valores Mobiliários). The Brazilian government has declared that bitcoin is an asset and is subject to taxes on capital gains. The Brazilian Parliament is presently debating a bill that would regulate cryptocurrencies reported as a financial asset in a proposal made by Brazil's Ministry of Finance. The Brazilian Internal Revenue Service has also released new tax guidelines for cryptocurrencies.

Europe - United Kingdom: All enterprises in the United Kingdom that deal with cryptoassets must comply with the Financial Conduct Authority (FCA) [7]. The FCA requires cryptocurrency trading to register. Under UK legislation, all licensed Cryptoasset enterprises must adhere to counter-terrorist financing (CFT) and anti-money laundering (AML) regulations. Crypto-assets were recently recognized as property under the UK legal system by the UK High Court. It has also established rules for virtual asset service providers (VASPs). The FCA and the Bank of England have issued several cautionary statements and recommendations regarding their utilisation. The UK Crypto Asset Task Force was established by the FCA, the Bank of England, and HM Treasury to determine when and how Cryptoassets should be controlled. The lack of legislative and financial protections, the nature of cryptocurrencies as repositories of value, and the perils of market manipulation and instability all sparked worry. The task force underlined the United Kingdom's willingness to incorporate some cryptocurrencies under the "Financial Promotions Regulation".

Asia - China: The People's Bank of China (PBOC) outlawed banking firms from trading in cryptocurrencies, eventually expanding the prohibition to include virtual currencies and initial coin offerings (ICOs). There is no rule prohibiting Chinese citizens from owning or dealing in cryptocurrency. The Chinese government will crackdown on bitcoin mining and trade, according to China's Financial Stability and Development Committee. The People's Bank of China recently stated that all crypto-related operations are prohibited in China. The development of China's digital yuan and central bank digital money most likely motivated the Chinese government to make this decision. China is also attempting to meet its environmental commitments, as mining cryptocurrencies such as bitcoin consumes a lot of energy.

Asia - India: Previously, the Reserve Bank of India (RBI) barred Indian banks from working with cryptocurrency exchanges due to concerns about consumer safety, anti-money laundering, and financial stability. However, the Indian Supreme Court overturned the order, stating that there is no such restriction [11]. Despite all these, India has embraced blockchain technology and started developing a Central Bank Digital Currency (CBDC) backed by the Government of India.

Cryptocurrencies are currently deregulated and have no legal grounds in India. The proposed Cryptocurrency Bill, which is still pending Cabinet approval and submission to Parliament, is expected to define the future of virtual currencies in India.

Asia - Japan: In Japan, all cryptocurrency exchange platforms must be recognized by the Financial Services Agency (FSA). Japan's modified Payment Services Act (PSA) made it lawful to use virtual currencies as a form of payment [1]. Gains on cryptocurrencies should be classified as miscellaneous income and taxed proportionately, according to Japan's National Tax Agency, Financial Instruments Exchange Act (FIEA), and Act on Prevention of Transfer of Criminal Proceeds (APTCP). The Japanese Virtual Currency Exchange Association (JVCEA) was founded to foster compliance with regulatory requirements and provide a part in determining industry standards and maintaining regulatory compliance.

Asia - Singapore: The Monetary Authority of Singapore (MAS) regulates cryptocurrencies. The Securities and Futures Act covers digital payment tokens (DPT), public issues. PSA helps crypto firms address the impact of economic frauds and enforce guiding principles, such as KYC. The Inland Revenue Authority has stated that they will be subject to the Goods and Services Tax on income produced from or received in Singapore. Singapore's Blockchain and Crypto Assets Council (BACC) has taken preemptive measures to prevent unethical conduct, advocating for crypto sector rules.

Middle East - United Arab Emirates (UAE): The United Arab Emirates (UAE) has formed the UAE Blockchain Strategy [8] to become a frontrunner in Blockchain technology. The Dubai Financial Services Authority (DFSA) has established a crypto legislative regime for enterprises operating in the Dubai International Financial Center. The UAE Securities and Commodities Authority, Abu Dhabi Global Market (ADGM), and the Financial Services Regulatory Authority (FSRA) has defined the usage of Cryptoassets as a measure of wealth. Additionally, the Dubai Multi Commodities Centre (DMCC) and the Securities and Commodities Authority (SCA) have classified cryptocurrencies as products and assets.

As of late, the Saudi Arabian Monetary Authority (SAMA), the Central Bank of the Kingdom of Saudi Arabia (KSA), and Ripple are thinking of embracing the Blockchain and Cryptoassets as the future of economic and technological revolution for the years to come.

7.3 SOME PRACTICAL IMPLEMENTATION OF PRIVATE KEY CUSTODIAN

This section explores the projects: `TrustVerse`, `Safe Haven`, `DigiPulse`, `Casa Covenant`, and some other important initiatives in the field of Cryptoassets Inheritance. Those projects were started with the aim to provide an easy process of Cryptoassets inheritance by a nominee without involving technicalities into the scene.The aforementioned projects tries to solve the problem in a different manner. We assess the projects and report the practicalities of the same. Following we show the current status of the projects and put forward the discussions on how the projects meet our requirements.

`TrustVerse`: TrustVerse offers a compatible service for managing cryptoasset [12]. TrustVerse provides a wallet service, called `MarS` for digital asset management. The `MarS` wallet can handle ERC-20 (fungible) tokens. Tokes are different from *Ether*. Tokes are only associated with the contract. TrustVerse provides a "non-custodian" maintenance of encryption key, called `MasterKey` [6]. MasterKey would allow the users to recover the private key if they lose their private information. In fact, MasterKey allows the users to have some passwords (mnemonics) to make up the private key. The keys corresponding to the mnemonics are stored in different cloud locations. If user loses his private key, it can be easily recovered through a Two-Factor Authentication with the mnemonics. Currently, MarS wallet and Samsung Blockchain Wallets [7] are supported by MasterKey. Finally, TrustVerse integrates all these services in a digital wallet management DApp, called `Pluto`. Pluto allows the users to chalk out their plans to be put into effect for transferring cryptoassets ownership to their nominees. This helps the user identify conditions and circumstances under which the plan might be triggered and also the procedure to be followed if the said plan is put into effect.

In case of untimely dismissal, the nominees need to submit legally binding documents to ascertain the fact and subsequently access information stored by the user. The legally binding document needs to be ratified by all nominees before being processed for the release of assets.

`Safe Haven`: Safe Haven [18] is a cryptographic key management that system provides secure and decentralised control and storage of private cryptographic keys and other information. Owner's private keys, random seeds, passphrases, and other digitised information may be split into random subkeys and distributed to a group of people. The group gains the access to owner's private key or related information if and when a specified condition has been met. A quorum is defined with a threshold of member to gain the access of the private key.

Safe Haven implements the Shamir Secret Sharing mechanism to create the subkeys [19]. If there are T nominees for a cryptoasset, the owner defines a polynomial of degree T as $f(x) = p + a_1 x + a_2 x^2 + \cdots + a_T x^T$. Here p is the numeric value of the cryptoasset, a_i are random selection of the owner. Then every group member P_i privately receives the subkey as $f(i)$, for $i = 1, 2, \ldots, T$. The validator privately

---

[6]see https://www.the-masterkey.com/mars
[7]see GEMINI: https://www.gemini.com/samsung

receives the subkey as $f(T+1)$. The above distribution ensures the threshold of group members as T along with the validator.

The distribution of subkey prevents the validator from singlehandedly attaining the majority and revealing the private key. All T nominees and the validator must come to a consensus by reconstructing the secret from their respective shares and thereby revealing the private key. Safe Haven also introduces "Key Escrow" in the same way. A certain percentage of keys are kept in escrow with the validators. This is because the system is not completely non-custodial.

However, there is certain criticism on "Key Escrow." Jurgen Schouppe, the creator of Safe Haven, justifies this by stating that a third-party trust is needed for the proper functioning of the escrow. In particular, when validator possesses more than one subkeys and the number of nominees is $y < T$, the reconstruction of private key would be stuck in limbo as the validator acts maliciously and refuses to share the subkeys. Therefore, the preferable choice of nominees-validator ratio is $T : 1$.

`Digipulse`: DigiPulse provides a safe custody, called "vault," to store private information on the Ethereum Blockchain platform. User can store any inheritable assets in the vault. The vault is cryptographicall secured by applying the standard AES symmetric encryption. To transfer the asset from owner to nominee, the of AES and a passphrases are given to the nominees.

The vaults exist on the Ethereum Blockchain and are monitored by the community. That raises security concerns over the storage of user information. For this reason, DigiPulse allows encrypted data storage on the Blockchain. The system incorporates third-party software to monitor users activities. The user sets a "period of inactivity" by which instructing the monitor to overlook his activity. As the "period of inactivity" is over and user does not respond, the nominees are allowed to open the vault. This is called Dead-man's Switching.

`Casa Covenant`: Casa Covenant [4] platform is built on a multi-signature wallet. Casa might be drawn parallel to Safe Haven. However, Casa is fundamentally different from the above three. The idea behind Casa Covenant is the multi-signature used in Bitcoin transactions. There is a set of n public keys, and to execute a transaction, one has to produce at least $t+1$ private key information, where the threshold scheme in t-out-of-n. Ideally, those private keys are stored in different media to secure them from being compromised.

In addition, Casa also comes with a Dead-man's Switch. Casa monitors the users' activities on its portal. If a user is not activity for a stipulated period of time, then Casa attempts to contact the user using the user's preferred mode of communication. Failure, results in the triggering of the Dead-man's Switch, which transfers the assets to the nominees.

While the solution offered by Casa seems to be ideal at first glance, there are major criticisms. Firstly and foremost, Casa functions on a $(n-1, n)$ threshold scheme. This means that users are expected to create a new set of keys for a multi-signature if any one of the keys in the current set is lost or compromised. Maintaining a set of such keys over time can be cumbersome. Furthermore, the Casa transfers the cryptoasset to new address. This incurs no transfer fee, which is hardly the case in cryptocurrencies. Most cryptocurrencies require payment of transfer. Like, Bitcoin incurs mining fees, Ethereum consumes gas and mining fee, etc. Secondly, Casa recommends storing the keys in distant locations. This can be done by the use of cloud storage. However, that defeats the non-custodial property of cryptoasset wallets.

Last Will: The Bicoin BCH (Bitcoin Cash) can be inherited through "Last Will" platform. There is a smart contract for bitcoin inheritance. Users can create and administer BCH endowments using the Last Will protocol. Last Will is a non-custodial and permissionless inheritance. The project of Last Will is still in the development phase. The project is available for open development on the GitHub (see https://github.com/MyWishPlatform/lastwill).

PassOn: PassOn focuses on the succession of tangible items on the Blockchain platform. Unlike the cryptocurrency, the new concept of inheriting real estate, tokens, non-fungible tokens, artwork, shares, and bonds are addressed in the PassOn framework. When the testator dies, how do the beneficiaries get their parts?

7.4 CRYPTOASSET WILL

A will or testament is a legal document that expresses the wish of person(s), the testator, as to how their property, the estate, is to be distributed to the beneficiaries at death, and the names of one or more persons, the executor, to manage the estate until its final distribution. In Section 2(h) in The Indian Succession Act, 1925 it is stated as *"will" means the legal declaration of the intention of a testator with respect to his property which he desires to be carried into effect after his death.*

What is an estate of a person? An estate comprises every *net worth* of an individual, including all lands, real estate, possessions, financial security, etc. Generally, estate includes,

- Estate is the economic valuation of all investments, assets, and interests of an individual.
- Estate includes a person's physical and intangible belongings - land and real estate, furnishings, cars, sailboats, etc.

When we consider cryptocurrency as estate, it becomes difficult to preparation "will" becomes cryptoasset "will" differs form the traditional "will". The constraints of cryptoasset "will" are listed below:

i. The owners of cryptoassets are anonymous. In practice, there are addresses which hold cryptoassets. In Blockchain ecosystem, address acts as pseudonym pf owners.
ii. The cryptoasset owner usually has a wallet. Only owner, who knows the passcode and address of the wallet, can perform wallet operation. The knowledge of wallet address and the passcode is equivalent to releasing the control over the cryptoasset.
iii. Disclosing the wallet credential in "will" is complete catastrophe.

The cryptoasset "will" intends to transfer the testator's cryptoassets until the point when the heirs can enter into their rights. Moreover, "will" should not, compromise the anonymity of the owner nor it contains the access passcode of the wallet.

7.4.1   HOW TO "WILL" THE CRYPTOASSET

Is it a game or a policy? If someone wants to inform his heirs about his cryptoasset but not let them know how to access that ceyptoasset - it is something like a treasure hunt to the heirs. Or, if someone appoints a trustee to hold his wallet passcode and later passes on the passcode to the heirs on his demise - it is clearly centralised compromising the privacy and security of the asset.

The testator has to plan cryptoasset "will" not for the transfer of asset but also the security of the asset. Following we present some possible methods of cryptoasset "will".

Coincover: Now a days, people are using multiple wallets with different keys, passcodes, tokens, etc. People do not want to lose their keys, passcodes, or tokes. Coincove [5] is creating the infrastructure that applies cryptography to achieve a widespread adaptation of owners' secret to solve the problem. Coincover provides a Secure Key Storage (SKS) to the users. SKS is an offline emergency backup for the users' secrets, passcode, tokens. The storage is offline, fully encrypted, and has zero network exposure. Whenever there is a loss of key, the party may recover the key after proving his identity and credential.

Coinsafe: Similar to Coincover, another application is Coinsafe [20]. The Coinsafe application allows to prepare a backup of your keys using trusted devices and friends. A recovery policy has to be set up during the creation of the backup plan. You have the choice of either a 2-2, 2-3 or 3-5 recovery scheme. In a 3-5 scheme you would need five devices, and in case of loss, the recovery request has to be approved by at least three devices. Presently, Coinsafe supports the cryptocurrencies like Bitcoin, Ethereum, DAI, and Monero.

Cryptoasset in a Will: The possible way to include the cryptoasset in the "will" is to mention that you are the possessor of a wallet passcode. The "will" does not contain the passcode. The heirs cannot transfer the asset. Testator uses a separate memorandum and notes down the passcode of the wallet. The memorandum is kept in safe custody, like bank locker or trusted third party. Memorandum serves two purposes - firstly, memorandum does not commit on the asset value, but the asset itself. That means, owner can use or modify the asset, even after the asset has been nominated to the hires. Secondly, memorandum allows to update the wallet passcode or other related information.

One may adopt either Coinsafe or Coincover, and then write a "will" with a memorandum mentioning the reference of Coinsafe or Coincover. As heirs get the right to execute on the cryptoasset, he can recover the wallet passcode (or key) and takes the control.

7.5   BITCOIN SCRIPT AND SMART CONTRACT FOR CRYPTOASSET INHERITANCE

So far we have seen different mechanisms and policies to inherit the wallet (or private key) thereby the cryptoasset. Those techniques are offchain and human interaction is required. Therefore, the techniques are not decentralised. Blockchain does not

Table 7.1
How to Parse the nSequence **in Bitcoin Transaction.**

i^{th} bit	nSequence$[i] = 1$	nSequence$[i] = 0$
31	Absolute timestamp	Relative locking
22	Relative block height	Relative time
15-to-0	block height	second $\times$ 512

record those transactions. In this section we shall explore the possibilities of onchain transaction for cryptoasset inheritance. We are emphasising the protocols where the Blockchain network itself determines the conditions - when and how the cryptoassets would be transferred to the heirs.

The existing solutions are unsatisfactory. They are folklore solutions, basically rely on the traditional legal systems[8]. The popular adaptation is, the well known legacy, to leave the bequeath in a secure shelve. However, it does not ensure the testator whether the inheritors will indeed access the cryptoasset after his decease. An alternative solution is the cryptoexchanges, e.g. Coinbase, which provide a centralised mechanism to handover the cryptoassets to the heirs. Cryptoexchange allows the owners to nominate their heirs. Coincover and Coinsafe are the names of some cryptoexchages.

Our primary objective is to design decentralised self-sovereign cryptography "will". Testator wants to bequeath cryptoasset to his heirs without relying on any third party. The main problem of self-sovereign cryptographic "will" is to define the "event of death". Our ramification of the definition of death is inspired by the concept of *life certificate* used in the banking system. *A party is considered to be dead if he has not responded after elapsing certain time, T*. The parameter T is publicly known. We believe that there may be other useful and meaningful definitions of "event of death", but working with the concept of *life certificate* helps to simplify the design of cryptographic "will".

7.5.1 BITCOIN AND CRYPTOGRAPHIC "WILL"

Bitcoin transaction is a record of transfering coins from a set of input to a set of output addresses. The transaction also records some other useful parametrs. Input->nSequence is one of the useful fields in the transaction record. nSequence is a 32 bit field describing the relative time parameter to include the inputs in the transaction. If nSequence is *OxFFFFFFFF* then Bitcoin network ignores the field. Otherwise defines a specific locking time, before which the input would not be included in the transaction. The locking time may be an absolute time or a relative block height. Table 7.1 explains how to parse the nSequence field.

A straightforward approach of designing a cryptographic "will" is to define a locking time and release the transaction. The transaction ensures that heirs cannot

---

[8]see https://www.gobankingrates.com/investing/crypto/what-happens-to-your-bit coin-when-you-die/

redeem the coins during the locking period. The nave approach does not satisfy the "event of death", rather imposes a time constrain on "event of death". There are two fundamental drawbacks in this solution - firstly, if the owner of Bitcoin died before the elapse of locking period, then also transaction would not be functional due to the locking period. Secondly, if the owner of Bitcoin is alive after the locking period, yet the transaction would be successful, and the control would be transferred to the heirs.

The second problem, i.e. transfer of control to the heirs even the owner is alive, has a countermeasure. Bitcoin Improvement Proposal BIP65 introduces an opcode CheckLockTimeVerify (CLTV). Similar to nSequence, Bitcoin defines another time parameter, called nLockTime. Unlike *nSequence* which is associated with the inputs, *nLockTime* is associated with the transaction. The time restricts the miner to mine transactions with nLockTime greater or equal to the current block height. Intuitively, nLockTime is the earliest time or block height when the transaction would be included in the block. CLTV compares the user's define time with the nLockTime. The CLTV script fails unless the nLockTime. If the transaction is released after the nLockTime, it will eventually fail and the coins will not be transfered from the owner's address. To overcome the problem - owner forms the transaction with a nLockTime and the script with a CLTV. The nLockTime is set to a time in the future. If the transaction is not released before the nLockTime, it would never succeed, and owner retains the coins.

⟨nTimeLock⟩ OP_CheckLockTimeVerify OP_Drop OP_Dup
OP_Hash160 ⟨PubKeyHash_heir⟩ OP_EqualVerify OP_CheckSig

Figure 7.4 Bitcoin Script with CLTV

Now, owner may construct transactions with nTimeLock with CLTV. Figure 7.4 shows a typical example of CLTV. The first row has a OP_CheckLockTimeVerify operator. The operator marks the transaction invalid if STACK top item is greater than the nLockTime. Otherwise, the script evaluation continues. The transaction is also invalid if nSequence is invalid or relative block height. When the first row of the script evaluates as true, the second row of the script is a normal PayToPuhclikeyHash (P2PKH).

Testator signs the transaction but does not release the transaction immediately, rather he keeps it in a safe custody. On demise, the transaction is released. If the nLockTime expired, the testator creates another transaction with new nLockTime, signs, and keeps the new transition in the custody. The advantage of the protocol is owner never losses control of his cryptocurrencies.

Yet, we do not have a decentralised protocol for cryptographic "will". The above two protocols are not completely onchain. The involvement of "custody" digresses the concept of decentralised protocol. The elimination of "custody" will make the protocol self-sovereign and decentralised. This can be done with a second layer network. Lightning Network, a second layer transaction channel, is often used for off-chain transactions [16]. Transactions are happening on the Lightning Network, but those transactions are not included in the Blockchain. Lightning Network is aimed to boost the transaction processing times with real-time settlements and lower the prices connected with Bitcoin's blockchain. It also uses less energy.

Before we present the decentralised protocol, we want to clarify another concept, i.e SIGHASH_NOINPUT. To redeem an UTXO, the user has to sign the transaction. Depending on the application, the transaction may be signed in different ways. The transaction structure has a specific field, called SIGHASH, that indicates how the inputs and outputs are signed. Bitcoin protocol has implemented some standard SIGHASHs. The most common SIGHASHs are:

- SIGHASH_ALL signs every inputs and outputs of the transaction.
- SIGHASH_NONE sines all the inputs, but no outputs
- SIGHASH_SINGLE signs all inputs and only one output of same index.
- SIGHASH_ANYONECANPAY signs all outputs. This SIGHASH is used with either of the above three. Depending on the conditions the inputs are signed. For example, SIGHASH_SINGLE| ANYONECANPAY signs all outputs and only one input.

There have been many proposed improvements for the SIGHASH types. SIGHASH_NOINPUT is one proposed modification that is widely used in the payment channel [16]. Specifically, SIGHASH_NOINPUT, describes the scenario where the transaction does not care what specific input will be provided, however it cares about the amount.

The decentralised Bitcoin protocol for cryptographic "will" is based on the Lightning Network. Let owner has Bitcoin at his address #owner, wants to bequest the asset to his heirs. For simplification, we consider two heirs, owing to the addresses #heir1 and #heir2, respectively. The protocol works as below:

i. Owner generates an alternative address #ownerX and publishes a transaction with the input address #owner with Bitcoin B and output address as #ownerX with Bitcoin B with the nLockTime to a future time T_1. This transaction indicates a dummy transfer of B Bitcoin from address #owner to address #ownerX. The transaction is not included in the Blockchain unless the time T_1 reaches. In Figure 7.5, Step 1: shows that #owner made a transaction with CLTV that delayed the transaction to be included in the Blockchain.

ii. Owner creates another transaction with no input and #heir1, #heir2 as two output addresses. The transaction is signed with SIGHASH_NOINPUT. This transaction is made on the Lightning Network, thus not included in the Blockchain. In Figure 7.5, Step 2: shows the second layer transaction (Lightning Network). The transaction has no input but transfers B_1 to #heir1 and B_2 to #heir2. The heirs could include the input if they know the private key of some source.

iii. Owner provides the private key corresponding to the address #ownerX to the heirs. In Figure 7.5, Step 3: shows that owner communicates the private key of the address #ownerX. Thus, the transaction at Step 2 is only applicable unless the transaction at Step 1 is completed.

The above setting implies the following.

- Heirs know the private key corresponds to the address `#ownerX`. So they can complete the NOINPUT transaction by includding the address `#ownerX` in the input.
- However this is only possible after the locking time of T_1. The dummy transaction will be effective and included in the Blockchain only after the time T_1.

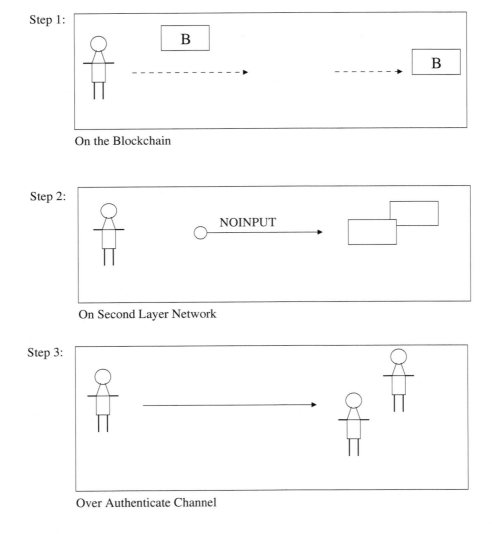

Step 1:

On the Blockchain

Step 2:

On Second Layer Network

Step 3:

Over Authenticate Channel

Figure 7.5   Decentralised Bitcoin protocol for cryptographic "will"

Now, if owner is fortunate to be alive after the time T_1, he just releases another transaction with higher nSequence, prior to time T_1. This transfer is valid, because non-final transaction is replaceable with transaction that includes the same inputs with a higher nSequence number. This owner gradually increments the locking period with his life span.

7.5.2   SMART CONTRACT AND CRYPTOGRAPHIC "WILL"

In 1990s, Nick Szabo introduced the concept of smart contract and defined it as *a set of promises, specified in digital form, including protocols within which the parties perform on the other promises.* The concept of smart contracts had evolved especially after the arrival of decentralised cryptocurrency, Bitcoin, in 2009.

Smart contract is simply a computer program. The program is immutable i.e., once deploy, the code cannot be changed. The only way is to destroy the contract and deploy a new contract. Smart contract is deterministic in nature. That means, code's execution only depends on the characteristic of the caller (owner of the contract or other addresses).

There are different programming environments for writing a smart contract. The popular choice is solidity [13]. Solidity is a high-level, object oriented language. The compilation of solidity smart contract produces Bytecode which can be deployed on the Blockchain. Every smart contract can be uniquely identified with an address. A contract only runs if it is invoked by some entity - user or contract.

Transaction are atomic. A transaction may involve multiple contract calls. Failure of any contract (i.e. function of the contract) eventually "roll backs" all the states of the present and preceding contracts. Ethereum Blockchain is a popular choice of DApps. In this section we present the cryptographic "will" on the Ethereum Blockchain. The programming environment is solidity. Ethereum smart contract is functionally superior then Bitcoin *Scripting*. Ethereum smart contract allows us to define some data structure and program to operate the data. It also provides functionalities to invoke other contracts as well as to transact *Ether* to other contract or address. Therefore, modelling "event of death" is rather simpler that Bitcoin *Scripting*.

Figure 7.6 shows a smart contract, named willTimeLock, that simulates the cryptographic "will". The contract declares three interfaces - the constructor function, assetTransfer and extendTimeLock. The constructor is invoked once only, when the contract is deployed. The function initialises the variables. assetTransfer is invoked by other address, may be the hier. The function transfers the asset if and only if the current block time is greater than elaspeTime + createTime. The variable createTime is the relative creation time of the contract. The *owner* of the contract can reset the creation time to the current block time through the extendLockTime. The contract captures the current block time from system argument *block.timestamp*. The block.timestamp is used to retrieve the current *block.timestamp*.

```solidity
1   // SPDX-License-Identifier: GPL-3.0
2
3   pragma solidity 0.7.0;
4 ▾ contract willTimeLock {
5       uint assetValue;
6       uint createTime;
7       uint elaspeTime;
8       address owner;
9       address heir;
10
11      event Transfer(address indexed _to, uint value);
12      event ExtendTimeLock(uint time);
13
14 ▾   constructor(address add){
15          owner = msg.sender;
16          heir = add;              // Only one heir
17          createTime = block.timestamp;
18          elaspeTime = 259200; //One month
19      }
20 ▾   function assetTransfer() public {
21          require(createTime+elaspeTime < block.timestamp);
22          require(msg.sender == heir);
23          msg.sender.transfer(assetValue);
24
25          emit Transfer(msg.sender, assetValue);
26      }
27
28 ▾   function extendTimeLock() public{
29          require(msg.sender == owner);
30          createTime = block.timestamp;
31
32          emit ExtendTimeLock(block.timestamp);
33      }
34  }
35
```

Figure 7.6   Ethereum cryptographic "will" based on time lock

The contract work in the following way:

i. The owner of the asset deploys the contract and sets the createTime and elaspeTime. *Elaspe time* is the locking time before which heirs cannot transfer the asset. Owner also defines the address of the heir. In Figure 7.6, owner had declared only one heir.

ii. If the *elaspe time* is over and owner has not reset the createTime, the heirs can claim the asset.

iii. If the owner is alive just before the elaspeTime, he immediately resets the createTime.

7.5.3 ERC20 AND ERC721 TOKENS

Ether is the inbuilt valuation that exists in the Ethereum Blockchain network. Ethereum has a function modifier, called *payable*, that indicates the function receives *Ether* while being called. Moreover, Ethereum defines the concept of *fallback* function call. *Fallback* function executes when the function identifier does not match any of the available functions in a smart contract or mismatch of argument. The function declared in the contract as below is a *fallback* function.

```
function() payable{ .... }
```

The *fallback* function is responsible for collecting the sent *Ether*, if the called function fils.

The tokens are not an integral part of Ethereum contract. They are simply a data item, but tokes define a standard set of interfaces to transfer tokes from one contract to other. Tokens are generally used to represent the valuation of some items different from *Ether*. In the cryptographic "will", we can represent assets in terms of token.

The ERC20 token has an inbuilt data structure. The first one is

```
mapping(address => uint256) balance
```

The data structure is used to track the balance of every entity (by his address). The second one is

```
mapping(address=> mapping(address=> unit256)) delegate
```

This data structure is used to delegate another entity to spent the token on behalf of the owner (see the approve and allowance functions). The mapping is from the owner to the delegated entity followed by the token amount.

The ERC721, on the other hand, defines another data structure as below.

```
mapping(uint256=> address) private deedOwner
```

The non-fungible tokens are having a *deedID*. As we have mentioned in the subsection 7.0.1 that the entity car may have a *deedID* as the VehicalNumber. To map the *deedID* to the ownership, the contract maintains the mapping *deedOwner*. As a use case, we take the example of case as described in subsection 7.0.1. We present a snippet of solidity to describe how to represent car as a non-fungible token. We also show the transfer of ownership using the transfer function of ERC721. Figure 7.7 is a contract named *Car*, that inherits the ERC721 token. The *constructor* initialises the vehicle with the _vehicalID and _owner. It also maps the vehicle ID to the owner's address. It is analogous to track the *Car* from the VehicleNumber.

```
1   pragma solidity ^0.8.7;
2
3 ▾ contract Car is ERC721 {
4       :
5       :
6     mapping(uint256 => address) deedOwner;
7     mapping(address => uint256) balance;
8
9 ▾   constructor(uint256 _vehicalID, address _owner){
10        deedOwner[_vehicalID] = _owner;
11        :
12        :
13    }
14 ▾   function transfer(address _to, uint256 _deedID) external payable{
15        address postOwner = deedOwner[_deedID];
16        deedOwner[_deedID] = _to;
17        balance[postOwner] += msg.value;
18        :
19        :
20    }
21    :
22   :|
23 }
```

Figure 7.7   A snippet of smart contract that implements the token car.

Now, consider the transfer of ownership. The transfer does the following.

- update the deedOwner mapping with the new entity's address (line#16 of Figure 7.7).
- Transfer the *Ether* to the previous owner's address (line#17 of Figure 7.7).

The contract *Car* may inherit the contract *willTimeLock* (presented in Figure 7.6) and overload the assetTransfer function as below.

```
function assetTransfer(address _to, uint256 _deedID)
external payble{
    :
    :
    msg.sender.transfer(_to, _deedID);
}
```

7.6   CONCLUSION

This chapter brings to light different pros and cons of cryptoasset inheritance. We started with the wallet security, the derivation of private keys, and their recovery. Following, we present the available services, either online or offline, to maintain safe custody of private keys. We find that the current solutions are unsatisfactory and undermine the basic properties of Blockchain philosophy. The solutions are either centralised or threshold trust models. Moving forward, we try to define the cryptographic "will", and the bequeath of cryptoassey. We find some existing solutions which are centralised. Finally, we propose some self-severing solutions, both on Bitcoin and Ethereum platforms.

Bibliography

1. Financial Services Agenc. Financial instruments and exchange act. `https://www.fsa.go.jp/en/policy/fiel/index.html`. Last accessed: September 2021.

2. Andreas M. Antonopoulos. *Mastering Bitcoin: Unlocking Digital Cryptocurrencies*. O'Reilly Media, Inc., second edition, 2017.

3. Andreas M Antonopoulos and Gavin Wood. *Mastering Ethereum : Building Smart Contracts and DApps*. O'Reilly Media, Inc., 2018.

4. Casa. Comprehensive bitcoin inheritance. `https://keys.casa/bitcoin-inheritance-plan`. Last accessed: September 2021.

5. Coincover. The safety standard for crypto. `https://www.coincover.com/`. Last accessed: September 2021.

6. FinCEN. United states department of the treasury financial crimes enforcement network. `https://www.fincen.gov/resources/statutes-regulations/fincens-mandate-congress`. Last accessed: September 2021.

7. United Kingdom Government. Financial conduct authority. `https://www.fca.org.uk/`. Last accessed: September 2021.

8. UAE Governtment. Emirates blockchain strategy 2021. `https://u.ae/en/about-the-uae/strategies-initiatives-and-awards/federal-governments-strategies-and-plans/emirates-blockchain-strategy-2021`. Last accessed: September 2021.

9. New Delhi India Today. Cryptocurrency firm ceo dies in jaipur, rs 1,000 crore may vanish from face of earth. `https://www.indiatoday.in/business/story/quadrigacx-ceo-gerald-william-cotten-canada-cryptocurrency-wallets-missing-passwords-1449538-2019-02-06`, February 6 2019. Last accessed: September 2021.

10. Cremation Institute. Cryptocurrency estate planning 2021 study. `https://cremationinstitute.com/crypto-estate-planning-study/`. Last accessed: September 2021.

11. Manavi Kapur. India's supreme court lifts ban on banks facilitating cryptocurrency trade. `https://qz.com/india/1812540/top-indian-court-lifts-ban-on-banks-dealing-with-cryptocurrency/`, March 4 2020. Last accessed: September 2021.

12. Digifinance Pte. Ltd. Trustverse digifinance. `https://www.trustverse.io/`. Last accessed: September 2021.

13. Ritesh Modi. *Solidity Programming Essentials: A Beginner's Guide to Build Smart Contracts for Ethereum and Blockchain.* Packt Publishing, 2018.

14. United States of America. United states department of the treasury financial crimes enforcement network. `https://www.fincen.gov/`. Last accessed: September 2021.

15. Government of Canada. Financial transactions and reports analysis centre of canada. `https://www.fintrac-canafe.gc.ca/intro-eng`. Last accessed: September 2021.

16. Joseph Poon and Thaddeus Dryja. The bitcoin lightning network: Scalable off-chain instant payments. `https://github.com/lightningnetwork/paper/blob/master/paper.tex`, May, 5 2017. Last accessed: September 2021.

17. Sanya Jain, NDTV. Man accidentally throws away hard drive with bitcoin worth $280 million. `https://www.ndtv.com/offbeat/british-man-james-howells-accidentally-throws-away-hard-drive-with-bitcoin-worth-280-million-2354148`, January 18 2021. Last accessed: September 2021.

18. Jurgen Schouppe. Methods and systems for cryptographic private key management for secure multiparty storage and transfer of information, May 21 2018. Patent No: EP3654578A1, European Patent Office.

19. Adi Shamir. How to share a secret. *Communications of the ACM*, 22(11):612–613, 1979.

20. Arnav Vohra. Coinsafe never lose your bitcoins ever! `https://medium.com/coinsafeapp`, May 2019. Last accessed: September 2021.

21. Lawrence C. Washington. *Elliptic Curves: Number Theory and Cryptography.* Chapman & Hall/CRC, second edition edition, 2008.

8 Blockchain in Healthcare

Healthcare sector has witnessed a lot of changes in the last decade. With the applications of various modern technologies in the fields of information technology, communication engineering, and bio-electronics, the overall healthcare service sector has upgraded itself to provide better level of services. Healthcare infrastructure is one backbone of any country. Lack of proper healthcare infrastructure denies many citizen affordable and proper medical treatment. In some developed countries, the healthcare service is entirely provided by government. But in most of the developing and under-developed countries, government hospitals as well as private hospitals cater the medical treatments to it's people. For any medical service provider (MSP), effective treatment not only depends on doctors alone, but also on better coordination of different sections such as clinical diagnostic section, pharmacy section, record section, billing section, etc. Sometimes, a patient or medical user (MU) suffers from multiple diseases. So, intra-MSP coordination between different units is required. Again, a MU may have undergone medical treatment in one MSP and presently undergoing medical treatment in a different MSP. So, inter MSP coordination is very vital for exchange of MU medical records. Now, different MSPs may not trust each other. Therefore, when it comes to sharing records and reports among different mutually non-trusted MSPs, use of blockchain technology helps out to overcome the issues that exist among different non-trusted entities. Similarly, a medical insurance company (MIC) may not trust a MSP regarding billing of MU who is admitted in the hospital. This is also a very good scenario where use of blockchain resolves issues that arise between non-trusted entities. Basically, with the emergence of body area network (BAN) and Internet of Things (IoT) in the arena of automated healthcare service, the amalgamation of different recent technologies such as Cloud, IoT, and blockchain makes the area of e-healthcare very prominent interdisciplinary research topic. In this chapter, we discuss the adoption of blockchain in different areas of healthcare. The organisation of this chapter is as follows. The next section discusses the evolution of healthcare industry from Healthcare 1.0 to Healthcare 4.0. Next, an introduction to blockchain has been given. Thereafter, application of blockchain in maintaining the healthcare records, medical insurance, health status monitoring, clinical research, automated contact tracing, and automated responses to medical emergency have been discussed in the subsequent chapters.

8.1 HEALTHCARE INDUSTRY 4.0

From the introduction of automated electronic healthcare diagnostic instruments during the 1970s, the emergence of Healthcare 1.0 was observed. During this period, healthcare systems uses were specific. Healthcare systems were not coordinating with other kind of digital systems. In this era, mostly paper-based or typed medical treatment prescriptions and medical reports were in use.

DOI: 10.1201/9781003355052-8

The Healthcare 2.0 era started around beginning of 1990s and continued till the middle of first decade of present millennium. During this period, information technology (IT) was combined with healthcare to provide next level of healthcare systems. In this period, many newer concepts like microcontroller-based medical instruments, digital tracking, Internet, tele-medicine emerged. With the advent of Internet, social media began to very important role in creating online communities for sharing healthcare information and personal experiences and views. Healthcare systems networked with electronic health management enabled doctors to have secured access to patient health record on time. However, experts also raised the issues of privacy and security in different aspects of Internet-enabled healthcare provisions.

Arrival of Healthcare 3.0 enabled customised access or retrieval of healthcare data. Concept of Electronic Healthcare Records (EHRs) were introduced. Electronic sensor became available in the market for use in healthcare. Wearable and implanted sensors made real-time and ubiquitous tracking of MU a reality.

Healthcare 4.0 era started from the middle of second decade of current millennium. This period is closely associated with the advent of Industry 4.0. Several pathbreaking technologies such as cloud, artificial intelligence (AI), machine learning (ML), big data, and blockchain have started to revolutionise healthcare. This amalgamation of different technologies with healthcare paved the ground for smart healthcare [15]. The major objective of this age is to provide real-time and patient-centric healthcare services.

In this age of Healthcare 4.0 age, MSPs are using more and more smart technology based applications. Such applications help a lot in proper diagnosis, treatment and management of MU illnesses, and help in better management of electronic health record (EHR) of MU. Records are often found to be stored in duplicate, mismatched in format, made available on different health networks. The correctness of EHR data is very crucial. Any significant error in EHR data may affect adversely the success of the MSP which is using this erroneous EHR data. So, the EHR data must be free of errors and security vulnerability and be tamper proof. The security of EHR is becoming very important. If unauthorised persons or hackers get access to MU data, privacy of MU gets compromised.

8.2 BLOCKCHAIN

Concept of digital cryptocurrency was introduced by anonymous researcher(s) Satoshi Nakamoto in [9] in 2008. In this report, blockchain was introduced and proposed as the underlying technology behind the bitcoin cryptocurrency. Bitcoin is free from many of the disadvantages that exist in traditional centralised banking system. Apart from bitcoin, numerous other crypto currencies are in circulation today. Few prominent example of such currencies are Etherium, Litecoin, Peercoin, Teether, Syscoin, etc. Now, the use of blockchain is not confined to cryptocurrencies alone. This technology has been found to be immensely useful in diverse field of applications. The reason of such wide application of blockchain is due to it's peer to peer (P2P) distributed nature, tamper-proof feature, resiliency against system failure.

As a result, blockchain is being considered as a breakthrough technology that has potential to bring huge benefits to wide range of industries.

What is there inside a blockchain? As the name suggests, blockchain is a chain of blocks. Every block contains data or certain number of transactions and some metadata as block header. The metadata includes message digest of previous block produced by using cryptographic hash functions [10], a time stamp, nonce value. Every node keeps a copy of node that gets added in the blockchain network. We can say that, a blockchain is a linked chain of blocks. First block of a blockchain is known as genesis block. The linked chain of blocks is shown in the Figure 8.1.

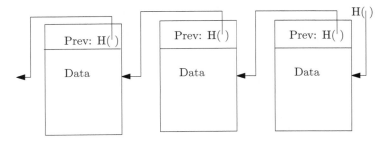

Figure 8.1 Blockchain as linked chain of blocks

Every block records and preserves transactions from specific time period. These transactions are maintained as a binary tree data structure with hash pointers. This kind of binary tree is known as Merkle tree. Merkle tree root is pointed by the block data field. The Figure8.2 shows a Merkle tree.

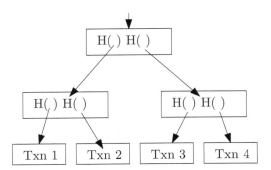

Figure 8.2 Merkle tree

However, one drawback of blockchain is that it is massive computation and storage intensive. Every node needs to store every block, and often the time to add a new block into the blockchain is in the order of several minutes.

8.2.1   CONSESNUS

Any recorded transaction in blocks of blockchain are verifiable, immutable, and permanent. Whenever a new block is to be appended in a blockchain, majority of nodes, that is, more than 50% of nodes must reach in a consensus to add this block. This consensus building is achieved in the distributed P2P blockchain network by using a consensus algorithm. Use of consensus algorithm to add new nodes is a salient feature of blockchain network. There are quite a few consensus algorithms such as practical byzantine fault tolerance (PBFT) algorithm, proof-of-work (PoW), proof-of-stake (PoS), and delegated PoS, etc. The PoW consesnus algorithm is used to secure the transactions from malicious tampering, where a node gives proof of work by solving a computational intensive hash puzzle. Note that there is no centralised server to verify authenticity, integrity, and correctness of transactions. The resourceful nodes in P2P network take this responsibility in the absence of centralised server. This process is called mining. Miner nodes possess significant computational resources. Whenever there is a request to add a block, several miners attempt to solve the computational puzzle such as a hash puzzle. The miner who wins in solving the hash puzzle, broadcasts the block gets the valid block appended into the blockchain receives a reward for it's computation efforts on behalf of the whole network. Blockchain security stems from this proof of work concept. It is necessary that majority of the miners are honest in the blockchain network. In general, any arbitrary node can not be authenticated to join a blockchain network and run consensus algorithm.

As per the access control mechanism of unserlying blockchain network, a node may / may not join into the blockchain network. A blockchain platform is classified as permissionless (public blockchain) or as permissioned (private blockchain and consortium blockchain).

Example of public blockchain is Ethereum. Public blockchain suffers from considerable amount of time for blockchain operations. IBM has released Hyperledger Fabric platform that hosts and promotes many blockchain based applications. Private blockchain such as Hyperledger is free from some disadvantages of public blockchain.

8.2.2   SMART CONTRACT

The Blockchain proposed by Satoshi Nakamoto was smart ledgers meant for recording only the financial transactions. Later on, concept of smart contract was introduced in blockchain. Smart contracts are executed to perform many desirable functions. A smart contract can access any internal data structure in blocks. However, a tweak known as cryptlet permits blockchain to access external data structure securely.

The idea of a smart contract is not a new concept that has been used in blockchain. But it is only with the blockchain technology, in particular, the Ethereum that smart contracts are now unleashing its full potential.

Bitcoin has the provision for execution a script which has very limited and specific functionality. However, Ethereum supports encoding of wide range of scripts or rules to process transactions. These scripts are called smart contracts. A smart contract is triggered or executed only when some pre-specified conditions are satisfied. In fact, a smart contract is capable of encoding any given set of conditions. For example, a smart contract execution can enable a fund transfer when certain event happens such as insurance policy matures. Smart contracts are being used in different types of applications, such as banking, insurance, education, healthcare, etc. Smart contracts are written using programming languages such as Solidity. In fact, the provision of writing smart contracts according to the need of application and the immutatble, tamper-free distributed nature of blockchain, are the main reason behind the wide use of blockchain in different types applications.

Like a block, a smart contract also has an address. A smart contract is executed when a transaction is sent to it's address. When a blockchain accepts a transaction with a smart contract's address as recipient, then every miner execute the smart contract. With this, we conclude the section on blockchain introductory concept, and move on to the applications of blockchain in different sectors of healthcare in subsequent chapters.

8.3 HEALTHCARE RECORD MANAGEMENT

Blockchain has a great potential in resolving the interoperability issues that exist in the current healthcare systems. Te greatest problem faced by traditional healthcare system is incompatibility of data format of patient health data or electronic health record (EHR). This causes hindrances in sharing EHR data of same MU when MU visits from one MSP to another. This is shown in Figure 8.3. This can be used as

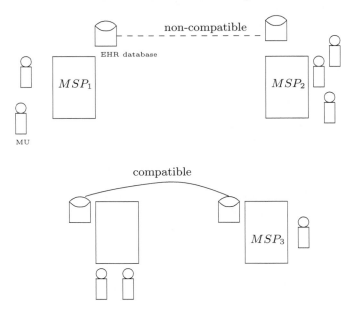

Figure 8.3 Incompatible EHR format in different MSPs

a standard that permits the different stakeholders such as doctors, other healthcare personnel, researchers, etc to share EHR in a secure way. Sharing of EHR in a seamless way allows to improve the healthcare service quality. In this section, we briefly describe few existing works that use blockchain to manage EHRs.

[2] proposed a EHR management system, MedRec. It is a decentralised EHR management system that uses blockchain. This system provides MU tamper-proof log and easy retrieval of her PHI information stored across multiple MSPs. Leveraging unique properties of blockchain, it manages data sharing, confidentiality, authentication, and accountability which are very crucial when sensitive information like PHI is dealt with. This scheme provides incentives to different stakeholders of healthcare such as researchers, public health officials for taking the responsibility of miners. As a result, miners get access to aggregated and anonymised data as rewards. However, it engages MUs and MSPs to decide on their choice in releasing PHI metadata.

MUs leave data scattered across various MSP sites as different medical treatments are done across multiple MSPs in the course of life. As a result, MU lose easy access to her own past PHI and other EHR data, as the MSP retains primary stewardship of MU's EHR and PHI data during her medical treatment under that particular MSP. Interoperability of EHRs is a challenging issue and it creates additional difficulties to effective data sharing among MSPs. To navigate the large amount of EHRs, this system structures them on blockchain by using three kinds of contracts: summary contract, patient-provider relationship contract, and registrar contract.

[1] proposed a blockchain-supported PHI exchange with an underlying mechanism to monitor and enforce policies attached to MU data. MUs in the system define polices during registration time that determine functions that are allowed on their PHI data. The policies are enforced in terms of smart contracts and controls the access of PHI data or metadata.

[16] proposed a system for efficient storage and maintenance of EHRs using blockchain. It provides efficient and secure access of EHR to MUs, MSPs, and any other third party and at the same time preserves MU's privacy. This is very suitable for adoption in the healthcare 4.0 era where the MU is given the ownership and supreme control over her EHR. MU can monitor any access to her EHR transactions that are taking place. This framework has four major parts: blockchain, patient node, provider network, and voter node. Patient node is the end-user node where the EHRs are created. Provider network hosts the health record database. Voter node helps in validating the nodes that are added and verifying integrity of transactions that are taking place over the network. Example of vital tasks that are performed on the blockchain are addition of a block, addition of a MU, grant/change/revoke access permission, addition/retrieve/transfer EHR.

[15] studied some limitations of healthcare systems and proposed solutions using blockchain. It proposed an improved access control policy for smooth data access among MSPs. The EHR sharing system has four different kind of participants: MU, administrator, doctors, and paramedical staffs. For each kind of participants, a separate algorithm in terms of smart contract is used.

[3] proposed a storage scheme to manage personal EHR based on blockchain and cloud. It has also proposed a service framework for sharing EHRs.

Now, we summarise all these works on EHR management using blockchain as follows. EHR is very private to MU. To grant different levels of accesses to the MU's EHR stored across multiple sites, MU defines the access policy for herself and other different category of stakeholders in terms of blockchain smart contracts.

8.4 MEDICAL INSURANCE

Medical insurance is an integrated part of modern healthcare services. In countries like United States, it's very difficult for common citizen to afford medical treatment bill if they are not covered under any medical insurance scheme. In countries like India, some state governments tie up with insurance companies to provide minimum healthcare insurance cover which is sufficient for most of the cases. Now, when a MU is under insurance cover, its very natural to undergo medical treatment without payment of any cash. But, that is not what happens often. The MU needs to pay fully or partially to the MSP billing section and insurance company reimburses later on. This occurs due to lengthy and manual process of verifying the insurance claim and examining the billing and then releasing the amount. This traditional process of insurance claim and release of claimed amount is depicted in the sequence diagram shown in Figure 8.4. This lengthy and manual process of insurance claim,

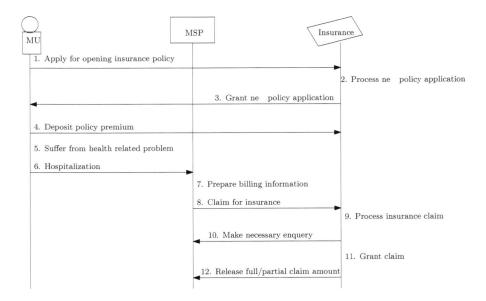

Figure 8.4 Sequence diagram of traditional medical insurance policy and claim

examination, and release amount can be automated to make it very fast and hassle free process using blockchain. In this section, we mention few such existing solutions.

The insurance sector begun to explore the application of blockchain technology for improving its services and in 2016, the first blockchain-based insurance consortium, B3i has come into existence. [6] outlined a blockchain based scheme where smart contracts have been used to speed up the claim processing and reduce the manual processing of claims or settlement costs. The smart contract encodes the complex rules to enable automatic fund transfer from insurance company to the MU or from the insurance company to the MSP directly.

[19] proposed a blockchain-based storage scheme for medical insurance . Here, the stakeholders are MSP, MU, insurance company and n number of servers. The MSP executes a (k, n)-threshold protocol among all servers. Any blockchain node can join into the protocol to become a server if other nodes and the MSP permits so. MU's clinical expenditure data is maintained by the MSP in blockchain and is secured by n servers. Any k servers can help the insurance company to get a sum of patient's spending data by using homomorphic computations by following [7]. However, any server remains unaware of the MU spending data, stored in the blockchain, as long as the number of honest servers is $> n - k$.

[13] discussed design of an efficient transaction processing of general insurance on a blockchain-based platform. This scheme can be extended to cover the healthcare insurance use case also.

We now summarise the application of blockchain medical insurance. The process of releasing medical insurance is often very complex one and needs rigorous verification of documents. This complex and rigorous document verification involving mutually non-trusting entities are automated by the use of blockchain where the smart contracts ensure the automatic fund transfer/release from insurance company to MU/MSP when all the conditions are met.

8.5 HEALTH STATUS MONITORING BY BAN AND IOT

Different types of sensors are being used used in medical frontiers. These sensors can be categorised into three types: physiological sensors, bio-kinetic sensors, and ambient sensors. Sensors that measure blood glucose, blood pressure, oxygen level in blood, body temperature, etc. are examples of physiological sensors. Bio-kinetic sensors track and measure movements human body or parts of it in terms of acceleration and angular rotation during motion or movement. Ambient sensors are not directly used by MU but they are used to measure the surrounding environmental parameters such as temperature, light, humidity, etc. Table 8.1 summarises a list of different types of sensors available commercially.

Over the last two decades, several bio-sensors have been developed. These bio-sensors make a kind of network in a human body, called body area network (BAN). A sink node or gateway node is used by the human to accumulate the physiological readings by sensors. A hand-held device such as smart phone which acts as sink node and forwards these PHI readings to servers in MSPs for analysis. However, MSPs

Table 8.1

Common Bio-sensors

Sensor	Description of Sensor Measurement
Accelerometer sensor	Acceleration due to user movement
Blood pressure sensor	Systolic and diastolic blood pressures
CO_2 sensor	CO_2 content in blood
ECG sensor	Heart's electrical signal
EEG sensor	Brain's electrical signal
EMG sensor	Muscle's electrical activity
Glucometer	Blood sugar
Heart rate sensor	Heart contraction count (per minute)
Humidity sensor	Humidity in surrounding environment
Oximeter	Oxygen saturated hemoglobin
Pedometer	Step count of user in motion
Respiration rate sensor	Chest rise count (per minute)
Spirometer	Respiratory flow rate
Thermometer	Body temperature

may not have adequate infrastructure for continuous PHI data analysis. Cloud is an alternative for this continuous physiological condition monitoring without a fail. [11] has discussed a cloud-enabled body area network. Blockchain infrastructure can also be used for storing this PHI data similar to the EHR. However, it would put heavy burden to store continuous PHI data in blockchain. But the appropriate filtering can be used which only keeps the important PHI feature data in blockchain instead of keeping the continuous PHI data.

IoT is the network of wearable devices with sensors, actuators, software, and Internet that allows the sensors and actuators to be connected and to exchange data. Wearable devices collect MU's PHI data and transfer it to MSPs for continuous health monitoring, exact diagnosis of disease, and subsequent treatment through actuators up to a certain extent till a full fledged treatment is provided by MSP. However, direct adoption of blockchain with IoT is not very much viable as use of blockchain implies high computational power for solving PoW, and prolonged latency for confirming transaction in blockchain.

[5] proposed a framework that adopts blockchain for IoT. This scheme reduces high computing power of a node associated with blockchain by eliminating the use of PoW to make it preferable for IoT. This scheme preserves anonymity and authenticity of the MU. To support anonymous transactions, it uses a lightweight ring signature scheme. It uses double signature. First, a lightweight digital signature used to make PHI tamper-proof. Second, a signer uses ring signature to sign anonymously. It first encrypts the PHI data using symmetric encryption. Then it encrypts the key using public key encryption. The PHI data is sent to a smart devices to format and aggregate

data. Thereafter, the aggregated PHI is forwarded to the relevant smart contract for complete analysis. When the PHI data is not normal, then smart contract execution triggers an alert to the MU.

So, the resource constrained BAN and IoT can use tailored blockchain network where some computation intensive consensus and mining process is simplified to monitor the continuous health status of PHI and whenever abnormality is found in PHI data, an alarm is sent to MU and other appropriate entities.

8.6   CLINICAL RESEARCH

Clinical research is a very important area of healthcare involving developing and release of new medicines and vaccines. It examines the safety and effectiveness of medicines and vaccines. The ecosystem of clinical research includes a complex network of application sites, multiple pharmaceutical and research organisations. The normal course of actions to study clinical data trails methodically is a prolonged process. To make it faster, it is necessary to automate different operational factors including data processing of clinical trial. Clinical trials of new drug formulas are generally classified into four phases. This process continues through all four phases over several years. Use of technology helps a lot in reducing this lengthy clinical trial. This need is more easily explained when we see the processes adopted during the discovery of Covid-19 vaccines and it's clinical trial. Blockchain can play a significant role in clinical research. Clinical trials need large number of MU's data. A meta analysis is performed during last phases of clinical trial. It requires that MUs give their consent to share their EHR for clinical research. Now, it is very much essential to preserve privacy of these MUs who are volunteering for clinical trial. If proper care is not adopted, the cases lack of transparency, unavailability of data traceability, difficulty of accessing clinical data and results real time, and a risk of malicious data tampering are not uncommon. [14] proposed a scheme for such trust-leveraging effort by using the blockchain which results in better transparency. An MU can use the IoT infrastructure to store her own EHR data in blockchain network. and facilitate the secure clinical information that paves the way to build a large EHR repository of correct and complete clinical data.

[17] has used data from a successfully accomplished clinical trial and simulated the clinical trial. It also examined its resiliency against data tampering. It assessed the prospects of furnishing traceable audit trail of trial data to regulatory boards. This study has advocated that use of blockchain offers an improved data management of clinical trial, bolsters trust in clinical research eco system, and facilitates supervision of clinical trial by regulatory boards.

[4] has stressed that the expenditure of carrying out clinical trials over multiple sites has increased many fold over the period. In general, data management practices of clinical trial depends on centralised database. This work has proposed a framework for clinical trial spanning over multiple sites using permissioned blockchain to reduce the administrative cost, effort and time that ensures data privacy and integrity. It has used Hyperledger Fabric to utilise its unique features like private channel, private network and smart contract. Smart contract can verify specific criteria before

entering MU data into the system. Smart contracts are also used to record and keep track of any adverse effect of medicines or vaccines on MU.

So, clinical trial management which is very time taking process spanning over multiple years involves a very complex eco system. The effective data processing and management of clinical trial can be fastened using blockchain.

8.7 CONTACT TRACING

Contact tracing is an important step in curbing spread of viruses that has potential to cause an epidemic or even pandemic such as Covid-19. Governments are finding it very difficult to stop the fast-pace spread of pandemic. When a MU is detected to be infected with virus such as Novel coronavirus, the task of correctly identifying all the persons who have come in contact with the MU in previous fortnight is a hilarious task. Identifying these contact persons manually is a very challenging job and often produces incomplete result. Some governments have applied digital technology for contact tracing of its citizens. But this approach is easily prone to compromising privacy of citizens.

[12] has proposed an architecture of blockchain based solution for recording each transaction in a secure manner for contact tracing of novel coronavirus. It records the communications between MUs who are equipped with cloud-enabled BAN and maintains privacy of MUs. Whenever a MU is found to be Covid-19 positive, the concerned officials immediately finds only those blockchain transaction records corresponding to the infected MU for identifying contact tracings. Further, can also check if a contact person is already having any known symptoms of Covid-19 such as high fever or breathing problem which is also detected automatically by this system.

[18] has discussed a blockchain based privacy-preserving contact tracing scheme. It preserves the identity and location of users. It adopted blockchain to link the MU and authorised solvers to decouple MU's identity and location. Moreover, it combines blockchain, encryption and anonymisation to protect identity of MU. Also, use of blockchain paves the way for global contact tracing, not limited to boundary of a country.

In essence, contact tracing, which is very important to restrict spreading of infectious epidemics, can be done automatically and without compromising the identity of MU's using blockchain.

8.8 MEDICAL EMERGENCY

Medical emergency is an important event in any healthcare management facility. Medical emergency demand special care and a prompt service and proper medical treatment is necessary for timely cure of the MU. However, a single lapse in monitoring or treatment may lead the MU in medical emergency to succumb to death. There is a direct relationship between number of death of emergency patients and the inability to timely access EHR data of patient in medical emergency and the time taken to hospitalise the patient. The timely access to the MU's EHR data and current PHI data can help the paramedics and doctors to start diagnosing the status of MU and the next course of treatment to be started immediately. [8] introduced a blockchain-based solution for recording MU's emergency relevant EHR data as MU moves from one MSP to a different MSP, maintaining continuous in-transit footprints of MU. Thereafter, the ambulance crews can access and urgent prescription from the doctors and can start the quality pre-MSP care. In a medical emergency, previous knowledge of MU's EHR can certainly create a difference, particularly when MU is in very critical condition. It adopts blockchain as a viable solution for data management during medical emergency. It uses file transfer tool based on File Transfer Protocol Secure based and Hyperledger Fabric to provide a secure and complete view of medical emergency data on the blockchain ledger. When an MU moves from one MSP to another, her PHI gets recorded into a chain of blocks, that gives consistent report on the present health condition of MU.

So far, different blockchain based solutions for e-healthcare systems have been discussed. The distributed P2P nature of blockchain along with it's immutable and tamper proof ledger is creating foundations for many innovative applications in different sectors including healthcare. However, major concern is that blockchain demands huge computation and storage overhead in every node. However, the smart healthcare involves many components such as IoT which do not support such heavy computational and storage resources. Tuning the blockchain feature according to the underlying network's computing and storage resources is a major challenge that lies ahead. One very important open and innovative research area is to use intelligent smart contracts where smart contract codes use machine learning algorithms for different applications such as automatic diagnosis of some diseases. Also, there is a need to give thoughts on scope of discarding blocks selectively which will no longer be required by the host applications. Another important issue is that researchers should not blindly attempt to use blockchain technology unnecessarily for any use cases involving healthcare.

8.9 CONCLUSION

In this chapter, we have introduced the blockchain technology and it's application in various fields of healthcare services. With the emergence of Healthcare 4.0 along with Industry 4.0, innovative applications of latest computing technology are paving the way for smart healthcare without compromising the privacy of user while maintaining security of EHR data. Blockchain is a path-breaking technology that has capability to revolutionise working of different industries such as banking, insurance, pharmaceutical and healthcare. We have discussed various existing works that uses blockchain to solve different drawbacks of traditional centralised healthcare services and it's allied industries. We have mentioned important works in the field of EHR management, settling medical insurances, health status monitoring using BAN and IoT, managing clinical trials, smart contact tracing in the context of pandemic situation, and medical emergency management - all using blockchain based solutions. This chapter would serve as a brief and compact state of art in the field of healthcare solutions using blockchain technology for the researchers who are making foray into this area. With the amalgamation of cloud, IoT and the lightweight blockchain technology, the society is going to witness more innovative solutions, in near future, to some problems that healthcare industry is trying to find out.

Bibliography

1. Sandro Amofa, Emmanuel Boateng Sifah, O-B Kwame, Smahi Abla, Qi Xia, James C Gee, and Jianbin Gao. A blockchain-based architecture framework for secure sharing of personal health data. In *2018 IEEE 20th International Conference on e-Health Networking, Applications and Services (Healthcom)*, pages 1–6. IEEE, 2018.

2. Asaph Azaria, Ariel Ekblaw, Thiago Vieira, and Andrew Lippman. Medrec: Using blockchain for medical data access and permission management. In *2016 2nd International Conference on Open and Big Data (OBD)*, pages 25–30. IEEE, 2016.

3. Yi Chen, Shuai Ding, Zheng Xu, Handong Zheng, and Shanlin Yang. Blockchain-based medical records secure storage and medical service framework. *Journal of medical systems*, 43(1):1–9, 2019.

4. Olivia Choudhury, Noor Fairoza, Issa Sylla, and Amar Das. A blockchain framework for managing and monitoring data in multi-site clinical trials. *arXiv preprint arXiv:1902.03975*, 2019.

5. Ashutosh Dhar Dwivedi, Gautam Srivastava, Shalini Dhar, and Rajani Singh. A decentralized privacy-preserving healthcare blockchain for iot. *Sensors*, 19(2):326, 2019.

6. Valentina Gatteschi, Fabrizio Lamberti, Claudio Demartini, Chiara Pranteda, and Victor Santamaria. Blockchain and smart contracts for insurance: Is the technology mature enough? *Future Internet*, 10(2):20, 2018.

7. Craig Gentry et al. *A fully homomorphic encryption scheme*, volume 20. Stanford Uuniversity, 2009.

8. Shirin Hasavari and Yeong Tae Song. A secure and scalable data source for emergency medical care using blockchain technology. In *2019 IEEE 17th International Conference on Software Engineering Research, Management and Applications (SERA)*, pages 71–75. IEEE, 2019.

9. Satoshi Nakamoto et al. Bitcoin: A peer-to-peer electronic cash system. 2008.

10. Anupam Pattanayak. Revisiting dedicated and block cipher based hash functions. *IACR Cryptology ePrint Archive*, 2012:322, 2012.

11. Anupam Pattanayak and Subhasish Dhal. Cloud enabled body area network. In *Cloud Network Management*, pages 67–85. Chapman and Hall/CRC, 2020.

12. Anupam Pattanayak, Subhasish Dhal, and Sourav Kanti Addya. Automatic privacy-preserving contact tracing of novel coronavirus infection by cloud-enabled wban using blockchain, IACR cryptology eprint archive, no. 1479, 2020.

13. Mayank Raikwar, Subhra Mazumdar, Sushmita Ruj, Sourav Sen Gupta, Anupam Chattopadhyay, and Kwok-Yan Lam. A blockchain framework for insurance processes. In *2018 9th IFIP International Conference on New Technologies, Mobility and Security (NTMS)*, pages 1–4. IEEE, 2018.

14. Partha Pratim Ray, Dinesh Dash, Khaled Salah, and Neeraj Kumar. Blockchain for iot-based healthcare: background, consensus, platforms, and use cases. *IEEE Systems Journal*, 15(1):85–94, 2020.

15. Sudeep Tanwar, Karan Parekh, and Richard Evans. Blockchain-based electronic healthcare record system for healthcare 4.0 applications. *Journal of Information Security and Applications*, 50:102407, 2020.

16. Jayneel Vora, Anand Nayyar, Sudeep Tanwar, Sudhanshu Tyagi, Neeraj Kumar, Mohammad S Obaidat, and Joel JPC Rodrigues. Bheem: A blockchain-based framework for securing electronic health records. In *2018 IEEE Globecom Workshops (GC Wkshps)*, pages 1–6. IEEE, 2018.

17. Daniel R Wong, Sanchita Bhattacharya, and Atul J Butte. Prototype of running clinical trials in an untrustworthy environment using blockchain. *Nature communications*, 10(1):1–8, 2019.

18. Hao Xu, Lei Zhang, Oluwakayode Onireti, Yang Fang, William J Buchanan, and Muhammad Ali Imran. Beeptrace: blockchain-enabled privacy-preserving contact tracing for covid-19 pandemic and beyond. *IEEE Internet of Things Journal*, 8(5):3915–3929, 2020.

19. Lijing Zhou, Licheng Wang, and Yiru Sun. Mistore: a blockchain-based medical insurance storage system. *Journal of medical systems*, 42(8):1–17, 2018.

9 Blockchain Privacy and Its Security Challenges

Software systems can be of two types, i) Centralised Software System and ii) Decentralised Software System.In Centralised, all nodes are distributed and linked to a single node of coordination [7]. Decentralised refers to the connection of several nodes without the need for a central node for coordination. Figure 9.1 below shows the Centralised and Decentralised Software System.

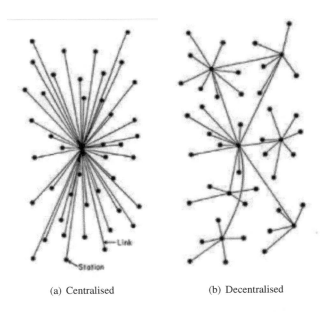

(a) Centralised   (b) Decentralised

Figure 9.1   Centralised Software System [49], and Decentralised Software System [49]

Blockchain is a distributed/Decentralised software system. It is a "purely peer-to-peer"(P2P) system that is comprised of independent nodes of the network [7]. Blockchain technology is popular due to its decentralisation, P2P transaction, and blockchain's immutability [18]. It can be referred to as a publicly available "digital-ledger" [18] (data structure) that has full real-time access. It is applied for storing data or transactions on a trusted platform and has no intervention from a third party. The idea of blockchain is based on Santoshi Nakamoto which is described in 2008 [1, 47]. The bitcoin-cryptocurrency is the first blockchain application. [22] Bitcoin is a digital currency that is built upon blockchain technologies and used for trading items on the internet [22], similar to money which people use in today's world. Because of the

DOI: 10.1201/9781003355052-9   **193** successful outcomes in Bitcoin, now people could use blockchain technologies in every field, which includes the finance, government, powergrid supply-chain, storage, IoT, e-voting, and healthcare [25], etc. Because we all utilise these products and services on a daily basis, cybercriminals have opportunities to commit cybercrime [2, 3]. 51% of the attacks are mostly a security issue in Bitcoin, cryptocurrency. In this, using the same technology bases, the attacker tries to control the system's mechanism. An extensive survey has been taken out up to 2021. This research paper mainly discuss the applications and working of the Blockchain, apart from this, it also explains the issues which are related to the implementation of the blockchain in different-different technology.

In Table 9.1, numerous surveys have been conducted through research papers published in recent years, and it will illustrate the survey results as well as the work done on blockchain technology till now. To begin this, research papers were collected from a variety of sources, which includes ScienceDirect, IEEE EXplore, Springer, and Google Scholar, and these survey papers were reviewed and evaluated to learn more about the contributions made by researchers in a particular year.

This research-based paper is mainly based on the following topics: Section 2 present the overview of the blockchain which includes the blockchain's concept, working, structure, types, and its advantages. Section 3 briefly state the uses of blockchain technologies in various domain. Section 4 provides detailed information about blockchain technology's security and privacy issues. And at the last, Section 5 summarises and concludes this paper.

9.1   OVERVIEW

9.1.1   THE CONCEPT OF BLOCKCHAIN

It contains cryptography mechanisms, algorithms, model which combines P2P networks and uses consensus an algorithm, for solving all the traditional methods of distributed database synchronise problem, which is also known as a "multi-field infrastructure construction" [1, 12, 13].

This technology has the following properties:

Decentralised: Blockchain eliminates the use of any centralised node, Apart from that, all the data can be recorded, updated, and stored distributively.

Transparent: Whatever the data is recorded by the blockchain systems, these data is transparent to each node, and blockchain systems also help to have a transparent on updating data, because of these reasons the blockchain the technology could be trusted.

Open Souce: Many technologies of blockchain are open for all, which means that all records are visible to the public [38], and anyone may utilize blockchain networks for creating the new technologies in the market whenever required [25].

Autonomy: As the foundation for consensus, any node on this system may communicate and update information in a secure manner [25].

Immutable: This refers to all the data records that will be reserved for the future. It cannot be changed, until and unless one could take control equal to or more than 51% nodes at a particular time.

Table 9.1

Comparison Based on a Survey of Blockchain Technology

Year	Survey Papers	Remarks
2016	Macro Conoscen [4]	This addresses the effect in integrity and adaptability.
2016	Zbin Zang [5]	The application field for a blockchain-related consensus system was addressed
2017	BayuAdhi Tama [7]	Applications of Blockchain technology were reviewed.
2017	Lakshmi SivaShankar [8]	A survey was conducted on several consensus algorithms as well as reviewed their efficiency and feasibility.
2017	Xiaoqi Li [9]	A security study was conducted, and the real threat linked to the blockchain was discovered.
2017	Iuon-Chang Lin [10]	Security issues and different challenges are addressed.
2017	Madrita Banerjee [6]	Addresses how blockchain might aid in the secure transaction of the IoT dataset & identified 9 potential challenges
2018	Yaga D [16]	From a technological standpoint, blockchain advancements were examined..
2019	Ali MS [17]	The use of Blockchain in IoT was the subject of a thorough investigation
2020	Yassine Issaouni [29]	This paper discusses the trends as well as applications of Blockchain in a nutshell.
2021	Mohd Javaid [32]	There was a discussion about how blockchain technology is helpful to the industry.
2021	Anup Kumar Paul [31]	There was a discussion about the benefits and problems of using Blockchain with IoT
2021	Proposed Work	Researched all applications and their issues in a particular domain, what are the services it offers

Anonymity: Blockchain technologies, remove all the trust issues related between all the nodes so that all the transactions can be done anonymously, we are only required to know the blockchain address of the person. Below (Figure 9.2) shows the blockchain's technology advantages.

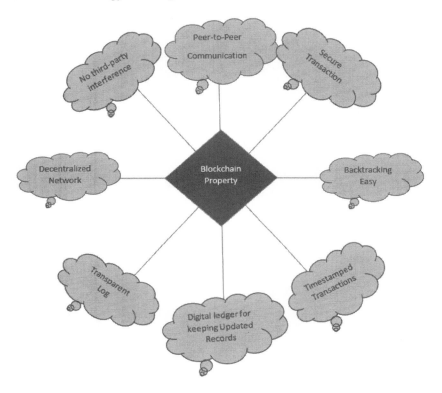

Figure 9.2   Advantages of Blockchain

9.1.2   HOW BLOCKCHAIN WORKS

Step1: First, the sending node will record the new data, and then it will broadcast it to the network.

Step2: The receiving node, whatever it is, will first check the message from the data it has received. Following that, it will check to see if the message received is accurate, and if it is, it will be recorded in the block.

Step 3: The Proof of Work(PoW)or Proof of Stake(PoS) will now be applied to the block by all receiving nodes which are present in the network [39].

Step 4: Finally, block is recorded in a chain. After the execution of the consensus algorithm, all nodes present in the the network would be admitting this block and, after that, it would then continuously extend the chain based, on those blocks. The below (Figure 9.3) depicts the working of blockchain technology.

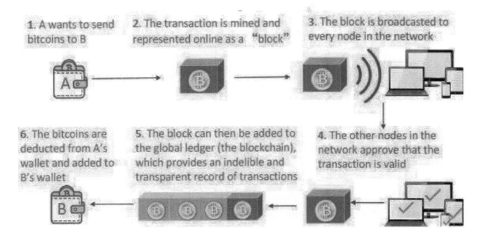

Figure 9.3 How blockchain works [50]

9.1.3 THE BLOCKCHAIN'S STRUCTURE

In the blockchain block, generally, contains the following data, i) Main-data, ii) hash of the previous and iii) the current block, iv) timestamp and v) other information. Below this, (Figure 9.4) shows the blockchain's structure.

Main data: It depends upon what services the blockchain application gives, Few examples of main data are IoT data records, bank clearing methods, transaction methods.

Hash: When the transaction is completed, it is hashed into the program and, it will be broadcasted to every node. Each block contains thousands of transaction records [19]. The "Merkle tree" function, also known as the "Merkle-tree-root," is used by blockchain technology to construct the final hashed value. In a hash of a current block, the final hash value will be stored in the block header [19]. Computing resources might be rapidly decreased by employing the aforementioned code.

Time-stamp: In this, the block's time is generated.

Other information: It just looks like a block's signature, which is a "Nonce value," a user defines it as other data. In figure 9.4, the Structure of the Blockchain is shown.

9.1.4 HOW TO GET CONSENSUS ?

Consensus, used for making all the blockchain nodes agree on the same message and it also aids in ensuring that the most recent block is accurately put to the chains. It guarantees the message which is stored by the node is the same one [46] and it also

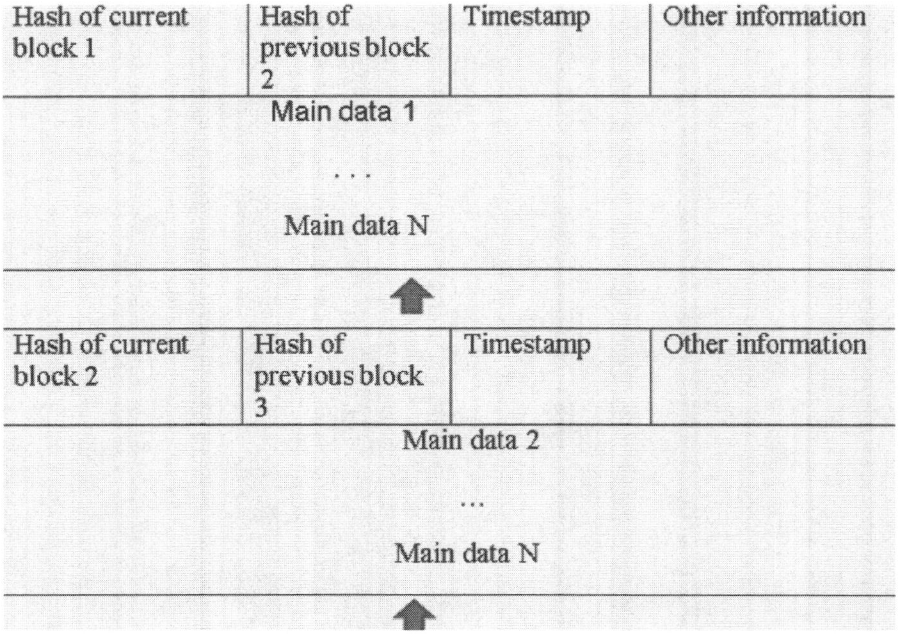

Hash of current block 1	Hash of previous block 2	Timestamp	Other information

Main data 1

. . .

Main data N

⬆

Hash of current block 2	Hash of previous block 3	Timestamp	Other information

Main data 2

. . .

Main data N

⬆

Figure 9.4 Blockchain Structure

guarantees that the "fork attack" won't happen and protect us from any malicious. Based on the different types of consensus algorithm, there is two different consensus algorithm, "Proof-of-Work and Proof-of-Stake." The below figure, (Figure 9.5) shows how the PoW Mechanism and PoS mechanism works.

9.1.5 PROOF OF WORK (POW)

It is very difficult to produce, because it is a piece of data, and Proof of work is very easy for others that they could be able to verify it. Producing a Proof of Work (PoW) might be a random process with a very low likelihood that many trial and error approaches will be necessary on average before a genuine POW is created. Hashcash POW algorithm is used by Bitcoin.

"Mining" is the process of computing the Proof of Work. Every block has some random value, which is termed as "Nonce" value in the block's header [36]. On modifying this value, Proof of Work would be generating a value, that would make the header of the block, which has a hash value less than a "Different Target." Difficulty in this refers to the amount of time taken to calculate the hash value whose value is less than the target value.

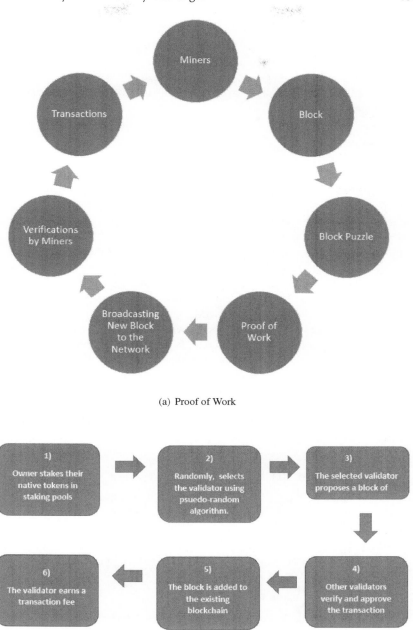

(a) Proof of Work

(b) Proof of Stake

Figure 9.5 fig (a) Shows Working of Proof of Work(PoW) (b) Shows Working of Proof of Stake(PoS)

9.1.6   PROOF OF STAKE (POS)

Since Proof of Work uses lots of electricity, and computation power, it is like wastage of power. Proof of Stake (PoS) does not need a lot of computational resources [22, 37]. With PoS, the resource, i.e., the amount of Bitcoin held by a miner, is 1 percent (percent) of the Proof-of-Stake blocks [11, 22]. It may give enhanced network security against malicious attacks.

9.1.7   TYPES OF BLOCKCHAIN

9.1.7.1   Public Blockchain

In this blockchain, everyone present in the node may review and validate the transaction. Everyone in the node may take part in the process of reaching a consensus or agreement. Bitcoin, as well as Ethereum, can be an example of Public Blockchain.

There are several drawbacks to this type of blockchain, they are as follows, As it is publicly available to everyone in the blockchain, so it might be the case that it will get attacked by the attacker in the node. Designing a blockchain technology is a complex task, it requires multiple machines to coordinate with the different-different algorithm. Bitcoin, Ethernum uses public blockchain technology, as these technologies believe to replace banks, credit cards, and debit cards. So the transaction will be slow as compared to the VISA. It is known that VISA can handle approximately a thousand (1000) transactions per second. Bitcoin uses Proof of Work (PoW) as an algorithm, it could able to process only around 7-10 transactions per second. Thus, bitcoin cannot handle the speed as today's VISA can. Wastage of Resources happens in bitcoin, as it requires a lot of energy to solve a block puzzle. A public blockchain, it is consisting of many miners, which solves the problem, around 10 minutes of work will require a large number of resources, then the transactions' block will be added to the blockchain.

9.1.7.2   Consortium blockchain

In this blockchain, the node which is authorised could choose in advance, mainly it has partnerships like B2B (business-to-business) [48]. Pieces of information in the blockchain's technology could be open or could be private [48], and also Partly Decentralised. Hyperledger is consortium blockchains. No matter how much advantage it has, but the process of launching this type of blockchain is much more critical.

9.1.7.3   Private blockchain

In a private blockchain, nodes are restricted, everyone in the node cannot take part in the blockchain. For data accessing, it has strict authority management. Below this the Figure 9.6 shows public, consortium, and private blockchain. There are some disadvantages in a private blockchain, this type of blockchain has a smaller number of people which includes businesses. as in this blockchain, there are very amount of

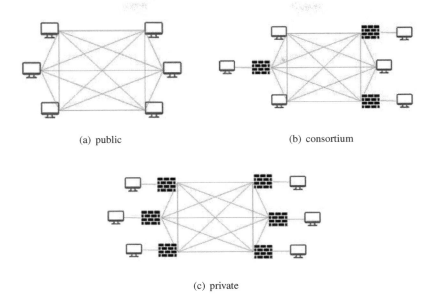

(a) public   (b) consortium

(c) private

Figure 9.6 fig (a) shows Public [9], fig (b) Shows Consortium [9] and, fig (c) Shows Private [9] Blockchain respectively

nodes, so it is prone to the security breach and threats, bad people in the network can able to get access easily.

Each type of blockchain has some advantages as well as disadvantages. We require public blockchain because it is much more convenient than other types. Then, for private control we need private or consortium blockchain depending upon what services it offers. Figure 9.6 shows the private, public, and consortium blockchain.

9.2 APPLICATION OF BLOCKCHAIN

Very first, the blockchain technology concept was only used for the Bitcoin cryptocurrency, now this concept has been widely moved to many other domains. Below this all, the domains have been explained briefly. The below Figure 9.7 depicts the application of Blockchain.

9.2.1 HEALTHCARE

Healthcare System is mainly an essential part of our life. This healthcare system provider uses blockchain so that their patient's medical reports can be stored securely and safely. Whenever the medical record of a particular patient is generated and signed, after that, it is written to the blockchain, so that the healthcare department can able to provide particular patient's medical report with proof and at that time, they have also full confidence about the particular patient's record that could not

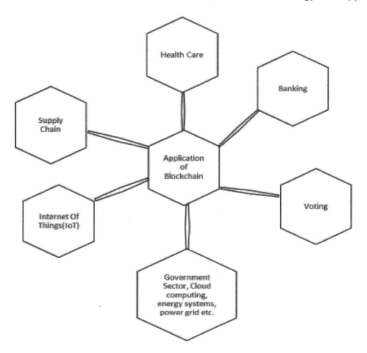

Figure 9.7   Application of blockchain

be changed. Whatever the personal health record of a person, it might be encrypted and preserved on the blockchain system using some private key [45], such that the particular record can be accessible by only particular person, it helps to give privacy and security. Figure 9.7 depicts the application of Blockchain. The below Figure 9.8 depicts benefits in healthcare because of blockchain.

9.2.2   BANKING AND FINANCE

According to a survey, blockchain has been helping, banking and finance area, more than any domain. In the the financial institution, they can be operated only in business hours, for example, suppose if we people deposited the check-in the bank on Friday at 6 pm., so we have to wait for Monday morning to see if the money hit our account. However, if blockchain technology has been integrated into banks [41], then the customer will be able to see his/her transactions processed within 10 minutes. Because of the blockchain networks, banks got the the opportunity of exchanging funds within several institutions and it can be done more securely and quickly.

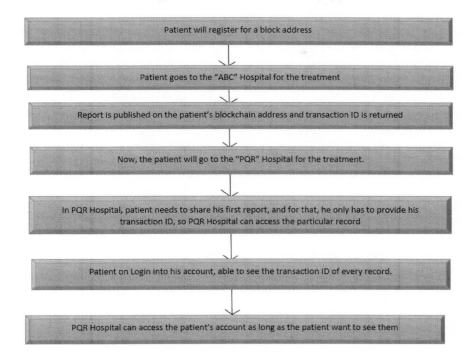

Figure 9.8 Benefits in healthcare because of blockchain

9.2.3 INTERNET OF THINGS

A material object refers to a "thing". When any material- object has an ON or OFF switch, which connects to the internet or to each other is referred to as "Internet of Things(IoT)". This describes the data that could be sent or received between the wirelessly connected devices. It determines the reliability of devices on the network and, will do continuously for the devices for entering as well as leaving the network [31]. Examples are Smartphones, Smart-cars.

9.2.4 VOTING

This blockchain technology can also be used to give the facility in the modern voting system. Blockchain on voting helps in eliminating fraud that had been done in voting and it also helps to boost the voter's turnout, and tampering in voting is also reduced. Apart from these pros, the blockchain will also maintain transparency in the voting process and it also helps to give instant results. And hence, it will eliminate the recount of the voting process. Figure 9.9 depicts banking, internet of things, and voting system in blockchain.

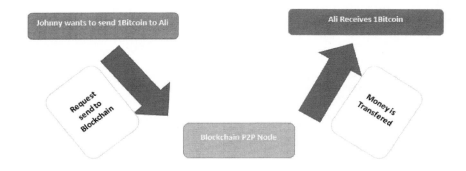

(a) Independent nodes in Blockchain to verify and approve the transaction

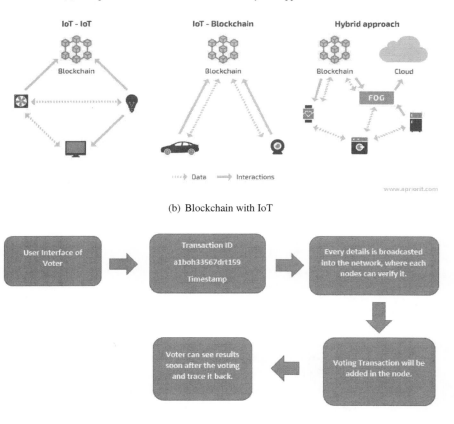

(b) Blockchain with IoT

(c) Voting System In Blockchain

Figure 9.9 Banking, iot and, voting in blockchain respectively

9.2.5 SUPPLY CHAIN

The supply chain can be used as the blockchain technology, such that it can record all the origins of the materials, which has been purchased. This will help the companies to check whether the products are authentic or not i.e. the authenticity of the products that have been purchased and also with the labels Fairtrade, Locals, and organic.

9.2.6 OTHER USES OF BLOCKCHAIN

Other than these applications, there are many domains, where blockchain technology is used as well. These are government sector, intellectual property's protection, certification of identity, energy systems, legal perspective, the intelligent transportation system, commercial world, the regulation system, E-business, cloud computing, power grid, insurance, smart contract: Ethernum, Hyperledgers, market's prediction, and many more domains.

9.3 SECURITY CHALLENGES OF BLOCKCHAIN

Apart from privacy, this technology also gets many security attacks, it faces [14, 15] many challenges and issues related to security. Some of the security attacks are described below. Figure 9.10 depicts types of attacks based on Blockchain.

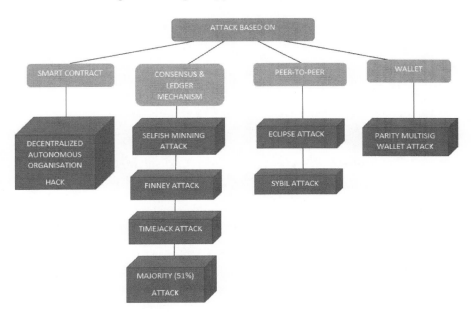

Figure 9.10 Various attacks on blockchain

9.3.1   ATTACKS BASED ON SMART CONTRACT

These are automated. These execute the transactions and also agree on the contract between the parties, with taking all the inputs from today's era, and there is no the intervention of any middlemen. When the transactions are once written into a blockchain then they became immutable, it gives the guarantee to the participants, in which the returns are based on its performance, which is as agreed as on the contract. Apart from immutability, there may be the cases when these contracts can have bugs.

9.3.1.1   The Decentralised Autonomous Organisation(DAO) Hack

This hack is the biggest exploitation in cryptocurrencies. Decentralised Autonomous Organisation (DAO) was the most popular feature of the Ethereum application. "The DAO" the project was started by a company name slock and this company was crowdfunding for the particular project. The crowdfunding campaign had such a large response that it was decided to collect dollar 12.7 million in ether, which was worth dollar 150 million at that time and is now worth dollar 2 billion. But while crowdfunding, the attacker found the vulnerabilities in a code, where he uses recursive withdraw function without settling the current transactions. So with the use of a recursive function, the hacker started the attack by giving the small amount as well as demanding the money every time with the use of a recursive function. Thus this request allows the attacker to take around dollar 70 million from crowdfunding. It takes an interesting turn after the occurrence of this event and the "Ethereum Foundation" forced the attacker for stopping the attack, as well as the foundation also told him that they will freeze the attacker's account. At that time, the attacker responded to it, by telling that was working as written into the contract and there would be intervention in a "soft or hard-fork" which would constitute a breach of contract that he might prove in court [35]. After a certain time, the hacker stopped the attack, and at a later time, "Ethernum Foundation" uses a "hard-fork," so that they can recover all the hacked money.

9.3.2   ATTACK BASED ON CONSENSUS AND LEDGER MECHANISM

9.3.2.1   Selfish mining attack

In this attack, there are many blocks that consider that, the longest chain will be considered as a very "upremium version of a ledger." So the greedy miner could tried to keep all the constructing blocks in a stealth mode at the very top of an existing chain, and also create more than one blocks in a current chain of a network and soon after this he will publish him/her private fork, that could be accepted by him/her as a new truth value i.e., this will be the "longest chain." After that, he could conduct transactions on the public network before releasing the "longer stealth chain." This gives him a limited window, so that he can be able to do double-spending.

9.3.2.2 Finney attack

These attacks can be defined as if we could use one of our transaction, we can mine any block with and keep it in, "stealth-mode," then an opportunity for us for spending the money twice. And if the merchant recognises that the transaction is not confirmed, then we could be able to send him this earlier transacted currency. And in the next step, we can also able to publish, whatever the earliest mined block was, as it was in stealth-mode before our new transaction is confirmed in the blockchain [33,35].

Assuming the situation, shown in figure (FIGURE 5 (b)).

STEP 1: The attacker begins the attack by creating a secret chain that contains txt21 in the 1st block(1).

STEP 2: If the attacker's chain is shorter than the chain of honest nodes, the attacker abandons the attack and begins again.

STEP 3: Attacker gains a lead of 2-block.

STEP 4: After that he sends the transaction that he wants to double spend, which is part of the block.

STEP 5: Transaction has now received sufficient confirmation, allowing the attacker to collect his rewards. He then makes his secret chain public and double-spend it.

9.3.2.3 Timejack attack

This type of attack happens in some nodes in blockchain networks. For example, its Bitcoin application depends on the internal timing that is calculated using the median time recorded by its neighbor nodes [33, 35]. Like, to the time we rely on our friends. Take a scenario, when the hacker manages to place lots of suspicious or bad people in our friend's list, then they will be able to modify the time. An eclipse attack in a target node can be the very initial move to a time jack attack [35]. When the eclipse attack is completed, the targeted node will refuse to take blocks from the actual network [35], since a block's timestamp is not in line with its time-stamp.

9.3.2.4 Majority (51%) attack

This type of attack comes when more than or equal to 51 percent of the mining power of a network is controlled by a "miner/group of miners". As difficult for very large networks to occur, there is the possibility of 51 percent attacks in the small networks are more likely to happen. If a the group has the majority control over the transactions on the blockchain network [33,35], then that could be prevented by reversing the older transactions. Figure 9.11 depicts selfish mining, finney and 51% attack.

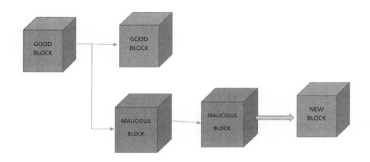

(a) Selfish-Mining Attack

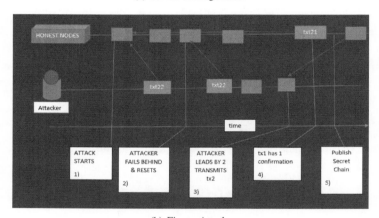

(b) Finney Attack

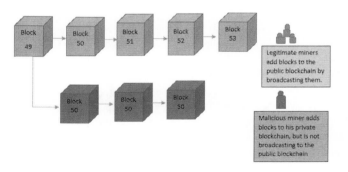

(c) Majority 51% Attack

Figure 9.11 Attack based on consensus mechanism (a) Selfish-mining, (b) Finney and, (c) Majority 51% attack respectively

9.3.3 ATTACK BASED ON P2P(PEER-TO-PEER) NETWORK

9.3.3.1 Eclipse attack

Eclipse attack could be defined as when anyone node will be depending upon some "m" number of nodes, and the the selection was done using the "peer-selection" strategy, so it could be seen as a "distributed ledger." If the hacker could able to control the node and [33] selects all the "m" no. of nodes from its legitimate node, then be able to eclipse the view of the original ledger [33, 35], and show the node with his own manipulated ledger.

9.3.3.2 Sybil attack

A hacker would try to flood the network by using a huge no. of nodes in this attack and, then the hacker will have an impact on the network. These nodes as of now appear to be unconnected individuals at the moment [33, 35]. In this type of attack, the aim is not to target only one user, but to target the whole network, and then the attacker generated a fork in the ledger, and if it is possible, and then allows the hacker to do a double-spending. Figure 9.12 depicts eclipse and sybil attack.

9.3.4 ATTACK BASED ON WALLET

9.3.4.1 Parity Multisig Wallet Attack

This attack took place when the vulnerability is known and it is hacked by a hacker and it results in holding-up 500,000 Ether. i.e., dollar 77 million by today. These walled-based contracts are having additional logic, that can be able to design for "regular automated payments" based on a user wallet. For minimizing the transaction fee, the "Parity Multisig" Wallet functions use a "Centralised Library Contract" [35]. However they leave some important components unprotected, which results in a breach, and it is then exploited. The attacker then added himself as an owner to the "library contract" [35], so that the wallets introduced after a certain date, would become a "Joint Owner" for the hacker. Then after that, he triggered the kill feature, which would be freezing the currency in the wallet.

9.4 CONCLUSION

There is no denying that blockchain technology has grown its importance in several past years, utilizing blockchain as a Decentralised network, it has enhanced the security over the centralised software system. Although there are some topics we are required to see, and this is also important to know about the blockchain technology that is not completely immune to cyberattacks. Apart from this, some problems have been improved with the new ideas, techniques and, majority of the security attacks could be eliminated by taking security best practices and proper governance strategy and also damage can be minimised.

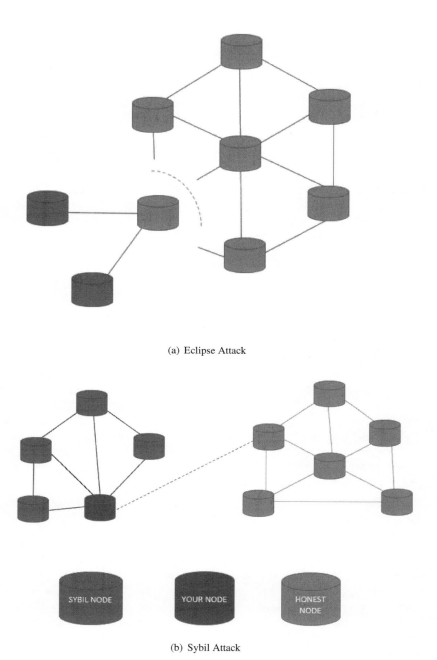

(a) Eclipse Attack

(b) Sybil Attack

Figure 9.12 Attack based on P2P network (a) Eclipse, (b) Sybil attack, respectively

As we all people are enjoying the advantages of blockchain technologies that are brought to us, but at the same point of time, we all people must stay cautious on its boon and also, be aware of the security issues.

Bibliography

1. S. Nakamoto *Bitcoin: A peer-to-peer Electronic Cash System*; Feb 24, 2013. (http:// bitcoin.org/bitcoin.pdf).

2. E.U. Opara, O. A. Soluade, *"Straddling a next cyber frontier: A emperical analysis on the network security, vulnerabilities, and exploitation"*; International Journal of Electronics and Information Engineering, vol. 3. no. 1, pp 10-18, 2015.

3. J. Singh, *"Cyber-attacks in cloud computing. A case study,"*; International Journal of Electronics and Information Engineering, vol. 1. no. 2, pp 78-87, 2014.

4. M. Conoscenti, A. Vetro, J.C. De Martin. *Blockchain for the Internet of Things: A systematic literature review*; 2016 IEEE/ACS 13th international Conference of Computer Systems and Applications (AICCSCA), IEEE, pp. 1-6, 2016.

5. Z. Zheng, S. Xie, H. -N. Dai, X. Chen, H. Wang. *Wang, Blockchain challenges and opportunities: A survey*; International Journel of Web and Grid Services 14 (4) 352-375, 2018

6. M. Banerjee, J. Lee, K.K.R Choo, *A blockchain future to Internet of Things: A position paper*;International Journel of Web and Grid Services 14 (4) (2018) 352-375, 2018.

7. Bayu Adhi Tama, Bruno Joachim Kweka, Youngho Park, Kyung-Hyune Rhee, *A critical review of blockchain and its current applications*; 2017 International Conference on Electrical Engineering and Computer Science (ICECOS), IEEE, 2017.

8. L.S. Shankar, M. Sindhu, M. Sethumadhavan. *Survey of consensus protocols on blockchain applications, in*; Proceedings of the 2017 4 th International Conference on Advanced Computing and Communication Systems (ICACSS), IEEE, pp. 1-5, 2017.

9. X. Li, P. Jiang, T. Chen, X. Luo, Q. Wen, *A survey on the security of blockchain systems*; Fut. Gen Comput. Syst. (2017),

10. L -C. LIN, T.-C. Liao, *A survey of blockchain security issues and challenges,*; IJ Netw. Secur. 19 (5) (2017) 653-659, 2017

11. S. King and S. Nadal, *Ppcoin: Peer to peer Crypto-Currency with Proof-of-Stake*; 2012

12. J. Garay, A. Kiayias, and N. Leonardoes,*The Bitcoin Backbone Protocol: Analysis and Applications*; pp. 281-310, Springer Berlin Heidelberg, Berlin, Heidelberg, 2015.

13. A. Gervais, G.O Karame, V. Capkun, and S. Capkun, *"Is bitcoin a Decentralised currency ?"*; IEEE Security Privacy, vol.12, pp. 54-60, May 2014.

14. J. Bonneau, A. Miller, J. Clark, A.Narayanan, J.A.. Kroll, and E.W. Felten, *"Sok: Research perspectives and challenges for bitcoin and cryptocurrencies"*; in IEEE Symposium on Security and Privacy, pp. 104- 121, May 2015.

15. E. Heilman, A. Kendler, A. Zohar, and S. Goldberg. *"Eclipse attacks on bitcoin's peer-to-peer network," in 24th USENIX Security Symposium,*; pp. 129-144, Washington, D.C., 2015

16. Yaga D, Mell P, Roby N, Scarfone K *Blockchain technology overview*; Draft NISTIR 8202:1–68, 2018

17. Ali MS, Vecchio M, Pincheira M, Dolui K, Antonelli F, Rehmani MH *Applications of blockchains in the internet of things: a comprehensive survey*; IEEE Commun Surv Tutorials 21(2):1676–1717, 2019

18. Bhabendu Kumar Mohanta, Debasis Jena, Soumyashree S. Panda, Srichandan Sobhanayak. *"A survey on applications and security privacy challanges"*; Internet of Things, 2019

19. D. Jeyabharati, D. Kesavaraja, D. Sasireka. *"Cloud Based Blockchaining for Enhanced Security"*; Elsevier BV, 2020

20. Lian Yu, Lijun Liu, Yanbing Jiang, Qi Jing, Bei Zhao, Chen Zhang (2020) *"Attack Graph Auto-Genation for Blockchains based on Bigraphical Reaction Systems"*; IEEE 20th International Conference on Software Quality, Reliability and Security(QRS), 2020

21. Yousif Abuidris, Rajesh Kumar, Wang Wenyong(2019) *A Survey of Blockchain Based on E-voting Systems*; Proceedings of the 2019 2nd International Conference on Blockchain Technology and Application, 2019

22. Abhyarthna Sontakke, Shivam Shadangi, Abhavya Verma, Roshani Pradhan. *Chapter 61 A Study on Securing Non-financial Data Using Blockchain Mechanism*; Springer Science and Business Media LLc, 2020

23. S. Gomathi, Mukesh Soni, Gaurav Dhiman, Ramya Govindaraj, Pankaj Kumar.*A surrvey on applications and security issues of blockchain technology in business sectors*; Proceedings, 2021

24. Mingli Wu, Kun Wag, Xiaoqin Cai, Song Guo, Minyi Guo, Chunming Rong *A comprehensive Survey of Blockchain: From Theory to IoT Applications and Beyond*; IEEE Internet of THings Journal, 2019

25. Ganguly Ananya, Das Priyanjali, Das Baisakhi, Das Abhishek. *Chapter 59 Secure Blockchain: Assessing Specific Security Threats*; Springer Science and Business Media LLC, 2017

26. Daniel Drescher *Blockchain Basics*; Springer Science and Business Media LLC, 2017

27. Sana Moin, Ahmad Karim, Zanab Sadar, Kalsoom Safdar, Ejaz Ahmed, muhammad Imran, *Securing IoTs in distributed blockchain: Analysis, requirements and open issues*; Future generation Computer Systems, 2019

28. I. Bentov, A. Gabizon, and A.Mizrahi, *Cryptocurrencies without proof of work*; 2014

29. Yassine Issaoui, Azeddine KHIAT, Ayoub Bahnasse, Ouajji Hassan *Smart Logistics: Blockchain trends and applications*; 2020

30. Mansoor Ali, Hadis Karimipour, Muhammad Tariq. *Integration of blockchain and federated learning for Internet of Things: Recent advances and future challenges*; Computer and Security, 2021

31. Anup Kumar Paul, Xin Qu , Zheng Wen. *Blockchain–a promising solution to internet of things: A comprehensive analysis, opportunities, challenges and future research issues*; Peer-to-Peer Networking and Applications 14(2):1-26, 2021

32. Mohd Javaid, Abid Haleem, Ravi Pratap Singh, Shahbaz Khan, Rajiv Suman *Blockchain technology applications for Industry 4.0: A literature-based review*; 2021

33. Blockchain *https://www.fool.com/*; 07 July, 2021

34. Proof-of-Work, *https://capital.com/proof-of-work-pow-definition*; 08 December, 2021

35. Aruba Marketing, 10 Blockchain and New Age Security Attacks You Should Know *https://blogs.arubanetworks.com/solutions/10-blockchain-and-new-age-security-attacks-you-should-know/*; 06 July, 2021

36. Jian Yang, Hong Shen *Blockchain Consensus Algorithm Design Based on Consistent Hash Algorithm*; 20th International Conference on Parallel and Distributed Computing Applications, and Technologies (PDCAT), 2019

37. Robin Singh Bhadoria, Vaibhav Agasti *The Paradigms of Blockchain Technology*; International Journal of Information Systems and Social Change, 2017

38. Harald Vraken *Sustanability of bitcoin and blockchains*; Current opinion in Environmental Sustainability, 2017

39. *Blockchain and Trustworthy Systems*; Springer Science and Business Media LLC, 2020

40. Consensus, *https://eprints.lancs.ac.uk*; 5 May, 2021

41. Banking and Finance, *https://www.mdpi.com*; 25 December, 2020

42. Peer-to-Peer Networ,k *https://www.jetir.org*, 6 May, 2021

43. Blockchain, *https://cms.digital-transaction.com*; 5 May, 2021

44. Blockchain technology, *https://ijcttjournal.org*; 7 July, 2021

45. A Review on Privacy Preservation Techniques in Surveillance and Health Care Data Publication *https://www.ijert.org*; 7 July, 2021

46. Review Introduction to Blockchain Technology. *https://hennyportman.wordpress.com*; 7 July, 2021

47. A Survey on Blockchain Technology and its Proposed Solutions *https://www.researchgate.net*; 6 May, 2021

48. Consortium, *https://link.springer.com*; 10 June, 2021

49. What's a DApp?, *https://www.stateofthedapps.com/whats-a-dapp*; 8 May, 2021

50. Security and Privacy on Blockchain, *https://dl.acm.org/doi/fullHtml/10.1145/3316481*; 8 May, 2021

51. Kevin C. TOFEL, Blockchain 101: How distributed trusted data can boost the IoT, *https://staceyoniot.com/blockchain-101-how-distributed-trusted-data-can-boost-the-iot/*; 10 September, 2021

10 Protocol for E-Voting Using Blockchain

The usefulness that is provided by a distributed database spans the whole world. Capped with the advantages provided by these databases was the innovation of Blockchain, which has transformed the current mode of business transactions and sharing of resources. Blockchain is a shared distributed ledger or a decentralised database that keeps a continuous digital record of who owns what record. The notion of a centralised authority to regulate the recording of records is dropped by Blockchain by having a network of replicated databases, that is synced via the internet network and is visible to all within a network. A consistent state of the ledger is maintained by a consensus mechanism amongst the nodes in the decentralised network. The ledger can also be combined with some logic-building support, like "smart contract", so that any business process or legal settlements can be done in a transparent, accountable, and trustful manner. Since the introduction of Bitcoin [16], many other variants have come up such as Ethereum, Hyperledger Fabric, R3Corda, etc have come.

The organisation of the chapters is such:

i. Introduction
ii. Literature Review
iii. Blockchain Implementations
iv. Contribution Work
v. Implementation Details
vi. Analysis and Result
vii. Comparison between HBasechainDB and Ethereum
viii. Conclusion
ix. Future Work

The below subsections starts with discussing the pros and the cons of Blockchain

10.0.1 PROS PROS AND CONS OF BLOCKCHAIN

Advantages and disadvantages of the bolockchain is discussed in this section

10.0.1.1 ros:

Following are the Pros of a Blockchain: Dissemination: The fundamental design on which blockchain stands is that it enables a database to be directly shared across a network with no involvement of a central institution. It has its logic for validation and authorization which is deterministic and decentralised.

DOI: 10.1201/9781003355052-10

- Cost-Effective: Blockchain enables a deterministic execution of logic codes, it is cheaper and easier to automate business processes and legal complaints which can be tailored to a specific group of business needs. The drawback of the centralised institution that employs a complicated design process to prevent their databases from being tampered with and protection from adversary attack is offloaded by blockchain.
- Transparent Control: Users have transparent control over all the transactional information published on the blockchain. As any usage requires the owner of the transaction which only a particular user holds.
- Availability Of Data: Blockchain data is public and due to its consistent and public nature, all the data becomes highly available to all the network users.
- Durability, And Reliability: Being a decentralised network, blockchain has a redundancy factor in terms of the number of nodes in a network. So, there is no concern about a single point of failure or a malicious attack.
- Immutability: All the records are stored as a block of chain which is cryptographically linked. Any change to a particular record will be viewable to all.

10.0.1.2   Cons:

Following are the Cons of a Blockchain:

- `Performance`: The consensus mechanism in blockchain though helps to maintain a consistent state in a decentralised environment, it has a slower transaction throughput. Likes of Bitcoin and Ethereum take 10 mins and 15 secs respectively to create and validate a block of transactions in a blockchain. Each having a transaction throughput of 7 transactions per second in Bitcoin and 10-30 transactions per second in Ethereum.
- `Governance`: All current existing currencies and data in use have been created and regulated by national governments and organisational institutions. For the blockchain to cross this hurdle would require a good protocol, transaction format, and specification to be well established and made a standard.
- `Control, Security, and Privacy`: The current use cases of blockchain are only limited to private and permissioned networks where the players are a few financial and business institutions. This use case is supported by strong cryptography. But, for the blockchain to work in a public domain still requires a lot of security standards and measures to be adopted and developed.

10.1   LITERATURE REVIEW

E-Voting has always tried to encompass and replace the traditional Paper or EVM-based Voting System. The benefit of making a voting process easier, more accessible for people, especially for remote areas, and lower the cost of the whole voting process set up, has always attracted the development of many protocols and frameworks. The concern of votes' privacy and user's anonymity looms very high. Fraud and

Coercion/vote-buying are the major setbacks as in the case of E-Voting no physical authority stands by in-person to prevent it.

Following is the literature for voting, which is Normal, Electronic and Blockchain-based.

10.1.1 NORMAL-VOTING SCHEMES

Paper-based Voting has always been the norm for all the voting process. Due to a stringent voting mechanism with the presence of a physical authority, this process is accepted and widely used.

Punched card or punch card [13], which is a stiff paper that contains digital information represented by the presence or absence of holes in predefined positions. The punched card was the earlier used voting scheme where the votes were defined as a set of defined holes in the card which was later read by a machine.

Optical Scan Voting System [4], uses an optical scanner to read marked paper ballots and tally the results. Different kinds of Systems are used for optical mark recognition. Mark sense system is one such system wherein a voter's choice of the vote which is filled in a rectangle, circle or oval marked paper is optically recognised.

Electronic Voting Machine (EVM) [11][22] is the most widely used machine. The design of it is simple to use together with the process being monitored in a controlled environment has led to it being the most opted-for device for the Voting Process.

10.1.2 ELECTRONIC-VOTING SCHEMES

Chaum [7] who proposed Votegrity, was the first to give end-to-end (E2E) voting schemes. E2E verifiability means that the voter can verify that their own vote has been cast as intended. The voter would be assured that their vote has been counted correctly and included in the final tally and that the public members can verify an election externally without being involved in an election. These voting protocols, also provide a way to audit the voter's votes and the ballots before picking the candidate and casting the ballot.

Pret a Voter [20] is an E2E voting system devised by Peter Ryan. It aims to provide guarantees of the accuracy of the count and ballot privacy that are independent of software, hardware, etc. Pret a voter involves a process of encoding a vote using a random list of candidates. Each slip consists of the random arrangement of candidate names with a value printed at the bottom of the slip. This encrypted value is the key that points the vote to a particular candidate. The random arrangement of the candidate names in the slip ensures the secrecy of voter's votes. After the election, voters can visit the Web Bulletin Board (WBB) and confirm their receipts appear correctly. Once this is over, the tellers take over and perform anonymising mixes and decryption of the receipts. All the intermediate stages of this process are posted to the WBB and are audited later.

The Helios Voting [2] by Ben Adida is a web-based Voting system. It is based on advanced peer-reviewed cryptographic techniques that enable the vote to remain secret while providing an intelligent ballot tracker to verify that the ballot was received and counted properly. A script capable of monitoring user traffic, capturing passwords entered by the user, and getting access to the web page. There has been use of the public Web bulletin Board (WBB) [18] for storing the encrypted form of a voter's vote. This board serves as a board of public verifiability by broadcasting these encrypted votes through a channel.

Homomorphic tally or Homomorphic based encryption is another technique described by Cohen and Fisher [8] which is used in voting. Homomorphic tally involves modifications, usually additions, and multiplications, to the ciphertext which are preserved upon decryption to reveal the operations that have been done on the ciphertext while recovering the modified decrypted value.

Auditability and verifiability of the voter's vote in case a voter disputes their vote or proves that they have voted contrary to what the system has recorded are essential. Transparency and integrity of votes during the voting process are necessary to avoid any conflict.

10.1.3   BLOCKCHAIN-BASED SCHEMES

Votebook [21] proposed by Kevin Kirby, Anthony Masi, Fernando Maymi, uses Blockchain as a "permissioned blockchain", where the distribution of keys enables voters to vote and the whole voting process is overlooked and controlled by a centralised authority. This proposal allows an individual to check if his vote was counted, the whole process of voting is transparent on the part of the voter, but the coercion of votes by the centralised authority desalinates the very basis of Blockchain being decentralised and transparent.

BitCongress [6] by Morgan Rockwell gives another voting model where their primary aim is to eliminate corruption of votes by a centralised authority. BitCongress is a decentralised, peer-to-peer, open-source voting system protocol. It works on the same principle as Bitcoin, which uses the Proof-of-Work consensus model to put a vote on the Blockchain. It augments the security of voter's votes using the public-key cryptosystem. BitCongress which is implemented in the Ethereum Network tallies and verifies the vote whose logic is written as a smart contract. This smart contract is deployed on the Blockchain where all the connected node or people can see and check. The Blockchain registers the votes, keeps a tally of everything voted on in the public eye. This scheme provided a decentralised environment for voting. This proposed scheme gave a good insight into Voting in the decentralised environment augmented by cryptographic systems for privacy or security. But, the practical implementation together with the basic features of voting; voter anonymity, transparent vote auditing was a major concern. Like a normal crypto transaction model, this model was configured to work in a voting model.

10.1.4   OUTCOME OF LITERATURE SURVEY

Blockchain is a relatively new technology, it's gaining enough traction and has been adopted by all the fields and domains, such as financial services, medical, IoT, supply chain management, E-Voting, etc. Electronic Voting has always attracted an aversion, with a significant number of people not being able to trust authenticity, integrity, and centralization. Paper-based voting is easily coercible, still, people acknowledge and trust this system more than Electronic voting. Now, Blockchains' emergence has set forth a new thought in people's minds regarding the inherent security flaws present in the current system. Blockchain can be used as one of the main components for designing a hybrid protocol or scheme for voting. We propose a Blockchain-based E-voting using the concept of Zero-knowledge Proof. We create a protocol design for a voting system using blockchain and show that a voting system can be decentralised, giving anonymity to voters, the privacy of votes, and a transparent election process.

10.2 BLOCKCHAIN IMPLEMENTATIONS

The following topics discusses various Blockchain implementations. These discussed blockchain platforms implementations gives an idea as to how and what various methodologies and concepts are used so as to achieve the functionalities of Blockchain.

10.2.1 BITCOIN

Bitcoin was started by a person or a group named Satoshi Nakamoto, is a decentralised peer-to-peer cryptocurrency. This implementation revolutionized the idea of a decentralised system. The underlying framework of Blockchain, which is transparent, tamper-resistant, and decentralised, opened up the possibility of using it for financial businesses, IoT, e-voting, medical data sharing, supply chain, etc.

All the transactions happen through a shared ledger, called Blockchain. The inclusion of a block into a blockchain happens by solving a consensus algorithm called proof-of-work. The hash function used for chaining the previous block to the current block is SHA-256. This is how tamper-resistance of data in blockchain is achieved. A change in the previous block leads to a change in the current and the following blocks. This chaining of blocks is what gave the name *"Blockchain."*

Mining: Bitcoin follows a distributed consensus mechanism called proof-of-work. Proof-of-work involves taking the hash of the previous transaction and adding it to a nonce where the concatenation of the two and passing it through a hash function gives a hash which is less the target hash. The finding of this nonce is compute-intensive for every miner node. The target hash is changed every 2016 block to make a block time creation of 10 minutes. This consensus mechanism is to confirm a transaction, add a block into chronological order. For the transactions to be confirmed, transactions are packed into a block and strict cryptographic rules are applied which are verified by other nodes in the network. These validation rules make a chain of block tamper-resistant.

Transaction: The transfer of bitcoin, in satoshis, happens through transactions. For the transaction to be successful any transfer of bitcoin must be a transfer from one or more previous transactions. Each transaction consists of input and output fields. The input field consists of one or more bitcoin received from previous transactions and the output fields are the bitcoins that are yet to be spent. These outputs of the transactions are called Unspent Transactions Outputs (UTXOs). So, the input of a transaction is an output of the previous transaction. The output of a particular transaction is allowed to be spent only once. For any transfer of bitcoins, in satoshis, to be valid must be used from only one of these UTXOs.

For spending a UTXO in the later transaction the spender must satisfy a verification rule called *Pay-To-Public-Key-Hash (P2PKH)*. This P2PKH is an instruction on the Blockchain to transfer ownership of satoshis from the current to the new owner.

`Pseudonymity`: Bitcoin is pseudonymous, that is, the real-world identity is not linked to the bitcoin funds but rather to a public address. As long as the user does not get involved in a real-world transaction that links his public address or the user does not publish his public address on a public forum, the user maintains his pseudonymity.

10.2.2 ETHEREUM

Ethereum [5][23] was started by Vitalik Buterin in 2015. Ethereum is a decentralised peer-to-peer Blockchain platform, which enables the deployment of a decentralised application. It follows the same consensus protocol as Bitcoin and offers the features of tamper-resistant and transparency. Unlike Bitcoin which is focused on a cryptocurrency and is used to identify the owner of the currency (Bitcoin), Ethereum is meant to run a decentralised application developed and deployed by the user. Ethereum network is meant to work with zero downtime and no third-party indulgence. The Proof-of-Work consensus protocol is used to update the global state of the Ethereum network. The support of a legally binding smart contract logic on the Blockchain network gives the capability of correct execution without any fraud. The support of this smart contract logic using an Ethereum virtual machine (EVM) makes the network a world computer. The development of EVM which is a Turing complete language, allows the creation of an arbitrary rule for ownership, transaction formats, or cryptocurrency called Ether on the network. The use of Smart contracts enables the deployment of a large variety of decentralised applications like supply chain management, e-voting, IoT, etc.

`Ethereum Accounts`: Ethereum state is made up of objects called accounts which is a 20-byte address. Any transfer of transactions happens between these accounts. An account contains:

- *Nonce*
- *Accounts current ether balance*
- *Accounts contract code, optional*

Ethereum has its cryptocurrency called "Ether", and whatever transactions take place in Ethereum happens with these Ether values. There are two types of accounts; an "externally owned account" which is owned by a private address and a "contract account" which is owned by a contract code. Any transfer of transaction takes place between two externally owned accounts. A contract account is activated and run either by a message from an externally owned account or by a message from another contract account, which in turn is activated by an externally owned account. Any execution of these externally owned accounts or contract code accounts must be paid in Ether. This Ether is given to the miners as a transaction reward for mining a block that would incorporate the transactions and append it on the Blockchain network. The execution of the contract code from the externally owned account enforces a strict deterministic execution. This deterministic execution enables the smart contract to be tamper-resistant and verified correctly by all the ethereum networks.

Smart Contract: Smart contract is just logic that includes both code and data. This logic or code can be used to transfer money, assets, or anything that can be represented by a value. The execution of this smart contract on the blockchain leads to a correct deterministic execution with zero downtime, no fraud, or no third-party interference. The smart contract enables credible transactions which are irreversible and easily verifiable by the network. Smart contract code can be used for a validation rule, transferring assets only when certain conditions are met, etc. This smart contract is deployed on the Blockchain as bytecode. This bytecode contract is replicated by all ethereum nodes and whenever this contract logic is activated, this bytecode is run and all the ethereum node executes this logic and performs the necessary actions for the state updation. There are many high-level languages for writing this smart contract. This contract is compiled into the EVM bytecode and stored in an Ethereum Blockchain.

Mining: Ethereum Mining includes using a Proof-of-Work consensus protocol same as Bitcoin. Mining in Ethereum is memory hard and computationally hard, which is more ASIC resistant; specialised mining chips. Mining involves taking the hash of the previous block header, trying a different nonce, and check if the resulting hash is less than the target hash. Solving this by using different nonce is computationally intensive. Any miner which solves this puzzle is given a reward in Ether. The block is then propagated to the network who themselves validate the block and add to their copy of the blockchain. This mining reward in Ethereum is fixed to the constant reward of 5.0 Ether. For any cheating miner or node, it is difficult because it involves solving a heavy computational puzzle. Finding a block in Ethereum is fixed to 10-12 secs. For any miner who finds it in less than 10-12 secs or more than 10-12 secs, the difficulty algorithm readjusts to keep the block creation time by the miner to 10-12 secs.

Ethereum uses the "Greedy Heaviest Observed Subtree" protocol, which is an innovation first introduced by Yonatan Sompolinsky and Aviv Zohar. Unlike a bitcoin network where a valid blockchain is considered the longest blockchain formed so far, in Ethereum the valid blockchain is considered the heaviest blockchain.

Fees and Contract Execution: Executing code or transferring a transaction in Ethereum results in the updation of the Ethereum state. This computation requires the usage of resources and Ethereum has defined a fee structure that is paid in a value called Ether. Each operation in Ethereum is assigned a gas which specifies the minimum amount of computation which this operation requires for successful execution. For example; ADD uses 3 gas, MUL requires 5 gas, basic transaction transfer costs 21000 gas, and contract transaction takes 21000 gas plus extra gas for further complex operation execution.

The gas per operation is fixed but the price to be paid per gas, called gasPrice is dynamic and depends on market value. gasPrice represents the value that the user will be willing to pay for the execution of the required operations. The users specify the gas price in Gwei. The total fees that a user pays for an operation execution is measured as: `totalfees = gasPrice × gasUsed`

The gasUsed is dependent on the operation execution and the gas used by EVM. The total gas for a transaction execution is specified by the user at the start of the transaction execution as gasLimit.

10.2.3 BIGCHAINDB

BigchainDB [14] was started by Trent McConaghy. BigchainDB provides an abstraction of blockchain which is built on a distributed database. It is meant to fill the gap in a decentralised ecosystem. This strategy gives a transaction throughput of million transactions per second, storing tera to petabytes of data and sub-second latency. BigchainDBs' permissioning capability ranges from a permissioned and a private blockchain network to an open public blockchain database. It is complementary to a decentralised blockchain processing platform like Ethereum, Bitcoin and a decentralised file system like the InterPlanetary File System (IPFS).

The underlying design of BigchainDB is a Distributed Database, MongoDB. The characteristics of a Blockchain are added to this database using concepts like "Blockchain Pipelining." These features give BigchainDB the unique characteristics of decentralised control, immutability, and creation and movement of digital assets. Unlike Bitcoin where the performance is restricted with 8000-10000 nodes, BigchainDB scales linearly in throughput with the increase in the number of nodes. BigchainDB relies on the consensus algorithm used in the distributed database, viz., Paxos, etc. for the correct ordering of the transactions and the correct copy of all the transactions in all the nodes. It inherently uses the features of a distributed database like sharding for improving performance throughput and conserving storage. BigchainDB aims to allow the underlying distributed database to improve performance and capacity while providing the Blockchain characteristics. BigchainDB operates or provides these Blockchain features by building a consortium of nodes called the federation of nodes. This federation of nodes is a peer-to-peer node where their main objective is to vote for a transaction. For a transaction to pass through, it must have a certain quorum of votes.

BigchainDB is meant to scale wherein the scaling capability allows the legally binding contract and certificates can get stored directly on the distributed databases. It can be used side-by-side with decentralised storage; *IPFS, processing; Ethereum, and high-level computation and communication systems.*

10.2.4 HYPERLEDGER FABRIC

Hyperledger Fabric [3] is a Blockchain framework underpinning distributed ledger solutions. It has a modular architecture that delivers a high degree of confidentiality, resiliency, flexibility, and scalability. It is one of the Hyperledger Project started by the Linux Foundation and is being actively developed with the coordination of IBM. It aims to support and integrate a global industry transaction solution by bringing the fragmented Blockchain protocol and parties into the standards built by the Hyperledger Fabric framework. It claims to do this with high reliability and security. It recognises that for long-term transparency, longevity, and interoperability of the blockchain technology to be adopted into the business requires good support and collaboration between the open-source and the business community.

It is designed to support a modular plug-and-play implementation of different components; the consensus algorithm, data store, cryptographic algorithms, and the membership services. It supports the creation, storage, and execution of custom-built logic or rules by leveraging container technology. This smart contract or logic is called chaincodes. The chaincode dictates the flow of transaction flow between two entities. It accommodates the complexity and intricacies of the current economic system.

The key features of Fabric include:

- Inclusion of PBFT (Practical Byzantine Fault Tolerant) consensus algorithm for achieving consensus among nodes.
- It provides chaincodes for confidential information sharing.
- Segregation of chaincode execution from ordering services enables the network to be more fault-tolerant and provides more scalability and performance.
- Fabric modularity enables the framework to fit in for a specific business need. All these features enable the fabric to cater to any business needs.

`Fabric Architecture`: The fabric consists of many nodes who all coordinate and communicate with each other. Each node runs the chaincode which has a program embedded in it. This chaincode is used for maintaining the state and ledger data. The chaincode is the main component in the architecture as all transactions are executed via chaincodes. Any Transactions which are considered valid have to be endorsed by a certain node and only a valid endorsed node can affect changes to the state of the blockchain. There are one or more special chaincodes, called system chaincodes for the management of the network to execute in a deterministic order.

The nodes in the fabric network play several roles. The nodes can be a committer, endorser, peer, or client. The client is a node that invokes an actual transaction, invokes an endorser, and broadcasts the transaction to the ordering service. A peer is a node that commits transactions and maintains the ledger state. Each peer has a local copy of the ledger state in its CouchDB database. A peer node can be an endorser where they endorse a transaction submitted by a client, simulate the transaction execution before the transaction gets submitted. The endorser nodes are specific to particular chaincodes and follow an endorsement policy. This policy specifies the necessary and sufficient conditions for the valid transactions to be endorsed. There is the orderer who commits the transactions to the database. This group of orderers forms the ordering service; they provide delivery guarantees. The ordering service can be implemented as a centralised or a decentralised protocol suite. Ordering service provides a shared communication channel for peers and clients. It is this channel where a client broadcasts its message which is then delivered to the peers.The channel is a private communication route that is being shared and used only by a specific number of nodes in a network. There can exist multiple channels at one instance of a fabric execution. A channel is defined by the peer, channel configuration, orderers, and the shared ledger. Each member on the channel must be authorized and authenticated for transacting messages. Each member or node has an identity established on the channel. This identity is established by a membership service provider (MSP). This MSP authenticates a peer node in the channel peers and services.

`Transaction Flow`: The transaction is first submitted by a client to a set of endorsing peers, of his choice. The set of endorsing peers becomes known to a client via a peer pertaining to a particular chaincode. The endorsing peer upon receiving a transaction simulates the execution of the transaction by invoking a chaincode that pertains to a particular transaction and then endorses the transaction by saving the result of the execution in its local state. The endorsed result is then sent to the client which acts as a valid message and signature to conclude that the transaction is endorsed. The client then sends the endorsed result and the transaction to the orderers who form the ordering service. The orderers order the transaction into a block and then sends it to the peer for committing it into a database. Before committing the transaction to the ledger or database the peer validates the transaction using the endorsement policy from the transactions chaincode against the ledger for the consistency of the result. When the validity gets established then the transaction is successfully recorded in the ledger.

10.2.5 COMPARISON TABLE FOR THE BLOCKCHAIN IMPLEMENTATIONS

	Description	Consensus	Currency	Mining Reward	Mode of Operation	Governance	Smart Contract	Privacy
Bitcoin	CryptoCurrency	PoW	Bitcoin	Yes	Public	Bitcoin Developers	Limited	Open
Ethereum	Generic Blockchain Platform	PoW, PoS	Ether	Yes	Public or Private	Ethereum Developers	Solidity	Open
BigchainDB	Generic Blockchain Platform, but more scalable	Voting	None	No	Public or Permissioned	BigchainDB Developers	None	Open
Hyperledger Fabric	Modular Blockchain platform	PBFT	None	No	Private or Permissioned	Linux Foundation	Chaincodes	Private

Figure 10.1 Comparison of blockchain implementations

Figure 10.1 provides the various parameters on which the various discussed blockchain implementations differ and what are the advantages and disadvantages.

10.3 CONTRIBUTION WORK

This Contribution provides the various concepts and fundamentals used in designing the protocol for voting.

10.3.1 ZERO-KNOWLEDGE PROOF (ZKF)

Zero-Knowledge Proof [10] was proposed by Shafi Goldwasser, Silvio Micali, and Charles Rackoff at MIT. The main idea behind ZKF is that a prover provides proof to demonstrate to the verifier that a prover has a secret knowledge to the proof without revealing this secret. The proof is valid only with this secret, otherwise it always results in false.

ZK proof varies from the traditional mathematical concept proofs. The mathematical proofs use statement/s which are already well-established proofs or statements which are considered to be true and based on it, it tries to derive the next true statement. ZK Proofs are more dynamic as it involves a series of information exchanges between a prover and a verifier wherein the prover tries to prove the truth of the proof statement, obviously without revealing the secret statement.

A Simple Example To Illustrate ZKF proof:

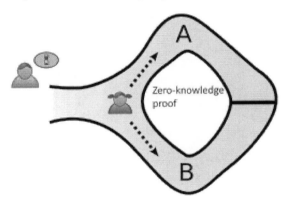

Figure 10.2 Illustration for zero-knowledge proof

Figure 10.2 illustrates the work as follows: Consider, a cave that has a circular tunnel. A door is present at the other end of the cave which needs a secret key to open it. Now, the prover and the verifier enters into a game where the prover tries to prove that he knows the secret password to this door without telling the verifier of what this password is.

The following events take place:

  i. The Prover chooses to take one (A or B) of the path of this cave. His choice of path is not known to the verifier.
 ii. Now, the verifier stands at one of the path (A or B) of the cave and asks by calling the Prover to come out from the path in which the verifier is standing.

iii. The Prover can come out of the path as told by the verifier every time they play this game. If the prover actually knows the secret to the door then he will convince the verifier that he knows the secret password. If the prover is lying about the secret then he has only a 50% chance of fooling the Verifier.

The correctness of the above proof lies in repeating the protocol a certain number of times. Such protocol also shows that the verifier is convinced probabilistically about the prover knowing the secret key to the door. But, the verifier cannot convince others as he does not possess the secret. Even if the verifier were to record all the process, such recording would be futile as it would appear to an outsider that the whole process was forged and set up by both prover and verifier.

Zero-Knowledge Proofs are subsystems of Interactive Proof Systems. A system in which prover and verifier exchange challenges based on some random number input with a secret where each response to the challenge. The proofs are probabilistic rather than absolute as in the mathematical sense. These proofs need only be correct with a certain bounded probability. Interactive proofs are also called proofs by protocol.

Three Main features which zero-knowledge proof must meet are:

- Completeness: An honest prover will eventually convince the Verifier that he has the secret knowledge to the proof.
- Soundness: An honest prover can always convince the verifier of the proof being correct if the statement of the proof is true.
- Zero-knowledge: The Verifier does not learn any information from the interaction with the prover about the proof.

The first two properties are the basis for zero-knowledge proof. The third property makes the proof, zero-knowledge.

10.3.2 SOME PROTOCOLS BASED ON ZERO-KNOWLEDGE PROOFS (ZKF)

The following gives the various methods and concepts of how the ZFK are used as a protocols.

10.3.2.1 Schnorr Identification Protocol

Claus-Peter Schnorr [9] proposed the identification protocol based on ZKF. The assumption made by Schnorr was that the key-pair would be of a specific type format. He took into account a "cyclic group of prime order."

The Following explains how Schnorr used this "cyclic group of prime order" for developing the protocol. Let "p" and "q" be two co-prime numbers and "g" be a generator of this cyclic group of prime order q. Generation of key-pair by "A(Alice)" would begin by picking a random integer "a" between 1 and q, and computing the key-pair as: $PK_A = g^a mod p, SK_A = a$

Alice will keep her secret key "a" to herself, but she freely publishes her public key PK_A. So, whenever she wants to prove knowledge of her secret key "a", she follows the simple protocol with the verifier "B(Bob (say))":

- Alice picks a random "k" in range 1 to q. She computes h = g^k mod p and sends h to Bob.
- Bob picks a random "c" in range 1 to q. He then sends "c" to Alice.
- Alice then computes: s = ac + k mod q and sends s to Bob.
- Bob then checks, if $g^s \equiv PK^c$. h mod p If the check evaluates to true then Bob accepts the proof.

CHECK FOR COMPLETENESS:

If Alice is honest and she is executing the protocol with Bob, then Bob will be convinced of the proof.

To check that the proof is complete it can be checked as follows:

$g^s \equiv PK^c.h mod p$
$g^{ac+k} \equiv (g^a)^c.g^k mod p$
$g^{ac+k} \equiv g^{ac+k}.mod p$

CHECK FOR SOUNDNESS: For the soundness of a proof of knowledge, we should show the existence of a simulator M. This simulator M is a special type of Verifier that interacts with a Prover, and if the Prover succeeds in completing the proof, simulator M should be able to extract the Prover's original equivalent secret. So, to prove soundness for proof of knowledge, we must show that such simulator M exists for every possible Prover.

Illustrating the above in terms of a protocol workflow:

- Prover picks a random "k" in range 1, $\cdots$, q. He computes h = g^k mod p and sends h to the simulator.
- Simulator picks a random "c1" in range 1, $\cdots$, q. The simulator then sends "c1" to Prover.
- Prover then computes s1 = a(c_1) + k mod q and sends s1 to the simulator.
- Now, say the simulator succeeds in impersonating the Prover and the prover completes the protocol by asking the simulator to sends a random value again. The simulator then picks a second random value "c_2" in range 1, $\cdots$, q and sends c_2 to Prover.
- The prover then computes s2 = a(c_2) + k mod q, again and sends s2 to the simulator.

So, the key observation is that if simulator M succeeds in impersonating the protocol execution then, M can *trick* the Prover, and ask for two different proof transcripts using the same "k". This shouldn't happen in a real protocol execution, where the Prover specifically picks a new k for each execution of the protocol. If the Simulator succeeds in tricking the Prover into doing this, then the simulator can solve the following simple equation to recover Prover's secret:

$(s_1 - s_2) \div (c_1 - c_2) mod q = ((ac_1 + k) - (ac_2 + k)) \div (c_1 - c_2) mod q = a(c_1 - c_2) \div (c_1 - c_2) mod q = a[Secret value]$

ZERO-KNOWLEDGE: The correct execution of the protocol between the Prover and the Verifier will ensure that the Verifier learns nothing about the secret which the prover does not intend to reveal. This makes the protocol with the basic issuance of completeness and soundness, a zero-knowledge-proof protocol.

10.3.2.2 Fiat-Shamir Protocol

Fiat and Shamir [19][1] proposed the *"non-interactive zero proof of knowledge (NIZK)"* for a secret key "a." The corresponding public key is g^a. Turning Schnorr protocol into a non-interactive proof requires the picking of a random challenge "c" without any interaction with the verifier. So, the verifier is replaced by a hash function.

Thus, the non-interactive version of the protocol for proving knowledge of a secret "a" with respect to a public key g^a is as follows:

- The Prover picks a random value "k" in range 1 to q (just as in the interactive protocol). Computes $h = g^k$ mod p and sends h to the Verifier. Now, the prover computes the challenge *"c"* as:$c = H(g^k || M)$ Where: H() = hash function, M = (optional) and arbitrary message string. || = concatenation, and k = a random value chosen in range 1,..., q (as described above in interactive version of protocol)
- Prover computes s = ac + k mod q and sends s to Verifier.
- Verifier then checks if $g^s \equiv PK^c . h mod p$ (just as in the interactive protocol)

Here, the key difference was the use of a hash function to pick a random challenge "c" without any interaction with the Verifier. In principle, if the hash function is *strong and has a uniform distribution of values then the proof becomes completely non-interactive.*

Where does this zero-knowledge proof protocol fit into our problem area of E-Voting on Blockchain?

10.3.3 PROTOCOL DESIGN

We have used this NIZK protocol for *voter anonymity* validation without revealing the real identity of the voter. The validation part of the NIZK proof is put on the blockchain which simply takes a list of public parameters sent by each anonymous voter. This proof on the Blockchain validates that a particular anonymous voter is valid and has a right to vote without his real identity being exposed on the Blockchain. Then, the voter can vote whose vote is encrypted using a symmetric key cryptosystem. We have used the Fiat-Shamir protocol for providing anonymity to the voters in the Blockchain ecosystem. We have used a Double-Discrete logarithm [15] for implementing the proof.

10.3.3.1 Voter Anonymity

For every n-voters in the network, all of them initially generate two random numbers using private key/number. A random number generation function such as SHA256 padded with some private strings/numbers is used. The two random numbers are designated as serial number(sn) and a random secret(r_1).

Several each Voter then generates too concerning some (say) commitments (cm^i) as follows:

$$cm^i = H1(sn, r_1) \qquad (10.1)$$

Where: H1 = SHA256 hash function.

A second private key or number is again used by all n-voters using the same generation function, SHA256 padded with some string or number to generate a random number which is to use for publishing commitment(cm^i) on the Blockchain.

The resulting random number is designated as *'publishCM address'*. Such addresses are used by each voter to publish their commitment(cm^i) on the Blockchain:

$$publishCMaddress = H1(sn, r_2) \qquad (10.2)$$

Where: H1 = SHA256 hash function, r_2 = random secret,

After each voter vi publishes his commitments on the Blockchain network, the voter's v^i will have to vote for a candidate or any proposed query on the network.

Each voter v^i can vote for a candidate or the proposed query as follows: Voters v^i generates the proof saying:

"I know some random numbers/information such that one of the commitments amongst commitments i.e cm^i, is created and put by me on the BlockChain"

The proof does not reveal any information about the particular commitment that a particular voter v^i claims to have created

Each Voter generates their respective proof as follows: $y^i = (g^{cm}i * g^x i) \; t^i = (g^v i * g^z i) \; h^i = Hash(g^i, y^i, t^i) \; r^i = g^i + z^i - cm^i * h^i - x^i * h^i$

PROOF (PRF) CONSISTS OF: (t^i, r^i, h^i)

Any voter in the network can verify the proof as follows: $t^i \equiv g^r i * y^h i$

Where, y^i = temporary variable to store the result of $g^{cm}i * g^x i$, g^i = generator of a large chosen finite cyclic group, cm^i = random number generated as described in (1), x^i = random number generated using SHA256 hash function with some number/string padded, t^i = temporary variable to store the result of $g^v i * g^z i$, v^i = random number generated using SHA256 hash function with some number/string padded.

z^i = random number generated using SHA256 hash function with some number/string padded.

Hash = SHA256 hash function. CORRECTNESS OF THE PROOF(PRF) CAN BE VERIFIED AS FOLLOWS: $= g^v * g^z \equiv g^v * g^z * g^{-(cm*h)} * g^{-(x*h)} * g^{(cm*h)} * g^{(x*h)}$

since: $y = (g^{cm} * g^x)$ and $r = v + z - cm * h - x * h$ So, $g^v * g^z \equiv g^v * g^z$

After generating the above proof, the voter v^i would then be able to cast his vote. Each voter v^i will use sn^i, the random number generated above, as the voting address to cast the vote.

The use of sn^i for voting serves two purposes:

- **No Double-Voting:** Once *"sn"* gets used, voters won't be able to vote again with the same *sn*. This is because once *sn* gets used, it will be published on the Blockchain and will be known to all other nodes that someone has used it. Moreover, the generated *sn* is some random number generated using a Hash function with a random private number. So, getting the same *sn* for the same voter again would be infeasible.

- **Voter Anonymity:** Since sn is also used to generate cm with some random value r_1 which is private to a voter, and that cm is put on the Blockchain. Knowledge of sn won't reveal anything about voters because sn is just some random value that is used by the voter. Co- relating sn to cm is also not feasible because it requires knowledge of random r_1 which the individual voter never discloses. Moreover, cm is also used for generating proof as shown above (1). Because the voter reveals only the proof, knowledge of cm will also not be of use for adversary for generating proof as it requires knowledge of **x** which again voter never reveals.

Padding with a unique string/number is like adding nonce to prevent the attack on private keys such as dictionary attack and rainbow table attack.

NOTE: THE PUBLISHCM ADDRESS (2) used by each voter to publish cm on the Blockchain is also the valid address of a voter because the same sn and some large random r_2 which the voter never discloses, is used. Knowledge of sn won't link which voter's sn it is, because this would require knowledge of r_2.

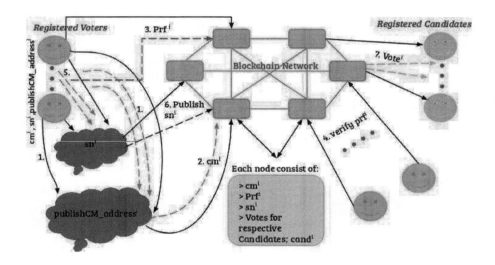

Figure 10.3 Protocol design for voter anonymity

DISCUSSION OF FIGURE 10.3:

   i. represents as a process where each voter v^i generates a *publishCMaddress^i*; which is random, as shown in Figure 10.4.
  ii. represents as putting cm^i on the Blockchain Network by the voter's v^i.
 iii. represents as putting proof prf^i on the Blockchain Network by the voter's v^i.
 iv. represents as verifying the prf^i by the other nodes/voters v^i on the Blockchain Network.

v. represents as a process where each voter v^i generates a sn^i; which is random, as shown in Figure 10.4.

vi. represents as publishing (sn^i on the Blockchain Network by the voter's v^i.

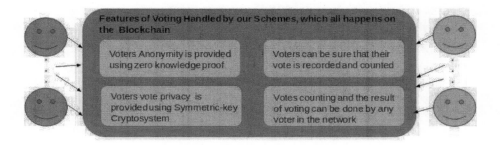

Figure 10.4 Voting Features handled by our protocol design using Blockchain

10.3.3.2 Registration of Voters and Candidates/proposed query

Registration of candidates and voters can be done by the registration authority. For each of the valid and registered voter, a unique serial number is given. This serial number is used later for opening the voting ballot page for Voting. This serial number is issued only once per voter for opening a ballot page once.

The candidates/proposed query for whom voting is to be done is pre-defined before the voting process. The administrator's job is to put the list of candidates or the query on the Blockchain. The administrator cannot do any manipulation because the elected candidate will already be known to all voters

10.3.3.3 Votes Privacy and Votes Counting

Each voter then sends the vote in an encrypted form using the Symmetric key cryptosystem such as AES on the Blockchain. Each voter reveals his Secret key on the Blockchain only when the voting period is over. Since every voter wants privacy of their vote, so revealing their Secret key during voting process will be against their privacy need.

The counting of votes at the end of the voting is done using the Smart Contract which is deployed on the Blockchain. After receiving the Secret keys, any voter can retrieve the encrypted vote by querying the Blockchain. All the encrypted votes can then be decrypted by using the Secret key which is published on the Blockchain by all the voters after the voting period. This can be done for any candidate by any voters. Predicting the total votes for a particular candidate by looking at the total number of encrypted votes for that candidate on the Blockchain would reveal nothing, as the encrypted vote can contain either a *"yesVote"* or a *"noVote."* Only the *"yesVote"* gets counted.

Each voter can then tally the votes by counting the total votes for each or all the candidates. *Following Figure 10.4. shows the features of E-Voting handled by our scheme.*

10.3.4 SECURITY CONSIDERATION

10.3.4.1 Voters Device Coercion:

Security of the voters voting machine can become a bottleneck wherein a coercer can influence the outcome of the vote by compromising the voter's device. The coercer can infect the voter's machine and get hold of the voter's private keys/numbers. This problem can be mitigated by enforcing voting in private or in a security bounded place.

10.3.4.2 Denial-of-Service (DoS):

The problem of the Denial-of-Service (DoS) attack is mitigated because once *sn* is used for voting, it becomes viewable to everyone on the Blockchain.

10.3.4.3 Sybil attack:

The problem of Sybil attack wherein a dishonest voter can generate several *"sn^i"* and *"r^i"* and repeatedly vote for a candidate of his choice. To mitigate this problem for each of the valid and registered voters, a unique *id number* is given. This *id number* is used later for opening the voting ballot page for Voting. This *id number* is issued only once per voter for opening a ballot page once.

10.3.4.4 Insider Attack:

Insider attack which can compromise the election and generally takes place in a centralised setting is taken care of has the whole process is decentralised. The work of the central authority is just to verify and validate the voters before the voting process begins.

10.3.4.5 Trojan Horse Spywares:

There are widely available tools for infusing this attack on the voter end device which acts as a point of contact to the blockchain network. To countermeasure, this regular update of the device software against any malicious activity can be done.

One significant attack on the entire blockchain is called the 51% attack [17]. This is one of the major flaws in Bitcoin and Ethereum Blockchain. Group of a miner who owns more than 50% of mining power will be able to over-power the whole networks hash rate capacity. This would significantly bias the block validation rule allowing only a selected number of blocks can to be mined and validated. The adversary would be able to halt voting for a particular candidate or reverse votes for a candidate. This means an adversary would be able to double-spend [12] the votes. Preventing this attack requires careful examination and incentives for the miner nodes.

10.4 IMPLEMENTATION DETAILS

At a higher level the normal process in a *client-server model* for a web app to work is as follows:

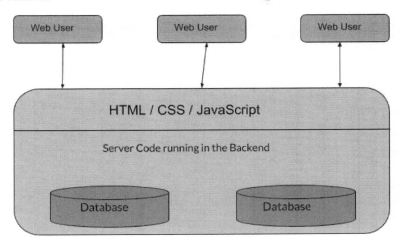

Figure 10.5 Centralised web app development

The above-mentioned Figure 10.5., is the normal process of how a client makes a request to the server, the client interacts with the centralised module which does the necessary processing and responds to the client request by retrieving the information. This architecture works well most of the time, but certain applications like e-voting, land registration, medical records sharing, etc., would require the database to be publicly and securely accessible to the concerned parties removing the need to depend on the web app for the data.

So, one way to solve the above problem would be the development and deployment of a *decentralised application (DApp)*. DApp involves running the backend code in a decentralised peer-to-peer network. DApp supports the deployment of a deterministic logic called smart contract to run which has public visibility and any concerned party can talk to the DApp using this smart contract. The front end can be any normal web browser. Ethereum is one such framework that follows a blockchain architecture and supports an easy way to build and use DApps.

As shown in the Figure 10.6, below, each client app connects and communicates to its own instance of the application. There is no centralised server to which all clients connect to. So, any node/person who wants to connect to DApp should have a full copy or act as a light client (i.e. have an instance of recent blockchain headers) on their computer node, phones, server, etc. Running any application would require every node to have this copy of the consistent blockchain. This introduces lots of redundancy but it's the way around to provide security and do away with a centralised server.

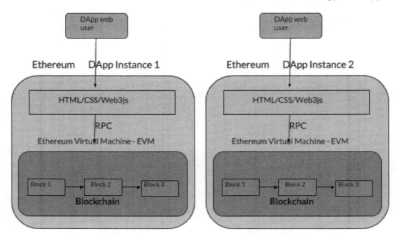

Figure 10.6 Ethereum DApp development

10.4.0.1 On Ethereum

The main components for the development of E-voting on Ethereum consist of:

- Geth: Ethereum Blockchain developed using GO. This geth implements a full Ethereum node Blockchain.
- Web3js: Web3js library which acts as an API for talking to smart contracts and geth Blockchain. Web3js uses remote procedure call (RPC) to talk to the geth Blockchain.
- Nodejs: Nodejs and HTML for the development of the front end which serves a client request on the blockchain.
- Solidity: A smart contract that is deployed on the geth nodes. Solidity is a contract-oriented, high-level language influenced by C++, Python, and JavaScript and is designed for the Ethereum Virtual Machine (EVM). Each of the geth nodes uses EVM for running the smart contract and the blockchain code.

Solidity is:

- statically typed,
- supports inheritance,
- libraries, and
- user-defined types.

The following gives the description of various components: COMPONENT DESCRIPTION:

The registration of the voters is assumed to be valid and is done securely by an honest authority.

USER/VOTER: Every user/voter generates random numbers using a *private key/number*. A random number generation function, *SHA256* padded with salt is used for getting the hash of these numbers. These hashes serve as *"voter addresses"* for voting and publishing *"commitments"* on the Blockchain. Each voter is also responsible for generating the proof parameters. The public parameters of the proof are deployed on the blockchain. All the public parameters are generated using *"Big-Integer" prime numbers*. These prime numbers belong to a *"multiplicative cyclic group"*. The arithmetic operations in these groups are based on *"double discrete logarithm"*.

The *private key/number* is hashed and kept after use which can only be extracted using the voter's passwords. This password is not stored by the voters *nodejs* file.

Each voter also uses *AES*, an asymmetric encryption technique for encrypting the vote. This encrypted vote is then published on the blockchain. The secret key for *AES* encryption is published by each voter on the blockchain only after the voting process.

SMART CONTRACT: The contract function is responsible for storing the votes in encrypted form, consists of the proof, and initializsing the candidate's address on the *geth blockchain*. The candidate's names are passed as constructor parameters at the time of initializsing and deploying the contract. Each of the names will be assigned a *"bytecode address"*. This address serves as a ballot per candidate on which votes have to be cast. This address is public and viewable to all. The contract stores the votes per candidate using *"mapping,"* which is a key-value store datatype in solidity. The keys are the candidate's addresses and the values are the list of encrypted votes.

CANDIDATE REGISTRATION, VOTING, VOTE COUNTING, AND VOTES VERIFIABILITY BY VOTERS: Candidate registration is done by invoking the constructor of the smart contract class. This constructor function deploys the candidate names on the blockchain. The deployment of a code in the blockchain is immutable. Every update made on the contract which consists of both the old and the new instance is retained by the blockchain, unlike the client-server model where every deployment of the code overwrites the old code.

The voting process involves storing the votes per candidate on the *bytecode address* by calling the function of the contract class. If by error the voter who uses an address for voting uses the same address again for voting, this will instantaneously be captured by the function class and will alert an error. All the vote values are encrypted using *AES* before storing them on the *geth blockchain*. It does not reveal the plaintext vote. The vote values can either be a *"yes"* or *"no"* vote. These votes can only be decrypted when each voter publishes their secret key on the blockchain.

When all the secret keys get published, all voters can decrypt the vote values and can individually count the votes for each of the candidates.

Whenever a voter puts their votes in encrypted form on the blockchain, the voter can always view that it has been stored on the blockchain, as it is transparent. For verifying if a particular voter's votes is counted, the voter after decrypting all the votes including his, can count and verify that the total votes tally with the rest of the voter's nodes. If it tallies then the voter can be sure that his vote has been counted.

A high-level view of E-voting application on Ethereum is shown in Figure 10.7.

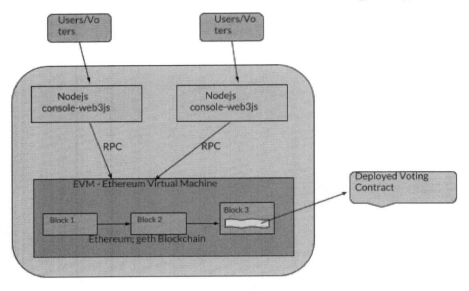

Figure 10.7   E-voting on Ethereum

10.4.0.2   On HBasechainDB

HBasechainDB is an in-house implementation by *High-Performance Computing and Data (HPCD) Group, Sri Sathya Sai Institute of Higher Learning.* HBasechainDB is a super peer-to-peer network operating using a federation of nodes. All the nodes in the federation have equal privileges which give HBasechainDB its decentralization. HBasechainDB provides a blockchain layer on top of the HBase database. HBase is a distributed, scalable, reliable, and versioned storage system.

Components Description USERS/VOTERS: This component follows the same procedures as discussed in the implementation of Ethereum. The only difference being the usage of *Java* instead of *nodejs*.

ZK PROOF FOR VOTING: HBasechainDB does not support the creation and deployment of smart contracts. So, to circumvent this problem a fixed public address that is known to all the voters is generated and used. This is the address for storing the proof. Generation of public addresses is done using *SHA-256*. The proof consists of the arithmetic *"double discrete logarithm"* operations, which are stored in a string format. To verify this proof, every voter must read the proof from this address, convert the string to an appropriate *BigInteger* format and apply the necessary parameters on this arithmetic proof. The proof does the job of verifying whether the parameters evaluates to *"true"* or *"false"*. The parameters for the proof are based on the *"multiplicative cyclic group"* of large prime numbers.

CANDIDATES REGISTRATION, VOTING, VOTE COUNTING, AND VOTES VERIFIABILITY BY VOTERS: Candidate's addresses are again generated using *SHA-256* hash which is fixed and acts as a public address. For any voter to vote, the voter has to provide this address as the destination address. All the votes per candidate are passed as a *"HashMap"* data type. The key per voter consists of a *"voteid"* and the value is the *"zero" or "one"* vote. This *"voteid"* is a unique per candidate. The voter can vote on any one of these addresses. Each vote is encrypted using *AES* before voting, so the content of the vote remains a secret. After the voting period, all the voters again publish their secret key on a public *"publish SecretKey"* address.

Any voter can pick up the key from this address, decrypt the vote and see the content and count the total number of votes.

All the voting process happens as a transaction transfer. Each of the transactions can be viewed and checked using the *"transaction ID"* by the voters. To get the list of votes per candidate, the voters can get the list of transactions of candidates using this *transaction ID*. These *transaction IDs* for each of the candidates are stored in a public address on *HBase*. This transparent store of *transaction ID* on *HBase* ensures that the voter can be sure that his votes are being stored.

For verifying that the voter's votes are counted, each of the voters can retrieve the transactions using these *transaction IDs*, count the total votes per candidate, and tally with the rest of the voter's votes count.

10.5   ANALYSIS AND RESULT

The following shows the analysis done on Ethereum and HBaseChainDB platforms using our protocol

10.5.1   ON ETHEREUM

Any transactions performed on Ethereum require the consumption of gas which is paid in a currency called Ether (virtual currency, like bitcoin). This payment of Ether is calculated via an intermediary benchmark called *"gasPrice" and "gasUsed"*.

The Equation for Ether calculation is: Ether= gasPrice * gasUsed.

On Ethereum, the gas used is measured in the unit of *"gas"*. Gas is a unit that gets translated into *Ether (ETH)* as a cost of performing that action (or work); a measure of computational effort. To each operation, a fixed amount of gas is assigned (e.g. adding two numbers costs 3 gas, calculating a hash costs 30 gas, sending a transaction costs 21000 gas).

Since computation is expensive as it has to be done by every full node in the network, excessive consumption of gas needs to be discouraged. There- fore, each unit of gas must be paid for (in Ether) by the sender of the trans- action that triggered the computation. *"gasPrice"* is the price to be paid for burning a gas by executing the smart contract code or a normal transaction operation. *gasPrice* is measured in a unit of *Gwei*. For 5 lines of code that need 5 units of gas, this would cost *5 Gwei*.

"gasUsed" is the amount of gas used for performing a particular operation. This *gasUsed* is deducted from *"gasLimit"*.

It is not known in advance the amount of gas a transaction will burn. So, every transaction has a field called *"gasLimit"* which puts a limit on the maximum amount of gas a sender is allowed to burn to execute a transaction. Transaction execution is stopped if it exceeds this limit. The gas utilised by the transaction processing is deducted even if the full execution takes more than the *gasLimit*. This limit prevents the user from over utilising the resources, as the termination of transaction execution frees the resources from the user. The field for *"gasLimit"* is initialised by the sender before executing a transaction or smart contract.

Blocks, also have a field called *"gasLimit"*. This defines the maximum amount of gas all transactions are allowed to use in a block. This field sets a block size in constant with the network bandwidth so that the block propagation and processing time is kept to a minimum, and the transaction throughput is not affected by being a decentralised network. This *gasLimit* specifies the number of transactions that can sit in a block. The higher the gas used by a transaction, the fewer is the number of transactions in a block.

WHAT IS DIFFICULTY AND HASHRATE? Like all blockchain technologies, Ethereum's continual usage and security is driven by block reward or incentive. This incentive is provided when a consensus algorithm fulfills the block validation rule and generates a hash which is less than the target difficulty hash. All the nodes are called miners who produce blocks, while the other nodes check for validity. This consensus algorithm is called *"proof-of-work (PoW)."*

The *"proof-of-work (PoW)"* algorithm used in Ethereum is called *"Ethash"* which involves finding a *nonce* and trying as an input to the algorithm so that the result is below a certain threshold than the set difficulty. The difficulty gets changed if the block is produced under 10 sec or more than 14 sec.

The point of this algorithm is to keep the block production time between 10-14 sec. The verification of a solution is fast and easy. The possibility of finding the *nonce* such that it less than the difficulty threshold governs the block creation time by a miner node.

Any node participating in the network can be a miner and their expected time to mine a block is directly proportional to their *"mining power or hashrate,"* i.e., number of *nonces* tried per second to find a value smaller or equal to the defined difficulty value.

Using this model, we have measured the transactions per seconds for upto four nodes. Initially we started with a setup of a private network of two nodes. The difficulty is set to a predefined value of 131056 in decimal or 0x1fff 0 in hex. The *hashrate* of each node is 159824 hashes/sec (H/s). We have kept the block time between 0.5 to 1 sec.

Blocktime is the time taken by a miner node to produce a block after solving the *PoW* difficulty target algorithm.

We can calculate the Blocktime of a node as: Blocktime = difficulty / hashrate = 131056/159824 = 0.82 secs.

Blocktime for a block is kept under 1 sec (in our case). Blocktime for two nodes is $(2 \times 131056)/(159824 \times 2) = 0.82$ secs

Increasing the *hashrate i.e., adding a node*, requires increasing the difficulty, otherwise a fork can lead to a delay in the block formation in a miner node.

A network of three nodes $(3 \times 131056)/(159824 \times 3) = 0.82$ secs

Network of four nodes = $(4 \times 131056)/(159824 \times 4) = 0.82$ secs

So, as the number of nodes, i.e., hash power, gets added we had to increase the difficulty to make a consistent block time of 0.82 secs

The network propagation time for the block depends on the "gasLimit" of the block. With the given "gasLimit" of 1,000,000 gas and the gas for each transaction of 37,000. With each transaction having a base gas requirement of 27,000. We have taken the average gas requirement of 37,000 for sending the transaction and running the smart contract. So, the number of transactions per block is = 1000000/37000 = 27

In our private setup of four nodes we have the following configuration.

- Ubuntu 16.04 OS
- Intel Core i5-4670 CPU @ 3.40GHz4 processor
- 16 GB RAM
- 1 TB hard drive, and
- LAN of 15 Mbps

This configuration of nodes has almost negligible block propagation delay. Thus, transactions/sec= (27 * 60)/0.82 = 1976. So, to find the number of transactions/votes per day, it will be: (86400 * 27)/0.82 = 28, 44, 878

Given a number of voters: 21,924,151 (say). The number of days to vote is: 21924151/28, 44, 878 = 7.7 or 8 days

The figure 10.8 lists the different parameters for measuring transactions/sec against the number of nodes.

no of nodes	Hashrate (hashes per sec)	Difficulty	gasLimit/block (Gas)	gas/transaction	transactions/sec
1	159824	131056	1000000	37000	1976
2	319648	262112	1041592	37000	2048
3	479472	393168	1050010	37000	2049
4	639296	524224	1321013	47000	2049

Figure 10.8   Parameters for Measuring Transactions/sec against number of nodes

Figure 10.9 shows that when the number of nodes increases there is not much increase in the number of transactions per seconds.

As, it can be seen from Figure 10.10, that the increase in the number of nodes i.e., hashrate, requires the increase in difficulty, for the block creation time to be consistent. So, to keep up with the number of voters/transactions per sec, there should be a linear scaling of hashrate and difficulty. Also, the increase in gasLimit/block and gas/transactions does not incentivize the transaction throughput as the increasing hashrate and difficulty of the nodes takes the major share of block- time.

Number of Nodes vs Transactions per second

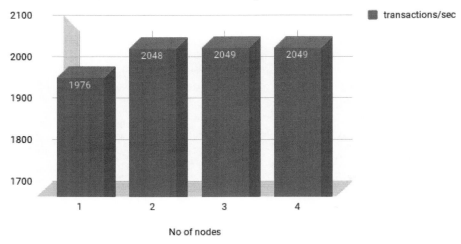

Figure 10.9 Ethereum transactions per sec v/s no of nodes

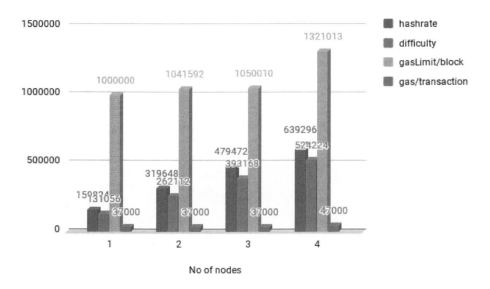

Figure 10.10 Block parameters for measuring transactions/per sec against number of nodes

10.5.1.1 On HBasechainDB

On HBasechainDB, the transactions throughput per node shows an al- most linear scaling. The main reason being that the computation is moved towards the data, rather than moving data to computation.

Moreover, there is no overhead of all nodes participating in a consensus to maintain the consistent state of the blockchain. This is done by a small set of dedicated federation of nodes. Also, the computation of the proof is done off-blockchain, by each of the individual nodes.

We have shown the results on three nodes. Each node has a configuration of:

- Ubuntu 16.04 OS
- Intel Core i5-4670 CPU @ 3.40GHz4 processor
- 16 GB RAM
- 1 TB hard drive, and
- LAN of 15 Mbps

transactions/sec vs. no of nodes

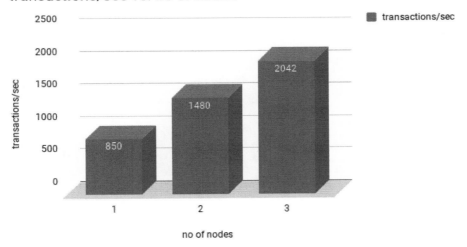

Figure 10.11   HBasechainDB transactions per second v/s no of nodes

So, with the result in Figure 10.11, if the number of voters is 2192 (say, taking the number of voters at a linear scale and equivalent to the transaction throughput) and transactions per second of 2042, it takes 1 day to complete a voting process.

Thus, increasing the number of nodes will be able to handle an increase in the transactions/voters per second as shown by Figure 10.12.

10.6   COMPARISON BETWEEN HBASECHAINDB AND ETHEREUM

The following graphs shows and discusses the implementations comparison between HBasechainDB and Ethereum platforms using our proof-of-work protocol design.

Figure 10.13 shows the increase in number of nodes linearly. The increase in nodes being a linear integer.

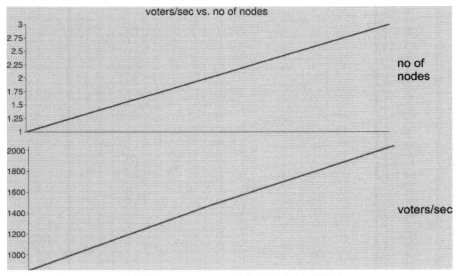

captionVoters per second v/s Number of Nodes

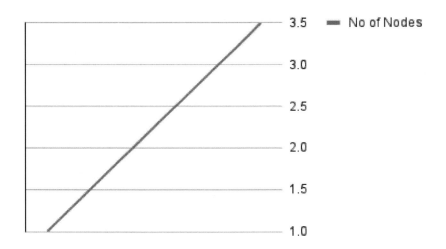

Figure 10.12   Number of Nodes used for Experiment

The graph in Figure 10.14 shows the voters per second on HBasechainDB. From our observation, the voters per second on HBasechainDB is better than in Ethereum. The main reason being the underlying support provided by HBasechainDB is in tune with the protocol design.

HBasechainDB makes a linear scaling of transaction throughput as it moves the computation to the data nodes. This decreases the heavy load of moving large amounts of data to the processing nodes over a limited band- width channel.

Figure 10.13 Voters per sec on HBasechainDB

Figure 10.14 Voters per sec on Ethereum

In case of Ethereum there is a constraint of block time to be consistent, and to make this happen there is an overhead of adjusting the difficulty with each increase in hashrate or node. This adjustment of consistent block time which is to be followed by all the nodes prevents the transactions throughput from scaling. Added to it is that the gas consumed by the smart contract prevents writing of complex code, which limits writing complex arithmetic or logical operation on the Ethereum Blockchain.

10.7   CONCLUSION

A great dilemma of adopting E-voting has always troubled mankind. With the history of widespread misuse of E-Voting in many government agencies, a full-fledged voting solution is yet to come to the fore. There have been several good proposals for it, but each comes with inherent security issues which makes its adoption unsuitable for election. As this domain has been left void by the earlier technologies, using a new technology such as Blockchain could be used to complete this gap. With rapid development and adoption of Blockchain, its reach has spread to all domains making it a good and viable solution for E-voting.

So, we have looked at various blockchain technological solutions to try and see if it addresses the need. The key take away was that solutions and frameworks are being designed and considered by many private institutions.Looking for a viable framework for our work required quite an evolved logic handling platform. So, Ethereum was our choice of platform for our voting protocol. One of the reasons for this is that Ethereum supports creation of contracts, which are accounts operated by the Ethereum Virtual machine (EVM). Voters anonymity and privacy is an important piece of any voting protocol and is not yet handled by EVM transactions.

We have even extended this protocol to be used in HBasechainDB. HBasechainDB gives good scalability of transactions. Though it's still in its de- velopment phase and does not provide strong logic handling features and security, the transaction throughput which it provides is excellent.

10.8   FUTURE WORK

- Though the current protocol implementation on Ethereum and HBasechainDB shows the working, still more security testing needs to be done. A strong security mechanism always has the possibility of reducing the performance of the network nodes.
- Zero Knowledge proof can have an implementation using Elliptic Curve, as Elliptic Curves are meant to give good security with much less computation on the part of the user nodes.
- While we believe that protocol design should scale even with added cost of security features, extensive tests for the same have not been done. We recommend that scalability tests and more security threat tests be performed to provide empirical validation of the protocol.
- Parameters generation for zero knowledge proof is done completely on the user nodes. Upcoming features on Ethereum such as zk-snark can be used and leveraged wherein the parameter generation can be more computationally secure against adversary threats

Bibliography

1. Michel Abdalla, Jee Hea An, Mihir Bellare, and Chanathip Namprempre. From identification to signatures via the fiat-shamir transform: Minimizing assumptions for security and forward-security. In *International Conference on the*

Theory and Applications of Cryptographic Techniques, pages 418–433. Springer, 2002.

2. Ben Adida. Helios: Web-based open-audit voting. In *USENIX security symposium*, volume 17, pages 335–348, 2008.

3. Elli Androulaki, Artem Barger, Vita Bortnikov, Christian Cachin, Konstantinos Christidis, Angelo De Caro, David Enyeart, Christopher Ferris, Gennady Laventman, Yacov Manevich, et al. Hyperledger fabric: a distributed operating system for permissioned blockchains. In *Proceedings of the thirteenth EuroSys conference*, pages 1–15, 2018.

4. Tigran Antonyan, Seda Davtyan, Sotirios Kentros, Aggelos Kiayias, Laurent Michel, Nicolas Nicolaou, Alexander Russell, and Alexander A Shvartsman. State-wide elections, optical scan voting systems, and the pursuit of integrity. *IEEE Transactions on Information Forensics and Security*, 4(4):597–610, 2009.

5. Vitalik Buterin et al. A next-generation smart contract and decentralized application platform. *White Paper*, 3(37), 2014.

6. Francesca Caiazzo and Ming Chow. A block-chain implemented voting system. *Computer System Security*, 2016.

7. David Chaum. Secret-ballot receipts: True voter-verifiable elections. *IEEE security & privacy*, 2(1):38–47, 2004.

8. Josh D Cohen and Michael J Fischer. *A robust and verifiable cryptographically secure election scheme*. Yale University. Department of Computer Science, 1985.

9. David Derler and Daniel Slamanig. Key-homomorphic signatures and applications to multiparty signatures. *IACR Cryptol. ePrint Arch.*, 2016:792, 2016.

10. Oded Goldreich and Yair Oren. Definitions and properties of zero-knowledge proof systems. *Journal of Cryptology*, 7(1):1–32, 1994.

11. Md Murshadul Hoque. A simplified electronic voting machine system. *International Journal of Advanced Science and Technology*, 62:97–102, 2014.

12. Ghassan O Karame, Elli Androulaki, and Srdjan Capkun. Double-spending fast payments in bitcoin. In *Proceedings of the 2012 ACM conference on Computer and communications security*, pages 906–917, 2012.

13. Friedrich W Kistermann. Hollerith punched card system development (1905-1913). *IEEE Annals of the History of Computing*, 27(1):56–66, 2005.

14. Trent McConaghy, Rodolphe Marques, Andreas Müller, Dimitri De Jonghe, Troy McConaghy, Greg McMullen, Ryan Henderson, Sylvain Bellemare, and Alberto Granzotto. Bigchaindb: a scalable blockchain database. *White Paper, BigChainDB*, 2016.

15. Kevin S McCurley. The discrete logarithm problem. In *Proc. of Symp. in Applied Math*, volume 42, pages 49–74. USA, 1990.

16. Satoshi Nakamoto and A Bitcoin. A peer-to-peer electronic cash system. *Bitcoin.–URL: https://bitcoin. org/bitcoin. pdf*, 4, 2008.

17. Christopher Natoli and Vincent Gramoli. The blockchain anomaly. In *2016 IEEE 15th International Symposium on Network Computing and Applications (NCA)*, pages 310–317. IEEE, 2016.

18. Arnis Parsovs. Homomorphic tallying for the estonian internet voting system. *IACR Cryptol. ePrint Arch.*, 2016:776, 2016.

19. Charles Rackoff and Daniel R Simon. Non-interactive zero-knowledge proof of knowledge and chosen ciphertext attack. In *Annual International Cryptology Conference*, pages 433–444. Springer, 1991.

20. Peter YA Ryan, David Bismark, James Heather, Steve Schneider, and Zhe Xia. Prêt à voter: a voter-verifiable voting system. *IEEE transactions on information forensics and security*, 4(4):662–673, 2009.

21. Christoph Van der Elst and Anne Lafarre. Blockchain and the 21st century annual general meeting. *Eur. Company L.*, 14:167, 2017.

22. Scott Wolchok, Eric Wustrow, J Alex Halderman, Hari K Prasad, Arun Kankipati, Sai Krishna Sakhamuri, Vasavya Yagati, and Rop Gonggrijp. Security analysis of india's electronic voting machines. In *Proceedings of the 17th ACM conference on Computer and communications security*, pages 1–14, 2010.

23. Gavin Wood et al. Ethereum: A secure decentralised generalised transaction ledger. *Ethereum project yellow paper*, 151(2014):1–32, 2014.

11 Secure Permission-based Medical Blockchain Framework for the Exchange of Electronic Health Records

In recent years, "blockchain" innovation has been acquiring more attention from the predominant media. In the simplest form, blockchain is a more look-alike new type of data structure. Blockchain is demonstrated to be immutable, which ensures trustworthiness, confidentiality and manageability of data through a pair of public and private keys. Blockchain has been at the centre of attention after the effective boom of Bitcoin. There have been numerous endeavors to utilise noteworthy features of blockchain for different applications and use cases. This article investigates the proficiency of blockchain technology in healthcare systems in particular it focuses on how Electronic Health Records (EHR) such as scan reports, medical images etc., can be preserved by adopting blockchain networks in a telehealth environment. This section provides the insights into the background of the research says blockchain networks, distributed storage and image encryption for ensuring the privacy of EHR.

11.0.1 BLOCKCHAIN NETWORK

A blockchain network is a decentralised, distributed database that is utilised to hold a persistently growing list of records, known as blocks that are interlinked and secured by using cryptography techniques. Each block contains a timestamp, transaction details and hash of the previous block in such a way that these transactions are rigid. Immutability is the primary characteristic of blockchain which guarantees the integrity or trustworthiness of data that are distributed in the blockchain technology. Practically, a blockchain can act as an open, distributed ledger that can contains transactions between different nodes productively and in a provable and perpetual manner. Figure 11.1 (a) depicts the schematic representation of a centralised ledger and Figure 11.1 (b) shows the distributed ledger. From Figure 11.1, it is depicted that, multiple ledgers can connect in a centralised ledger however all transactions are held and verified by the central authority here it is termed as bank server. Therefore, it requires a trusted third party for verifying the transactions. Consequently, blockchain technology runs in a peer-to-peer network where all nodes have some level of access to the ledger without trusted third-party verification. In a blockchain network, each

DOI: 10.1201/9781003355052-11

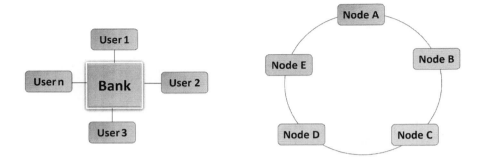

Figure 11.1   Centralised vs distributed ledger

transaction is securely broadcasted to all nodes in the network by adopting cryptographic techniques. Generally, in a blockchain framework, miners/nodes are used to collect all the new blocks by executing proof of work for appealing transactions. Thus, in a distributed ledger, miners are responsible for verifying the transactions. The running example of the blockchain network is given in the following scenario.

Scenario 1: Alice wants to spend X amount to Bob: Without blockchain: Alice sends a request to the bank account stating that the debit of X from Alice's account and credit to Bob's account by mentioning bob's account details. The bank server verifies the request say: Is Alice's account has enough money for transfer, Account credibility, etc. After these verifications, the bank server executes the transaction and sends X amount to bob. With blockchain: Alice creates a transaction of X to Bob and broadcasts it over the internl miners check whether the transaction is valid. If yes, Bob receives amount X from Alice. The major building blocks of blockchain technology are (i) authentication – through which the distributed framework ensures legitimate users, (ii) encryption for preserving the confidentiality of the data or transaction details (iii) digital signatures are said to be a digital stamp established as a proof for validating task, and (iv) hashing is used for converting the data files into unique code. The primary components in the blockchain framework are distributed ledger, smart contracts and distributed applications.

11.0.1.1   Types of Blockchain

Blockchain framework can be categorised into (i) permission-based framework and (ii) permissionless framework.

- Permission-based blockchain: Blockchain network is open to limited participants among the available users. These allowed users are approved by the access control authority. It maintains access control privileges for available users in the network.
- Permissionless blockchain: In a permissionless distributed blockchain network, transactions are open to all users available in the network. It is also

referred to as a public blockchain where anyone without prior permission can read/write the data.

11.0.1.2 Fundamental elements in blockchain

The building blocks of any blockchain technology are Database, Block, Hash, Miner/node, and Transaction.

- Blockchain as a database:
  The blockchains are normally treated as a database but not as a traditional database structure where it is treated as rows and columns. Rather blockchain is viewed as a ledger of previous transactions.
- A block: Each block in a blockchain comprises of following components as shown in Figure 11.2 Every block in a blockchain contains previous

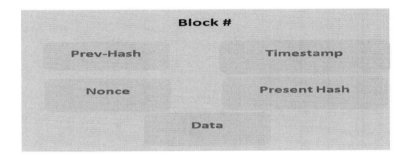

Figure 11.2   Elements of blockchain

and present hash values which are utilised to determine the order of transactions that occurred. Data holds the details about transactions and nonce represents the random number accompanied with the block.

- Hash
  Hash is the mathematical expression, that miner or node has to solve for identifying the block. Initially, a nonce, random number is generated and added at the end of the data block. The complete block undergoes a hash operation, SHA 256 and if the resultant has started with zero, a new block is found else the node should continue the process.
- Miner/node A miner or node is a system that tries to solve the mathematical expression associated with the block. By solving the mathematical problem, it can easily identify the blocks in the network.

11.0.2 INTER-PLANETARY FILE SYSTEMS (IPFS)

IPFS stands for Interplanetary File System and that keeps tracking of further versions of the file in case of update. It also defines how files circulate across a network, making it a distributed file system. IPFS uses the concept of content addressing i.e. labeling and finding content using the content of the file. During the upload of the file, the IPFS breaks the file into different chunks and distributes it over the network and returns the single cryptographic hash value to the user while maintaining a cryptographic Hash of chunks itself required for content addressing

11.0.3 CHAOTIC IMAGE ENCRYPTION

Nowadays, networking and digital communications are developing rapidly which empowers individuals to perceive images in a frequent manner. The network is an open medium, and while transmitting the images through the internet there is a chance of attacks and leakage of sensitive data. Thus, guaranteeing the digital images more specifically sensitive images from intruders or attackers is the most significant task. Generally, due to the special characteristics of digital images, conventional algorithms are not recommended for image encryption. Thus, to ensure the secrecy of digital images, chaotic systems are adopted for encrypting the images in the digital forum. The chaotic image encryption procedure follows Friedrich's architecture for performing pixel shuffling and diffusion. The process involved in chaotic image encryption are shown below:

11.1 BLOCKCHAIN TECHNOLOGY IN HEALTHCARE

Initially, the blockchain framework was coined for economics and cryptocurrencies, but nowadays its efficacy is widened for several applications which include biomedical, government bodies, and etc. The capability of blockchain technology can be seen in the medical field as illustarted in Figure 11.4

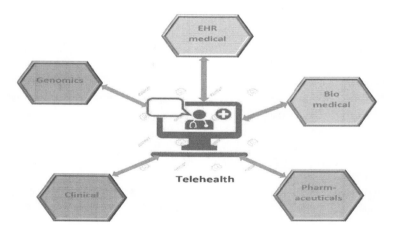

Figure 11.3   Blockchain in healthcare

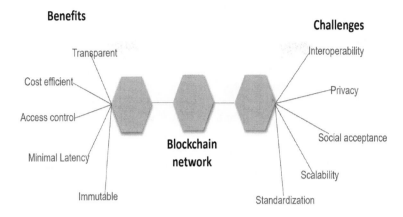

Figure 11.4 Blockchain opportunities and challenges

Health care is an information-escalated domain with huge amounts of medical information such as medicine prescription, medical images say MRI, CT scan, X-rays, lab reports and so on are produced, processed, and disseminated daily. However, patients' records are mostly hospital or institution centric which is termed as Electronic Health Records (EHR). This hospital-centric database results in inefficient coordination of data sharing during emergencies. Timely sharing of EHR across the healthcare centre and patients is essential for clinical consideration. For example, efficient and timely coordination of cancer patients is a prominent one where patient's medical history, test reports and diagnosis provides necessary information for the physician. Access to EHR is also important for patients and their caretakers. Conventional medical record exchange consists of three phases **Upload** – sending information say medical images, reports from one location to another through the internet, **Download** – obtaining information from the source or database, **View** – can read the medical records for consultation. Though it allows the exchange of medical records from one location to other, yet it is not suitable for patient-centric approaches or massive records. Thus, to ensure efficient transmission, blockchain technology is adopted in the healthcare environment.

Electronic Health Records (EHR) usually contain critical and highly sensitive data which is frequently shared among hospital judiciaries, researchers, lab technicians for better diagnosis and appropriate treatment. In conventional data exchange medium, during storage and transmission, there is possibility to compromise in patient's treatment. Thus, ensuring consistnet patient's medical history is highly important for guaranteeing the better treatment. To achieve this, blockchain based legder framework is adopted in the healthcare domain.

As a sign of emerging innovative technology, blockchain research has attracted many applications in recent years, as a result, blockchain-based patient data sharing platform has emerged. OmniPHR is a patient-centric blockchain where patient health records are shared among hospitals, patients and caretakers. In OmniPHR, data are stored in an off-chain manner. Also, another well-known application called MedRec from MIT researchers introduced Ethereum based information-sharing portal for medical records. The MedRec links the patient identities to the record that are held in hospitals. Through MedRec patients can view their records anywhere and anytime. Similarly, other blockchain methodologies are introduced with supply chain management perspective, health surveillance, and etc. Additionally, the outbreak of COVID-19 demonstrates the need for timely risk management of patient's data in accordance with hospital, testing lab and scan centres. The primary concern of timely risk management is medical record sharing among physicians, patients and their caretakers. The timely management of clinical record sharing can be ensured by adopting blockchain methodology.

11.1.1 RESEARCH CHALLENGES FOR ADOPTING BLOCKCHAIN TECHNOLOGY IN HEALTHCARE

Recently, blockchain technology gains more popularity as a result it is universally adopted in various sectors. The technology has its own benefits and challenges which are depicted in Fig.5.

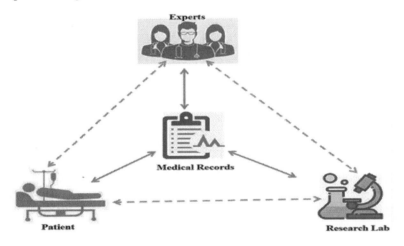

Figure 11.5   Medical records for various stakeholders

- Security
  The most important challenge in implementing a blockchain framework is data security. With blockchain technology, the application can be implemented without third-party services, yet it allows all miners/nodes to verify the transaction/records. This results in the security and privacy risk for the data that is being outsourced. In a healthcare domain perspective, the patients should nominate one or two caretakers for accessing their medical

information in case of emergencies. Simultaneously, the nominee has the chance to add further set of users to access the data which results huge privacy violation.

- Storage

  The healthcare data such as lab reports, health history and medical images MRI, CT scan and X-rays consume more storage for processing and transmission. Also, the fundamental principle of blockchain is distributed ledger with transaction oriented hence the database must have the capability to grow proportionally with respect to the incoming medical records.

- Standardisation

  For healthcare data, international Standardisation and data normalisation are required for medical records such that they can easily be shared among experts in other countries. The uniformity includes data size, format and sensitivity level of data that are yet to be considered while designing blockchain applications.

11.2 NOVEL PERMISSION BASED SECURE MEDICAL BLOCKCHAIN FOR ELECTRONIC HEALTH RECORD

Electronic Health Records (EHRs) are used to store the critical and highly sensitive private information of patients for diagnosis and treatment. If a person suffers from serious medical issues like cancer, or kidney disease then the long history of the treatment undertaken, post-treatment taken and recovery should be maintained. Accessing complete history like radiation doses and lab results are crucial for the patient's treatment. At sometimes, the patient may wish to go for a different diagnosis and treatment plan. For a consultation, the patient may visit multiple hospitals as every patient has their own rights to look and receive his health information. If the person moves from one country to other the situation still becomes worsen. Sending patient records through e-mail is not advisable as it has many security leaks. Moreover, these investigations are rarely shared among various health practioners who are involved in patient's care and it is isolated in the medical institution itself. The quality of patient's care suffers in this situation as other institutions do not know the patient's complete history. This, in turn, may lead to the increased cost to patients, unnecessary delays, incorrect decision making and in the worst case it leads to patient death due to fatal medical errors. Sometimes, anonymised data collected from various sources of the same patient may lead to patient de-identification, privacy violation, etc. and it has various consequences from inefficient caring of patients to information lack during critical and emergency situations. Unfortunately, EHR records are normally stored in the centralised environment for an institution which results in fragmentation and security breaches irrespective of de-identification and access control.

Blockchains are decentralised and distributed repositories to store information securely using different cryptographic primitives. The various participants like patients, health care professionals and research institutions upload medical records to the chain in an authenticated and secure fashion. In order to ensure privacy to the medical documents before feeding into blockchain technology, those records should be encrypted using symmetric key cryptography. If hypermedia data of EHRs is encrypted using traditional symmetric encryption schemes like AES, Triple DES then they lead to high computation cost. Hence chaotic encryption methods are preferred in this case. After encryption, these records can be stored in an Interplanetary File System (IPFS) with suitable regulatory jurisdiction. IPFS protocol uses a Peer-to-Peer network for secure storage of inofrmation which is protected from any form of alteration. The data stored on IPFS holds a cryptographically generated hash value which acts as a unique identifier. This strategy for secure storage makes it a good choice for storing sensitive and critical information. The unique cryptographic hash identifier can be stored on decentralised applications to minimise the extensive computations on the blockchain. Internet of Things (IoT) links various smart devices to provide solutions during emergencies. When a patient requires emergency treatment, the request will be sent to various entities like hospitals, medical practitioners, ambulances, etc. so that such situations can be easily handled. Hence, a practical real-time implementation of a system that uses a blockchain framework can be integrated to handle medical emergency situations. The proposed methodology employs permissioned blockchain framework to preserve metadata together with an access control policy. An IPFS service is also integrated to store encrypted patients' data. As per the access control defined by the patient, these technologies permit us to promise the security of the data, privacy as well as availability.

11.2.1   RELATED WORKS

Telemedicine offers clinical scientists with extended access to huge patient populations throughout the globe, which can bring about quicker and other remarkable clinical preliminaries. The innovation empowers investigation studies to proceed further legitimately to patients, disseminating the procedure and allow investigators extended access to patients with uncommon illness. While conventional clinical preliminaries frequently experience long retard, transportation limitations, and high dropout tariffs, telehealth can relieve these issues by utilising tools such as the remote assortment of biometric information, telecasting forum, and secluded medication observation. Global expansion generates more innovative models towards telemedicine. The telemedicine programme is an entire autonomous framework which conveys different services such as permitting, observing patient's records as well as gives continuous synchronal indispensable signals handling and deploying of in-patient. In this manner, such stage incorporates different actors and endorses different entails inside a consideration place. Baccar [3] introduced a new online e-health manifesto called Human Machine Interface (HMI) by utilising Zigbee modules, sensors to transmit the data acquisition panel and ascertains the patient's geographical location in addition to physiologic telemonitoring. Since HMI gathers the data through Zigbee modules, the signal strength for data coverage is very low and it is confined to a single building i.e., inside the hospital. Also, legal data fusion and clustering with respect to security are very tedious. Boric [4] discussed privacy and security threats towards the outsourced medical data. Additionally, authors explore remote monitoring systems for senior people who suffered from Obstructive Sleep Apnea (OSA).

Security is guaranteed by imposing access rules to the clinical and public authorities. Though researchers profess security and privacy preservation through access control, it imposes a very low degree of protection to sensitive data.

For ensuring significant level of security, researchers have a shift towards the blockchain based data outsourcing. Blockchain is a ledger that is shared over a network of computers. Blockchain innovation provides new devices for security and protection concerns. Moving towards digitisation and analytics, this innovation developed as a provable answer for security and authorisation issues. The fundamental subject behind the technique is once the data has been added to the chain it is hard to alter it. Though it offers a promising answer towards preserving sensitive data only a few researches are existing for incorporating blockchain in medical data. Padmavathi [13] presented a survey about the research impact of blockchain in healthcare. The author enlisted the opportunity for the utilisation of blockchain in E-health. With the assistance of blockchain, information can be managed effectively and efficiently. There is no requirement for the patient to have a bundle of clinical history files and results with them each time they visit a hospital. In addition, the utilisation of blockchain innovation could lessen capacity costs, support effectiveness, decline the requirement for manual documentation.

Gordon [9] focused on interoperability in healthcare especially patient-driven interoperability. The author examines how blockchain technology felicitates the patient data exchange through digital access controls, aggregation and immutability. It is considered that Blockchains empowers a consolidated and dispensed component for the administration of validation and approval rules encompassing the information. For instance, a blockchain can have "Smart Properties" which is a unit whose proprietorship is overseen between a blockchain for permitting a few types of computerised property to have clean possession. The caretaken of the information (for instance, the patient), is distinctly represented on the blockchain, and can eventually allocate access regulations and agreements around their data, empowering simpler sharing. Dubovitskaya [8] employed permissioned blockchain method to preserve metadata and usage regulation policy and cloud utilities to collect encrypted patients' data. Clinical data are stored through patients' secret keys. The system performs a hash on the shared data and signer using a secret key before it gets uploaded. The system shares only the text data rather than sharing radiology images which is crucial for consultation.

Al Omar [2] proposed MediBchain, a privacy-preserving platform for healthcare information using cryptographic functions with blockchain. The author ensures pseudonymity, privacy, integrity, accountability availability and security of the clinical data. Liu. X. [12] suggested a medical data sharing and security conspire dependent on the hospital's private blockchain to enhance the electronic health system of the hospital. The scheme achieves various properties like decentralization, tamper proof etc., Furthermore, a symptom matching dashboard is given to the patient who can analyse the symptoms prior to consulting the clinical authorities. The model also makes data sharing between doctor and patient in a protected way by utilising proxy re-encryption technology. Hylock [11] introduced Healthchain – a patient-centered health record and exchange. The secured information exchange is carried out by utilising smart contracts. Smart contracts are self-transactions performed when specific conditions of an agreement are met. In a smart contract, the re-encryption key is generated and deposited in a block. The authors employed an encryption mechanism which has a huge key length that led to computational overhead. Abid [1] suggested a methodology for sharing clinical information through blockchain. The secrecy of the clinical information is maintained by employing a history-based blockchain. A validated digital disseminated ledger of information in blockchain is created and utilised in a distributed environment. A blockchain based medical service framework is introduced by Chen Y [6]. Information repository and access control are the primary exchanges in the information trade. The information has not been altered with the assist of hash function and also public key cryptography is employed for confidentiality. Author guaranteed that one cannot decrypt the patient's information without providing the secret key.

Vazirani [15] proposed that cloud-based clinical information is related to authorisations and information retrieval guidelines, in this way utilising blockchain to maintain information via smart contracts. When an expert generates a record, it is confirmed, and its review consents are approved by the patient and stocked in a smart contract. The document can never be altered without understanding a greater part of hubs. Provisional access can be constrained by the utilisation of tokens, made by clients and circulated to hospital jurisdictions and insurance companies. The limitation is the operational cost involved in concealing this medical information from various legitimacy systems. Roehrs [14] presents an article about implementing a Personal Health record model using blockchain. The model is shaped through a private P2P network, where health records are sorted out into data blocks including a linked list and a disseminated ledger of clinical information. This course of action permit all clients related to the system to refresh their information proactively, i.e., data blocks can be sent and received automatically. These researches empower the secrecy of the patient data by incorporating blockchain over medical data but for tele-medicine or E-healthcare, the patient medical image is also equally important. For improving the secrecy of medical image outsourcing, a reversible watermarking technique is used. Bouslimi [5] introduced joint encryption and watermarking scheme for securing medical image outsourcing. It combines substitutive watermarking algorithm, quantization with stream cipher encryption. The author confirms the image integrity after it gets encrypted.

Similarly, Hussein [10] suggested a genetic algorithm-based blockchain for preserving medical data. The author proposed a system using Discrete wavelet Transform for enhancing the universal security and a Genetic algorithm for optimizing search and also hash function is utilised once there is a requirement of fetching a new record. Christo [7] ensures the secrecy of the sensitive data and also efficient retrieval using Securechain and SHA algorithms. The medical data is encrypted and the corresponding private cloud address for identification is stored in the blockchain and the information can be fetched after authenticating the user. Though they are about preserving the data which is at rest, there is a need for continuous processing of data which will contribute for alerting emergency services. In view of these examinations, it is imperative to work towards the direction of preserving health care data in a secure manner and processing those data under distributed ledger network for effective consultation and diagnosis.

11.2.2 CONVENTIONAL HEALTHCARE APPROACH

The high-level block diagram of various stakeholders of medical health records is shown in Fig. 11.5. These stakeholders participate in creating, accessing and updating the medical sensitive records.

Fig. 11.6 shows the conventional healthcare approach. As Fig.7 portrays that, the conventional healthcare approach is composed of different stakeholders at different locations like patients, hospitals, medical practitioners, testing labs and scan centre.

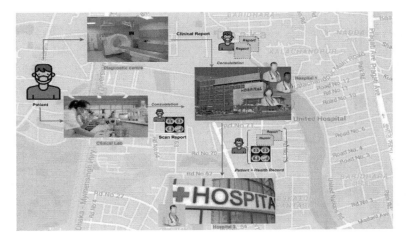

Figure 11.6 Conventional Healthcare approach

Habitually, these entities are interrelated i.e., the medical practitioners plan their treatment according to the lab test report and scan report. In general, if any patient faces an illness, he/she first visit the hospital for doctor consultation irrespective of the location. Later, as per the medical practitioner's advice, the patient may direct to a diagnostic centre or clinical laboratory for analyzing the illness. Usually, the diagnostic centre and clinical laboratories are situated at different locations. Thus, in the conventional approach, the patient needs to carry their diagnostic reports (CT scans, MRIs, PET scans) and test report whenever they visit the hospital. The situation will get even worse when the patient plans to travel within or outside the country as they need to carry all their medical history documents. Also, in the conventional healthcare approach, if any patient willing to get a second opinion from different medical practitioners they need to undergo the same set of diagnoses or tests which is very expensive in terms of money and time constraints. Thus, to overcome these difficulties and to ensure transparency, it is necessary to build a distributed ledger framework for connecting all the entities irrespective of their location.

11.2.3 PROPOSED APPROACH

To address the challenges of the conventional healthcare approach, the proposed system introduces Medical blockchain, a paperless medicinal service in a patient-centric manner. The detailed architecture of the proposed methodology is illustrated in Fig. 11.7. The main objective of the suggested Medical blockchain is, to link the government hospitals, medical practitioners, clinical laboratory, and patients at different locations by developing a common portal which acts as a distributed ledger system for exchanging the Electronic Health Records (EHR). In the conventional healthcare approach, patients must visit the same hospital and same medical practitioner throughout their treatment as the concerned experts/hospitals only knowing his/her medical history. This incurs an additional burden to the patients and their families who are forced to afford the cost for their travel and shelters apart from treatment.

To overcome these challenges, the proposed distributed Medical blockchain ledger framework can also act as a medium for online consultation, patient can share their queries with the medical experts irrespective of their location.

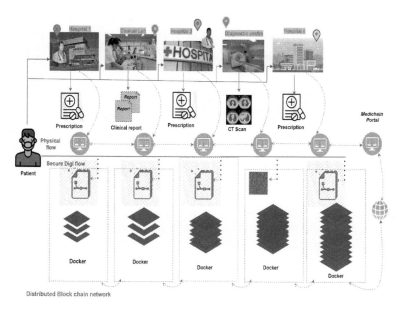

Figure 11.7   Systematic diagram of the proposed architecture

As depicted in Fig. 11.7, initially, if any patient visits any hospital which is connected in distributed networks for consultation towards his illness, a congruence form will be obtained from that patient stating that he agrees to share the EHR to all the entities in the ledger network or particular entities. Consider, patient P_1 visits hospital H_1 for consultation / treatment. The medical practitioner in the H_1 diagnose the disease and provides necessary supplements (Medicines) meanwhile doctor update the patient details and its medical history in the Medical blockchain portal. As the framework is designed using the blockchain Hyperledger framework, the data entered in H_1 will get reflected among all hospitals. To gurantee the confidentiality and integrity of the EHR, the suggested secure medical blockchain can define privileges for accessing EHR. Meanwhile, after getting the initial consultation, P_1 maybe suggested to approach clinical lab and diagnostic centre in the ledger framework for getting a medical report about their body fluids and medical images. The patient P_1 is uniquely identified by his ID proof. As these centres are interconnected through the suggested blockchain framework, the test reports and diagnostic images are shared among the portal by defining the access privileges to the hospitals. Now reports, prescription and diagnostic image for the patient P_1 will be available in distributed ledger framework and equipped with access control privileges. Once patient's records are available in the medical blockchain, he/she can visit any hospitals or can approach any doctors in the network for treatment and online consultation. While sharing these EHR in distributed frameworks among hospitals, clinical lab and diagnostic centres, it is very crucial to maintain the confidentiality and integrity of records. Thus, a secure permissioned medical blockchain framework is equally equipped with a dedicated security framework for preserving these data. The systematic representation of the suggested security framework is given in Fig. 11.8.

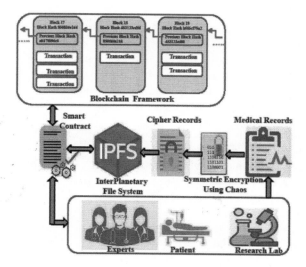

Figure 11.8 Systematic represenattion of the proposed secure medical blockchain framework

i. Generation of *Medical_Record*:

To illustrate the methodology, let us consider a scenario of a patient P_1 approached expert E_1. E_1 started diagnosing P_1 by admitting him to the corresponding hospital H_1. For sake and simplicity, the admission procedure is ignored over here and E_1 monitors P_1's situation continuously. The prescription of medicines and P_1 status are recorded lively and submitted to Medichain portal through smart contract. E_1 updates a file to keep the recording of medication called *Medical_Record*. This *Medical_Record* is shared among granted experts, labs and corresponding patients. For patients, only READ access whereas for E and granted labs READ/WRITE permission is there. During diagnosis, E may refer to some labs for required tests. The Experts and Labs update the *Medical_Record* file.

ii. Users:

In the detailed view, there are three kinds of active users namely Experts, Patient and Research Lab or clinical lab or diagnostic centres. Experts are the professionals in the medical field like Cardiologists, Anaesthesiologists, Dermatologists, Endocrinologists, Nephrologists, Neurologists etc. Patients are the person who is taking medical treatment under the Experts. The role of research labs is to perform different tests like blood tests, urine test, to generate diagnostic image, etc. and generate reports accordingly. Three users are interrelated entities through mutual understanding or because of some trust factor. It is assumed that only one file is maintained for each patient.

11.2.3.1   Symmetric encryption using chaos

In the proposed system, the file containing medical records is encrypted using Symmetric Encryption System. The encryption logic uses Chaotic maps to generate keystreams required for encryption as traditional schemes are time-consuming. The control values of the keystream depend on the input medical record file. So, for the attackers, it is very hard to perform chosen-plaintext attack. The details of medical record encryption are given in Fig. 11.9.

i. Keystream Generation

In the first step, the seed key is generated from the input image. From these seed values, the control parameters of chaotic maps are generated. Chaotic maps are the mathematical functions that generate chaotic order values for certain control values. These maps can be one-dimensional, two-dimensional like logistic map, Arnold cat map. Multidimensional maps are also there. However, if dimensions are more, complexity will be more. By executing chaotic maps keystreams are generated. These keystreams are used in permutation and diffusion operations.

ii. Permutation

It is the process of shuffling values. Shuffling indexes are created using the chaotic map.

iii. Diffusion

In this step pixel values are modified. Generally, bitwise XOR operation of values with keystreams is performed.

Note that Permutation and Diffusion should be reversible so that decryption is also possible. To increase the level of security the permutation and diffusion are repeated for m and n times. The value of m and n can be 4, 5 respectively.

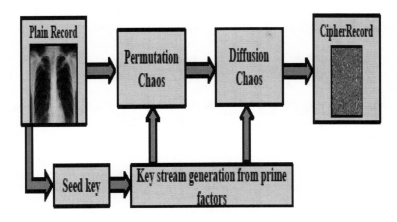

Figure 11.9   Symmetric key encryption using chaos

11.2.3.2   Secure storage – IPFS

The property of IPFS is a tamper-proof system. The encrypted files are uploaded to IPFS, IPFS chunks the file, distributes it over the network and returns the cryptographic Hash of that file. This Hash value is used for further references and it is illustrated in Fig. 11.10.

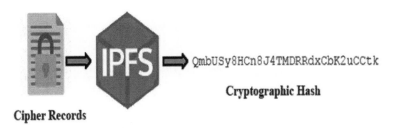

Figure 11.10   Usage of IPFS System

11.2.3.3   Medical Blockchain Framework

Next, a blockchain is a linked list of blocks that contain digital records which is a shared and distributed ledger of information. Blockchain utilises cryptology and rules for accessing the information in a secure manner. Each transaction is composed permanently to the blockchain. Transactions are only the records. Throughout the procedure, participants keep a duplicate of the mutual ledger and consent to its precision, guaranteeing consensus. In the proposed system, the transactions or data i.e., Encrypted Medical Record files Hash is uploaded to the blockchain. The transactions include a Hash of encrypted medical records, details related to smart contracts, details related to Patient, Experts and Research Labs. Smart contracts also can be embedded in the blockchain to make tamper-proof, transparent, immutable and decentralised.

Transactions: On the network, any kind of communications with EHRs are documented as transactions. Only to the participants related to the transaction, these transactions are accessible. Here some of the instances of transactions are illustrated in the following scenarios.

i. Granting Access of patients

- Patient X grants right to use EHR to Medical Practitioner P
- In Patient X's authorised asset (ledger) the Medical Practitioner P's Identification is added.
- Patient X's Identification is added to authorised asset (ledger) of Medical Practitioner P .
- The secret key of EHR is deciphered with private key of Patient X.
- The secret key is then enciphered with public key of Medical Practitioner P.

ii. Revoking Access of patient

- Patient X cancels access from Medical Practitioner P.
- From the authorised asset of Patient X, Practitioner P's Identification is detached.
- From the authorised asset of Medical Practitioner P, Patient X's Identification is detached.
- The private key of Patient X is utilised to decipher Secret key of EHR which is further used to decipher HER.
- Using a new secret key, the EHR is enciphered again.
- Using Patient A's public key, and all remaining IDs public keys that have permission the new secret key is enciphered.

iii. Medical Practitioner who refers Patient

- Medical Practitioner A updates the permissions of Medical Practitioner B to allow and access the Patient's EHR.
- Blockchain code checks for Permission of Medical Practitioner A on the EHR.
- Private key of Medical Practitioner A is used to decipher EHR's secret key.
- Public key of Medical Practitioner B is used to encipher the secret key.
- To the Patien tA's authorised asset, Medical Practitioner B's Identification is added.

- To the Medical Practitioner B's authorised asset, Patient A's Identification is added.

Data structure The overview of the required data structure is shown below. Four classes need to be designed namely Expert, Patient, Research Lab and *Permission_Medical_Record*. The *Permission_Medical_Record* defines the constraints for reading and writing the *Medical_Record* file.

Expert data structure

```
class Expert
{
int Expert_id;
string Name,
string Qualification;
float Experience;
Patient list[];
void getdata();
```

Patient data structure

```
class Patient
{
int Patient_id;
string Name,
FILE Medical_Record;
Expert list[]
```

Research Lab data structure

```
class Research_Lab
{
int LabId;
string Name;
void
referLab(PatientId);
```

Permission Data structure

```
class Permission_Medical_File

{

int FileID;

FILE Patient_Medical_Record;

PatientRead(patientID);

ExpertReadWrite(expertID)
```

11.2.4 PERFORMANCE METRICS FOR EVALUATION

This section provides insights into performance metrics that are commonly adopted for evaluating the performance of a secure blockchain framework.

11.2.4.1 Performance evaluation for blockchain - Hyperledger Caliper

One of the most critical aspects of blockchain users is the performance of a blockchain solution. However, presently there is no general tool for providing performance reviews of various blockchain technologies based on a collection of impartial and generally agreed guidelines. Some studies exist on the performance of various blockchain implementations in different contexts, but a blockchain benchmarking tool is not widely accepted. Hyperledger Caliper is a benchmark method for blockchain frames and is a benchmark goal for working on blockchain implementation. However, tools that can create a blockchain network quickly are ideal for working with Caliper. Hyperledger Caliper can generate reports containing various evaluation metrics, such as transactions per second, transaction latency, usage of resources, etc. The goal is to use Caliper results by other Hyperledger projects as they develop their applications and support the option to implement a blockchain that meets the unique needs of a user.

11.2.4.2 Performance evaluation for secure medical image records

The proposed framework introduces a secure blockchain-based distributed ledger for sharing medical health records usually medial images. Thus, the performance can be analysed in terms of chaotic image encryption. Some commonly used metrics for analysing the capability of image encryption against cryptographic attacks.

Keyspace analysis: To break the encryption strategy, intruders usually perform a brute-force attack to identify the secret keys that are used for the image cryptosystem. Generally, a total number of keys used for encrypting and decrypting the plain and cipher images are termed as keyspace. An effective encryption mechanism should possess a large keyspace to make the brute-force search infeasible. Strong image encryption should possess a keyspace of at least 2^{100} keyspace to withstand the brute-force attack. The total number of keys utilised for image cryptosystem always relies on both keys used in image pixel confusion and diffusion methods.

Key sensitivity analysis: Effective image encryption should guarantee high sensitivity towards the secret key i.e. a minimal change in the secret key should exhibit significant changes in cipher image. The sensitivity of secret keys can be evaluated by calculating the cipher image difference which can be calculated as:

$$K_{\text{sensitivity}} = \frac{\delta(\mu, \mu_1) + \delta(\mu, \mu_2)}{2(I.J)} \times 100\% \tag{11.1}$$

$$\delta(\mu, \mu_1) = \sum_{p=0}^{I} \sum_{q=1}^{J} D(\mu(p,q), \mu_1(p,q)) \tag{11.2}$$

$$D(\mu(p,q), \mu_1(p,q)) = \begin{cases} 0; & \text{if } \mu(p,q) = \mu_1(p,q) \\ 1; & \text{if } \mu(p,q) \neq \mu_1(p,q) \end{cases} \tag{11.3}$$

Here μ, μ_1, μ_2 are the original cipher images and its variants with small changes in the key space. The key sensitivity is evaluated by computing differences among different cipher images encrypted using different keys. Theoretically, the difference value for cipher images should be 99% for any image cryptosystem.

Correlation analysis: The adjacency pixel correlation is the fundamental property of images through which it can convey meaningful information or pictures. Yet for cipher images, in order to withstand the statistical attack, the cipher image should possess zero correlation among adjacency pixels. Because, if the pixel correlations are high, the intruder can easily break the encryption methodology and obtain plain images. Generally, cipher image correlations are calculated in three directions viz. horizontal, vertical and diagonal as given below:

$$c_{mn} = \frac{E((m - E(n))) - E((m - E(n)))}{\sqrt{V(m)V(n)}} \tag{11.4}$$

where,

$$E(m) = \frac{1}{x} \sum_{x=1}^{n} m_x \tag{11.5}$$

Similarly,

$$V(m) = \sum_{x=1}^{n} (E(x) - E(x)^2 \tag{11.6}$$

Here, m, n represents the neighbouring pixels and x is the number of pixels in the images.

Histogram analysis: Histogram plots of an image give information about the pixel patterns exhibiting in the image. Thus, an efficient image encryption scheme should possess uniform or flatten histogram plots to withstand the statistical attacks. The sample histogram plots of the plain and cipher images are given below. The figure depicts that the plain image reveals the pixel pattern whereas the cipher image possesses uniformity in the image pixel histogram. The qualitative analysis of histograms can be carried out by computing histogram variances. Histogram variance is another important metric to evaluate the image pixel uniformity. The ideal image cryptosystem should possess minimal variances with higher uniformity. The mathematical expression for calculating histogram variance is given below.

$$\text{Var}(H) = \frac{1}{x^2} \sum_{i=1}^{x} \sum_{j=1}^{x} \frac{1}{2}(h_i - h_j)^2 \tag{11.7}$$

where H is the array of histogram values and h_i, h_j be the number of pixels at particular cipher images.

Shannon entropy analysis: Shannon entropy analysis is the commonly used metric for investigating the amount of randomness in the image encryption scheme. The Shannon entropy or information entropy is expressed as:

$$S(T) = \sum P(T_i) \log \frac{1}{P(T_i)} \tag{11.8}$$

Where $P(T_i)$ is the probability of pixel-level values T_i. To achieve a maximum entropy value i.e. $H(T) = 8$, T_i should exhibit the same probability for uniform distribution. The entropy metric which is defined in (8) tends to be a global randomness measure, however, any encryption scheme that results in a good randomness value (nearer to 8) is not enough to conclude the true randomness as it computes global pixel value distribution. Subsequently, it is necessary to measure the randomness among local non-overlapping block pixels of an encrypted image. The local Shannon entropy is determined as

$$LT_{L,B}^{-} = \sum_{i=1}^{L} \frac{H(s_i)}{k} \tag{11.9}$$

where L is the number of blocks and B is the size of local blocks.

Differential attack measure: The differential attack is the form of attack in which the attacker tries to obtain the plain image by calculating the cipher image difference. Strong image encryption should possess maximum plain image sensitivity which makes it infeasible for an attacker to perceive original images. The common metric used for calculating the plain image sensitivity is the Number of Pixel Change Rate (NPCR) and Unified Average Change Intensity (UACI). An effective encryption should possess 99% of NPCR and 34% of UACI. The mathematical expression for NPCR and UACI is given below:

$$NPCR = \frac{\sum_{m=1}^{I} \sum_{n=1}^{J} P(m,n)}{IXJ} \times 100\% \tag{11.10}$$

where,

$$P(m,n) = \begin{cases} 0; & \text{if } C_1(m,n) = C_2(m,n) \\ 1; & \text{if } C_1(m,n) \neq C_2(m,n) \end{cases} \tag{11.11}$$

here, $C_i(m,n)$ are the encrypted images whose plain image is differed by one bit also I×J be the size of the image. Similarly, UACI is expressed as:

$$UACI = \frac{1}{I \times J} \sum_{m,n=1}^{I,J} mn \frac{|C_1(m,n) - C_2(m,n)|}{256} \times 100\% \tag{11.12}$$

11.3 CONCLUSION

In the healthcare domain, the suggested secure permissioned medical blockchain framework can act as an immutable and transparent architecture where all patients and hospital jurisdiction can efficiently access the Electronic Health Records. To ensure the secrecy of the medical records, the system introduced chaotic-based image encryption for medical images. The proposed system investigates various performance metrics for the efficacy of the framework with respect to blockchain and image security. This prototype guarantees the availability, security and access controls over sensitive health records.

Bibliography

1. Rabia Abid, Bakhtawar Aslam, Muhammad Rizwan, Fahad Ahmad, and Mian Usman Sattar. Block-chain-security advancement in medical sector for sharing medical records. In *2019 International Conference on Innovative Computing (ICIC)*, pages 1–9. IEEE, 2019.

2. Abdullah Al Omar, Mohammad Shahriar Rahman, Anirban Basu, and Shinsaku Kiyomoto. Medibchain: A blockchain based privacy preserving platform for healthcare data. In *International Conference on Security, Privacy and Anonymity in Computation, Communication and Storage*, pages 534–543. Springer, 2017.

3. Noura Baccar and Ridha Bouallegue. A new web-based e-health platform. In *2014 IEEE 10th International Conference on Wireless and Mobile Computing, Networking and Communications (WiMob)*, pages 14–19. IEEE, 2014.

4. Olga Boric-Lubecke, Xiaomeng Gao, Ehsan Yavari, Mehran Baboli, Aditya Singh, and Victor M Lubecke. E-healthcare: Remote monitoring, privacy, and security. In *2014 IEEE MTT-S International Microwave Symposium (IMS2014)*, pages 1–3. IEEE, 2014.

5. Dalel Bouslimi, Gouenou Coatrieux, Michel Cozic, and Christian Roux. A joint encryption/watermarking system for verifying the reliability of medical images. *IEEE Transactions on Information Technology in Biomedicine*, 16(5):891–899, 2012.

6. Yi Chen, Shuai Ding, Zheng Xu, Handong Zheng, and Shanlin Yang. Blockchain-based medical records secure storage and medical service framework. *Journal of Medical Systems*, 43(1):1–9, 2019.

7. Mary Subaja Christo, Partha Sarathy, C Priyanka, et al. An efficient data security in medical report using block chain technology. In *2019 International Conference on Communication and Signal Processing (ICCSP)*, pages 0606–0610. IEEE, 2019.

8. Alevtina Dubovitskaya, Zhigang Xu, Samuel Ryu, Michael Schumacher, and Fusheng Wang. Secure and trustable electronic medical records sharing using

blockchain. In *AMIA Annual Symposium Proceedings*, volume 2017, page 650. American Medical Informatics Association, 2017.

9. William J Gordon and Christian Catalini. Blockchain technology for healthcare: facilitating the transition to patient-driven interoperability. *Computational and structural biotechnology journal*, 16:224–230, 2018.

10. Ahmed F Hussein, N ArunKumar, Gustavo Ramirez-Gonzalez, Enas Abdulhay, João Manuel RS Tavares, and Victor Hugo C de Albuquerque. A medical records managing and securing blockchain based system supported by a genetic algorithm and discrete wavelet transform. *Cognitive Systems Research*, 52:1–11, 2018.

11. Ray Hales Hylock and Xiaoming Zeng. A blockchain framework for patient-centered health records and exchange (healthchain): evaluation and proof-of-concept study. *J Med Internet Res*, 21(8):e13592, 2019.

12. Xiaoguang Liu, Ziqing Wang, Chunhua Jin, Fagen Li, and Gaoping Li. A blockchain-based medical data sharing and protection scheme. *IEEE Access*, 7:118943–118953, 2019.

13. U Padmavathi and N Rajagopalan. A research on impact of blockchain in healthcare. *International Journal of Innovative Technology and Exploring Engineering*, 8(9):35–40, 2019.

14. Alex Roehrs, Cristiano André da Costa, Rodrigo da Rosa Righi, Valter Ferreira da Silva, José Roberto Goldim, and Douglas C Schmidt. Analyzing the performance of a blockchain-based personal health record implementation. *Journal of Biomedical Informatics*, 92:103140, 2019.

15. Anuraag A Vazirani, Odhran O'Donoghue, David Brindley, and Edward Meinert. Blockchain vehicles for efficient medical record management. *NPJ Digital Medicine*, 3(1):1–5, 2020.

12 The Use of Blockchain in Taxing Digital Products and Services: A Conceptual Model Proposal

Taxes, which are the core financing sources of the government, are usually collected on income, wealth, and expenditures. Various types of tax areas have been in question and have changed during the evolution of humanity. One of the reflections of this change is the digitalisation process experienced in every field. From the invention of the telegraph to smartphones; From Electronic Numerical Integrator and Computer (ENIAC) [1], which can process data thousand times faster than the calculators, to today's computers with terabytes of processing capacity and network structures that connect digital devices, all technological developments, we have the opportunity to observe talking about the fourth industrial revolution (Industry 4.0) period [2] and the digital economy. Today, a new economic era, also called the network economy, is experienced as the concept of digitalisation.

Economic developments in the digital field require new regulations in the taxation areas of the states. The traditional understanding of taxation is attempted to be evolved in a way that does not fall behind the digital age. Indeed, areas such as robot tax [3], space-mining tax [4], and taxation of cryptocurrencies [5] have become debatable. Here, one of these areas is the taxation of digital services.

The first applications of this new tax, conceptualised as digital service tax in practice, started in countries such as France, England, and India. Nowadays, when the global dimensions of the digital economy have reached the level of three trillion dollars annually [6], states are expected to make an effort to obtain financing from these countries. The purpose of this attempt is not only to generate income but also to try limiting non-tax areas, which is a requirement of the principle of fairness in taxation, which is one of Adam Smith's taxation principles. However, ensuring fairness in taxation necessarily requires effective tax control. At this stage, it is critical to underline the importance of an adequate control system for taxing revenue sources in digital sectors. It is necessary to equip traditional tax control tools (tax review, inspection, search, and information gathering) with the technical infrastructure that can provide high levels of success in the conventional tax areas in a digital environment.

On the other hand, parallel to the rapid developments in technology, the electronic circulation of money in money markets has begun to substitute the physical circulation of money. In this way, distributed, traceable cryptocurrencies that do not belong to any country have emerged. Furthermore, blockchain concepts have also

DOI: 10.1201/9781003355052-12

emerged by allowing these coins to circulate freely in the global market. This new monetary system has become superior to existing ones, especially with the feature that the owner of the money is anonymous, transactions are traceable, verified, un-changeable, distributed, non-fungible, and reliable [7]. The blockchain platforms, on which these cryptocurrency systems operate independently, have started using other social, public, and economic reasons [8]. One of the technologies used in this context is smart contracts that have carried the Ethereum cryptocurrency to a priv-ileged place as systems that work on blockchain, transform the electronic contracts between the parties into computer algorithms and ensure the correct operation of contract clauses electronically. Studies and practices regarding the use of smart con-tracts in government affairs and bureaucratic processes have also attracted attention recently [9, 10, 11, 12].

The problem statement in this study is how blockchain technology could solve the problems in the taxation of digital services. The main objective is to describe the problem domain and the contemporary issues that could serve to propose a model framework. The second objective in the paper is to provide lossless trace-ability and taxation process of digital services. Additionally, the third objective is to provide a conceptual model based on blockchain, smart contracts, and even a centrally controlled cryptocurrency which will have an innovative and future-compatible operation for countries to monitor commercial activities in the electronic environment.

In the first part of the study, digital service tax applications for countries; in the second part, blockchain and smart-contract concepts; in the third part, a conceptual model proposal and the introduction of the process, and in the discussion and con-clusion part, the proposed model, its applicability and future potential are discussed.

12.1 DIGITAL SERVICES

Digital services include the electronic production, delivery, and consumption of dig-ital assets that create benefits for the consumer. The most important feature of digital services that differentiates them from traditional service types lies in the fact that the service is partially storable. For example, an abstract digital service, such as a commercial music file or audiobook, electronically recorded in a studio environment and delivered to customers from storage areas in the cloud, can theoretically re-main forever in the information storage media in the cloud, without deterioration and no change until the user requests it. Another remarkable feature that distin-guishes digital services from traditional services, although not generalisable for all digital services- can be made available to consumers in as many identical copies as the number of consumers who request them. For instance, a game delivered via the Google Play Shop, or another online store could be downloaded and installed on computers, tablets, game consoles, or mobile phones, and could also be played online or offline, alone or in groups, interactively. Another characteristic that distinguishes digital services from traditional services is their independence from place and time, although this inference is not true for all digital services. For instance, for accommo-dation services, businesses such as hotels and hostels are needed as a physical asset.

However, it is possible to make reservations and complete all payment processes for an accommodation business by accessing digital brokerage services from anywhere. Another important distinction is that, with few exceptions, conventional services are delivered and consumed in the same place. For example, a consultancy service, transportation service, or accommodation service is utilised as soon as it is delivered. However, digital services do not have to be used immediately upon delivery, and the deliverer and consumer do not need to be in the same place. In the Covid-19 pandemic conditions, we are in, mostly consultancy, training, and event services have been conducted by bringing individuals and institutions together online or offline from different locations. Especially from the perspective of taxation, digital service applications based on countries that may be subject to taxation included in the [13] report can be summarised as follows:

 i. To earn ad revenue, sell ad space on a digital platform;
 ii. Selling user data generated from user activities on a digital platform;
 iii. Providing digital intermediary services to users of a digital platform by facilitating the exchange of goods or services between these users;
 iv. The introduction of a digital platform that allows users to interact to sell goods or services;
 v. Providing a digital interface that allows users to connect and interact with others (intermediary services);
 vi. Income derived from providing tourist rental services on digital platforms;
 vii. Providing services to advertisers who intend to place targeted advertising messages in a digital interface based on data collected about users and generated by consultation with this interface (advertising services based on users' data);
 viii. Income from short-term rentals in the sharing economy through digital platforms;
 ix. Online sale of e-commerce operator products;
 x. Online provision of services provided by the e-commerce operator;
 xi. Payments for certain digital services, such as downloading or accessing images, movies, text, information, video, sound, music, games (including gambling), other multimedia content, multiplayer media, mobile ringtones, online news, outside the country's borders, traffic information, weather forecasts and statistics, online clubs, dating sites, long-distance training or testing;
 xii. Payments for offshore digital services such as online advertising, designing, creating, hosting, or maintaining websites, uploading, storing, or distributing digital content, collecting online, or providing any facility or service for the processing of user-related data within the borders of the country, any facility or other online facility for the online sale of goods or services performed by non-persons;
 xiii. Payments for online advertising to foreign service providers and fees for e-services such as online games, videos, audio broadcast, movies, TV series, music, and online platform services;
 xiv. To generate revenue by displaying internet search engine service and product and service links to users;

xv. To earn income through social media services;

xvi. To generate revenue with cloud computing services;

xvii. Earning income through standardised online education services. Various approaches exist for classifying products and services in the world. The Nice universal classification system, which is implemented by the Nice Agreement for digital services and all other products and services listed, can be accessed at [14].

12.2   ELECTRONIC PAYMENT SYSTEMS

Towards the end of the 1960s, the first arrangements for Electronic Data Exchange in commercial transactions [15] and Electronic Funds Transfer in 1978 [16] were actually like the footsteps of a new era. In the 1980s, before the transfer of commerce to the electronic environment, processes for transferring money from the physical environment to the electronic environment began to emerge as prepaid systems such as telephone cards and restaurant payment cards [17]. In this context, first among banks, then between banks and institutions and individuals, and finally among individuals, money transfers have become possible through banks. The physical circulation of money has started to decrease with the widespread use of electronic cards, credit cards, and ATMs worldwide [18]. In the second half of the 1990s, with the development of the Internet and communication technologies, Internet banking transactions via mobile phones and WAP replaced traditional processes such as money transfers and bill payments [19]. In 2000, the European Parliament and the Council defined electronic money in the directive [20]. Today, many individual and corporate banking and payment transactions and payment of debts, such as fines and taxes to the state are conducted intensively through all mobile devices, laptops, desktop computers, and the Internet. The most important advantage of these monetary transactions in an electronic environment in government administration is to monitor money movements. Considering that electronic commerce has started to replace traditional one with a large extent, it is a fact that all processes, especially for payment and taxation, between buyer-seller-intermediary-bank-state bodies, occur in an electronic environment. Although credit cards are already available as a payment option, the emergence of digital wallet-based global initiatives such as PayPal, Alipay, GooglePay, and ApplePay, as well as national initiatives such as IyziCo and Turkcell Payment (see [21] for a comprehensive list) demonstrates a demand for faster, easier, and more efficient payment processes [22, 23]. Recently, one of these payment systems, PayPal, will begin accepting cryptocurrencies [24], and other payment systems are also in this trend. In the decentralised finance (Defi) system, money does not move physically, but only in the electronic environment in a digital wallet where any person, institution, organisation, or government other than the account holder cannot access and intervene [25]. These systems promise a high level of protection of the financial privacy of the person, the security of their digital wallets, and extremely easy-to-use, fast, and efficient processes in payment processes.

In taxing the digital services, if all monetary processes are processed via digital wallet and payment systems as described here, inevitably, the governments will need some changes to guarantee the tax traceability of these processes where blockchain technology could be the best alternative.

12.3   BLOCKCHAIN TECHNOLOGY

In the first emergence of Bitcoin, blockchain technology and cryptocurrency as a whole represented Bitcoin. However, after the separation of cryptocurrencies and blockchain technologies, a rapid increase was observed in applications of blockchain technology. It has shown that blockchain can be used in the tracing of food processes [26], the supply chain process, tracking the process from the first stage to the delivery of the product to the end-user [27, 28], health systems [29], maritime transport [30, 31, 32] and even in elections [33, 34, 35]. Apart from cryptocurrency, platform-based blockchain infrastructures such as Hyperledger [36] have been developed and opened to enterprises [37].

Blockchain applications are differentiated from conventional ways that they can be fully open to the use of everyone for a fee or free of charge or only for the usage of some private individuals and institutions [38]. Nowadays, anyone who wishes can build their own blockchain infrastructure, cryptocurrency and smart contracts, and even own cryptocurrency; for income-generating activities around a business or provide infrastructure services for use by others after training through online training activities [39]. Blockchain technology, which is both the subject and the source of inspiration for many applications and research since its introduction, has reached a remarkable position in the relevant literature in a short time [40].

The blockchain can be considered a general ledger (ledger) that businesses keep their accounting journal transactions [41]. The transparency of the blockchain is that a copy of this general ledger can be shared by anyone who wants it, where all these shared general ledgers could confirm this transaction [7]. Such a decentralised distributed structure ensures that the ownership of the system in the entire network cannot be controlled by a unique center. Anyone can be a part of this network, download the large notebook to their computer system and keep the records in themselves, or anyone who wishes can take part in this network anonymously to make transactions to buy and sell.

Blockchain technology means that every commercial transaction (especially in Bitcoin transactions, this corresponds to the exchange of cryptocurrency), in order for the transaction to be carried out in a complete manner, accessing and reviewing the record blocks with existing records, anonymous (unless the identity is clearly identified a single hexadecimal code is assigned to him / her by the system) whether the person actually owns this money, processing the records that the person receiving the money actually transferred this money to his / her account, the date the receiver and the sender perform the transaction, after which block this transaction will take place in the block to be created, the sender and All information, such as what the last balances of the receiving anonymous people are, what the registration number of the new block is added to the system due to this transaction, is securely processed electronically in the system by all users with the ledger (for detailed info, see [42].

Blockchain.com [43, 44, 45, 46, 47, 48] shows cross-sectional examples of data reflecting transactions performed by users and miners with Ethereum cryptocurrency accounts. Blockchain.com [43] presents transactions based on blockchain technology. As seen from Blockchain.com [43], the time-based change in the Ethereum cryptocurrency can also be seen in a separate graphic and can be viewed live on blockchain.com. Blockchain.com [43] shows that under the title of the last blocks, the sequence numbers of the newly created blocks, when they were created (mined column), the record (miner column), the number of transactions (transactions) in that block, and the size (size of the block). The Last transactions section includes a unique number (hash column) of each transaction created by the time of the transaction, the monetary size transferred within the scope of this transaction (in separate amount columns in ether/dollar).

Blockchain.com [44] contains information about the individual transactions, the sender-receiver, and the account holder who engages in cryptocurrency mining. Although this information is shared publicly, the real identity of the person is kept anonymous. The person who owns the account hides his real identity through a digital wallet, etc. He has created and performed his transactions with a hash code, which can be encoded and scanned by a QR code converter and reader. As in Blockchain.com [44], anyone can view the total number of transactions of the account holder, the total amount of money sent in Dollars or Ethereum (ETH), the total amount received, the total amount paid to the network for the transactions (transaction fee), and detailed information about the transactions with a time stamp. The Gas expression in the transactions section shows how much money is paid to the network as a transaction fee for each transaction performed. The demand for gas for transactions here is money that is a variable amount (i.e., a higher cost to perform instantaneously) of ETH or Dollars.

Blockchain.com [45] shows a block structure in the blockchain, which also includes many consecutive transactions. This block structure contains all data about the block, such as a unique identifier hash code, the number of accounts that confirm this block, the reward assigned to the record, the number of transactions related to the block, the block owner (miner), the difficulty level of the block, and the number of other nodes (node or uncle). In Blockchain.com [46], the transaction code (hash code) of all transactions in the block, from whom (hash code), to whom (hash code), how costly (ETH or dollars) a transfer is, how much transaction fee (Gas) paid when it occurs. The green arrows towards the right in the middle characterise a vectorial (directional) flow from the left account to the right.

Blockchain.com [43] and Blockchain.com [48] are examples of unapproved and approved procedures, respectively. In cryptocurrency transactions, the transaction needs to be verified by other account holders in the network to transfer the transaction to the block. Until the transaction is verified, it is temporarily included in the registry, but the accounts are updated after the verification occurs. When Blockchain.com [48] is examined, it is seen that 6272 account holders in the network have verified the relevant transaction. In money transfer through blockchain, Bitcoin and Ethereum are the most known and intensive cryptocurrencies. In line with technological developments and digitalisation, many cryptocurrencies are emerging [49].

12.3.1 SMART CONTRACTS

Smart contracts were first introduced by Szabo [50] in 1990 as "a set of commitments defined on a digital platform, including protocols that define the obligations of the parties to each other"." In 1998, as part of the Stanford Digital Library Project, the rights and obligations of the Stanford Infobus System were used to define the objects in the management service layer [50].

The model proposed by this study includes smart contracts as an essential component. Many different definitions of a smart contract are in the literature [50]. In technical terminology, a smart contract is a computer program or a transaction protocol working as a controller and an executor that automatically documents actions and events designed according to the provisions of an agreement or contract signed between the parties [52, 53, 54, 55]. The purpose of the smart contract is to reduce the costs of reliable intermediaries, arbitration and sanctions, and fraud losses, malicious and undesired exceptional circumstances [50, 53].

From a conceptual viewpoint, a smart contract, in its simplest form, allows the written commitments between the parties in business processes to be automatically controlled and audited by the system without any external intervention by humans. Encoding the written commitments between the parties in the digital environment does this control. Smart contracts are built with the help of the programming languages for each commitment clause beyond the documents created with word processors. Thus, smart contracts ensure that these commitments work autonomously, precisely, transparently, and swiftly in a protected and distributed manner, rather than being administered by a single person or institution.

Smart contracts are self-executing contracts that define rules for negotiation and provide complete confirmation of commitments and execution of the contract using official code. These contracts work over the blockchain and become a part of it. When all the appropriate conditions are met, the smart contract runs and operates itself. Confirmation of this process may occur at different stages through confirmation by formal means or by simulation. Optionally, this confirmation can be done through the queries executed the blockchain [56].

Vending machines can be considered the oldest technological equivalents of smart contracts [54]. A technical report [57] on Ethereum describes the Bitcoin protocol as a version of the smart contract that is first defined by Szabo, a computer scientist, lawyer, and cryptographer. Other blockchain, such as Ethereum, have emerged as second-generation blockchain that enable complex and distributed applications beyond cryptocurrencies. Smart contracts constitute the base items of this generation [58]. Various cryptocurrencies like Ethereum that support scripting languages allow for a more advanced smart contracts between untrusting parties [51].

Smart contracts, as an illustration, could be applied to control the bank clients' credit card limits, interest rates, loan requests, and payments. Sample contracts can be created for various domains and shared on online platforms [59]. Appendix 1 presents a sample of an Ethereum-based smart contract for asset transfer. Just a decade ago, contracts were made through written documents and with mutual wet signatures in physical environments, in the presence of a witness or guarantor. As the implementation steps were followed by manual, the documents were digitally confirmed between the parties. Business processes have evolved by the direct intervention of individuals. Undoubtedly, even this evolution has advanced the efficiency of business processes towards a time gain in terms of time, cost, and agility that stretches from weeks or days to days or hours. Today, many business processes have been transferred to digital and continue in this way. On the other hand, with the adaptation of smart contracts to this existing system, business processes are moving towards a completely different dimension. Today, communication companies have numerous deals for mobile subscribers. The different subscription tariffs they offer could be an example of demonstrating the benefits of smart contract applications. In such cases, where many agreements, notifications, warnings, and approvals between the parties are realised with SMS and sometimes email confirmation, the process of leaving the control to computer algorithms and codes has already become mandatory. It is simply necessary that these systems meet the expectations promised by smart contracts. Otherwise, these new business processes created in the digital environment may turn into an inextricable situation. Assessment and collection of various taxes arising from commercial transactions between the parties on a contractual basis by the relevant legislation make the government a legal party to smart contracts. As one of the parties is the government, they play a crucial role in delivering digital services in controlling and auditing tax situations based on income-related articles.

Digital services and all their footprints in the digital environment depend on electricity. There may be a need to access these documents when there is no electricity for the affairs of the government. Therefore, both multi-confirmation and multi-archive features make the system robust.

12.4 DIGITAL SERVICE TAX REGULATIONS IN COUNTRIES

Previous studies on the taxing of the digital economy can be processed as regulations implemented by the OECD, the European Union, and states' initiatives. The goals of such efforts include preventing tax evasion and increasing tax revenues. This section deals with the taxing of digital services in some countries. Among the primary factors influencing the selection of these countries is their leadership role in taxing the digital economy within their community (France), their ability to steer or motivate many other countries (United Kingdom), the presence of numerous software companies, and the existence of a user network (India).

One of the first examples of the taxation of the digital economy came into effect with the publication of the Digital Services Tax (DST) Law numbered 2019-759 in the Official Gazette dated July 24, 2019, in France. The tax rate has been set at 3% and companies whose annual worldwide income from services in the previous year exceeded 750 million Euros and whose income from services in France exceeded 25 million Euros [60] would be held accountable under the legislation.

In France, the digital service tax will cover Google, Apple, Facebook, and Amazon (GAFA), most notably the big four companies in the USA, and is called GAFA Tax. The UK has not yet enacted a new tax law in the digital service tax area. However, the budget proposal for 2020 (UK Finance Bill 2019-2020) proposed a 2% digital service tax on search engines, social media platforms, and online markets.

This new tax, targeting an annual income of £515 million by 2025, is associated with the revenue generated by British users using social media platforms, search engines, or online sales platforms (excluding financial and payment service providers). The prerequisite for the inclusion of the tax is that the company concerned has obtained at least £500 million globally and at least £25 million of it from British users [61].

Austria, the Digital Service Tax Law entered into force on January 1, 2020, and the digital service tax has changed since this date. Law imposed a digital service tax on advertisements on digital platforms such as banner advertising, search engine advertising, and product comparison services imposed as 5%. The companies that provide these advertising services determine the tax of the taxpayers in the law. They also set lower limits in terms of taxing these services. According to the law, earning 750 million Euros worldwide from such services and at least 25 million Euros in Austria has been determined as the minimum conditions for liability. The taxpayer calculates the tax monthly and pays it on the 15th day of the following month [62].

The digital service tax application in Italy has entered into force as of January 1, 2020, with the 2020 Budget Law. This tax covers the advertising activities on the digital interface only, instead of all digital services, the multilateral digital interface that allows users to buy/sell goods and services, and the transmission of user data generated using a digital interface. In a 3% digital service tax, the lower limit liability is 750 million Euros for global revenues and 5.5 million Euros for revenues from activities in Italy [63].

Many sectors of the Indian economy, which has half a billion Internet subscribers, are transforming into a digital field. This situation brings new employment opportunities for tens of millions of Indians. The rising technology and falling costs in the smartphone market have made India one of the world's largest digital economies. In India, there is an average of 17 hours of social media usage per person per week, and 80% of society has at least one Internet banking account [64].

With these developments, Balancing Tax is the first regulation for taxing the digital economy in the country in 2016. The delivery of online advertising, cloud services, e-books, movies, music, software, and other intangible assets on the Internet is all subject to the balance tax. Balance tax applies to any person who receives data or information electronically via a computer network or otherwise provides data or information and games. This tax is 6% of the cost of online advertising services provided by foreign companies. After the annual sales of digital service providers registered in India exceed 100,000 Indian Rupees (INR), they are subject to the Balancing Tax [65].

More than half of European Union countries have legalised the taxation of digital services, while many other countries are on the way. However, it is possible to reach a global agreement on the taxing of digital services through the negotiations conducted by the OECD with 130 countries [66]. Notably, they are currently making or planning regulations more suitable for their conditions. Not only are direct or indirect taxes adopted for digital services, but also sometimes both are at the same time. Alternatively, when KPMG [13] examined, it is seen that the tax rates show a distribution between 0% and 15%.

There are clusters of countries that have adopted digital taxation as direct or indirect taxation. Of course, it is not mandatory to choose only one of these in a country, and countries could adopt different procedures according to the type of digital service. For example, countries that apply indirect taxing other than Tunisia and Pakistan have chosen direct taxing. However, 56 of the 77 countries do not prefer the direct tax basis but have adopted indirect taxes. Naturally, it is not surprising that many countries prefer a more indirect taxation. Indirect taxes are adopted as an additional tax to current consumption taxes and included in the price. This inclusion contributes to reducing tax pressure and fostering a low degree of tax resistance because of financial anesthesia. Thus, society adopts the new tax type more.

The transition process to digital service tax in Turkey is under Article 1-7 of Law No. 7194 of 5/12/2019 on Digital Service Tax and the Amendment and Decree No. 375. It entered into force on March 1, 2020, according to clause (a) of the first paragraph of Article 52 of the relevant Law. The Official Gazette published The Digital Service Application General Communique numbered 31074 on 20/03/2020 and is valid as of March 1, 2020 [68]. The scope of the digital service tax was examined and summarised under specified headings of the relevant law and the related General Communique [69]. Whether the digital service provider, which conducts its service activities in Turkey and exceeds the exception limits, is a taxpayer in terms of income or corporate tax in Turkey does not affect digital service tax liability[1]. According to the second paragraph of the 3rd article of the relevant law, in cases where the taxpayer does not have a residence, legal workplace in Turkey, or in other cases deemed necessary, the Ministry of Treasury and Finance authorised for securing the tax receivable and authorised to hold all parties accountable.

In the relevant legislation context, the accounting period of the digital service tax is a calendar year. The taxation period is monthly, and the Ministry of Treasury and Finance is authorised to determine a quarterly taxation period when necessary-according to the types of services and the activity volumes of the taxpayers. The entire revenue obtained is accepted as the tax base. On the other hand, discounts shown in invoices and similar documents affect specifying this base. The tax base is set by the "Equivalent Value and Equivalent Fee" as included in the provisions of Article 267 of the Tax Procedure Law No. 213 if the revenue is from values other than money (i.e., goods and services).

Within the scope of the same law and general communique, the revenue does not contain the value-added tax paid by digital service providers. The discounts made after the taxation period cannot be deducted from the tax base either. Additionally, the taxpayer cannot deduct the expenses incurred by a digital service from the tax base. Alternatively, the digital service tax paid by the taxpayer, or their responsibility can be shown as an expense in determining the net income of the relevant taxpayer

---

[1]Those who have less than 20 million Turkish Lira (TL) in revenue in Turkey or less than 750 million Euro or TL equivalent in foreign currency are exempt from digital service tax. If the taxpayer is a member of a consolidated group in terms of financial accounting, the total revenue obtained from the group regarding the services covered by the tax is taken as the basis in the application of these limits.

based on income and corporate tax. Additionally, the digital service tax amount is excluded from invoices or similar documents substituted for invoices.

In terms of liability, these arrangements, which will be entered into by digital service providers in Turkey, in particular, have no bearing on the taxpayer. Although it is controversial in the literature that a tax is levied on income or expenditures, it is mainly constructed as a kind of expenditure tax [71]. Although the procedures and principles regarding taxing the digital services are defined by the legislation, the processes for monitoring, inspection, and collection serve the relevant public units to the extent and sensitivity of the current business processes and technological infrastructure. This research develops a feasible conceptual model including business processes and technological infrastructure, usage of digital money and the money market, blockchain infrastructure, and the adaptation of digitally created, binding, unchangeable smart contracts. In this way, we aimed at enabling the operation of all activities regarding the taxation of digital services and the collection process in a verifiable, auditable, and unchangeable manner.

12.5 SMART CONTRACTS AND TAXATION PROCESS BASED ON BLOCKCHAIN TECHNOLOGY

This section employs smart contracts from a conceptual perspective in the context of blockchain technology. Additionally, we propose a model to explain its relationship with taxation to ensure its efficiency in auditing the digital service tax.

Technological development and progress have an undeniable role in the digital economy. Therefore, the taxation process should involve digital services in this economy like other components. Many countries and associations such as the European Union, the OECD, and the USA study different definitions and processes for taxation [72, 73]. The effective management of this taxation process requires a systematic and verifiable approach to the definition. Examining the updated implementations shows that the audit processes based on mutual verification use the blockchain and related technological infrastructures. Therefore, it is indisputable that a digital mechanism, by which digital platforms open for auditing, are essential for effective taxation of a commercial transaction where digital services involved, and all stages of the service occur on digital platforms [74, 75]. This status as technological infrastructure, not only for digital service tax but also for effective management of all tax types, is something that the leading audit firms have recently emphasised the international platform [76]. One of the main reasons for this trend is that these technologies support chained smart contracts, which can run digital applications in decentralised platforms.

A blockchain-based smart contract must conduct the taxation and tax collection process effectively. Here, in this study, laws, and regulations in Turkey and the digital services taxation ecosystem within the scope of the relevant parties will be discussed. As an alternative to a taxing system based on declarations, taxing a service on digital platforms where all payments performing through electronic payment systems can be made strictly effective with the help of a technological infrastructure in which all parties are involved as stakeholders. In such an ecosystem where service recipients, service providers, the estate, banking practices, and electronic payment system platforms can play a part as the main stakeholders, banks and companies that are executors of the payment systems bear the heaviest responsibility. Because the moment when the digital service purchase is verified corresponds to the instant that the payment is recognized, the blockchain, consisting of smart contracts that will enable communication and verification of transactions between relevant stakeholders, affects ensuring efficiency in taxation.

First, before structuring the blockchain, digital services need to be standardised through classification and coding. Furthermore, expressing digital service purchases, which also have an international dimension, by using international standard codes for all parties will prevent the risks of misidentification and classification. At this point, it is also necessary to define smart contracts and blockchain conceptually. Such a definition is essential in terms of the terminology of the relationship between the blockchain and taxation.

Establishing an audit mechanism with a robust infrastructure in the taxation process of digital services and the digitalisation of this mechanism due to these services will be essential for the effective management of the process. It would be easy for service providers to be involved in an automation system to be built, assuming that they have the infrastructure to distribute such services to large audiences regardless of location. If payment systems and information system infrastructures used by tax administrations already exist, integrating them will be possible through setting connections to each other. The incomplete system component here is the automation infrastructure that the service consumer must create. One can find support and incentive applications for infrastructure development.

Considering the conventional structure of the tax system and tax collection processes, the collection of digital service taxes requires an automation system for both data flows and an audit system based on the declaration in this flow. The incomplete dimension of such a business model is the absence of transaction confirmation and tax collection on confirmed transactions beyond the declaration. In this context, blockchain is one of the essential technologies of our present age and could be used. In other words, the automation system needed to be configured on the blockchain. Thus, the parties in all stages associated each other on the blockchain, and confirmation or smart contract audits all transactions mutually. Within this context, the study proposes a blockchain model that can run on smart contracts concerning the tax payment process of digital services. As a result, all parties involved in this model form different layers, with the blockchain at the core. The layer just above the blockchain (Figure 12.1), is made up of smart contracts and defines the rules regulating the interaction between the parties to secure the blockchain's operation. The layer above the smart contracts is optional where it exhibits the money flow defined in the blockchain for smart contracts designed as cryptocurrency issued by the Central Bank. In the upper layer, there is information and payment systems that can regulate the information-document-money flow. On the outermost layer, some parties play an active role in this model. Parties are classified into two groups. In the first group, there are individual and corporate taxpayers, banks, and intermediary organizations. In the second group, there are government agencies (Tax Administration, Central Bank, etc.) that are responsible for regulations, audits, and tax collection processes. There is an

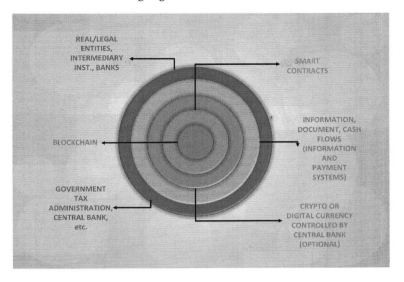

Figure 12.1 The proposed framework for the taxation of digital services.

intensive interaction between layers within this structure. Figure 12.2 systematises this interaction in the data flow, data on the blockchain, and the working principles of the model. The coloured symbols in this flow highlight the essential steps for constructing the blockchain.

According to the presented model, the digital service demand of a service consumer triggers the process flow. Service consumers must first define the terms of the digital service they need. This stage is sub-process because the corporate or the individual who is the consumer for the service performs these transactions with the steps determined sui generis. At this stage, the digital service codes should also include the terms of service in the commitments. At this stage, the consumer could run a process where he/she creates alternatives for digital service providers, establishes selection criteria, and selects the most suitable service provider through customised steps. Thus, the consumer sends the necessary terms to the service provider, and the service provider designs a smart contract to this specification. The customer receives this specially designed smart contract. Within the scope of the service user-service provider bilateral relationship, it is achievable for the corporate receiving the service to provide the contract, depending on the level of development of the corporate.

The manner and format in which the smart contract is operated (especially in terms of response time–for example, a higher contract price like a gas fee is required for instant transactions) may vary depending on the level and frequency of interaction between the service provider and its clients. It is possible to construct a digitally enabled coaction. The service client can examine the transmitted smart contract, approve it according to its suitability, request and update to the smart contract, or cancel the request and turn to another service provider. The same goes for the

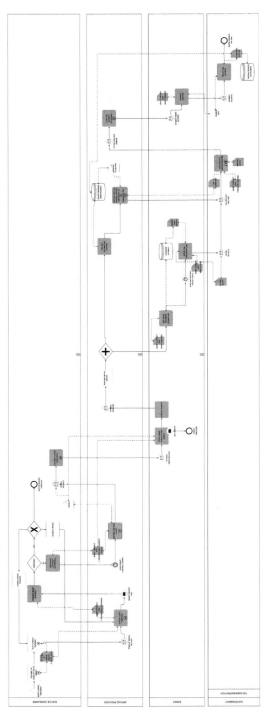

Figure 12.2   The workflow of the proposed model.

service provider, but this detail is excluded from the figure to keep the flow simple. If deemed appropriate, the client confirms the commitment electronically.

For most of the applications, using the service also corresponds to the approval of the smart contract. At the time of confirmation, the information system of the service provider generates an electronic invoice, and the invoice is delivered to the client. The service client initiates payment transactions immediately. A customised sub-process performs the payment transactions according to the conditions of the consumer. A simple electronic money transfer could be done, or the system could be integrated with a custom electronic payment system and configured based on a digital currency. The payment system is the center of the proposed model since the tax occurs at the moment of payment and constitutes a link in the blockchain. Therefore, banks must keep the payment records through the smart contract between the provider and the client, either directly or through a payment system. Also, if the commitments between the client-bank and the provider-bank are defined as smart contracts, the chain will be even more substantial.

In the process outlined above, a service provider can close numerous sales by providing related services to multiple service clients. The service provider records these sales details and revenues in its information system. Besides, the system creates reports from the information system during the tax collection period. Eventually, the regulations guarantee this reporting process of the tax administration. Thus, when the tax declaration and payment periods are due, the relevant return is effortlessly obtained from the service provider. The bank information system also keeps track of these records within its structure and periodically reports them to the tax administration simultaneously with the service provider. Alternatively, the tax administration receives and confirms periodic reports based on the smart contracts signed with the bank and the service provider. Unless the confirmation, the tax process remains pending, and the tax administration request updates from the service provider to make this verification possible. For this reason, the relevant stage is like a cyclical sub-process within the workflow. Since these reporting processes will run through smart contracts and interactive information systems running on the blockchain, taxing will take less time. After the confirmation occurs, the service provider makes the tax payment with the specified payment system, and the tax administration system records it. The service provider gets the tax records based on the smart contract between the service provider and the tax administration. Finally, the periodic tax cycle is over.

The parties in the layers given in Figure 12.1 will be in interaction according to this process on the blockchain. Since all activities and controls conducted can be audited through digitally signed smart contracts between the parties and information systems that provide data flow for related operations and security for bilateral interactions, an effective and fair taxation process will be ensured. Considering that the information system infrastructure is already adequate, such a holistic system can be commissioned in less time by combining the smart contracts to be prepared with these systems.

DISCUSSION AND CONCLUSION

In parallel with the technological developments in today's world, digital products and services are developing rapidly in terms of both variety and volume. The global crisis triggered by the Covid-19 pandemic has accelerated the digitalisation trend of the economy. It has also increased the need to address tax challenges arising from digitalisation. Besides, the acceleration in digitalisation has increased the relative importance of automated digital services (ADS), focusing on the connections in the digital network environment and profit distribution [77]. Accordingly, several new business models in the digital medium have begun finding a place in our economic life. Money, which we can describe as the exchange measure of the economy, began losing its physical importance and began to be replaced by cryptocurrency. In particular, cryptocurrencies such as Ethereum, which has the basis of smart contracts, are preferable to others in this regard. This global digital transformation has brought up the issue of how to tax digital services. Looking at the world practices, for example, England, France, Italy, Austria, Turkey and India are making progress in tracking and taxing the earnings from digital services and making legal regulations. Other countries also try fulfilling the preparations and legal rules to adapt to the digital environment quickly. On the other hand, when examining the practices of various countries, we conclude that digital service taxing could use the same approach in the declaration principle that is a traditional tax assessment.

In terms of taxing digital services, a model that will support the declaration basis and ensure efficiency in taxation can serve as a function that integrates taxing digital services. The blockchain ensures that transactions are securely confirmed, and nodes are aware of these transactions and enter their registers if they choose, especially in distributing the money between the parties. Blockchain technology is also constantly developing to close the system's vulnerabilities. The most striking example of this is Ehtereum's experimentation to evolve into the second version.

Additionally, smart contracts also ensure the non-fungible structure of the commitment between the parties, guarantee the correct implementation of the contract provisions and ensure its traceability. When viewed from the perspective of countries, the problem here is that people anonymously exist in the system. Anonymity can complicate taxation processes in case the system is audited for compliance against legal issues and taxation. The USA, for example, as a country with declaration taxation, recently introduced a regulation requiring the reporting of cryptocurrency transactions above ten thousand dollars [78]. However, if the government can establish the stages of the commercial relationship with a smart contract for all parties, it could control the delivery of digital services more. Within the scope of this study, we propose a conceptual model of how such a structure could be possible. If this model is applied, the accrued tax can be automatically reflected in the accounts of legal entities and individuals, instantly or in periods after the digital service-oriented activity occurs.

FUTURE DIRECTIONS AND FINAL REMARKS

For the model to operate effectively, a central bank-controlled cryptocurrency could replace the current currency in circulation. Thus, this cryptocurrency or the other existing cryptocurrencies in the market could help payment transactions under control for the commercial activities originating from all digital services in the country and the digital services offered outside the country. New legal regulations and infrastructure are necessary for the realisation of the model. Considering that digitalisation will become more crucial in a pandemic exposure such as COVID-19, the return on investment will be short.

Bibliography

1. Goldstine, H.H.; Goldstine, A. The Electronic Numerical Integrator and Computer (ENIAC). Mathematical Tables and Other Aids to Computation. **1946**, 2(15), 97–110.

2. Ustundag, A.; Cevikcan, E. Industry 4.0: Managing the Digital Transformation. Springer: Switzerland.

3. Gasteiger, E.; Prettner, K. A Note on Automation, Stagnation, and the Implications of a Robot Tax. *Discussion Paper.* 2017. https://refubium.fu-berlin.de/handle/fub188/22056 (accessed Dec 21, 2020).

4. Muzyka, K. The Problems with an International Legal Framework for Asteroid Mining. In *Deep Space Commodities.* 2018; pp. 123–140. Palgrave Macmillan, Cham.

5. Akins, B.W.; Chapman, J.L.; Gordon, J.M. A Whole New World: Income Tax Considerations of the Bitcoin Economy.*Pitt. Tax Rev.* **2014**, *12*, p.25.

6. UNCTAD. Digital Economy Report. 2019; New York, USA. https://unctad.org/system/files/official-document/der2019_overview_en.pdf (accessed Oct 12, 2020).

7. Nakamoto, S. Bitcoin: A peer-to-peer electronic cash system.2008. https://bitcoin.org/bitcoin.pdf (accessed Oct 7, 2020).

8. Singh, J.; Michels, J. D. Blockchain as a Service (BaaS): Providers and Trust. In *2018 IEEE European Symposium on Security and Privacy Workshops (EuroS&PW).* 2018; pp. 67–74. IEEE.

9. Shermin, V. Disrupting governance with blockchain and smart contracts. *Strategic Change.* **2017**, *26*(5), 499–509.

10. De Souza, R.C.;Luciano, E.M.; Wiedenhöft, G.C. *The uses of the Blockchain Smart Contracts to reduce the levels of corruption: Some preliminary thoughts.* In Proceedings of the 19th Annual International Conference on Digital Government Research: Governance in the Data Age, Delft, The Netherlands, May 30, June 1, 2018; pp. 1–2.

11. Jalakas, P. Blockchain from Public Administration Perspective: the Case of Estonia. Master Thesis. Tallinn University of Technology: Tallinn, Estonia. 2018. https://digikogu.taltech.ee/en/Download/d591ed87-3350-44a1-acb3-f0e184f9dc18/PlokkahelavalikuhaldusevaatenurgastEestiKaas.pdf (accessed Dec 25, 2020).

12. Stefanović, M.; Ristić, S.; Stefanović, D.; Bojkić, M.; Przulj, D. *Possible Applications of Smart Contracts in Land Administration.* In 2018 26th Telecommunications Forum (TELFOR), Belgrade, Serbia, November 20–21, 2018; pp. 420–425. IEEE.

13. KPMG. Taxation of digitalised Economy. https://tax.kpmg.us/content/dam/tax/en/pdfs/2020/digitalised-economy-taxation-developments-summary.pdf (accessed Nov 15, 2021).

14. Nice Classification NCL. Advance Publication. https://www.wipo.int/ classifications/en/news/nice/2020/news_0004.html (accessed Oct 18, 2020).

15. Gibson Jr, G. E.; Bell, L.C. Electronic Data Interchange in Construction. *Journal of construction engineering and management.* **1990**, *116*(4), 727–737.

16. Hsia, D.C. Legislative History and Proposed Regulatory Implementation of the Electronic Fund Transfer Act.*USFL Rev.* **1978**, *13*, p.299.

17. Hartmann, M. E. E-payment Evolution. In Handbuch E-Money, E-Payment & M-Payment. 2006, 7–18. Physica-Verlag HD.

18. Avino, M. Ann Leven Using the First ATM in the National Air and Space Museum. 1986. https://siarchives.si.edu/collections/siris_sic_12960 (accessed Oct 15, 2020).

19. Kaynak, E.; Harcar, T. D. Consumer Attitudes toward Online Banking: a New Strategic Marketing Medium for Commercial Banks. *Int. J. Technology Marketing.* **2005**, *1*(1), 62–78.

20. EP2000.*European Parliament and Council Directive (2000/46/EC)- JIBC.* April 20 08, 13, No: 1–17.

21. Ozdemir O.; Kukmen K. *Turkiyede Odeme ve Elektronik Para Kurulusslari ve Mali Analizi,* Yavuz Demirdogen Ed. *Dijital Donusum ve Finansal Teknolojilere Yansimalari.* 2020; pp 157–182: Nobel Yayinevi.

22. Wang, Y.; Hahn, C.; Sutrave, K. *Mobile payment security, threats, and challenges.* In 2016 second international conference on mobile and secure services (MobiSecServ). 2016; pp. 1–5. IEEE.

23. Di Maggio, M.; Yucaoglu, G. *iyzico: Fundraising in Emerging Markets (A).* 2018.

24. Reuters.	https://www.reuters.com/article/paypal-cryptocurrency/paypal-to-allow-cryptocurrency-buying-selling-and-shopping-on-its-network-idINL1N2HB14U (accessed Nov 22, 2020).

25. Swan, M. decentralised finance: blockchains, prediction, and valuation. *Economist: Finance Disrupted.* 2016; New York, NY.

26. Kamath, R. Food traceability on blockchain: Walmart's pork and mango pilots with IBM. *The Journal of the British Blockchain Association.* **2018**, *1*(1), 3712.

27. Dobrovnik, M.; Herold, D.M.; Fadcdreussrst, E.; Kummer, S. Blockchain for and in Logistics: What to Adopt and Where to Start. *Logistics.* **2018**, *2*(3), article no: 18. https://www.mdpi.com/2305-6290/2/3/18 (accessed: Sep 2, 2020).

28. Hackius, N.; Petersen, M. Blockchain in Logistics and Supply Chain: Trick or Treat? In digitalisation in Supply Chain Management and Logistics: Smart and Digital Solutions for an Industry 4.0 Environment. *Proceedings of the Hamburg International Conference of Logistics (HICL).* 2017, *23*, 3–18. Berlin: epubli GmbH.

29. McGhin, T.; Choo, K.K.R.; Liu, C.Z.; He, D. Blockchain in healthcare applications: Research challenges and opportunities. *Journal of Network and Computer Applications.***2019**, *135*, 62–75.

30. Czachorowski, K.; Solesvik, M.; Kondratenko, Y. The Application of blockchain technology in the maritime industry. In *Green IT engineering: Social, Business and Industrial Applications.* 2019; pp.561–577. Springer, Cham.

31. Yang, C.S. Maritime shipping digitalisation: Blockchain-based Technology Applications, Future Improvements, and Intention to Use. *Transportation Research Part E: Logistics and Transportation Review.* **2019**, *131*, 108–117.

32. Shirani, A. Blockchain for Global Maritime Logistics. *Issues in Information Systems.* **2018**, *19*(3), 175–183.

33. Kshetri, N.; Voas, J. Blockchain-enabled E-voting. *IEEE Software.* **2018**, *35*(4), 95–99.

34. Specter, M. A.; Koppel, J.; Weitzner, D. The Ballot is Busted Before the Blockchain: A Security Analysis of Voatz, the First Internet Voting Application Used in US Federal Elections. In *29th USENIX Security Symposium (USENIX Security 20).* 2020; pp. 1535–1553.

35. Ayed, A.B. A Conceptual Secure Blockchain-Based Electronic Voting System. *International Journal of Network Security & Its Applications.* **2017**, *9*(3), 01–09.

36. Cachin, C. Architecture of the Hyperledger Blockchain Fabric. In *Workshop on Distributed Cryptocurrencies and Consensus Ledgers.* July 2016, 310(4). http://www.zurich.ibm.com/dccl/papers/cachin_dccl.pdf (accessed Sep 1, 2020).

37. Bhuvana, R.; Aithal, P.S. Blockchain based Service: A Case Study on IBM Blockchain Services & Hyperledger Fabric. *International Journal of Case Studies in Business, IT, and Education (IJCSBE)*. **2020**, *4*(1), 94–102.

38. Lai, R.; Chuen, D.L.K. Blockchain–from public to private. In *Handbook of Blockchain, Digital Finance, and Inclusion*. 2018; Vol.2; pp. 145–177. Academic Press.

39. Udemy. Build a Blockchain and a Cryptocurrency from Scratch, https://www.udemy.com/share/101Wz2/ (accessed Oct 7, 2020).

40. Ozdagoglu, G.; Damar, M.; Ozdagoglu, A. The State of the Art in Blockchain Research (2013–2018): Scientometrics of the Related Papers in Web of Science and Scopus. In *Digital Business Strategies in Blockchain Ecosystems*. 2020; pp. 569–599: Springer, Cham.

41. Crosby, M.; Pattanayak, P.; Verma, S.; Kalyanaraman, V. Blockchain Technology: Beyond Bitcoin. *Applied Innovation*. **2016**, *2*, 6–10.

42. Bitcoin. Bitcoin Developer: Introduction. https://developer.bitcoin.org/reference/intro.html (accessed: Oct 7, 2020).

43. Blockchain.com. A Real Cross-section of Records and Transactions in Chain of Records Technology. https://www.blockchain.com/explorer?view=eth (accessed June 2–4, 2021).

44. Blockchain.com. A Sample of Ethereum User Account and Transactions. https://www.blockchain.com/eth/address/0x5a0b54d5dc17e0aadc383d2db43b0 a0d3e029c4c (accessed June 24, 2021)

45. Blockchain.com. A Sample of Record Content in Ethereum Blockchain Technology. https://www.blockchain.com/eth/block/0xcf7e37967d7cc644288d4fe 533e40f3cfbb80fe59be7792a946 d63da41a23fd3 (accessed June 24, 2021).

46. Blockchain.com. A Partial Example of Transactions Performed in an Ethereum Block. https://www.blockchain.com/eth/block/0xcf7e37967d7cc644288d4fe 533e40f3cfbb80fe59b e7792a946 d63da41a23fd3?view= standard (accessed June 24, 2021).

47. Blockchain.com. An Example of Real and Disapproved Transactions on an Ethereum Blockchain. https://www.blockchain.com/eth/unconfirmed-transactions (accessed June 24, 2021).

48. Blockchain.com. An Example of a Real and an Approved Transaction on an Ethereum Blockchain. https://www.blockchain.com/eth/tx/0x553bbfb16a29136 4c62def4553 5b657226ab3ce226c50241323 a551ba736aa4f (accessed June 24, 2021).

49. Sanlisoy, S.; Ciloglu, T. An Investigation on the Crypto Currencies and Its Future. *International Journal of eBusiness and eGovernment Studies.* **2019**, *11*(1), 69–88.

50. Szabo, N. Formalizing and Securing Relationships on Public Networks.1997 https://nakamotoinstitute.org/formalizing-securing-relationships/ (accessed Oct 07, 2020).

51. Alharby, M.; van Moorsel, A. Blockchain-based Smart Contracts: A Systematic Mapping Study. *Computer Science & Information Technology.* Dhinaharan Nagamalai et al. (Eds). 2017; pp. 125–140. arXiv preprint arXiv:1710.06372. doi:10.5121/sit.2017.71011.

52. Röscheisen, M.; Baldonado, M.; Chang, K.; Gravano, L.; Ketchpel, S.; Paepcke, A. The Stanford InfoBus and its service layers: Augmenting the internet with higher-level information management protocols. *Digital Libraries in Computer Science: The MeDoc Approach.* 1998; Springer: 213–230. doi:10.1007/bfb0052526.

53. Fries, M. and Paal, P. B. Smart Contracts (in German). Mohr Siebeck. ISBN 978-3-16-156911-1 (accessed May 04, 2020).

54. Savelyev, A. Contract Law 2.0: Smart Contracts as the Beginning of the End of Classic Contract Law. *Information & Communications Technology Law.* **2017**, *26*(2), 116–134.

55. Tapscott, D.; Tapscott, A. *The Blockchain Revolution: How the Technology Behind Bitcoin is Changing Money, Business, and the World.* May 2016; pp. 72, 83, 101, 127. ISBN 978-0670069972.

56. Duchmann, F.; Koschmider, A. Validation of smart contracts using process mining. In *ZEUS. CEUR Workshop Proceedings.*2019; 2339; pp.13–16.

57. Buterin V. Ethereum Whitepaper.2013, https://ethereum.org/en/whitepaper/ (accessed Sep 28, 2020).

58. Xu, X.; Pautasso, C.; Zhu, L.; Gramoli, V.; Ponomarev, A.; Tran, A. B.; Chen, S. *The blockchain as a software connector*; 13th Working IEEE/IFIP Conference on Software Architecture (WICSA). 2016, April; pp. 182–191. IEEE.

59. Azure Samples. Application and Smart Contract Samples. https://github.com/Azure-Samples/blockchain/tree/master/blockchain-workbench/application-and-smart-contract-samples. (accessed Oct 05, 2020).

60. BDO France. Digital Services Tax introduced. https://www.bdo.global/en-gb/microsites/tax-newsletters/world-wide-tax-news/issue-52-september-2019/france-digital-services-tax-introduced (accessed Sep 4, 2020).

61. The Digital Services Tax, Policy Paper (UK). https://www.gov.uk/government/publications/introduction-of-the-digital-services-tax/digital-services-tax (accessed Sep 8, 2020).

62. BMF. Digital Tax Act 2020. https://www.bmf.gv.at/en/topics/taxation/digital-tax-act.html (accessed Aug 28, 2020).

63. BDO Italy- Digital Services Tax. https://www.bdo.global/en-gb/microsites/digital-services-taxation/ countries-cit-map/italy-digital-services-tax (accessed Sep 1, 2020).

64. McKinsey. Digital India: Technology to Transform a Connected Nation. https://www.mckinsey.com/business-functions/mckinsey-digital/our-insights/digital-india-technology-to-transform-a-connected-nation (accessed Sep 04, 2020).

65. Akkaya, H.; Adnan G. OECD ve Seadcdressilmis Bazi adcdreusslkelerde Dijital Ekonominin Vergilendirilmesi: Tadcdreussrkiye iadcdressin adcdressikarimlar. *International Journal of Public Finance.* **2019**, *4*(2), 166–188.

66. Asen, Elke. What European OECD Countries are Doing about Digital Services Taxes. https://taxfoundation.org/digital-tax-europe-2020 (accessed Oct 15, 2020).

67. Dijital Hizmet Uygulama Genel Tebligi, 20/03/2020 tarihinde 31074 sayili Resmi Gazetede yayimlanmis https://www.gib.gov.tr/dijital-hizmet-vergisi-uygulama-genel-tebligi-0 (accessed Jun 5, 2020).

68. Resmi Gazete. 2017. https://www.resmigazete.gov.tr/eskiler/2019/12/20191207-1.htm (accessed Jan 5, 2021).

69. WTS. Digital Services Tax (An overview of the new Digital Services Tax in Turkey). https://wts.com/global/publishing-article/07042020-turkey-vat-nl publishing-article?language=en (accessed June 8, 2021).

70. KPMG. Taxation of the digitalised economy (developments summary, updated October 29, 2021)..https://tax.kpmg.us/content/dam/tax/en/pdfs/2021/digitalised-economy-taxation-developments-summary.pdf (accessed Nov 15, 2021).

71. Arikan, Z.; Gadcdreussrbadcdreussz, S. Tadcdreussrkiye'de Dijital Hizmet Vergisi Uygulamasi, Vergi Anlayisi ve Uygulamalarinin Biadcdressimsel ve Yapisal Karakterleri.*Magna Carta'dan Gadcdreussnadcdreussmadcdreussze Yasanan Gelismeler*, sahin Karabulut Eds., Legal Yayincilik, Maliye Kitaplari Serisi. 2. 2020; pp. 291–301.

72. Byrnes, W. Comments and Recommendations OECD Public Consultation Document Secretariat Proposal for a "Unified Approach" under Pillar One. 2019. https://ssrn.com/abstract=3487236 (accessed Sep 28, 2020).

73. Danescu, E. Taxing Intangible Assets: Issues and Challenges for a Digital Europe.Internet Histories. **2020**, *4*(2), 196–216.

74. Hrabcak, L. Vyzvy pre danove pravo v podobe Blockchain technologie [Challenges for tax law in the form of Blockchain technology]. In Zbornik prispevkov zo 6. rocnika Jarnej internacionalizovanej skoly doktorandov UPJs 2019, Kosice: safarik Press.

75. Hrabcak, L.; Popovic, A. On the Certain Issues of Digital Services Taxes.Financial Law Review. **2020**, *17*(1), 52–69.

76. Frankowski, E.; Barański, P.; Bronowska, M. Blockchain Technology and Its Potential in Taxes.Deloitte. 2017 (accessed Dec 21, 2018).

77. OECD Secretary-General Tax Report to G20 Finance Ministers and Central Bank Governors – October 2020, OECD, Paris. www.oecd.org/tax/oecd-secretary-general-tax-report-g20-finance-ministers-october-2020.pdf (accessed Oct 17, 2020).

78. CNBC. https://www.cnbc.com/2021/05/20/us-treasury-calls-for-stricter-cryptocurrency -compliance-with-irs.html (accessed June 5, 2021).

A A Partial Smart Contract Example Created for Asset Transfer

```
217 lines (192 sloc)   5.38 KB                                                          Raw   Blame   
  1   pragma solidity >=0.4.25 <0.6.0;
  2
  3   contract AssetTransfer
  4   {
  5       enum StateType { Active, OfferPlaced, PendingInspection, Inspected, Appraised, NotionalAcceptance, BuyerAccepted, SellerAccepted, Accepted, Terminated }
  6       address public InstanceOwner;
  7       string public Description;
  8       uint public AskingPrice;
  9       StateType public State;
 10
 11       address public InstanceBuyer;
 12       uint public OfferPrice;
 13       address public InstanceInspector;
 14       address public InstanceAppraiser;
 15
 16       constructor(string memory description, uint256 price) public
 17       {
 18           InstanceOwner = msg.sender;
 19           AskingPrice = price;
 20           Description = description;
 21           State = StateType.Active;
 22       }
 23
 24       function Terminate() public
```

Source: Azure Samples (Asset Transfer), 2020 [59]

DOI: 10.1201/9781003355052-A

Index

For Product Safety Concerns and Information please contact our EU representative GPSR@taylorandfrancis.com Taylor & Francis Verlag GmbH, Kaufingerstraße 24, 80331 München, Germany

Printed and bound by CPI Group (UK) Ltd, Croydon, CR0 4YY
08/05/2025
01863659-0001